Machine Learning in Signal Processing

Machine Learning in Signal Processing
Applications, Challenges, and the
Road Ahead

Edited by
Sudeep Tanwar, Anand Nayyar, and Rudra Rameshwar

CRC Press
Taylor & Francis Group
Boca Raton London New York

CRC Press is an imprint of the
Taylor & Francis Group, an **informa** business

A CHAPMAN & HALL BOOK

MATLAB® is a trademark of The MathWorks, Inc. and is used with permission. The MathWorks does not warrant the accuracy of the text or exercises in this book. This book's use or discussion of MATLAB® software or related products does not constitute endorsement or sponsorship by The MathWorks of a particular pedagogical approach or particular use of the MATLAB® software

First edition published 2022
by CRC Press
6000 Broken Sound Parkway NW, Suite 300, Boca Raton, FL 33487-2742

and by CRC Press
2 Park Square, Milton Park, Abingdon, Oxon, OX14 4RN

© 2022 selection and editorial matter, Sudeep Tanwar, Anand Nayyar, Rudra Rameshwar; individual chapters, the contributors

CRC Press is an imprint of Taylor & Francis Group, LLC

Library of Congress Cataloging-in-Publication Data
Names: Tanwar, Sudeep, editor. | Nayyar, Anand, editor. | Rameshwar, Rudra, editor.
Title: Machine learning in signal processing : applications,
challenges and the road ahead / edited by Sudeep Tanwar, Anand Nayyar, Rudra Rameshwar.
Description: First edition. | Boca Raton : Chapman & Hall/CRC Press, 2022. |
Includes bibliographical references and index. | Summary: "Machine Learning in Signal Processing: Applications, Challenges and the Road Ahead offers a comprehensive approach towards research orientation for familiarising 'signal processing (SP)' concepts to machine learning (ML). Machine Learning (ML), as the driving force of the wave of Artificial Intelligence (AI), provides powerful solutions to many real-world technical and scientific challenges. This book will present the most recent and exciting advances in signal processing for Machine Learning (ML). The focus is on understanding the contributions of signal processing and ML and its aim to solve some of the Artificial Intelligence (AI) and Machine Learning (ML) challenges"—Provided by publisher.
Identifiers: LCCN 2021032155 (print) | LCCN 2021032156 (ebook) |
ISBN 9780367618902 (hardback) | ISBN 9780367618926 (paperback) |
ISBN 9781003107026 (ebook)
Subjects: LCSH: Machine learning. | Signal processing.
Classification: LCC Q325.5 M3219 2022 (print) | LCC Q325.5 (ebook) |
DDC 006.3/1—dc23
LC record available at https://lccn.loc.gov/2021032155
LC ebook record available at https://lccn.loc.gov/2021032156

ISBN: 978-0-367-61890-2 (hbk)
ISBN: 978-0-367-61892-6 (pbk)
ISBN: 978-1-003-10702-6 (ebk)

DOI: 10.1201/9781003107026

Typeset in Palatino
by codeMantra

Contents

Preface

Recent advances in human-machine interactions give revolutionary experience to users through smartphones, Google Glasses, and many such applications. These innovations are due to the successful installation of various recent cutting-edge technologies such as voice recognition, object recognition, and motion recognition. Though many of these technologies are still far from perfection, these examples demonstrate the usefulness and importance of machine learning (ML) approaches in signal processing (SP) research.

These well-known recognition technologies have roots deeply in many aspects of academic research and industrial development. Moreover, signal processing machine learning (SPML) is also deeply involved in feature extraction and preprocessing. ML could take digital signals as raw features to learn rules, and several times, many statistical SP techniques are providing ML solutions. Illustrations like wavelet transform given for SP now have been widely used in preprocessing for many ML applications, while probabilistic graphical models often used in an expert system now show their potentials in image segmentation and recognition. The signal analysis techniques are used to analyze, model, and classify the signals. The data scientists coming from different fields, like computer science or statistics, might not be aware of the analytical power these techniques bring with them. The fundamental signal processing concepts and tools were needed to apply ML to discrete signals. The focus is on commonly used techniques for capturing, processing, manipulating, learning, and classifying the signals. The topics included as per advanced research, but were not limited to, the following areas: mathematical models for discrete-time signals, Hilbert spaces, Fourier analysis, time-frequency analysis, linear and nonlinear filters, signal classification and prediction, principal components, and basic image processing. With time, we will cover wavelets, compressed sensing, and deep learning (DL).

From a speculative perspective, there are various issues in SP (design of filter) and ML—SVMs that can be figures as curved optimization issues. Even more generally, optimization and streamlining expect a colossal activity in the two fields—when in doubt; the optimization issue is to confine some limit of noise/powerlessness subject to constraints that can be tunes, dependent upon the application. Incompletely, many can uninhibitedly consider the issue of choosing loads which extend the likelihood function in a logistic regression problem or issue an intently looking like choosing the FIR filter taps that may restrict swell over some frequency band of interest. From a sensible perspective, it is consistently critical to join procedures from both SP and ML to improve desired accuracy. Likewise, ML algorithms implemented or executed on hardware and embedded programming, for instance, DSP chips that have commonly been expected to oblige signal processing operations, for instance, convolution and FFTs. There are applications, for instance, well-being wearables in which latency and power use ought to be seen as when the gear performs both SP and ML. Hence, there will be an increasingly unmistakable interdependency between SP and ML, and low-level programming structure in applications on resource obliged contraptions.

This book presents the fundamental applications of digital signal processing (DSP) and challenges and solutions using ML techniques. The range of applications of DSP is huge. The DSP systems can be applied generally using DSP processors such as PC. This concept of DSP generally includes processing of discrete samples of data, due to the availability of elevated speed computers, as far as DSP operations such as correlation, convolution, filtering, FET, etc. can easily be installed quickly. In today's modern world, there are DSP processors widely available and used in modern electronic labs globally. These DSP processors are majorly designed based on quick switching response time and implementations of DSP operations, whereby these depend on different real-time applications using DSP processor-based systems.

Chapter 1 introduces DSP and its scope of applications using ML. The chapter begins with the essential definitions and ideas of signal processing focusing on its applications in the advanced period. The challenges identified with traditional DSP procedures and techniques just as the quick worldwide need to manage colossal information are accentuated. Several basic concepts of signal classification, distance metrics, discrete signal representation, sampling, quantization, change of basis, and the importance of the analysis of time and frequency domains are discussed to review the fundamentals of signal processing.

Chapter 2 presents learning theory, both supervised and/or unsupervised, for signal processing. Also, the chapter targets presenting the essentials of AI (ML) procedures valuable for different sign-handling applications. The chapter likewise includes the numerical and measurable philosophies utilizing for signal preparing alongside AI. The standard discrete time signals, properties of discrete time systems, linear time invariant systems, etc. are presented in the chapter.

Chapter 3 deals with supervised and unsupervised learning theory for signal processing. The chapter gives an indepth description with regard to Model Training, Algorithms of model training, regression problems and other related concepts.

Chapter 4 describes various applications of signal processing. Artificial intelligence and ML approaches will in general expand the exactness of the sign preparing performed. In the present registering world, ML is being used in numerous basic genuine applications, and it is likewise demonstrating its value regarding diminishing endeavors, cost, and time in preparing. The chapter has uncovered that applying AI and ML approaches like profound learning, fake neural organization, profound neural organization, or convolutional neural organization surely builds the exhibition of the framework by decreasing the exertion, time, and cost. In the chapter, ten applications and utilizations of sign preparing that are currently being utilized enormously in various processing conditions and are likewise using AI approaches have been examined. In particular, uses of AI approaches in sound sign preparing, audio compression, digital image processing (DIP), video compression, digital communications, medical services, seismology, discourse acknowledgment, PC vision, and monetary forecasting have been featured.

Chapter 5 provides an in-depth understanding of DL having computer vision, natural language processing (NLP), and signal processing (SP). The chapter proposes a thorough and inside-out investigation of the writing; how, where, and why DL models are applied in image processing, natural language processing, and signal processing. With late movements in profound learning-based PC vision models, applications are more straightforward to make than at some other time. This part explores PC vision calculations and profound convolutional neural networks (CNNs) to recognize, follow, and see constantly protests added with picture division. Regular language preparing considers relationship between PC and individuals using normal language.

Brain computer interfacing is discussed in Chapter 6. Brain investigating and far-off correspondence have their remarkable stand-out engrave in various fields. It makes a run of the mill appreciation among clients and the wrapping structures. The BCI system includes four key fragments. They fuse signal obtaining, signal preprocessing, highlight extraction, and course of action of orders. One of the troubles for researchers and psyche aces is to grasp and handle the issue of "'BCI Illiteracy." This part of ML shows the application zones in nuances that could be more helpful by the brain computer waves in engaging or accomplishing their objectives. Significant convenience and explicit difficulties that face brain computer signals in different bits of BCI framework are also examined.

Chapter 7 highlights the concepts and applications of adaptive filters and neural net. The chapter momentarily examines different sorts of versatile channels and various uses of something similar in the space of correspondence frameworks, biomedical sign preparing, clamor/reverberation dropping frameworks, and radar applications. The MSE of LMS and RLS channels shift arbitrarily; however, MSE of NLMS channel diminishes steadily. A counterfeit neural organization contains interconnection of an enormous number of non-straight electronic units called neurons. The advancement of neural networks has been inspired by the design and working of human mind, consequently its name. The chapter momentarily examines about single and multilayer neural net and utilizations of the equivalent in the space of media transmission frameworks, biomedical applications, and sign handling.

Adaptive decision feedback equalizer based on wavelet neural network is discussed in Chapter 8, with details proposed on the concept of WNN DFE preparing calculation dependent on cuckoo inquiry advancement which keeps away from nearby minima not at all like existing WNN preparing calculations. PC recreations are performed to assess the proposed equalizer design over blurring, nonlinear, and time-fluctuating channels, and contrast and existing procedures in writing. The results show that the proposed conspire and decrease in mean-square mistake (MSE) contrasted with the closest cutthroat plan in the event of benchmark straight channels. For nonlinear channels, the decrease in MSE is in the scope and contrasted with the closest serious plan. Comparative upgrades are seen in piece blunder rate (BER) for time-changing direct and for variety in eigenvalue proportion (EVR) of the channel.

Chapter 9 includes and highlights aspects of intelligent video surveillance systems using DL methods (DLMs). The chapter presents strong DL calculations for image classification and object detection. Primarily, the oddity in this part is introducing tweaked lightweight deep convolutional neural network (LW-DCNN) for image classification and image of characterization, and this model is adequately acted in arranging the functioning state of insulators which are utilized on electric surveys. The chapter presents a cross-breed application to sound sign and depicts the examination of different element extraction techniques to sound signs. In near future, through the achievement of profound learning calculations, PCs will talk like people and furthermore open new freedoms for different nondangerous strategies. The chapter also concludes with the results of investigation of the tweaked techniques and utilizations of DL models in genuine time environment.

Chapter 10 introduces the concept of stationary signal, auto correlation, and linear and discriminant analyses. The idea of autocorrelation measure in ML has explicitly been planned to help the cycle of comparability estimation among the slacked values and genuine worth inside the given time arrangement. Straight discriminant investigation (LDA), ordinary discriminant examination (NDA), or discriminant work analysis, a generalized form of Fisher's direct discriminant, is a strategy utilized in measurements, design acknowledgment, and AI to track down a straight mix of highlights which can describe or separate among at least two classes of articles or occasions. The resultant blend might be additionally used as a direct classifier or for dimensionality decrease before later arrangement. The chapter talks in detail about the job of fixed sign, autocorrelation, and linear and discriminant analyses in machine figuring out how to distinguish between different examples and unmistakable highlights in machine.

Chapter 11 describes an intelligent system for fault detection in rotating electro-mechanical machines. On account of electromechanical frameworks, a few disappointments can happen (bearing imperfections, burst of rotor bars, misalignment, unconventionality, breaks or broken cog wheels). To guarantee satisfactory degrees of dependability and wellbeing, viable demonstrative strategies (particularly at the soonest stage when deficiencies are arising) and observing and considering shortcomings are required to stay away from each stop or loss of creation and to decrease extra fix costs. The recognition of these issues by stator current investigation strategies has been broadly investigated and applied. Among these methods, head part investigation (PCA) or MCSA (motor current signature analysis) which is fundamentally founded on the examination of stator flows by cutting-edge signal preparing calculations.

Chapter 12 presents wavelet transformation and ML techniques for digital signal analysis in IoT systems; further, a productive advanced sign investigation should be included to recognize different occasions that are started. Numerical models and AI, and profound learning strategies are proficient approaches to play out these advanced sign examinations in IoT applications. Consequently, the chapter centers around different methods of sign preparing associated with the point of view of IoT. Furthermore, the chapter talks about different ML and profound learning methods to arrange and anticipate the occasions in IoT sensor gadgets. At last, a contextual analysis dependent on the forecast of IoT gadget occasions utilizing persistent wavelet change and ML models is introduced. Because of the tremendous advancement in the fields of innovation, IoT has been associated with different advances like wireless sensor networks (WSNs), cloud computing, and so on. IoT has associated people to objects that can be gotten to any place and whenever. IoT has its applications in each area. It has improved the medical care administrations as wellbeing checking should be possible progressively.

MATLAB® is a registered trademark of The MathWorks, Inc. For product information, please contact:
The MathWorks, Inc.
3 Apple Hill Drive
Natick, MA 01760-2098 USA
Tel: 508-647-7000
Fax: 508-647-7001
E-mail: info@mathworks.com
Web: www.mathworks.com

Editors

Sudeep Tanwar (M'15, SM'21) is currently working as a professor in the Computer Science and Engineering Department at the Institute of Technology, Nirma University, India. Dr Tanwar was a visiting professor at Jan Wyzykowski University in Polkowice, Poland and the University of Pitesti in Pitesti, Romania. Dr Tanwar's research interests include Blockchain Technology, Wireless Sensor Networks, Fog Computing, Smart Grid, and IoT. He has authored 2 books and edited 13 books, and also published and presented more than 200 technical papers in top journals and top conferences such as IEEE TNSE, TVT, TII, WCM, Networks, ICC, GLOBECOM, and INFOCOM. Dr Tanwar initiated the research field of blockchain technology adoption in various verticals in 2017. His *h*-index is 38. Dr Tanwar actively serves his research communities in various roles. He is currently serving the editorial boards of *Physical Communication, Computer Communications, International Journal of Communication System*, and *Security and Privacy*. He has been awarded the best research paper awards from IEEE GLOBECOM 2018, IEEE ICC 2019, and Springer ICRIC-2019. He has served many international conferences as a member of the organizing committee, such as publication chair for FTNCT-2020, ICCIC 2020, and WiMob2019; member of the advisory board for ICACCT-2021 and ICACI 2020; workshop co-chair for CIS 2021; and general chair for IC4S 2019, 2020, and ICCSDF 2020. Dr Tanwar is a final voting member for IEEE ComSoc Tactile Internet Committee in 2020. He is a senior member of IEEE, CSI, IAENG, ISTE, and CSTA, and the member of the Technical Committee on Tactile Internet of IEEE Communication Society. He is leading an ST research lab where group members are working on the latest cutting-edge technologies.

Dr. Anand Nayyar received his Ph.D. (Computer Science) from Desh Bhagat University in 2017 in the area of Wireless Sensor Networks and Swarm Intelligence. He is currently working in Graduate School, Duy Tan University, Da Nang, Vietnam. He is a certified professional with 75+ professional certificates from CISCO, Microsoft, Oracle, Google, Beingcert, EXIN, GAQM, Cyberoam, and many more. He has published 100+ research papers in various national and international journals (Scopus/SCI/SCIE/SSCI-Indexed) with high-impact factor. He is a senior and life member of more than 50+ associations. He has authored/co-authored cum edited 30+ books of computer science. He is associated with more than 500 international conferences as Programme Committee/Chair/Advisory Board/Review Board member. He has 10 Australian patents , 1 Indian Design and 1 Indian Utility patent to his credit in the area of Wireless Communications, Artificial Intelligence, IoT, and Image Processing. He is currently working in the area of Wireless Sensor

Networks, IoT, Swarm Intelligence, Cloud Computing, Artificial Intelligence, Blockchain, Cyber Security, Network Simulation, and Wireless Communications. He has received 30+ awards for teaching and research—Young Scientist, Best Scientist, Young Researcher Award, Outstanding Researcher Award, Excellence in Teaching, and many more. He plays the role of Associate Editor for Wireless Networks (Springer), Computer Communications (Elsevier), IET-Quantum Communications, IET Wireless Sensor Systems, IET Networks, IJDST, IJISP, and IJCINI. He is the Editor-in-Chief of IGU Global's US journal "International Journal of Smart Vehicles and Smart Transportation (IJSVST)."

Dr. Rudra Rameshwar (Ph.D.—IIT Roorkee, M. Tech.—IIT Roorkee, D.B.E.—EDII Ahmedabad, B. Tech. (Elect. Engg.)—DEI Agra, B.Sc.—DEI Agra) is a full-time management faculty working in LMTSOM, Thapar Institute of Engineering & Technology (Deemed-to-be-University) Patiala (Punjab State), India. He is associated with core MBA specializations working in the area of "Operations, Energy & Sustainability, and Analytics." Additionally, he is working in the area of Industry 4.0, Education 4.0, Business Analytics, HR Analytics, CSR, Service Operations Management, Sustainable Development, Warehouse Management, Sustainable Business Strategies, Industrial Marketing, Technology and Innovation, Research Methodology, Data Analytics, International Management, Business Statistics, Research Design and Statistical Tools—Techniques, Data Analysis, Interpretation—SPSS/EViews/Minitab Training, Meta-Analysis, Advanced Regression Analysis, Qualitative & Quantitative Research, and Academic Publishing and Integrity. He is actively working and involved in research and academic discussions, expertise/consultancy/workshop-training in techno-management domain comprising above areas of research and teaching involved in Ph.D. and Master's Thesis Guidance/Supervision, Data Analysis & Interpretation, Thesis/Article/Research Paper Writing, Project-Based Write-Up, Case Study Discussion, etc. He has been a recipient of first prestigious Ph.D. National Doctoral Fellowship (N.D.F.) Award from AICTE (Govt. of India) New Delhi and Institute of Public Enterprises Hyderabad for his Doctoral Research Program worked at IIT Roorkee (Uttarakhand) India. He has published 60+ research papers in reputed journals and conferences on subjects ranging from Science & Technology, Engineering to Management and won prestigious awards. He is a life member of Thomason Alumni Association (IIT Roorkee), Indian Science Congress Association (ISCA) Kolkata, and Confederation of Indian Industry (CII) Chandigarh.

Contributors

V. Ajantha Devi
AP3 Solutions
Chennai, India

Kumar Sanjay Bhorekar
School of Data Science
Symbiosis Skills and Professional
    University, Pune, India.

Anjanadevi Bondalapati
Department of Information Technology
MVGR College of Engineering
Vizianagaram, India

Saad Chakkor
LabTIC, ENSA of Tangier
University of Abdelmalek Essaâdi
Tangier, Morocco

Chandana G.
ECE Department
RV College of Engineering
Bengaluru, India

Anjana Mahaveer Daigond
ECE Department
RV College of Engineering
Bengaluru, India

Pascal Dore
LabTIC, ENSA of Tangier
University of Abdelmalek Essaâdi
Tangier, Morocco

Ahmed El Oualkadi
LabTIC, ENSA of Tangier
University of Abdelmalek Essaâdi
Tangier, Morocco

Ankit Garg
Department of Computer Science and
    Engineering
Amity University
Gurugram, India

Dhanalekshmi Gopinathan
Department of Computer Science and
    Engineering
Jaypee Institute of Information Technology
Noida, India

Bhuvan Jain
Senior Software Developer-
    DeliveryFulcrum Digital
DPU IDL
Pune, India

Ruby Jain
School of Data Science
Symbiosis Skills and Professional
    University
Pune, India

Rajalakshmi Krishnamurthi
Department of Computer Science and
    Engineering
Jaypee Institute of Information Technology
Noida, India

Bandana Mahapatra
School of Data Science
School of Symbiosis Skills and Professional
    University
Pune, India

Saikat Majumder
Department of Electronics and
    Communication
National Institute of Technology, Raipur,
    Chhattisgarh, India

Manjaiah D. H.
Department of Computer Science
Mangalore University
Mangalore, India

Mohd Naved
Department of Business Analytics
Jagannath University
Delhi, India

Manimala Puri
Symbiosis Center for Distance Learning
Symbiosis Open Education Society
Pune, India

Anuj Kumar Singh
Department of Computer Science and
  Engineering
Amity University
Gurugram, India

Paras Nath Singh
Department of Computer Science and
  Engineering
CMRIT
Bangalore, India

Kavitha Somaraj
Programs and Curriculum Department
Higher Colleges of Technology
Dubai, United Arab Emirates

Sowmya K. B.
Department of ECE
RV College of Engineering
Bengaluru, India

1

Introduction to Signal Processing and Machine Learning

Kavitha Somaraj

Higher Colleges of Technology

CONTENTS

1.1 Introduction

Signal processing has gained a lot of appreciation in the modern era with its applications growing virtually in all walks of life such as communications, entertainment, control, and environment, just to mention a few. Digital signal processing (DSP) is a main driver of a digital revolution that introduced compact disks, DVDs, digital cameras, mobile phones, and countless technological devices. The clinical diagnosis of various health ailments would be less efficient if medical equipment such as X-rays, electroencephalograph, and electrocardiogram analyzers that depend on DSP did not exist. Recent advancements have led to hi-tech gadgets and wearables based on human machine interface (HMI) technology such as Google Glasses, Xbox games, and Fitbits to name a few.

DOI: 10.1201/9781003107026-1

Signal processing can be defined as the process of extracting useful information from a signal. It depends on the nature of the signal and the type of information that needs to be extracted. It deals with the transformation, analysis, and synthesis of signals or information. The purpose of signal processing is to modify the given signal such that the quality of information is improved in some well-defined meaning [1]. Signal processing is classified as analog signal processing and digital signal processing. An analog signal varies continuously with time, and as described in [2], the term *analog* appears to have stemmed from the analog computers used prior to 1980. Those computers solved linear differential equations by means of connecting physical (electronic) differentiators and integrators using old-style telephone operator patch cords. However, present-day computers and technologies rely on digital signals, thereby making analog signals obsolete. DSP deals with the analysis of discrete or digitized sampled signals [3], and it has a number of advantages when compared to analog signal processing such as high processing accuracy, stability, and reliability.

DSP evolved in 1960, and since then, the use of DSP has been growing continuously, because of the development of powerful and efficient methods, particularly filter design techniques and fast Fourier transform (FFT) algorithms, opening several application areas [4].The traditional digital signal processing technique utilized specialized hardware to process signals which included data acquisition, signal transformation, analysis, synthesis, filtering, evaluation and identification, etc. in order to extract information [5]. However, with the advancement of technology and living standards, DSP has evolved even further, and the most recent development is the fusion of signal processing and machine learning referred to as SPML. The present-day wearable gadgets such as Google Glasses etc. mentioned earlier depend on human machine interaction and brain computer interface signals that must translate signals from the user's brain into messages or commands which can be achieved through SPML.

The current SMAC (Social, Mobile, Analytics, Cloud) technology trend paves the way to a future in which intelligent machines, networked processes, and big data are brought together [6]. A large volume of data or information is generated through various sources in this virtual world, and therefore, the modern society is facing the challenge of "information overload." There is an immediate need to deal with sheer volumes of data, which poses a significant constraint to traditional DSP techniques. Moreover, the data that needs to be processed is available in different formats. These challenges have led to the adoption of powerful machine learning algorithms. As described in [7], machine learning adequately fits the constraints and solution requirements posed by DSP problems: from computational efficiency, online adaptation, and learning with limited supervision to their ability to combine heterogeneous information, to incorporate prior knowledge about the problem, or to interact with the user to achieve improved performance. Few academic researchers have adopted ML and related algorithms for various applications such as detecting building or construction defects using image processing [8], automatically generating highlights of a broadcasted cricket match [9], secure data analytics [10], block-chain-based smart applications [11], traffic management [12], and distributed big data analytics [13]. Moreover, SPML is currently used in various real-world applications that depend on statistical data preprocessing and feature extraction techniques such as image processing, object detection, biometrics, and voice recognition, to mention a few. For these reasons, it is crucial for engineers, scientists, technologists, and alike to have the right knowledge in order to be able to join procedures from both signal processing and machine learning to achieve the desired accuracy while building such applications.

This book is a complete resource on SPML, and this introductory chapter basically aims to set the stage and provide a foundation for the various upcoming advanced topics that will be introduced throughout this book. The book is a one-stop reference including a comprehensive range of topics from technological developments in SP and ML, adoption of ML in SP, to societal impact and applications of SPML. The primary intent overall is to provide an insight into why SPML is the future.

1.2 Basic Terminologies

It is important to know some of the core concepts before we deep dive into the advanced concepts of signal processing, machine learning, and SPML. In this section, we will go over some of the basic terminologies related to signal processing and machine learning.

1.2.1 Signal Processing

1.2.1.1 Continuous and Discrete Signals

A signal is generally defined as a physical magnitude that changes with time [14], and examples include light, audio, images, and videos that are captured by sensors or measurement systems. It is a quantity that conveys information with respect to time. For example, a sound signal conveys information about the changes in air pressure over time.

A signal is classified according to whether it is continuous in time or discrete. Figure 1.1a and b represents the two different types. Continuous time signals have values for all points in time, and real-world signals are mostly continuous with time that varies from $-\infty$ to $+\infty$.

A general representation of a one-dimensional continuous-time signal $x[t]$ is given by Equation (1.1). As indicated, the signal $x[t]$ may be a complex ($\mathbb{C}$) or real-valued ($\mathbb{R}$) function of time, and $t \in R$, e.g., continuous time.

$$x[t]: R \rightarrow \mathbb{C} \text{ or } x[t]: R \rightarrow \mathbb{R} \tag{1.1}$$

A *discrete time signal* is represented by a sequence of numbers [14] denoted as $x[n]$ and $n \in Z$ where Z is a set of integers. A general representation of a discrete time signal is given in Equation (1.2).

$$x[n]: Z \rightarrow \mathbb{C} \text{ or } x[n]: Z \rightarrow \mathbb{R} \tag{1.2}$$

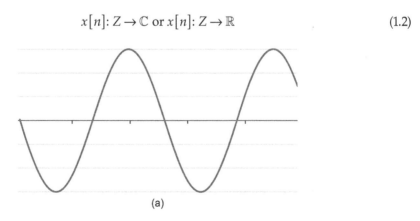

(a)

FIGURE 1.1
Representation of signal types: (a) continuous; (b) discrete.

(Continued)

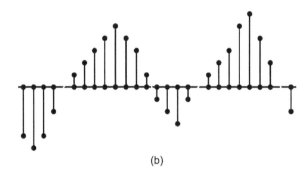

(b)

FIGURE 1.1 (*Continued*)
Representation of signal types: (a) continuous; (b) discrete.

In the current scenario, there has been an exciting move from the analog model to a sequence of discrete values, which has led to a major paradigm shift in digital signal processing. When compared to the traditional analog model, discrete models are simple and easy to use in terms of computational efforts. For example, if we want to find the average speed between two points using the analog model, the computation involves using calculus to determine the integral of the speed function $x(t)$ and then dividing it by the interval length. Conversely, if discrete speed measurements are used, the average can be easily obtained by dividing the sum of discrete values by the number of samples. The signals are processed in batches or samples, reducing the complexity and processing time, and discrete data storage is less complicated. Moreover, the noise levels can also be controlled effectively using digital signals. To summarize, the advantages of using the discrete model include the following: (i) easy storage of data, (ii) processing does not depend on the nature of the signal, and (iii) effective transmission with minimal noise.

1.2.1.2 Sampling and Quantization

Digital signals have two components: time and amplitude, and each sample can take values from a predetermined set of integers. Digitization is a two-step process and includes two distinct operations: sampling and quantization. Initially, through sampling, the analog signal $s[t]$ is converted to a discrete signal $s[n]$, and the signal is sampled at regular time intervals nT, where n is the number of samples, and T is the sampling period (seconds) as represented in Equation (1.3). However, through the process of sampling, the analog signal is transformed into a discrete time signal $s(nT)$ with continuous amplitude value [14].

$$s[n] = s(nT) \tag{1.3}$$

Since the sampled signal includes a continuous amplitude value, it is not yet a completely digital signal. So, there is a need for it to go through the process of quantization where the continuous amplitude is quantized by assigning a discrete number to represent its value for each sample. So, to summarize, a discrete time signal quantizes time as well as signal amplitude. An ideal sampler can be compared to a simple switch that turns ON and OFF every T seconds, and the period of sampling is given by Equation (1.4).

$$T = \frac{1}{f_s} \tag{1.4}$$

where

f_s = sampling frequency in hertz.

The *Nyquist–Shannon sampling theorem* states that a signal can be exactly reconstructed from its samples if the sampling frequency is greater than twice the highest frequency component in the signal. In practice, the sampling frequency is often significantly higher than twice the Nyquist frequency [14]. For this signal to be audible to the human ear, the sampling frequency must be 40 kHz.

1.2.1.3 Change of Basis

A majority of signal processing applications require decomposing a signal into its individual signal constituents for performing operations on each of those individual components. Signal decomposition can also be referred to as signal transformation where the signal is transformed from one domain to the other, for example, time domain to frequency domain. Signal transformation helps in analyzing the signal, and this requires a change of basis from one coordinate system to another.

A basis can be considered as the skeleton of a vector space. It is a set of vectors that span an n-dimensional vector space and are linearly independent of each other. A basic operation in vector spaces is a linear combination denoted by Equation (1.5) where α and β are coefficients or coordinates that are unique.

$$c = \alpha x + \beta y \tag{1.5}$$

If S is a set of k vectors, the fundamental building block is called a basis vector such that any vector can be expressed as a linear combination of this basis vector. The set of vectors can be denoted by $\left\{ s^{(k)} \right\}$ where k is the cardinal number of the vector. S is a basis for vector space V if we can express for all elements x belonging to V:

$$x = \sum_{k=0}^{K-1} \propto_k s^{(k)}, \text{ vector coordinate } \propto_k \in \mathbb{C} \tag{1.6}$$

For example, let us consider the canonical basis $\mathbb{R}^2$ of the Euclidean plane. Any vector in the Euclidean plane is a point on the plane that can be expressed as a pair of coordinates x_0 and x_1. Let us take two vectors $e^{(0)}$ and $e^{(1)}$ as follows:

$$e^0 = \begin{bmatrix} 1 \\ 0 \end{bmatrix} \quad e^1 = \begin{bmatrix} 0 \\ 1 \end{bmatrix} \tag{1.7}$$

Then, any vector in the Euclidean plane, $\mathbb{R}^2$, can be expressed as a linear combination of $e^{(0)}$ and $e^{(1)}$ as in Equation (1.8) where the coefficients are the coordinates themselves.

$$\begin{bmatrix} x_0 \\ x_1 \end{bmatrix} = x_0 \begin{bmatrix} 1 \\ 0 \end{bmatrix} + x_1 \begin{bmatrix} 0 \\ 1 \end{bmatrix} \tag{1.8}$$

For example, if $x_0 = 3$ and $x_1 = 3$, vector V1 in Figure 1.2 can be represented as $V1 = 2e^0 + 3e^1$.

Real-world signals in nature exhibit periodic behavior where the phenomena repeat after a certain period of time. Therefore, signal processing applications depend on oscillatory

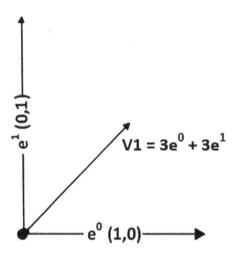

FIGURE 1.2
Representation of basis for a vector space.

functions such as sines and cosines to represent such periodic signals. A basis for a class of signals is a collection of signals in the class that have the property that any other signal in that class can be written as a weighted sum of those signals. Suppose we have the class of signals that are length N, and $x[n]$ is in that class (is of length N). If $y^{(k)}[n], \ldots, y^{(M-1)}[n]$ are also of length N and are a basis for these signals, we can find $c[1], \ldots, c[0]$ such that

$$x[n] = \sum_{k=0}^{K-1} c[k] y^{(k)}[n] \tag{1.9}$$

In a nutshell, signal processing applications require decomposing a signal into its individual signal constituents or transforming it from one domain to another. This requires a change of basis from one coordinate system to another.

1.2.1.4 *Importance of Time Domain and Frequency Domain Analyses*

The concept of domains is of utmost importance in digital signal processing and machine learning, as both time domains and frequency domains are used interchangeably depending on the application. For example, frequency domain methods are more effective than the time domain methods in certain applications, for example, fingerprint recognition and audio signal detection.

Time domain data representation shows how a signal varies with time, and it is also referred to as time-series data, whereas the frequency domain representation shows how much of the signal is present in a particular frequency band over a range of frequencies. Fourier transform is used to transform signals from time to frequency domain, and in this process, the time information is transformed into the magnitude and phase component of each frequency. The frequency domain representation is also referred to as spectrum because it includes a spectrum or range of frequency components. Figure 1.3 represents an audio signal in the time as well as frequency domains. Representing the audio signal in the frequency domain allows audio experts to alter frequencies to make it more pleasing for the human ear.

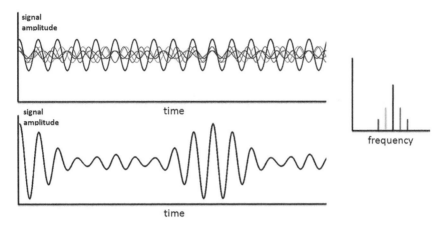

FIGURE 1.3
Audio signal in the time and frequency domain.

1.2.2 Machine Learning

In the previous section, we have reviewed the basic definitions and terminologies related to signal processing. In this section, we will learn about machine learning and how it is classified. We will also look at some of the commonly used terms and definitions.

Machine learning is a subset of artificial intelligence that can learn to perform a task with extracted data and/or models [15]. Machine learning is the branch of science that enables computers to learn, adapt, extrapolate patterns, and communicate with each other without explicitly being programmed to do so [16]. Machine learning algorithms can solve various real-world problems such as detecting frauds, analyzing the sentiments of customers to promote sales growth, translating languages, and so on. Machine learning algorithms learn from historical data and are mainly classified into three main categories as shown in Figure 1.4.

1. **Supervised Learning**: These algorithms require the knowledge of both the input or independent variable and the target or dependent variable. For example, predicting the price of a house falls under this category where the inputs can be the number of rooms, area of the house, and so on, and the target variable is the house price.

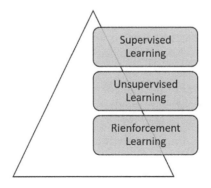

FIGURE 1.4
Classification of machine learning algorithms.

2. **Unsupervised Learning**: These algorithms do not have the knowledge of the target or dependent variable. For example, identifying different customer segments falls under unsupervised learning, and customers can be segregated based on gender, age, income, etc. for the purpose of marketing.

3. **Reinforcement Learning**: This type of machine learning algorithm uses the cause-and-effect method to learn in an interactive environment. It uses the method of trial and error using feedback and learns from its own actions and experiences. An example of reinforcement learning is a self-driving car where it has to learn several aspects including speed limits, parking zones, etc.

Machine learning requires data to make decisions and automates the process of creating algorithms which is referred to as model building. The process of model building includes taking data as input, identifying patterns in the data and finally summarizing the pattern mathematically. The effectiveness of machine learning depends on the data, type of data, scaling, noise factor, sensitivity, features selected, etc.

Organizations and businesses across the world consider several performance measures including growth in sales, customer satisfaction, customer retention, and so on for quantifying, benchmarking, and improving [15]. Machine learning algorithms could be used to identify various aspects that contribute to those key performance measures and thereby ensure quality service. In general, the following steps are adopted by a typical ML algorithm:

- Problem identification
- Identification of data sources and data finalization
- Data preprocessing and feature extraction
- Segregation of dataset into test, training, and validation sets
- ML model building
- Identification of the best model depending on performance
- Deployment of the model

The following are the key definitions of machine learning terminologies commonly used:

- **Deep Learning**: It is an advanced machine learning development or technique based on neural networks, which is capable of learning from enormous volumes of data.
- **Classification**: It falls under the category of supervised learning. It deals with discrete data and predicts the class to which the data belong. A simple example is categorizing emails as "spam" and "not spam." A classification problem can be either binary or multiclass.
- **Regression**: It falls under the category of supervised learning and provides predictions based on input features that are continuous values, for example, predicting the price of a house based on its features such as the plot size, location, etc.
- **Feature Extraction**: The process of extracting features from the given raw dataset necessary for building machine learning algorithms.
- **Test Set**: A subclass of the given dataset required to test the trained model. This set must represent the entire population and be large enough to yield meaningful results.

- **Training Set**: A subclass of the given dataset required to train the model.
- **Model Building**: The process of building a model using machine learning algorithm to solve the given problem.
- **Model Deployment**: The model is finalized based on multiple criteria and performance measures that include accuracy, costs, and performance speed. This is the final stage that involves developing strategies for deploying the model.

1.3 Distance-Based Signal Classification, Nearest Neighbor Classifier, and Hilbert Space

1.3.1 Distance-Based Signal Classification

Various real-world applications require machine learning algorithms to classify signals or objects. Identifying input data patterns is fundamental for such classification applications, and choosing the right distance metric is critical to make informed decisions. Good distance metrics can be used to enhance model accuracy and performance of machine learning algorithms. This section focuses on various distance metrics and how they contribute to SPML. Few key definitions are fundamental to distance metrics as that of metric space, normed linear space, and inner product space. From the definitions, you will notice that normed linear spaces and inner product spaces are just types of metric spaces that belong to the same family.

1.3.1.1 Metric Space

Metric space is simply a collection of objects (e.g., numbers and matrices), and a metric or distance function is a function that defines a distance between each pair of point elements of a set [17]. Some applications in SPML require the use of functions for measurement of distances in arbitrary spaces, and distance metrics belong to this class of functions. An arbitrary space can be any space including vector spaces. The simplest example of a metric space is a number line with real numbers, and the associated metric is $\|a-b\|$, where $a, b \in \mathbb{R}$.

Let us consider Z as an arbitrary space; a and b are two points in this space, and d is a distance function. The distance function d is a distance metric if it satisfies the following four conditions:

(a) The distance $d(a, b) \geq 0$
(b) The distance $d(a, b) = 0$ only if $a = b$ (implies that distance from a point to itself is zero).
(c) The distances must be symmetric which means $d(a, b) = d(b, a)$
(d) It must satisfy the triangle inequality property where $d(a, k) \leq d(a, b) + d(b, k)$

1.3.1.2 Normed Linear Space

A complex normed linear space is a linear space with a function $\|\cdot\| : L \to \mathbb{R}$ is called a norm called a norm [17]. The Euclidean distance and l_p norms fall under this category, and norms are used to measure distance as well as lengths in vector spaces. Let us consider a Euclidean plane $\mathbb{R}^n$ with n dimensions. The Euclidean distance or l_2 distance (where $p=2$) is the most commonly used distance metric. It is simply the distance measured between any two points in this plane using the Pythagorean theorem. For example, the Euclidean distance between two points a and b shown in Figure 1.5 can be calculated using Equations (1.10a).

$$l_2 = \|a - b\|_2 = \sqrt{\sum_{i=1}^{n} (a_i - b_i)^2} \tag{1.10a}$$

This is a two-dimensional Euclidean space, and a_i and b_i are the variables of vectors a and b in this space, i.e., $a = (a_1, a_2, a_3, \ldots)$ and $b = (b_1, b_2, b_3, \ldots)$.

Therefore, $a_i - b_i = (a_1 - b_1) + (a_2 - b_2) + \ldots + (a_n - b_n)$.

For example, the Euclidean distance between two vectors, let us say points a (1, 2) and b (3, 5) in the $\mathbb{R}^2$ plane can be calculated as follows:

$$l_2 = \|a - b\|_2 = \sqrt{(a_i - b_i)^2} = \sqrt{(3-1)^2 + (5-2)^2} = \sqrt{13} \tag{1.10b}$$

So, $\sqrt{13}$ is the Euclidean distance between a and b in two dimensions.

While Euclidean distance is sufficient to capture distance measurements in a given space, some applications require measurement of larger distances, and l_p norms are used for such applications. l_p norm where $p \geq 1$ is represented as in Equation (1.11).

$$l_p = \|a - b\|_p = \left(\sum_{i=1}^{n} |a_i - b_i|^p \right)^{\frac{1}{p}} \tag{1.11}$$

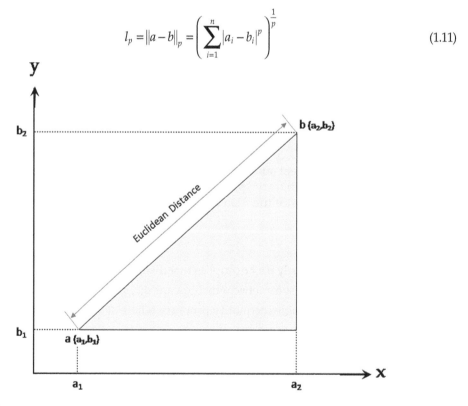

FIGURE 1.5
Representation of Euclidean distance.

Accordingly, l_1 and l_∞ distances can be computed as in Equations (1.12) and (1.13), respectively.

$$l_1 = \|a - b\|_1 = \sum_{i=1}^{n} |a_i - b_i| \tag{1.12}$$

$$l_\infty = \|a - b\|_\infty = \max_i |a_i - b_i| \tag{1.13}$$

1.3.1.2.1 l_p Norm for Signal Classification

Suppose we have a class of signals that are of length N, and $x[n]$ is in that class and is of length N. If we apply l_p norms to $x[n]$, the resulting l_1, l_2, l_p, and l_∞ norm distances will be as follows:

$$l_{1 \text{ norm}} (p = 1) = \sum_{n=0}^{N-1} |x[n]| \tag{1.14}$$

$$l_{2 \text{ norm}} (p = 2) = \left(\sum_{n=0}^{N-1} |x[n]^2| \right)^{\frac{1}{2}} \tag{1.15}$$

$$l_{p \text{ norm}} (p \geq 2) = \left(\sum_{n=0}^{N-1} |x[n]^p| \right)^{\frac{1}{p}} \tag{1.16}$$

$$l_{\infty \text{ norm}} = \max_{n \in \{0, \dots N-1\}} |x[n]| \tag{1.17}$$

1.3.1.3 Inner Product Space

A linear vector space F is an inner product space if it has an inner product function $\langle \, , \rangle : F \times F$, where $F \in \mathbb{R}, \mathbb{C}$. Inner products are used to measure distances and lengths as well as angles between vectors. Hilbert space is a complete inner product space which will be explained in this chapter at a later stage.

1.3.2 Nearest Neighbor Classification

The nearest neighbor classification is one of the oldest and robust distance classification methods that was introduced. Machine learning classification problems use two algorithms, namely, nearest neighbor (NN) and k-nearest neighbors (kNN), which have been successful in numerous machine learning classification problems such as image classification and pattern recognition to name a few. The difference between NN and kNN is that in NN, the value of k is 1. The value of k generally depends on the training set and typically $k=\sqrt{n}$ for a size of n.

To explain the concept of nearest neighbor, let us take an example of a classification problem in machine learning, where the dataset includes a training set and test set. kNN algorithm is used to identify similarities and dissimilarities in the data set. It follows a simple approach as in [18] where a query point t is classified depending on the category

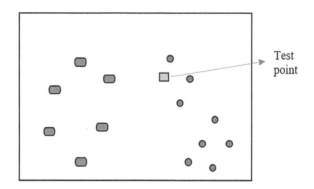

FIGURE 1.6
K-NN example.

of its nearest neighbors in the training set. It is labelled as belonging to that class which is most frequently represented among its *k*-nearest neighbors.

Referring to the example in Figure 1.6, the algorithm or classifier will find the nearest example to the test point using a distance function or metric and will assign the same class as that example. The distance metric commonly used in this classification to measure the similarity is the Euclidean distance. However, there are other distance metrics such as the Manhattan distance and the Minkowski distance that are also used.

1.3.3 Hilbert Space

The notion of a Hilbert space emerged from the efforts of a German mathematician David Hilbert to generalize the concept of Euclidean space to an infinite dimensional space. It expands the vector space from the two- and three-dimensional domains to domains with multidimensions or infinite dimensions. Hilbert space includes few additional properties to normal vector spaces such as an inner product operation that allows length and angle measurements. They are complete metric spaces that satisfy the following three properties [17]. Here, F is considered as a linear vector space.

(a) **Positive:** $x,\ x \geq 0$, for $x \in F; \langle x, x \rangle = 0$ only if $x = 0$
(b) **Symmetry:** $\langle x, y \rangle = \langle y, x \rangle$ for $F \in \mathbb{R}$; $\langle x, y \rangle = \langle \overline{y, x} \rangle$ for $F \in \mathbb{C}$
(c) **Distributive:** $\langle x, y_1 + y_2 \rangle = \langle x, y_1 \rangle + \langle x, y_2 \rangle$, $x, y_1, y_2 \in F$
(d) **Multiplicative:** $\langle \lambda x, y \rangle = \langle \lambda x, y \rangle$,   for $x, y \in F$ and $\lambda \in \mathbb{C}$

The advantage of Hilbert space is that there is no restriction on the vector dimensions— they can be finite, infinite, or even functions. Kernel methods in machine learning use Hilbert space to perform dot product computations.

1.4 Fusion of Machine Learning in Signal Processing

DSP has laid a foundation for various technologies in the information age including televisions, mobile phones, and MP3 players, to name a few. On the other hand, ML, which is a newcomer in this era, has led to the existence of sensational technologies such as face recognition, voice recognition, image classification, driverless cars, and stock market prediction. While DSP systems extract information through a sequence of processes that include data acquisition, signal conversion, and filtering, the ML technique depends on algorithms to extract information.

Signal processing and machine learning have undergone rapid transformations and seen significant improvements with the advancement in technology and the change in economic demands. Over the recent years, there has been an overwhelming demand for smart devices and gadgets that can interact with the environment which are referred to as human-machine interface (HMI) devices, for example, wearable tech gadgets that can track human activity. While such applications depend on machine learning techniques to mimic human intelligence to learn from the data and offer solutions to real-world problems, it is important to note that they also depend on statistical signal processing and feature extraction techniques. It is evident that modern applications require the fusion of SPML systems to maintain high performance while dealing with big data, high-tech digital sensors, and hardware.

1.5 Benefits of Adopting Machine Learning in Signal Processing

Machine learning algorithms learn from the data and continuously improve performance through experience. However, the data generated and stored by smart gadgets or systems are available in enormous volumes, and the term "big data" is used to describe this large-scale data set. Moreover, the data are available in diverse formats such as 2D signals, videos, and images, and traditional signal processing techniques will not come in handy to extract the information hidden in the data. Considering the enormous data sets and diverse formats, it is vital for ML algorithms to perform with high speed and efficiency. The great need to cope with big data and dissimilar formats has led to the adoption of ML algorithms that use intelligent learning methods to extract information and process data with high speed and accuracy.

Artificial intelligence techniques and ML algorithms are widely used in a number of vast and complex applications that require statistical signal processing including bioinformatics, astronomy, environment, and communications, just to name a few. For example, under bioinformatics, several academic researchers have adopted SPML techniques such as short-time Fourier transform (STFT) to detect epileptic seizures through EEG data as in [19] and [20]. As the data keep growing bigger and bigger, some applications in the modern world would even require advanced ML techniques. The performance of traditional ML algorithms may be slow as they require data to be fully loaded into memory for data mining and processing. The inability of such algorithms to learn all the data within a reasonable allotted time may pose a challenge.

Advanced ML techniques such as deep learning have gained a lot of importance in the recent years due to their state-of-the-art performance in terms of speed and deep architecture. Deep learning architecture can capture complex input data patterns outperforming traditional ML techniques in making informed predictions. Especially, the deep learning technique called convolutional neural networks (CNN) has been showing some promising results for future work. The continuous evolution of technology and research efforts will definitely give rise to modern applications in various domains with a requirement to learn from multifarious environments, and this is where ML algorithms will play a vital role.

1.6 Conclusion

In this chapter, we have given you a crash course on the fundamentals behind signal processing and machine learning including key concepts and terminologies required to proceed with the rest of the chapters in this book. This quick overview would have provided sufficient introductory background information that is enough to get you started with the upcoming chapters in signal processing and machine learning. Specifically, we hope you have developed a mindset and thought process for utilizing the statistical signal processing and machine learning tools for solving real-world problems.

In this chapter, we defined signal processing as a process of extracting useful information from a signal. We also touched base upon digital signal processing and compared it with the analog model. At this point, you would have understood that the digital model is preferred due to its simplicity and less computational efforts involved, in addition to easy data storage, less complicated processing, and effective transmission with minimal noise. We also discussed the process of digitization and how analog signals are converted to digital signals through sampling and quantization techniques. The concept of change of basis and its benefits in terms of transforming the signal from one coordinate system or domain to another for the purpose of signal analysis was also explained. The signal processing concepts and terminologies introduced in this chapter would have provided sufficient underpinning knowledge and understanding to proceed with advanced topics in the upcoming chapters.

We also provided an introduction to machine learning and related concepts. It is important to emphasize that machine learning algorithms learn from historical data to make intelligent decisions and are split into three main categories: supervised, unsupervised, and reinforcement learning. Also, the steps that a typical ML algorithm follows for model building are worth remembering as it will be used throughout in all machine learning applications. This includes problem identification, identification of data sources, data pre-processing and feature extraction, segregation of dataset into test, training, and validation sets, model building, identification of the best model, and finally model deployment. Moreover, SPML applications require machine learning algorithms to classify signals or objects, and identifying input data patterns is a key requirement for such classification problems. This is where distance measurement plays a crucial role and helps make informed decisions. Accordingly, we provided an introduction to the fundamentals of distance metrics and how they contribute to SPML. The basics of the nearest neighbor classifier and Hilbert space were also covered as they are used in all advanced machine learning algorithms.

To conclude, the knowledge gained through this chapter will help you appreciate the wide importance of signal processing and machine learning to the knowledge economy and how they link seamlessly with each other to develop essential tools and high-end solutions to real-world problems. The final sections discuss the fusion of SPML and describe the benefits of adopting machine learning in signal processing to cope with big data and dissimilar formats to extract information and process data with high performance and accuracy.

References

1. B. A. Shenoi, *Introduction to Digital Signal Processing and Filter Design*, John Wiley & Sons Inc., New York, 2021.
2. R. G. Lyons, *Understanding Digital Signal Processing*, Third edition. O'Reilly Media, Inc., USA, 2021.
3. B. P. Lathi, *Linear Systems and Signals*, Oxford University Press, Sacramento, CA, 2020.
4. C. D. M. Regis, *Digital Signal Processing*, Momentum Press, New York, 2018.
5. H. Lu, Y. Xiaoyu, W. Haodong, L. Jin, M. Xuejiao, and Z. Caihong, "Research on Application of Digital Signal Processing Technology in Communication", *IOP Conference Series: Materials Science and Engineering*, Vol. 799, no. 1, May 2020. doi: 10.1088/1757-899X/799/1/012026.
6. J. Alzubi, A. Nayyar, and A. Kumar, "Machine Learning from Theory to Algorithms: An Overview", *Journal of Physics: Conference Series*, Vol. 1142, No. 1, p. 012012, November 2018.
7. J. L. Rojo-Álvarez, M. Martínez-Ramón, J. Muñoz-Marí, and G. Camps-Valls, *Digital Signal Processing with Kernel Methods*, Wiley-IEEE Press, Hoboken, NJ, 2018.
8. J. Vora, M. Patel, S. Tanwar, and S. Tyagi, "Image Processing Based Analysis of Cracks on Vertical Walls", 2018, doi: 10.1109/IoT-SIU.2018.8519926.
9. S. S. Maram, N. Kumar, J. J. P. C. Rodrigues, S. Tanwar, and A. Jain, "Images to Signals, Signals to Highlights," *IEEE Global Communications Conference (GLOBECOM-2020)*, Taipei, Taiwan, 7–11 December 2020, pp. 1–6, 2020.
10. R. Gupta, S. Tanwar, S. Tyagi, and N. Kumar, "Machine Learning Models for Secure Data Analytics: A Taxonomy and Threat Model", *Computer Communications*, Vol. 153, pp. 406–440, 2020.
11. S. Tanwar, Q. Bhatia, P. Patel, A. Kumari, P. K. Singh, and W. C. Hong, "Machine Learning Adoption in Blockchain-Based Smart Applications: The Challenges, and a Way Forward", *IEEE Access*, Vol. 8, pp. 474–488, 2020.
12. S. Khatri, H. Vachhani, S. Shah, J. Bhatia, M. Chaturvedi, S. Tanwar, and N. Kumar, "Machine Learning Models and Techniques for VANET Based Traffic Management: Implementation Issues and Challenges", *Peer-to-Peer Networking and Applications*, Vol.14, pp. 1–27, 2020.
13. V. Anavangot, V. G. Menon, and A. Nayyar, "Distributed big data analytics in the Internet of signals", *2018 International Conference on System Modeling & Advancement in Research Trends (SMART)*, IEEE, Moradabad, November, pp. 73–77, 2018.
14. S. M. Kuo, B. H. Lee, and W. Tian, *Real-Time Digital Signal Processing: Fundamentals, Implementations and Applications*, Wiley, New York, 2013.
15. M. Pradhan and D. U. Kumar, *Machine Learning using Python*, Wiley India Pvt Ltd, New York, pp. 0–364, 2019.
16. S. Halder and S. Ozdemir, *Hands-On Machine Learning for Cybersecurity: Safeguard Your System by Making Your Machines Intelligent Using the Python Ecosystem*, Packt Publishing Ltd, Birmingham, 2018.
17. O. Ekin, P. L. Hammer, A. Kogan, and P. Winter, "Distance-Based Classification Methods", *INFOR: Information Systems and Operational Research*, Vol. 37, No. 3, 1999, doi: 10.1080/03155986.1999.11732388.
18. R. Chellappa and S. Theodoridis, *Academic Press Library in Signal Processing: Volume 1-Signal Processing Theory and Machine Learning*, vol. 1, Academic Press, Chennai, 2014.
19. M. Sameer and B. Gupta, "Beta Band as a Biomarker for Classification between Interictal and Ictal States of Epileptical Patients", *2020 7th International Conference on Signal Processing and Integrated Networks (SPIN)*, Noida, India, 2020, pp. 567–570. doi: 10.1109/SPIN48934.2020.9071343.
20. M. Sameer, A. K. Gupta, C. Chakraborty and B. Gupta, "ROC Analysis for detection of Epileptical Seizures using Haralick features of Gamma band", *2020 National Conference on Communications (NCC)*, Kharagpur, India, 2020, pp. 1–5, doi: 10.1109/NCC48643.2020.9056027.

2

Learning Theory (Supervised/ Unsupervised) for Signal Processing

Ruby Jain
Symbiosis Skills and Professional University

Bhuvan Jain
DPU IDL

Manimala Puri
Symbiosis Open Education Society

CONTENTS

DOI: 10.1201/9781003107026-2

2.1 Introduction

Signals are nothing but a function or a measurement that is used to convey information from one source to the destination. Signals can be in a form of voice, images, communication signals (digital), text signals, ECG signals, etc.

Signal preparing including examination, getting, identification, and assessment; displaying of the occasions and patterns, the manner in which they advance; and the irregularities and abnormalities influencing them have pulled the interest of numerous scientists around the world. Signal handling hypothesis starts from numerical establishments with shocking applications which help data technologists find and imagine new real factors diverging into correspondences, acoustics, discourse, music, biomedical designing, systems administration, control, and numerous different fronts in innovative work. A surprising harmony among hypothesis and uses of sign handling has been found with its gigantic impressions. Straight variable-based math, information changes, and sign dispersions maybe assuming the significant parts in the vast majority of these applications.

The spearheading work in fake neural organizations, motivated by the structure of the focal sensory system, by Warren McCulloch and Walter Pitts in the 1940s was another commended foundation in the zone of information evaluation and AI [1]. AI likes to make generative models for the issue under examination. Induction models and boundaries, inalienably depending on Bayesian learning, are dictated by the information and their surroundings.

AI and data hypothetical thoughts can assist measurable sign handling with conquering the obstructions of direct models and alleviate the requirement for Gaussianity and stationarity presumptions. Factual sign handling and inductive surmising calculations give a shared opinion at the cover between signal preparing and AI, which bring about some exquisite territories of exploration, for example, versatile and nonlinear sign handling, savvy frameworks, and perform various tasks and agreeable system administration [2].

2.1.1 Signal Processing

The innovation we use, and even depend on, in our regular day-to-day existences – PCs, radios, videos, and PDAs – is empowered by signal handling, a part of electrical designing that models and examines information portrayals of actual occasions. Signal handling is at the core of our cutting-edge world, fueling the present diversion and the upcoming innovation. It is at the crossing point of biotechnology and social associations. It improves our capacity to impart and share data. Signal handling is the science behind our computerized lives [3].

Signals are nothing but a function or a measurement that are used to convey information from one source to the destination. Signals can be in a form of voice, images, communication signals (digital), text signals, ECG signals, etc.

Signal processing is a method of translating, analyzing, and transforming of the signals obtained from different sources, so that it can be used in the real world for better processing of the information.

Some of the examples are using linguistics rules in speech recognition, image processing, and machine translating text from one language to other.

Signal processing implies handling any sort of sign whether it is simple or computerized in such a way that it tends to be deciphered by any sort of PC. For example, sound wave is additionally a sort of sign. At the point when a sound wave is heard by a gadget, the gadget just has some discrete or simple estimation of certain parameters, for example, recurrence, pitch, and so forth. The undertaking of signal processing is to deal with this sign in a particularity so a PC can decipher the sound as a human hears it, for example, regarding words and sound. This can be accomplished utilizing machine learning. This chapter will chiefly be tied in with preparing neuro flags otherwise called EEG signals [4].

Initially, let us comprehend the rudiments of EEG signals [4]. Neurons in our cerebrum speak with one another utilizing synthetic responses which produce electric signs. These electric signs are called EEG signals. You can receive these signs by utilizing a neuro headset. These signs when changed over into a dominate accounting page will give you discrete qualities for various boundaries, for example, alpha, beta waveform, and so forth. Our essential undertaking is to perceive the activity being performed by the client by perusing these qualities.

AI essentially implies causing a PC to do certain things for which it isn't unequivocally customized. For instance, you won't program a PC to foresee certain activity for a specific worth. The PC itself figures out how to decipher the information for a fact. You need to pick a few activities which you need the PC to learn. Let's state you pick applauding and flickering. Initially you will gather the signs for these activities and arrange them into a dataset. Signal processing includes a ton of preprocessing of the dataset. At that point, make a ML model from which we can figure out how to anticipate activity for new sign qualities from the recently gathered qualities [5].

The main piece of this cycle is preprocessing. Let's state at any one 10th piece of a second, you receive 20 estimations of 20 distinct boundaries. So, you need to consolidate these 20 *10 = 200 values in a solitary column of a dominate sheet. Presently, these 200 qualities are the highlights that describe a clap. Moreover, you should rearrange the information for each applaud in light of the fact that when you were gathering the information, you gathered the information for a few applauds of a similar individual. This rearranging abrogates the uniqueness related with the information for a specific individual. So thusly, you are preprocessing by deciphering the information. Preprocessing impacts significantly on accuracy for anticipating client's activities [6].

Subsequent to preprocessing, you can imagine your information utilizing charts to comprehend it more. In the event that your information is in multiple measurements, you can utilize principal component analysis (PCA). This strategy decreases the information from high dimensions to low measurements [7].

Signal processing predominantly is tied in with deciphering your information, and the part which you can't decipher is taken into consideration by machine learning. I spoke distinctly about EEG flags; however, all of the above strategies apply to all sorts of the signs. At long last, utilizing a ML model, your PC will have the option to perceive the sign as a human deciphers it [8].

This chapter is further divided into various sections. In the first section, the authors focused on machine learning concepts. The impact of train and test data is discussed further. Three primary slots of AI are discussed next in detail. Supervised, unsupervised, and semi-supervised learning with various applications are discussed in the next section. Various use cases of signal processing using supervised and unsupervised learning are discussed in the next sections. Regression, classification, multilevel classification, and various error methods are discussed in the next section. Regularization in machine learning is discussed next. Various clustering algorithms are discussed in the next section. Deep learning for signal processing is discussed in the next section. Time series analysis is discussed in the next section, followed by signal processing in various GPU-based frameworks. This chapter will end with a brief summary.

2.2 Machine Learning

- **Samuel (1959):** Field of study that gives computers the ability to learn without being explicitly programmed.
- **Kevin Murphy (2012):** Algorithms that automatically detect patterns in data use the uncovered patterns to predict future data or other outcomes of interest.

    AI is a science that manages the advancement of calculations gained from information. As per Arthur Samuel (1959) [9], AI is a "field of study that enables PCs

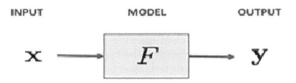

FIGURE 2.1
Machine learning algorithm.

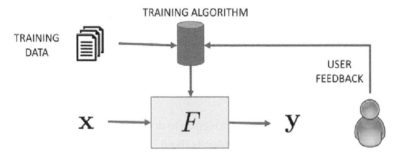

FIGURE 2.2
Train and test method.

to learn without being unequivocally customized." Kevin Murphy, in his original book [10], characterizes AI as an assortment of calculations that consequently identify designs in information that utilize the revealed examples to foresee future information or different results of interest.

Machine learning consists of different algorithms that are used by the computer to do a set of specified tasks without any external man-made rules and also, learning from the information (Figure 2.1).

Example:

Here, let the input be the brain signals that send signal to the model, i.e., a wheelchair. If the input is to turn left or right, the desired output would be the wheelchair moving to the given direction.

Basically, the ML should transform the given input into a desired output (Figure 2.2).

Here is the background of ML which is called training model where a huge amount of data is inserted into the training algorithm, and also user feedbacks are regularly taken to get the specified output from the model.

AI unites software engineering and insights to tackle prescient force, and gives the innovation behind different applications, including recognizing Visa misrepresentation, clinical diagnostics, and security exchange investigation and discourse acknowledgment.

As of late, AI strategies have been applied to parts of sign handling, obscuring the lines between technical studies, and causing many divided applications among the two.

Basically, an AI calculation may gain from information for the following:

- **Perceive Designs – Model**: perceiving text designs in a bunch of spam messages
- **Characterize Information into Various Classifications – Model**: grouping the messages into spam or non-spam messages.
- **Foresee a Future Result – Model**: anticipating if the approaching email is spam.

ML algorithms are isolated into three primary sorts:

- **Supervised Learning**: a prescient learning approach where the objective is to gain from a named set of information yield sets. The marked set gives the preparation guides to additional characterization or expectation. In AI language, inputs are called "highlights," and yields are called "reaction factors."
- **Unsupervised Learning**: a sort of less all around characterized information revelation measure; the objective is to learn organized examples in the information by isolating them from unadulterated unstructured commotion.
- **Reinforced Learning**: learning by collaborating with a climate to settle on dynamic assignments.

In view of the conversation up until now, we can begin to perceive how the cooperative energy between the fields of sign handling and AI can give another viewpoint to move toward numerous issues.

Examples of ML are as follows:

a. Amazon Alexa where it uses voice signals to do some specified tasks.
b. Model trying to learn what the image is about.
c. Example from the healthcare industry – EEG-controlled wheelchair, IBM Watson health cloud.
d. Video surveillance for traffic.

Having said that, ML consists of different algorithms to perform tasks with minimal external rules; however, a lot of hand-tuning is required for learning the algorithm, cost of data and consumption needs to be checked, and black-box makes it difficult for the researchers [11].

2.2.1 Why Do We Need ML for Signal Processing?

- SP is non-transparent to the tasks where man is interested in.
- The more the structure is inserted, the better the results generated.
- This helps in bringing both ML and SP together.

2.2.2 Speaker ID – A Utilization of ML Calculations in Sign Handling

Speaker ID (Figure 2.3) is the recognizable proof of an individual from the examination of voice attributes [12]. In this regulated characterization application, a named preparing set of voice tests (from a bunch of speakers) are utilized in the learning cycle.

Voice tests/chronicles can't be utilized as such in the learning cycle. For additional handling, it might require examining, cleaning (evacuation of commotion or invalid examples, etc.), or re-organizing the examples to reasonable configuration. This progression is called "data preprocessing" [9].

Likewise, we may need to change the information explicit to the ML calculation and the information on the issue. To prepare the ML model perceiving the examples in the voice tests, highlight extraction on voice tests is performed utilizing signal handling. For this situation, the highlights that are utilized to prepare the ML model are pitch and Mel-Frequency Cepstrum Coefficients (MFCC) [13] separated from the voice tests.

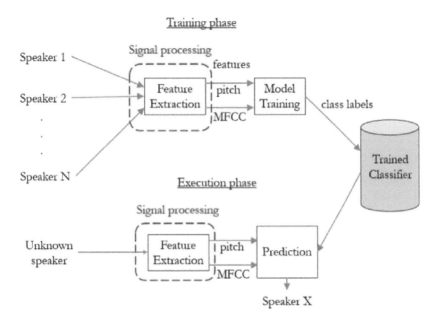

FIGURE 2.3
Speaker ID.

For the most part, the accessible dataset (set of information voice tests) is divided into two sets: one set for preparing the model, and the other set for testing needs (commonly in 75%–25% proportion). The preparation set is utilized to prepare the ML model, and the test set is utilized to assess the adequacy and execution of the ML calculation.

The preparation phase should endeavor to sum up the basic connection between the component vectors (contribution to the regulated learning calculation) and the class names (managed student's yield). Cross-approval is one of the check strategies for assessing the speculation capacity of the ML model.

The preparation phase ought to likewise evade over fitting, which may cause helpless speculation and incorrect arrangement in the execution stage. On the off chance that the exhibition of the calculation needs improvement, we need to return and make changes to the past advances. Certain measurement metrics like precision, recall, accuracy, F1 score, AUC-ROC frameworks are regularly used to assess the viability and execution of the ML calculation [14].

After the ML model is enough prepared to give fulfilling execution, we proceed onward to the execution stage. In the execution stage, when an unlabeled occurrence of a voice test is introduced to the prepared classifier, it recognizes the individual to which it has a place with.

2.2.3 Discourse and Audio Processing

Each phone, smart or not, depends vigorously on discourse preparing strategies to make voice correspondence between (at least two) individuals conceivable – from simple to computerized transformation to discourse improvement (separating, reverberation, commotion, and programmed pick up control) to discourse encoding on account side to discourse interpreting to discourse upgrade (regularly sifting and gain control) to advance to simple change on the playback side. Signal handling is the apparatus of decision consistently. Without signal preparing, present day computerized aides, for example, Siri, Ok Google, and Cortana, would not have the option to perceive a client's voice.

Sound pressure procedures, for example, MP3 and AAC, have changed the manner in which we tune in to music. We would now be able to hold the world's music melodic inventory in the palm of our hands and appreciate tuning in to music in a hurry, even totally untethered by means of Bluetooth. Once more, signal preparing got this going.

2.2.4 Discourse Recognition

Discourse acknowledgment is an indispensable utilization of sign handling; it's additionally likely the most straightforward to comprehend. Signal handling controls data content in signs to encourage automated speech recognition (ASR). It helps remove data from the discourse signals and afterward makes an interpretation of it into conspicuous words. Discourse acknowledgment innovation is found in warrior airplane, "converse with text" applications on advanced mobile phones, helpful applications, language interpretation and learning, and acknowledgment programs for individuals with incapacities [15].

2.2.5 Listening Devices

Would you be able to hear us now? The center of listening device innovation is four synchronized parts: amplifier, processor, and beneficiary and force source. Signal preparing is engaged with getting sounds in the climate and handling them to upgrade and enhance what the wearer hears. Immediately, sounds are changed over from simple to computerized and back to simple before sound is projected into the ear [16].

While the basic segments of the innovation will continue as before, portable amplifiers are getting progressively further developed – lessening commotion and criticism from the general climate to assist individuals with hearing fresh, clear sounds. Signal handling additionally decreases unexpected noisy clamors, for example, horns, and even permits amplifiers to interface remotely with a mobile phone or TV.

2.2.6 Independent Driving

When the stuff of sci-fi, self-sufficient vehicles are presently a reality. To work appropriately, these self-driving vehicles depend on contribution from a multiparticular arrangement of sensors, including ultrasound, radar, and cameras – and to forestall smashing, they should change over the gained data and channel it into information expected to control activity. Signal handling is indispensable to the innovation. It chooses whether the vehicle needs to stop or go and is essential for the radar used to translate climate conditions like downpour or mist [17].

2.2.7 Picture Processing and Analysis

Truth can be stranger than fiction. The inescapability of computerized cameras and screens in our everyday lives, for example, in our cell phones, vehicles, drones, reconnaissance frameworks, planes, emergency clinics, and our family room, interprets our always developing need to see, share, and interface with our visual climate, with expanding levels of detail. In medication, practically, all conclusions these days include a type of imaging. Notwithstanding, this quickly arising a piece of the ice sheet conceals a significant number of lesser-known yet exceptionally fundamental applications, quite in the social, military, wellbeing and logical exploration areas. Signal preparing is critical to a wide scope of utilizations, from procurement to show the following:

- Computerized reclamation of pictures and recordings
- Compacted detecting procurement (for example, single-pixel cameras)
- Picture improvement during procurement (inside camera chips)
- Picture recreation from non-picture sensors
- Picture quality appraisal
- Pressure and transmission across organizations and gadgets
- Picture to show advances (color planning, 3D to 2D projection)
- Recognition, including and following of highlights in pictures and recordings
- PC-helped conclusion in clinical imaging (for example, help for mammogram perusing)
- Computerized investigation of organic pictures (for example, cell following)

2.2.8 Wearables

The wearables market is arising and right now flourishing. Innovation and sensors incorporated into dress and adornments track wellness levels, pulses, actual area (GPS), rest examples, and the sky is the limit from there. Signal preparing helps gather these data and make an interpretation of it into valuable information to be utilized myriad – for example, announcing pulse to your primary care physician or increasing your exercise routine to get thinner [18].

2.2.9 Information Science

Each time you search on the Internet or post on Twitter, you're adding information to what exactly is prominently called "enormous data" sets. Organizations use this information to remove data, find out about practices and make answers to make our lives more proficient. Certain domains like neuroscience, medication, etc. depend on AI apparatuses blending imaging date in with clinical records and genomic to all the more likely comprehend and aggregate degenerative cycles and infections, anticipate reactions to treatment, and group patients into subgroups, for instance.

"Enormous data" is a quickly arising field, yet we're confronted with the test of concentrating huge arrangements of actually troublesome information. What's the critical part for investigating information and taking care of complex issues? Signal handling.

Like sign preparing, information science contacts our everyday lives in a bigger number of ways than we might suspect. Regardless of whether it's utilizing new information sources like arising web-based media stages, anticipating changes in the securities exchange, or contemplating information to tackle clinical issues going from diabetes to heart issues, signal handling makes it conceivable to examine information that improves our lives each day.

2.2.10 Wireless Systems and Networks

Have you ever considered speaking with extra-terrestrial creatures? Signal handling is necessary in looking for life past Earth. A significant perspective to compelling correspondences across satellite, video, radio, and remote frameworks, signal preparing makes the handling and transmission of information more proficient.

At the point when you're in a hurry and need web access or utilizing GPS to discover your direction, signal preparing is the in-the-background innovation changing and examining signs to assist us with imparting and gain from the innovation we use consistently – including phones, Wi-Fi, TVs, GPS gadgets, radar, sonar, radio, and cloud and versatile figuring [19].

2.3 Machine Learning Algorithms

ML is an application of Artificial Intelligence (AI) that gives frameworks the capacity to consequently take in and improve for a fact without being unequivocally modified. AI centers around the improvement of PC programs that can get to information and use it to find out on their own.

The way toward learning starts with observations or information, for example, models, direct insight, or guidance, to search for designs in information and settle on better choices later on dependent on the models that we give. The essential point is to permit the PCs adapt consequently without human intercession or help and change activities in like manner.

In any case, utilizing the exemplary calculations of AI, text is considered as an arrangement of watchwords; all things being equal, a methodology dependent on semantic examination impersonates the human capacity to comprehend the significance of a book.

AI empowers examination of monstrous amounts of information. While it by and large conveys quicker, more exact outcomes to distinguish beneficial freedoms or risky dangers, it might likewise require extra time and assets to prepare it appropriately. Consolidating AI with AI and intellectual innovations can make it significantly more powerful in preparing huge volumes of data.

Figure 2.4 [20] shows various categories of algorithms under supervised and unsupervised learning.

2.4 Supervised Learning

In supervised learning, the student is furnished with named input information. This information contains a grouping of info/yield sets of the structure (x_i, y_i), where x_i is a potential information, and y_i is the accurately marked yield related with it. The point of the student in administered learning is to take in the planning from contributions to yields. The supervised learning process is required to gain proficiency with a capacity of that represents the information/yield sets seen such a huge number, $(x_i) = y_i$, for all. This capacity f is known as a classifier if the yield is discrete and a relapse work if the yield is ceaseless.

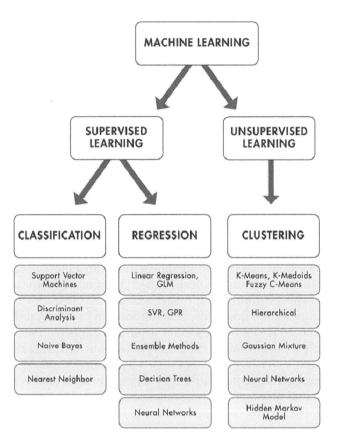

FIGURE 2.4
Tree structure of ML algorithms.

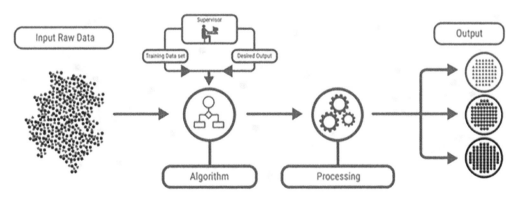

FIGURE 2.5
Supervised learning.

Supervised machine learning presently makes up maximum of the ML that is being used by systems across the world. The input variable (x) is used to connect with the output variable (y) through the use of an algorithm. As depicted in Figure 2.5, all of the input, the output, the algorithm, and the scenario are being provided by humans. We can understand supervised learning in an even better way by looking at it through two types of problems.

- **Classification**: Classification problems categorize all the variables that form the output. Examples of these categories formed through classification would include demographic data such as marital status, sex, or age. The most common model used for this type of service status is the support vector machine. The support vector machines are set forth to define the linear decision boundaries.

- **Regression**: Problems that can be classified as regression problems include types where the output variables are set as a real number. The format for this problem often follows a linear format.

2.5 Unsupervised Learning

Collecting marked information is though demanding but tedious, where precise naming is frequently difficult to accomplish. In unsupervised learning, the student is furnished with input information, which has not been named. The point of the student is to find the inalienable examples in the information that can be utilized to decide the right yield and incentive for new information occasions. The supposition here is that there is a structure to the info space, to such an extent that specific examples happen more regularly than others, and we need to perceive what for the most part occurs and what doesn't. In insights, this is called thickness assessment. Unsupervised learning calculations are exceptionally helpful for sensor network applications for the accompanying reasons – Collecting named information is asset and tedious – accurate naming is difficult to accomplish – sensor network applications are regularly conveyed in unusual and continually evolving conditions [21] (Figure 2.6).

During the process of unsupervised learning, the system does not have concrete data sets, and the outcomes to most of the problems are largely unknown. In simple terminology, the AI system and the ML objective is blinded when it goes into the operation. The system has its faultless and immense logical operations to guide it along the way, but the lack of proper input and output algorithms makes the process even more challenging. Incredible as the whole process may sound, unsupervised learning has the ability to interpret and find solutions to a limitless amount of data, through the input data and the binary logic mechanism present in all computer systems, depicted in Figure 2.6. The system has no reference data at all.

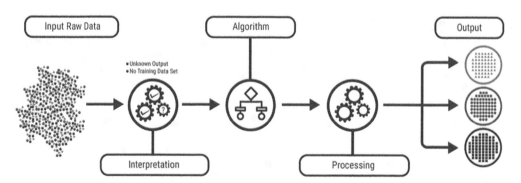

FIGURE 2.6
Unsupervised learning.

Since we expect readers to have a basic imagery of unsupervised learning by now, it would be pertinent to make the understanding even simpler through the use of an example. Just consider that we have a digital image that has a variety of colored geometric shapes on it. These geometric shapes needed to be matched into groups according to color and other classification features. For a system that follows supervised learning, this whole process is a bit too simple.

The procedure is extremely straightforward, as you just have to teach the computer all the details pertaining to the figures. You can let the system know that all shapes with four sides are known as squares, and others with eight sides are known as octagons, etc. We can also teach the system to interpret the colors and see how the light being given out is classified.

2.6 Semi-Supervised Learning

Semi-supervised learning calculations utilize both labeled and unlabeled data for preparing, as depicted in Figure 2.7.

The named information is regularly a little level of the preparation dataset. The objective of semi-supervised learning is as follows:

1. To see how joining marked and unlabeled information may change the learning conduct.
2. To plan calculations that exploit such a blend.

Semi-regulated learning is an extremely encouraging methodology since it can utilize promptly accessible unlabeled information to improve managed learning assignments when the named information is scant or costly features and classifiers.

Figure 2.8 shows two accelerometer signals corresponding to different activities [22]: resting vs. walking vs. running.

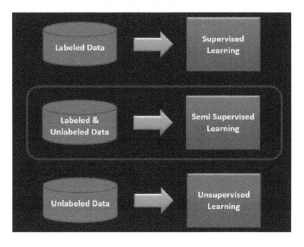

FIGURE 2.7
Semi-supervised learning.

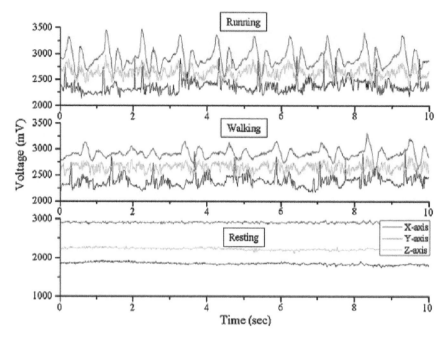

FIGURE 2.8
Different activities corresponding to signals.

The two signals are also themselves visually different. We will further assume that these are not the only patterns (signals) that are available to us, but we have access to a signal database with a number of patterns, some of which are known to originate from resting and some from walking [23]. The first step is to identify the measurable quantities that make these two regions distinct from each other. We can plot the mean value of the intensity in each region of interest versus the corresponding standard deviation around this mean. Each point will correspond to a different signal/region from the available database. It turns out that resting patterns (o) tend to spread in a different area from waking patterns (+). The straight line seems to be a good candidate for separating the two classes (o and +) and multiclass classification with three classes. Figure 2.9 [24] represents the example of binary and multiclass classification of various data points.

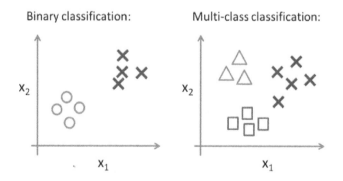

FIGURE 2.9
Binary and multiclass classification.

FIGURE 2.10
Reinforcement learning.

2.7 Reinforcement Learning

This ML algorithm is a learning technique that collaborates with its current circumstance by delivering activities and finds blunders or rewards. Experimentation search and postponed reward are the most significant qualities of fortification learning. Reinforcement learning is a type of machine learning technique that enables an agent to learn in an interactive environment by trial and error using feedback from its own actions and experiences [25,26].

Though both supervised and reinforcement learning use mapping between input and output, unlike supervised learning where feedback provided to the agent is correct set of actions for performing a task, reinforcement learning uses rewards and punishment as signals for positive and negative behavior.

As compared to unsupervised learning, reinforcement learning is different in terms of goals. While the goal in unsupervised learning is to find similarities and differences between data points, in reinforcement learning, the goal is to find a suitable action model that would maximize the total cumulative reward of the agent. Figure 2.10 represents the basic idea and elements involved in a reinforcement learning model.

2.8 Use Case of Signal Processing Using Supervised and Unsupervised Learning

2.8.1 Features and Classifiers

The preceding artificial classification task has outlined the rationale behind a large class of pattern recognition problems. The measurements used for the classification, the mean value and the standard deviation in this case, are known as features. In the more general case, l features x_i, $i=1, 2, ..., l$ are used, and they form the feature vector

$$x = [x_1, x_2, ..., x_l]^T$$

Each of the feature vectors identifies uniquely a single pattern [27]. Throughout this course, features and feature vectors will be treated as random variables and vectors, respectively. Measurements resulting from different patterns exhibit a random variation. This is due partly to the measurement noise of the measuring devices and partly to the distinct characteristics of each pattern. This is the reason for the scattering of the points in each class shown in the previous figure. The straight line in that figure is known as the decision line, and it constitutes the classifier whose role is to divide the feature space into regions that correspond to either class o or class +.

If a feature vector x, corresponding to an unknown pattern, falls in the class o region, it is classified as class o, otherwise as class +. This does not necessarily mean that the decision is correct. If it is not correct, a misclassification has occurred. In order to draw the straight line in the previous figure, we exploited the fact that we knew the labels (class o or +) for each point of the figure. The patterns (feature vectors) whose true class is known and which are used for the design of the classifier are known as training patterns (training feature vectors)

Having outlined the definitions and the rationale, let us point out the basic questions arising in a classification task:

- How are the features generated?
- What is the best number l of features to use?
- Having adopted the appropriate features, how does one design the classifier? (Optimality criterion).
- Once the classifier has been designed, how can one assess the performance of the designed classifier? (Classification error rate).

Figure 2.11 [28] shows the basic stages involved in the design of a classification system.
As is apparent from the feedback arrows, these stages are not independent.

2.8.2 Linear Classifiers

The major advantage of linear classifiers is their simplicity and computational attractiveness. We start assuming that all feature vectors from the available classes can be classified correctly using a linear classifier, and we will develop techniques for the computation of the corresponding linear functions. Next, we will focus on a more general problem, in which a linear classifier cannot correctly classify all vectors, yet we will seek ways to design an optimal linear classifier by adopting an appropriate optimality criterion.

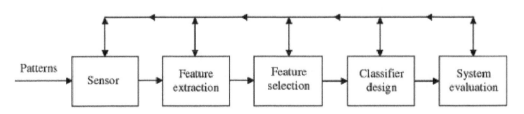

FIGURE 2.11
Stages of classification.

2.8.3 Decision Hyperplanes

Let us once more focus on the two-class case and consider linear discriminant functions. Then the respective decision hypersurface in the one-dimensional feature space is a hyperplane, that is,

$$g(x) = w^T x + w_0 = 0$$

where

$w = [w_1, w_2, \ldots, w_l]^T$ is known as the weight vector and w_0 as the threshold.

It can be shown that the vector w is orthogonal to the decision hyperplane.

In other words, $|g(x)|$ is a measure of the Euclidean distance of the point x from the decision hyperplane. On one side of the plane, $g(x)$ takes positive values and on the other negative [27].

2.8.4 Least Squares Methods

Although we know that the classes are not linearly separable, we still wish to adopt a linear classifier in many cases, despite the fact that this will lead to suboptimal performance from the classification error probability point of view. Remember, the goal now is to compute the corresponding weight vector under a suitable optimality criterion. So, in this section, we will attempt to design a linear classifier so that its desired output is again ±1, depending on the class ownership of the input vector. However, we will have to live with errors; that is, the true output will not always be equal to the desired one.

Given a vector x, the output of the classifier will be $w^T x$.

The desired output will be denoted as $y(x) \equiv y = \pm 1$.

The weight vector will be computed so as to minimize the mean square error (MSE) between the desired and true outputs.

The least-squares technique is an urgent factual strategy that is rehearsed to discover a relapse line or a best-fit line for the given example. This strategy is portrayed by a condition with explicit boundaries. The technique for least squares is liberally utilized in assessment and relapse. In relapse investigation, this strategy is supposed to be a standard methodology for the estimate of sets of conditions having a greater number of conditions than the quantity of questions.

The technique for least squares really characterizes the answer for the minimization of the amount of squares of deviations or the mistakes in the consequence of every condition. Discover the equation for amount of squares of mistakes, which help to discover the variety in noticed information.

The least-squares strategy is frequently applied in information fitting. The best-fit outcome is expected to diminish the amount of squared blunders or residuals which are expressed to be the contrasts between the noticed or exploratory worth and relating fitted worth given in the model.

There are two fundamental classifications of least-squares issues:

- Ordinary or linear least squares
- Nonlinear least squares

These rely on linearity or nonlinearity of the residuals. The direct issues are regularly found in relapse investigation in measurements. Then again, the non-straight issues are commonly utilized in the iterative technique for refinement in which the model is approximated to the direct one with every cycle.

2.8.5 Mean Square Estimation

Let y, x be two random vector variables of dimensions $M \times 1$ and 1×1, respectively, and assume that they are described by the joint pdf $p(y, x)$. The task of interest is to estimate the value of y, given the value of x that is obtained from an experiment. No doubt the classification task falls under this more general formulation. In a more general setting, the values of y may not be discrete. Take, as an example, the case where $y \in R$ is generated by an unknown rule $y = f(x) + \varepsilon$.

The task now is to estimate (predict) the value of y, given the value of x. Once more, this is a problem of designing a function $g(x)$, based on a set of training data points (y_i, x_i), $i = 1$, 2, ..., N, so that the predicted value

$$\hat{y} = g(x)$$

is as close as possible to the true value y in some optimal sense. This type of problem is known as a regression task. One of the most popular optimality criteria for regression is the MSE

The mean square estimate $\hat{y}$ of the random vector y, given the value x, is defined as

$$\hat{y} = \min \hat{y}$$

$E\left[|y - \hat{y}|2\right]$. Note that the mean value here is with respect to the conditional pdf $p(y|x)$. It can be shown that the optimal estimate is the mean value of y, that is,

$$\hat{y} = E[y|x] \equiv Z_\infty - \infty$$

$$y_p(y \mid x)dy$$

2.8.6 Support Vector Machines

Let x_i, $i = 1$, 2, ..., N, be the feature vectors of the training set, X. These belong to either of two classes, w_1 and w_2, which are assumed to be linearly separable. The goal, once more, is to design a hyperplane $g(x) = w^T x + w_0 = 0$.

This classifies correctly all the training vectors. As we have already discussed, such a hyperplane is not unique. The perceptron algorithm may converge to any one of the possible solutions.

A very sensible choice for the hyperplane classifier would be the one that leaves the maximum margin from both classes. Here we have touched a very important issue in the classifier design stage: it is known as the generalization performance of the classifier. This refers to the capability of the classifier, designed using the training data set, to operate satisfactorily with data outside this set. Let us now quantify the term margin that a hyperplane leaves from both classes. Every hyperplane is characterized by its direction (determined by w) and its exact position in space (determined by w_0). Since we want to give no preference to either of the classes, it is reasonable for each direction to select that

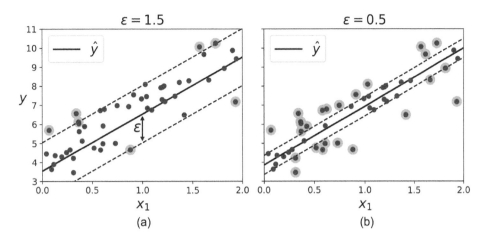

FIGURE 2.12
Two-class problem: (a) class 1 with w1; (b) class 2 with w2.

hyperplane which has the same distance from the respective nearest points in ω_1 and ω_2. Thus, our goal is to search for the direction that gives the maximum possible margin. Recall that the distance of a point from a hyperplane is given by equation below:

$$z = \left(| g(x) | \right) / \left(| w | \right)$$

Figure 2.12 shows an example of a linearly separable two-class problem with two possible linear classifiers.

Figure 2.12 shows a set of training data points residing in the two-dimensional space and divided into two non-separable classes. The full line in Figure 2.12a is the resulting hyperplane using Platt's algorithm and corresponds to the value $C=0.2$. Dotted lines meet the conditions given in (3.82) and define the margin that separates the two classes, for those points with $\xi_i=0$. The setting in Figure 2.12b corresponds to $C=\mathbf{1,000}$ and has been obtained with the same algorithm and the same set of trimming parameters (e.g., stopping criteria) [29,30].

2.8.7 Non-Linear Regression

NL model is more powerful than linear model and more difficult than linear regression. It uses NL equations that can take the form

$$Y = f\left(X, \, \beta\right) + \varepsilon,$$

where
    X=a vector of p predictors,
    β=a vector of k parameters,
    $f(-)$=a known regression function,
    ε=an error term.

Nonlinear regression is shown in Figure 2.13.

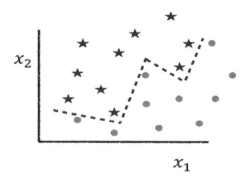

FIGURE 2.13
Nonlinear regression.

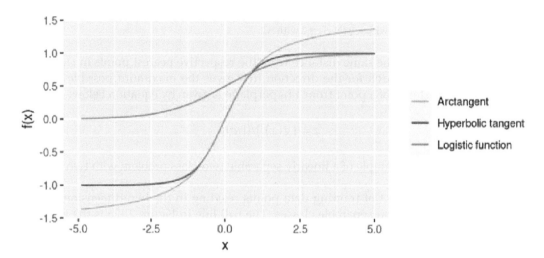

FIGURE 2.14
Sigmoid functions.

2.8.8 Non-Linearity of Activation Functions

2.8.8.1 Sigmoid Function

It is a mathematical function which takes the characteristics of S-shape. The common sigmoid functions are logistic, hyperbolic tan, and the arctangent presented in Figure 2.14 [31].

1. **Logistic Sigmoid Function Formula:** In the field of machine learning, this is commonly referred to as the sigmoid function.

$$S(x) = \frac{1}{1 + e^{-x}}$$

$$= \frac{e^x}{e^x + 1}$$

2. **Hyperbolic Tangent Function Formula**: It maps any real-valued input to the range between −1 and 1.

$$f(x) = \tan h(x)$$

$$= \frac{e^x - e^{-x}}{e^x + e^{-x}}$$

3. **Arctangent Function Formula**: This is the inverse of the tangent function.

$$f(x) = \arctan(x)$$

2.8.8.2 Rectified Linear Unit (ReLU)

This is the most widely used activation function in the deep learning models and it is represented as $f(x) = \max(0, x)$ and graphically as Figure 2.15.

2.8.9 Classification

2.8.9.1 Linear Classification

It is a classification algorithm (classifier) that defines its classification based on a linear predictor function combining a set of weights with the feature vector.

$$Y = f(\vec{w} \cdot \vec{x}) = f\left(\sum_j w_j x_j\right)$$

2.8.9.2 Two-Class Classification

It is also known as multiclass classification where the problem is classified into one or more classes.

$$y(x) = w^T X + w_0$$

and graphically as Figure 2.16.

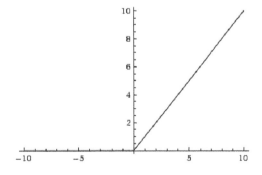

FIGURE 2.15
Rectified linear unit.

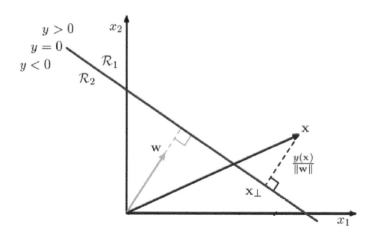

FIGURE 2.16
Two-class classification.

2.8.9.3 Geometrical Interpretation of Derivatives

Let AB be the line passing through the points $(x, f(x))$ and $(x+\Delta x, f(x+\Delta x))$. If Δx, that is, approaches zero, then the line approaches the tangent line at the point $(x, f(x))$ [32]. Accordingly, the slope of the tangent line is the limit of the slope of the line when Δx approaches zero, as shown in Figure 2.17.

Thus, the derivative $f'(x)$ can be interpreted as the slope of the tangent line at the point (x, y) on the graph of the function $y=f(x)$.

Whenever the function starts increasing at some interval, the slope of the tangent is positive at each point of that interval, and hence, the derivative of the function is positive.

Whenever the function starts decreasing at some interval, the slope of the tangent is negative at each point of that interval, and hence, the derivative of the function is negative.

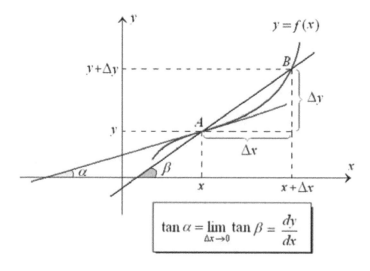

FIGURE 2.17
Geometric interpretation of derivatives.

2.8.9.4 Multiclass Classification: Loss Function

It is a machine learning classification functionality where there can be one or more classes or output.

As a feature of the optimization algorithm, the error of the present status of the model should be estimated consistently. This requires the option of an error function that is known as loss function, which can be utilized to estimate the loss of the model so the weights can be updated to prevent the loss.

2.8.10 Mean Squared Error

The MSE informs you about how close can the regression line be to a set of points. Examples are finding the line of regression, square of errors, etc.

Formula:

$$\text{MSE} = \frac{1}{n}\sum_{i=1}^{n}\left(Y_i \cdot \hat{Y}_i\right)^2$$

2.8.11 Multilabel Classification

As there is a continuous increase in the data available, there is need to organize those data. Hence, modern classification problem involves prediction of such multi-labels associated with the instance.

Accuracy in single label classification:

$$\frac{1}{N}\sum_{i=1}^{N} I\left[\hat{y}^{(i)} = y^{(i)}\right]$$

2.8.12 Gradient Descent

It is the most popularly used optimization technique in machine learning at the present time. These are used when training data models, can be combined with every algorithm, and is easy to understand and implement. In simple terms, it measures the change in the weights with regard to the change in error.

Working of GD:

Let's think of a climber hiking down a mountain, imagine GD as hiking down the valley.

See the below equation:

$$b = a - \gamma \triangle f(a)$$

where

b is the next position of the climber, while a is the current position.

– is the minimization;

γ is the waiting factor and rest as simply the direction of the downhill.

2.8.12.1 Learning Rate

- It moves faster in directions with minimal but consistent gradients.
- It moves slowly in directions with higher but inconsistent gradients.
- At the end of the learning, it reduces the learning rate.

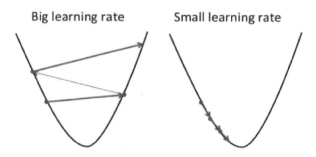

FIGURE 2.18
Learning rate in gradient descent.

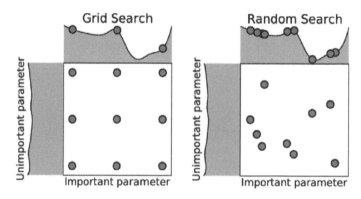

FIGURE 2.19
Grid search vs. random search.

Big and small learning rates [33] are represented in Figure 2.18.

2.8.13 Hyperparameter Tuning

It is a parameter where the value is set before beginning of the learning process. Few examples include loss in stochastic gradient descent and penalty in logistic regression. The difference between grid search and random search is depicted in Figure 2.19.

2.8.13.1 Validation

For implementation to be effective,

- Use different machines
- Decrease the data size
- Decrease the number of frequency of checks.

2.8.14 Regularization

In machine learning, the regularization is a process that regularizes or reduces the coefficient toward zero. In general, regularization means to make things regular or acceptable. This is exactly why we use it for applied machine learning. In the context of machine learning, regularization is the process which regularizes or shrinks the coefficients toward zero. In simple words, regularization discourages learning a more complex or flexible model, to prevent overfitting.

2.8.14.1 How Does Regularization Work?

The basic idea is to penalize the complex models, i.e., adding a complexity term that would give a bigger loss for complex models. To understand it, let's consider a simple relation for linear regression. Mathematically, it is stated as below:

$$Y \approx W_0 + W_1\ X_1 + W_2 X_{(2)} + \ldots + W_P X_P$$

where
Y is the learned relation, i.e., the value to be predicted.

$X_1, X_{(2)}, [\ldots,\ X]_P$ are the features deciding the value of Y.

$W_1, W_{(2)}, [\ldots, W]_P$ are the weights attached to the features $X_1, X_{(2)}, [\ldots,\ X]_P$, respectively.

W_0 represents the bias.

Now, in order to fit a model that accurately predicts the value of Y, we require a loss function and optimized parameters, i.e., bias and weights.

The loss function generally used for linear regression is called the residual sum of squares (RSS). According to the above stated linear regression relation, it can be given as follows:

$$\text{RSS} = \sum (j=1)^m \left(Y_i - W_0 - \sum_{(i=1)}^{n} W_i X_{ji} \right)^2$$

We can also call RSS as the linear regression objective without regularization.

Now, the model will learn by the means of this loss function. Based on our training data, it will adjust the weights (coefficients). If our dataset is noisy, it will face overfitting problems, and estimated coefficients won't generalize on the unseen data.

This is where regularization comes into action. It regularizes these learned estimates toward zero by penalizing the magnitude of coefficients.

2.8.15 Regularization Techniques

There are two main regularization techniques, namely ridge regression and lasso regression. They both differ in the way they assign a penalty to the coefficients.

2.8.15.1 Ridge Regression (L2 Regularization)

This regularization technique performs L2 regularization. It modifies the RSS by adding the penalty (shrinkage quantity) equivalent to the square of the magnitude of coefficients.

$$\sum_{(j=1)}^{m} \left(Y_i - W_0 - \sum_{(i=1)}^{n} W_i X_{ji} \right)^2 + \alpha \sum_{(i=1)}^{n} W_i^2 = \text{RSS} + \alpha \sum_{(i=1)}^{n} W_i^2$$

Now, the coefficients are estimated using this modified loss function.

In the above equation, you may have noticed the parameter α (alpha) along with shrinkage quantity. This is called a tuning parameter that decides how much we want to penalize our model. In other terms, tuning parameter balances the amount of emphasis given to minimizing RSS vs. minimizing the sum of the square of coefficients.

Let's see how the value of α alpha affects the estimates produced by ridge regression.

When $\alpha=0$, the penalty term has no effect. It means it returns the residual sum of the square as loss function which we choose initially, i.e., we will get the same coefficients as simple linear regression.

When $\alpha=\infty$, the ridge regression coefficient will be zero because the modified loss function will ignore the core loss function and minimize coefficients square and eventually end up taking the parameter's value as 0.

When $0<\alpha<\infty$, for simple linear regression, the ridge regression coefficient will be somewhere between 0 and 1.

That's the reason for selecting a good value of α (alpha) is critical. The coefficient methods produced by the ridge regression regularization technique are also known as the L2 norm.

2.8.16 Lasso Regression (L1 Regularization)

This regularization technique performs L1 regularization. It modifies the RSS by adding the penalty (shrinkage quantity) equivalent to the sum of the absolute value of coefficients.

$$\sum_{(j=1)}^{m}\left(Y_i - W_0 - \sum_{(i=1)}^{n} W_i X_{ji}\right)^2 + \sum_{(i=1)}^{n}|W_i| = \text{RSS} + \sum_{(i=1)}^{n}|W_i|$$

Now, the coefficients are estimated using this modified loss function.

Lasso regression is different from ridge regression as it uses absolute coefficient values for normalization.

As loss function only considers absolute coefficients (weights), the optimization algorithm will penalize high coefficients. This is known as the L1 norm.

2.8.17 K-Means Clustering

It is a simple yet powerful algorithm in data science.

Given: $S=\{x_1, ..., x_n\}$, a set S of n vectors of dimension d and an integer k

Goal: Find $C=\{\mu_1, ..., \mu_k\}$, a set of k cluster centers, that minimize the expression:

Formula:

$$f = \sum_i mi \left\| x - \mu_j \right\|^2$$

Regulated AI calculations are utilized to tackle characterization or relapse issues.

An order issue has a discrete incentive as its yield. For instance, "likes pineapple on pizza" and "doesn't care for pineapple on pizza" are discrete. There is no center ground. The similarity above of encouraging a youngster to distinguish a pig is another illustration of a grouping issue depicted in Figure 2.20.

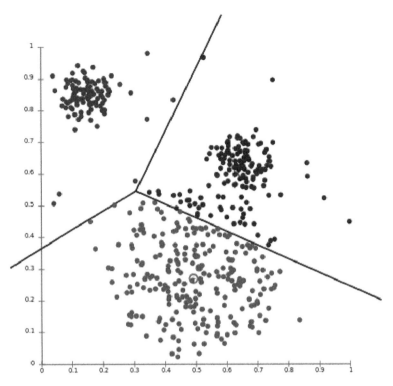

FIGURE 2.20
Classification example.

Table 2.1 shows an essential illustration of what characterization information may resemble. We have an indicator (or set of indicators) and a mark. In Table 2.1, we may be attempting to anticipate whether somebody enjoys pineapple (1) on their pizza or not (0) in light of their age (the indicator).

It is standard practice to speak to the yield (name) of a grouping calculation as a whole number, for example, 1, –1, or 0. In this occurrence, these numbers are simply authentic. Numerical activities ought not to be performed on them in light of the fact that doing so would be pointless. Think for a second. What is "likes pineapple" + "doesn't care for pineapple"? Precisely. We can't add them, so we ought not to add their numeric portrayals. In contrast to supervised learning that attempts to get familiar with a capacity that will permit us to make forecasts given some new unlabeled information, unsupervised learning attempts to get familiar with the essential structure of the information to give us more knowledge into the information.

The KNN calculation expects that comparable things exist in closeness. All in all, comparable things are close to one another.

There are alternate methods of ascertaining distance, and one way may be ideal relying upon the difficulty we are settling. Be that as it may, the straight-line distance (additionally called the Euclidean distance) is a mainstream and recognizable decision.

2.8.18 The KNN Algorithm

- Burden the information
- Instate K to your picked number of neighbors

TABLE 2.1

Age and Likes Pineapple on Pizza

Age	Likes Pineapple on Pizza
42	1
65	1
50	1
75	1
95	1
50	1
91	1
25	1
23	1
75	1
45	0
87	0
95	0
45	0
32	1
63	0
21	1
25	1
93	0
68	1
95	0

- For every model in the information
  - Calculate the distance between the inquiry model and the current model from the information
  - Add the distance and the list of the guide to an arranged assortment
- Sort the arranged assortment of distances and lists from littlest to biggest (in climbing request) by the distances
- Pick the principal K passages from the arranged assortment
- Get the names of the chose K sections
- On the off chance that relapse, return the mean of the K marks
- On the off chance that order, return the method of the K marks

2.8.19 Clustering

The strategy of group investigation can be separated into four phases, illustrated in Figure 2.21 given below:

1. **Feature Selection or Extraction**: Highlight choice picks recognizing highlights from a bunch of competitors and highlight extraction utilizes information changes to create valuable and novel highlights. Both are very urgent to the effectiveness of grouping applications. Rich determination of highlights can enormously diminish

FIGURE 2.21
Phases of clustering.

the outstanding burden and improve the ensuing plan measure. Ideal highlights ought to have a place with divergent groups, are resistant to clamor, and are anything but difficult to extricate and decipher.

2. **Clustering Algorithm Design or Selection**: This progression is normally joined with the determination of a relating vicinity measure. Examples are gathered according to whether they resemble each other, and the proximity measure directly affects the development of the subsequent bunches. There is no bunching calculation that can be generally used to take care of all issues. In this manner, it is significant to painstakingly research the attributes of the current issue, to utilize a fitting system.

3. **Cluster Validation**: Different approaches for the most part lead to different bunches, and in any event, for a similar calculation, boundary identification or the arrangement of information examples may affect the final results. Therefore, effective assessment guidelines and standards are essential to furnish the specialist with a level of confidence for the outcomes obtained from the preowned calculations. These appraisals should be unbiased and have no inclinations and should be valuable for addressing inquiries on the number of bunches covered up in the information, regardless of whether the groups acquired are important or why we pick some calculation as an option of another.

4. **Result Translation**: A definitive objective of bunching is to give significant experiences from the first information.

2.8.20 Clustering Methods

Time arrangement bunching can be partitioned into two principal categories: "entire clustering" and "aftereffect clustering." "Entire clustering" is the bunching performed on numerous individual time arrangements to aggregate comparable arrangement into groups. "Aftereffect grouping" depends on sliding window extractions of a solitary time arrangement and means to find likeness and differences among different time windows of a solitary time arrangement [34].

The clustering algorithms are usually classified as hierarchical or partition-based. These classifications will be briefly depicted underneath.

- **Hierarchical Algorithms**: This grouping instrument makes a various-levelled decay of the dataset utilizing some standard. The various levelled bunching calculation bunches information to frame a tree model structure and find progressive groups by utilizing ones recently settled. It very well may be separated into agglomerative various-levelled clustering ("bottom up") and troublesome progressive grouping ("top down"). In agglomerative methodology, all information focuses are viewed as a separate cluster, and on each iteration, clusters are joined based on criteria. In troublesome methodology, all information focuses are considered as a solitary bunch, and afterward, they are isolated into various groups dependent on specific rules.

- **Partition-Based Algorithms**: In this method, various partitions are constructed and then evaluated by some criterion. The parcel bunching calculation parts the information focuses into k segments, where each segment speaks to a group. The bunch should display two properties:

  1. Each gathering should contain in any event one article;
  2. Each item should have a place with precisely one gathering. The fundamental shortcoming of this calculation is that at whatever point a point is near another group's middle, it gives frail outcomes because of covering information focuses. In this exposition, a segment-based calculation, the K-means, is utilized. The primary thought of the K-means clustering is to define a circle with k centroids (focuses of the group) far away from one another, taking each direct having a place toward a given dataset and partner it to the closest centroid. Rehashing the circle, the centroid's position will change since they are re-determined by averaging all the focuses in the bunch, and after a few emphases, the position will settle, accomplishing the final groups [11]. The fundamental favorable circumstances of this calculation are its straightforwardness, efficiency, and speed, which are acceptable credits for huge datasets.

- **Distance-Based Methods**: As referenced previously, a distance put together grouping is worked with respect to the likeness between the information determined with a picked distance metric. Different distance measures can be applied to the information which will decide how the closeness of two components is determined. A simple Euclid and distance metric is sufficient to successfully group similar information cases. Notwithstanding, some of the times, a picked distance metric can be deluding, and therefore, it's important to know which will suit best the input data – this will influence grouping results, as certain components might be near each other as per one distance and farther away as indicated by another. Several approaches for time series comparison have been proposed. The most straightforward approach relies on similarity measures which directly compare observations or features extracted from raw data. In the time area, the auto connection and cross-relationship capacities are utilized to this end. Other than the estimations made straightforwardly between time arrangement, distances can likewise be processed from changes of the information. In the recurrence space, procedures utilizing discrete Fourier change of information and wavelets are additionally utilized.

  Liao [35] presented an overview on time arrangement information bunching, uncovering past explores regarding the matter. The research work arranges bunching in three gatherings: regardless of whether they work straightforwardly with the crude information, by implication with highlights extricated or in a roundabout way with models worked from the crude information. By demonstrating the crude information with a stochastic model, similitudes are recognized in the elements of different time arrangement.

2.9 Deep Learning for Signal Data

Deep learning for signal processing requires additional means when contrasted with applying deep learning or AI to other informational indexes. Great quality sign information is difficult to acquire and has such a huge number and fluctuation [36–38]. Wideband commotion, nerves, and twists are only a couple of the undesirable attributes found in most sign information depicted in Figure 2.22.

Likewise with all deep learning projects, and particularly for signal information, your prosperity will quite often rely upon how much information you have and the computational intensity of your machine, so a decent deep learning workstation is energetically suggested.

To sidestep utilizing deep learning, an intensive comprehension of sign information and sign handling will be required to utilize AI methods which depend on less information than deep learning [37] depicted in Figure 2.23.

1. The cycle would include putting away, perusing, and prepreparing the information. This will likewise include separating and changing highlights and parting into preparing and test sets. In the event that you are intending to utilize a managed learning calculation, the information will require naming.

2. Visualizing the information will be vital to recognizing the sort of prepreparing and highlighting extraction strategies that will be required. For signal handling, picturing is needed in the time, recurrence and time-recurrence areas for appropriate investigation.

3. Once the information has been imagined, it will be important to change and concentrate highlights from the information, for example, tops, change focuses, and signal examples.

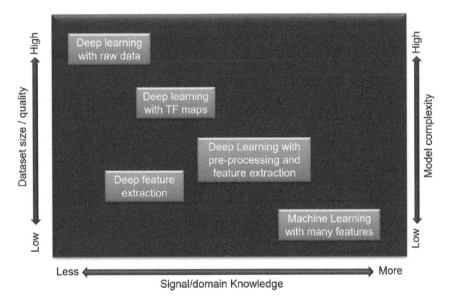

FIGURE 2.22
Deep learning.

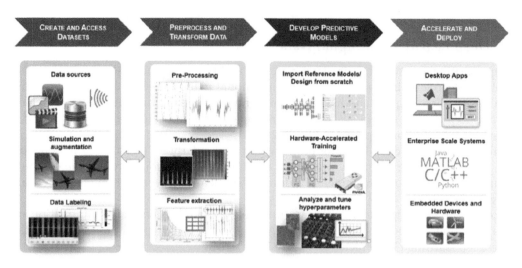

FIGURE 2.23
Phases along with tools.

Prior to the coming of AI or deep learning, traditional models for time arrangement investigation were utilized since signals have a period explicit area.

2.9.1 Traditional Time Series Analysis

This involves visual review of time arrangement, taking a gander at change over the long run, investigating pinnacles and box.

2.9.2 Recurrence Domain Analysis

As per MathWorks [37], frequency domain analysis is one of the critical parts of signal processing. It is utilized in zones, for example, communications, geology, remote sensing, and image processing. Time domain analysis shows a sign's energy appropriated over the long haul, while a recurrence space portrayal remembers data for the stage move that should be applied to every recurrence part to recuperate the first run through sign with a blend of all the individual recurrence segments. A sign is changed among time and recurrence spaces utilizing numerical administrators called a "change." Two well-known instances of this are fast Fourier transform (FFT) and discrete Fourier transform (DFT).

2.9.3 Long Short-Term Memory Models for Human Activity Recognition

Human Activity Recognition (HAR) has been picking up footing as of late with the appearance of propelling human PC communications. It has certifiable applications in ventures going from medical care, wellness, gaming, military, and route. There are two sorts of HAR:

Sensor-based HAR (wearables that are appended to a human body, and human movement is converted into explicit sensor signal examples that can be sectioned and distinguished). Most exploration has moved to a sensor-based methodology because of progression in sensor innovation and its ease.

2.9.4 External Device HAR

Deep learning methods have been utilized to conquer the deficiencies of AI strategies that follow heuristics framed by the client. Deep learning strategies that can consequently separate highlights scale better for more unpredictable assignments. Sensor information is developing at a fast speed (e.g., Apple Watch, Fitbit, person on foot following, and so forth), and the measure of information produced is adequate for deep learning strategies to learn and create more precise outcomes.

Repetitive neural networks are a reasonable decision for signal information as they inalienably have a period segment and accordingly a successive part. Deep Recurrent Neural Networks for HAR diagram some LSTM-based Deep RNNs to assemble HAR models for characterizing exercises planned from variable length input groupings.

Figure 2.24 above shows a proposed engineering for utilizing LSTM-based deep RNNs for HAR. The data sources will be crude signs obtained from multimodular sensors, fragmented into windows of length *T*, and took care of into LSTM-based DRNN model. The

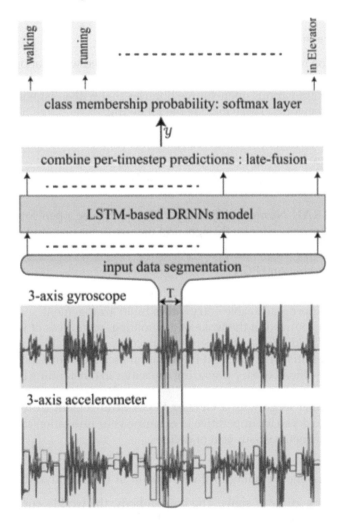

FIGURE 2.24
Utilizing LSTM-based deep RNNs for HAR.

model will at that point yield class expectation scores for each time-step, which are then combined through late-combination and took care of into the softmax layer to decide class enrollment likelihood [39].

The model performs direct start to finish planning from crude multimodal sensor contributions to action name characterizations. The info is a vector of discrete grouping of similarly dispersed examples seen by the sensors at time t. These examples are divided into windows of a most extreme time file T and took care of into a LSTM-based DRNN model. The yield of the model is a grouping of scores speaking to movement mark forecasts in which there is a name expectation for each time step (yL_1, yL_2, ..., yL_t), where $yL_t \in R_C$ is a vector of scores speaking to the forecast for a given information test x_t, and C is the quantity of action classes.

There will be a score for each time-step anticipating the kind of movement happening at time t. The expectation for the whole window T is obtained by consolidating the individual scores into a solitary forecast. The model uses a late-combination strategy in which the characterization choices from singular examples are joined for the general forecast of a window.

2.9.5 Signal Processing on GPUs

In the event that you're not previously utilizing a GPU-based workstation, you should consider changing from your slower CPU. You can ordinarily observe execution gains of 30x or more, and there are various open-source libraries that will assist with signal handling on GPU-based frameworks. These include the following:

- **NVIDIA Performance Primitives (NPP)**: Provides GPU-quickened picture, video, and sign handling capacities.
- **ArrayFire**: GPU-quickened open-source library for network, sign, and picture handling.
- **IMSL FORTRAN Numerical Library**: GPU-quickened open-source FORTRAN library with capacities for math, sign, and picture preparing, and measurements.

2.9.6 Signal Processing on FPGAs

An option in contrast to utilizing a GPU-based framework for signal handling is investigating a FPGA (field programmable entryway exhibit) arrangement.

FPGAs can be customized in the wake of assembling, regardless of whether the equipment is now in the "field." FPGAs frequently work coupled with CPUs to quicken throughput for focused capacities in figure and information escalated outstanding tasks at hand. This permits you to offload dreary preparing capacities in outstanding burdens to support execution of uses.

Concluding whether to go with a GPU or FPGA arrangement truly relies upon what you're attempting to do, so it's imperative to examine your utilization case with a business engineer to decide benefits versus cost of each.

2.9.7 Signal Processing is coming to the Forefront of Data Analysis

The actual world is a guide of signs. The human body, the world's current circumstance, space, and even creatures all produce flags that can be examined and perceived utilizing numerical and factual models. Signal preparing has been utilized to comprehend the human cerebrum, illnesses, sound handling, picture handling, and monetary signs, and that's just the beginning. Signal preparing is gradually coming into the standard of information investigation with new deep learning models being created to examine signal information [40].

2.10 Conclusion

Data-driven machine learning, especially deep learning technology, is fetching significant tools for treating big data issues in various domains. Machine learning and signal processing areas are parallel handling the need of todays' business domains. This chapter aims at introducing the fundamentals of machine learning (ML) techniques useful for various signal processing applications. It also discussed various mathematical methods involved in ML, thereby enabling the readers to design their own models and optimize them efficiently. This chapter focused on mathematical principles. Applications in machine learning, signal processing and communication, and the theory were tailored. Supervised, unsupervised, semi-supervised, and reinforcement learning were discussed along with subcategories.

References

1. Lettvin, J. Y., Maturana, H. R., McCulloch, W. S., & Pitts, W. (1959). What the frog's eye tells the frog's brain. *Proc IRE* 47:1940.
2. McCulloch, W. S., & Pitts, W. (1943). A logical calculus of the ideas immanent in nervous activity. *Bull Math Biophys* 5:115.
3. Kim, J. H., Lim, J. G., & Chung, S. K. (2009). DSP-based digital controller for multi-phase synchronous buck converters. *J Power Electron* 9:410–417.
4. Lastre-Domínguez, C., Shmaliy, Y. S., Ibarra-Manzano, O., Munoz-Minjares, J. and Morales-Mendoza, L. J. (2019). ECG signal denoising and features extraction using unbiased FIR smoothing. *BioMed Res Int* 2019. Article ID 2608547, doi: 10.1155/2019/2608547.
5. Sysel, P., & Krajsa, O. (2010). "Optimization of FIR filter implementation for FMT on VLIW DSP," *Latest Trends on Circuits, Systems and Signals*, available at http://www.wseas.us/e-library/conferences/2010/Corfu/CSS/CSS-29.pdf.
6. Jain, R., & Puri, M. (2019, March). Securing sensitive business data in non-production environment using non-zero random replacement masking method. *Int J Appl Innov Eng Manag* 8(3):382–390, ISSN 2319-4847.
7. Shruti Sehgal, H. Singh, M. Agarwal, Bhasker, V., & Shantanu. (2014). "Data analysis using principal component analysis," *2014 International Conference on Medical Imaging, m-Health and Emerging Communication Systems (MedCom)*, Greater Noida, 2014, pp. 45–48, doi: 10.1109/MedCom.2014.7005973. https://www.semanticscholar.org/paper/Data-analysis-using-principal-zcomponent-analysis-Sehgal-Singh/d85313272033783c5e68a67930ebdc129aa80d5b
8. Signal Processing Using Machine Learning, (2018). https://medium.com/@ariesiitr/signal-processing-using-machine-learning-9c4eac331d78, received on 15/12/2020 at 4: 00 pm.
9. Samuel, A. L. (1959). Some studies in machine learning using the game of checkers. *IBM J Res Dev* 44(1.2):210–229.
10. Murphy, K. P. (2013). *Machine Learning – A Probabilistic Perspective*. The MIT Press, Cambridge, ISBN 978-0262018029.

11. https://aws.amazon.com/blogs/machine-learning/k-means-clustering-with-amazon-sagemaker/ (accessed on 15 November 2020).

12. https://www.gaussianwaves.com/2020/01/introduction-to-signal-processing-for-machine-learning/ (accessed on 2 October 2020).

13. Chauhan, P. M., & Desai, N. P. (2014). "Mel Frequency Cepstral Coefficients (MFCC) based speaker identification in noisy environment using wiener filter," *2014 International Conference on Green Computing Communication and Electrical Engineering (ICGCCEE)*, Coimbatore, pp. 1–5.

14. Jain, R., & Puri, M. (2018, June). A robust approach to secure structured sensitive data using non-deterministic random replacement algorithm. *Int J Comput Appl* 179(50):17–21.

15. Benk, S., Elmir, Y., & Dennai, A. (2019). A study on automatic speech recognition. *J Inf Technol Rev* 10:77–85. doi: 10.6025/jitr/2019/10/3/77-85.

16. Cioffi, R., Travaglioni, M., Piscitelli, G., Petrillo, A., & De Felice, F. (2020). Artificial intelligence and machine learning applications in smart production: progress, trends, and directions. *Sustainability* 12:492.

17. Memon, Q., Ahmed, M., Ali, S., Memon, A. R., & Shah, W. (2016). Self-driving and driver relaxing vehicle. doi: 10.1109/ICRAI.2016.7791248.

18. Rainham, D., Krewski, D., Mcdowell, I., Sawada, M., & Liekens, B. (2008). Development of a wearable global positioning system for place and health research. *Int J Health Geogr* 7:59. doi: 10.1186/1476-072X-7-59.

19. Achki, S., & Gharnati, F. (2019). A study of wireless communications systems based on multiple correspondence analysis. *J Netw Technol* 10:1. doi: 10.6025/jnt/2019/10/1/1-8.

20. https://ecmapping.com/2018/02/21/the-10-machine-learning-algorithms-to-master-for-beginners/ (accessed on 20 October 2020).

21. Alloghani, M., Al-Jumeily, D., Mustafina, J., Hussain, A., & Aljaaf, A.J. (2020). A systematic review on supervised and unsupervised machine learning algorithms for data science. In M. Berry, A. Mohamed, & B. Yap (Eds.), *Supervised and Unsupervised Learning for Data Science*, pp. 3–21. Springer, Cham.

22. https://www.researchgate.net/figure/3D-accelerometer-signals-of-a-person-running-walking-and-resting-8_fig3_263963769 (accessed on 25 October 2020).

23. Bowles, M. (2015). *Machine Learning in Python: Essential Techniques for Predictive Analytics*. John Wiley & Sons Inc., ISBN: 978-1-118-96174-2. Available at https://www.wiley.com/en-in/Machine+Learning+in+Python%3A+Essential+Techniques+for+Predictive+Analysis-p-9781118961742

24. https://medium.com/@b.terryjack/tips-and-tricks-for-multi-class-classification-c184ae1c8ffc (accessed on 25 October 2020).

25. Kaelbling, L. P., Littman, M. L., & Moore, A. W. (1996). Reinforcement learning: A survey. *J Artif Intell Res* 4:237–285.

26. Alzubi, J., Nayyar, A., & Kumar, A. (2018, November). Machine learning from theory to algorithms: An overview. *J Phys* 1142(1):012012.

27. https://www.statisticshowto.com/nonlinear-regression/ (accessed on 2 November 2020).

28. https://www.researchgate.net/figure/The-basic-stages-involved-in-the-design-of-a-classification-system_fig10_251660138 (accessed on 23 October 2020).

29. Theodoridis, S., & Koutroumbas, K. (2009). Pattern Recognition (Fourth Edition). Academic Press: Cambridge, MA.

30. https://www.sciencedirect.com/topics/computer-science/training-data-point (accessed on 23 October 2020).

31. https://deepai.org/machine-learning-glossary-and-terms/sigmoid-function (accessed on 5 November 2020).

32. https://portal.tpu.ru/SHARED/k/KONVAL/Sites/English_sites/calculus/3_Geometric_f.htm (accessed on 7 November 2020).

33. https://builtin.com/data-science/gradient-descent (accessed on 10 Nov 2020).

34. Patel, D., Modi, R., & Sarvakar, K. (2014). A comparative study of clustering data mining: Techniques and research challenges. *Int J Latest Technol Eng Manag Appl Sci* 3(9):67–70.

35. Liao, T. W. (2005). Clustering of time series data – A survey. *Pattern Recognit Soc* 38:1857–1874.

36. https://www.kaggle.com/dansbecker/rectified-linear-units-relu-in-deep-learning   (accessed on 5 November 2020).
37. https://blogs.mathworks.com/deep-learning/2019/05/13/deep-learning-for-signal-processing-applications/ (accessed on 23 November 2020).
38. Anavangot, V., Menon, V. G., & Nayyar, A. (2018, November). "Distributed big data analytics in the Internet of Signals," *2018 International Conference on System Modeling & Advancement in Research Trends (SMART)*, pp. 73–77, IEEE, Moradabad, India.
39. https://www.mdpi.com/1424-8220/17/11/2556/htm (accessed on 25 November 2020).
40. https://www.minidsp.com/applications/dsp-basics/time-alignment (accessed on 28 November 2020).

3

Supervised and Unsupervised Learning Theory for Signal Processing

Sowmya K. B.

RV College of Engineering

CONTENTS

3.1 Introduction

An assignment involving ML may not be lined, but then it has numerous steps to be involved like stating the problem, preparing the required data, learning an underlying model, and improving the quantitative and qualitative evaluations of underlying model to present the model. Machine learning algorithms are alienated into labeled training data called supervised learning and an algorithm in which labeled training data is unavailable called unsupervised learning. Another class of machine learning method is termed as semi-supervised learning by making use of labeled data and unlabeled data training

DOI: 10.1201/9781003107026-3

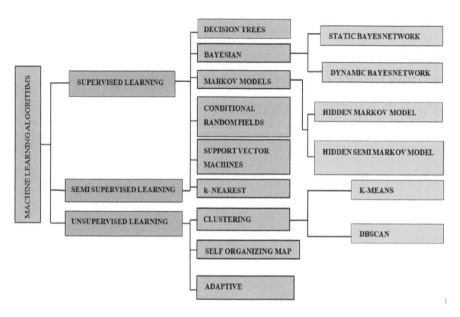

FIGURE 3.1
Types of machine learning algorithms.

set. Four categories of problems are noted in machine learning and pattern recognition. Figure 3.1 shows the types of ML algorithm.

3.1.1 Supervised Learning

The system has been given with example data inputs and their preferred outputs, given by an educator, and the objective is to learn a general rule of mapping inputs to outputs. Figure 3.2 shows the division of labeled and unlabeled data to obtain the learning methods [1].

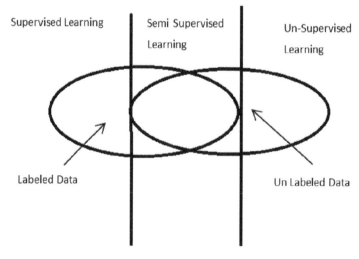

FIGURE 3.2
Division of labeled and unlabeled data.

3.1.2 Unsupervised Learning

In this learning, no labels are specified to the learning algorithm, making it independent to find construction in its input. Unsupervised learning is a goal in itself by realizing concealed patterns in data or a means in the direction of an ultimate termed as feature learning [2].

3.1.3 Reinforcement Learning

In this learning, system interrelates with a live situation where it has to perform a certain goal. When the system is navigating in the problem space, appraisal is provided in terms of plunders and penalties as it navigates its problem space [3].

3.1.4 Semi-Supervised Learning

Among supervised and unsupervised learning, there exist semi-supervised learning; here, the educator gives an inadequate training signal: by missing some of the target outputs.

3.2 Supervised Learning Method

The mainstream of applied machine learning practices is supervised learning. An algorithm is used to study the mapping function from the input to the output which has x as the input variable and Y as the output variable as depicted in equation 3.1. Here, the learner is given with input data that are labeled. The data contain a sequence of input pair and output pair. The intension of the learner is to know the mapping process from input data to output data. The function Y is termed as classifier if the output data are discrete data and function of regression if the output data are continuous.

$$Y = f(x) \tag{3.1}$$

The objective is to estimate the mapping function by having the input data (x) to predict the output variables (Y) for those data. The reason behind why supervised methods are also termed as supervised learning is that a teacher supervising the learning methodology is imitated as the procedure of algorithm learning after the dataset training. The learning discontinues as the algorithm accomplishes a tolerable level of performance [4–6].

Every supervised machine algorithm is centered on a previously well-defined set of labels C with the training set T encompassed of articles that are allocated one or more labels from C. An algorithm is shown to train the model by using C and T and application of model to categorize the unlabeled articles.

In the model, processing of the training set T and constructing a classification model with respect to the taxonomy C is carried out. The method includes three numbers of stages to correlate authors, keywords, and journals into single or many labels from C. Recording of many frequency values is utilized later by the classification algorithm to efficiently control the labels of the unclassified papers. The mainstream of the research articles comprises a set of keywords placed between the abstract and the introduction. Hence, the words arising in the title are also measured as representatives of the document's information and can be utilized in the training model.

Considering a paper p belonging to P tried in the training set T which comprises the keywords K_p and is branded into single or more research fields C_p belonging to C. The objective is to make correlations among every keyword of p and research fields of C_p. As the keyword k might appear in numerous papers belonging to various research zones, an algorithm similar to the k-NN algorithm is introduced. This is obtained by building of (k, c) pairs which we stock in a significance explanation vector K. By computing two frequency values $|P_k|$ and $|P_{k,c}|$, the former signifies the number of papers comprising the keyword k, while the last means the number of papers which consist of k and are plotted to the field c. The algorithm displays the steps important to train K. For every paper p of the training set, identifying all the research fields C_p and the keywords K_p is a bigger task. Creation of (k, c) pair for each research field c belonging to C_p [7–10] is done. Algorithms of Model Training in Article Classification is seen below:

Initialize K, A, J
for each paper p ∈ T
C^P ← ExtractResearchAreas(p)
Phase 1: Processing of the keywords
K^P ← ExtractKeywords (p)
for each keyword k ∈ K^P
$|P^k| \leftarrow |P^k| + 1$
for each research area c ∈ C^P
Create pair (k, c)
if K.search (k, c) =false
K.insert(k, c)
$|P k, c| \leftarrow 1$
else
$|P^{k,c}| \leftarrow |P^{k,c}| + 1$
Phase 2: Processing of the authors
A^P ← ExtractAuthors (p)
for each author a ∈ A^P
$|P^a| \leftarrow |P^a| + 1$
for each research area c ∈ C^P
Create pair (a, c)
if A.AP.search(a, c) = false
A.AP.insert (a, c)
$|P^{a,c}{}_{AP}| \leftarrow 1$
else
$|P^{a,c}{}_{AP}| \leftarrow |P^{a,c}{}_{AP}| + 1$
for each author a^0 ∈ A^P
Create tuple (a, a^0, c)
If A.AA.search (a, a^0, c) = false

A.AA.insert(a, a^0, c)

$\left|P^{\,a,c}_{\,AA}\right| \leftarrow 1$ else

$\left|P^{\,a,c}_{\,AA}\right| \leftarrow \left|P^{\,a,c}\right| + 1$

Phase 3: Processing of the journals

J ← Extract Journal (p)

$\left|P^{\,j}\right| \leftarrow \left|P^{\,j}\right| + 1$

for each research area $c \in C^p$

Create pair (j, c)

if Search(j, c) =false

J .insert (j, c)

$\left|P^{\,j,c}\right| \leftarrow 1$

Else

$\left|P^{\,j,c}\right| \leftarrow \left|P^{\,j,c}\right| + 1$

The stages incorporated in the supervised ML method are shown in Figure 3.3.

The six main steps in the expansion of a ML model are collection of data, choosing a measure of success, followed by setting an evaluation protocol, preparing the data, followed by developing a benchmark model, developing a good model, and altering its hyper-parameters.

Supervised learning problems are considered into regression problems and classification problems.

3.2.1 Classification Problems

In a classification problem, the output variable is a category. It involves assembling the data into classes. In an organization, if a person has to be given the appraisal, classification is used to know whether or not he would be the best appraisal taker. Two types of classification called binary classification and multiple classifications are

STEP 0	Determine the type of training examples
STEP 1	Collect the training Data Set
STEP 2	Determine the feature representation of the input
STEP 3	Choose a learning algorithm
STEP 4	Train the algorithm
STEP 5	Evaluate the algorithms accuracy using a test data test

FIGURE 3.3
Stages of supervised ML method.

considered. In binary classification, supervised learning algorithm labels input data into two distinct classes. Dividing data into more than two classes is termed as multiple classifications.

3.2.2 Regression Problems

In a regression problem, the output variable is an actual value. In regression, with the use of training data, a single output value is generated. These data are a probabilistic clarification, which is determined after seeing the strong point of association among the input data. Regression helps to predict the house price centered on its size, locality, etc. Recommendation and time-series prediction are the general types of difficulties built on top of cataloguing and regression. The discrete values of output data based on a group of independent variables are termed as logistic regression. This process can thrash when performing with nonlinear and numerous decision boundaries. It has no flexibility enough to arrest complex associations in datasets.

Few examples of supervised-machine learning algorithms are as follows:

- For solving regression problems, usage of linear regression.
- For solving classification and regression problems, usage of random forest.
- For solving classification problems, usage of support vector machines.

In the presence of a supervisor, supervised learning involves the usage of machine learning algorithms. Proper guidance in a proper direction gives proper feedback in the process; hence, it is termed as learning under supervision. Supervised learning goes through the reference of various categories of methods [11–14]. Training or teaching an algorithm uses information data and guiding a model by means of labels related with the data. Being humans, consumption of more information or data takes place, but noticing of these data points doesn't happen. When an image of a bird is shown, it is instantaneously known what the bird is centered on previous involvement. The scenario changes if the learner doesn't instantaneously identify the bird.

When the learner brands a guess and forecasts what the bird might be, it shows an opportunity to quantitatively appraise the learner for correct or wrong answer. It is likely because it has the correct labels of input.

Machine learning algorithm is commonly referred to as the model. If the model is giving a correct response, then there is nothing to do. The work comes into picture only when the response of the model is incorrect. The work is to exact the model when the response of the model is incorrect.

If the scenario continues, the model needs to be updated with necessary changes. If the hen image is shown, it recognizes it in a correct way. The presence of the input variable x and the output variable y and usage of algorithm help to learn the representing function w.r.t the input and output. The output y is shown as a dependent variable of input x as represented in equation 3.2.

$$Y = f(\mathrm{x}) \tag{3.2}$$

Approximation of the mapping function (f) leads to the prediction of the output variables (y) through the input data x (Figure 3.4).

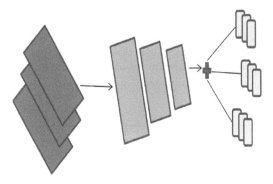

FIGURE 3.4
Approximating the mapping function [see Ref. 15].

3.2.3 Examples of Supervised Learning

The machine learning model learns to fit planning between the examples of input topographies with their related labels. When models are proficient with these examples, usage of new forecasts on unseen data is done.

The forecast labels can be both numbers and categories. For example, if the prediction of house fare is taken, then the yield is a number which gives rise to regression model. If we are forecasting if an e-mail is spam or not, the yield is a category giving rise to classification model [16–18].

Example: House Prices

Prediction of house fare is a bigger task which includes the process of machine learning. The information or properties which depict the complete information about the houses are number of rooms, square footage, features, whether a house has more rooms, and so on. The corresponding labels can be known by leveraging data coming from the numerous houses, their features, and prices. Hence, training a supervised machine learning model predicts a new house's fare based on the previous examples perceived by the model.

Scenario: a Cat or a Dog?

In the computer vision field, image classification is an important issue. The intension is to forecast which class an image fits to. Among several problems, the aim is to find the class label of an image. Does the image indicate an image of a cat or a dog?

Scenario: Weather Condition?

Considering various parameters forecasting weather in a specific location is a tough task. To do right forecasts for the weather, it is necessary to take into account numerous parameters as well as historical temperature data, precipitation, wind, and humidity. It is seen to be an interesting and very challenging issue required in developing the right answer by developing composite supervised models that comprise multiple tasks. Forecasting temperature every time is a reversion problem, in which the output labels are unremitting variables. By divergence forecasting it, is it successful to know snow or not is a binary classification problem?

Example: Text Classification

The data points are considered as meaningful structure and patterns in the annotations. Unsupervised learning is generally exploited for finding significant patterns and groupings innate in data, mining generative features, and investigative purposes [19,20].

3.3 Unsupervised Learning Method

In an unsupervised method, the input data x will be present, and the corresponding output variables will be absent. In some pattern recognition glitches, the training of data consists of a set of input vectors x without any of the consistent target values. The intension of unsupervised learning glitches may be to find groups of redundant examples within the data, which is termed as clustering, or to find how the data is spread in the space, called density estimation

The aim of unsupervised learning is ideal to the fundamental construction or distribution in the data suitable to learn about the data. It has different characteristics compared to supervised learning as it does not have educator or supervisor. Algorithms are permitted to realize its plans by bestowing the interested structure in the information.

Collecting and accumulating the labeled data is subject to resource constraint, and it is time consuming. In an un-supervised learning, achieving accurate labeling is very hard. It is a prerequisite that in an unsupervised learning, the learner is provided with unlabeled input data. For the new data instances, the intension of the learner is to find the inherent patterns in the information that is used to find the correct output information. The supposition is that there is a construction to the input space; hence, certain patterns occur more often than others which are termed as density estimation in statistics [21,22]. Unsupervised learning techniques are much useful in the sensor network applications. Sensor network applications are often organized in changeable and continuously changing surroundings. Figure 3.5 shows the clustering in machine learning.

The unsupervised learning method can be assembled into clustering problems and association problems.

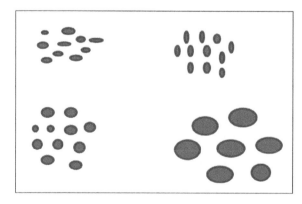

FIGURE 3.5
Clustering in machine learning.

- **Clustering Problems**: Discovering the inherent groups in the specific data is termed as clustering problem. An example is purchase behavior is particularly associated with clustering problem.
- **Association**: Ruling the learning problem is an association in which discovering rules define big portions of information or data.

Good examples of unsupervised learning algorithms are as follows:

- *k*-means for clustering problems.
- Apriori algorithm for association rule learning problems.

3.3.1 Illustrations of Unsupervised Learning

Below is the illustration toward different ways of unsupervised learning.

Example: Discovering Customer Segments

Clustering is a kind of unsupervised method with the intension to find natural groups or bunches in a feature space and infer the input data. It consists of many types of clustering procedures. One common methodology is to divide the data points in a way that each data point falls into a group that is similar to other data points in the same group depending on a predefined resemblance or detachment metric in the feature space. Clustering is frequently used for defining customer sections in marketing data. Marketing team members reach the customer segments in different ways to find different categories of customers. Gender, location, education, age, income, etc. are the features considered.

Example: Lessening the Complication of a Problem

Dimensionality lessening is a generally used unsupervised learning way; here, the aim is to reduce the number of random variables under concern. Having numerous practical claims, the most shared uses of dimensionality reduction are to overcome the complication of a problem by showing the feature space to a low-dimensional space. Hence, less correlated variables are measured in a machine learning system. PCA and t-SNE along with UMAP are the most commonly used algorithms [23–25]. Mainly, these are beneficial for lessening the complexity of an issue and also envisaging the data examples in an improved way.

Example: Feature Choice

Even though feature choice and dimensionality lessening aim toward reducing the number of features in the unique set of features, knowing the working of feature selection, good understanding of dimensionality lessening happens. Consider an example of banking system, in which the person wants to lend a loan and the bank has to predict whether the person is capable of repaying the loan. So, to know it intelligently, the bank should be accompanied with a machine learning system so that the bank can provide loan to the loan applicants who can only repay the loan amount. This requires tremendous information about each customer application to make assumptions. The most important attributes to be in the account of machine learning data base is the applicant's average monthly income, debit account, and credit history. Sometimes it is observed that the information collected during application does not contain all necessary documents

[26–28]. Some of the attributes are irrelevant to know whether he/she is repaying; for example, age, gender, and education of the person do not matter. Here, feature selection plays the role of deleting the unimportant attributes and adding the most important and helpful attributes by reducing the usage of less important information.

3.4 Semi-Supervised Learning Method

In this learning, a large amount of input data x and only some of the output data y are present; such learning problems are called semi-supervised learning. These have existence between supervised and unsupervised learning. In the photo collection of animals, few of the animal pictures are labeled example cat, dog and the mainstream are unlabeled. Most of the real-world ML problems come under this area. The domain expert labels the data, which requires more time and time consumption. Hence, the labeled data are costlier than unlabeled data. The unlabeled data are easy to store under collection as they do not require experts hence less time and less cost. Utilization of unsupervised learning methods is done to find out and learn the structure in the input data [29–31]. The supervised learning method is also used to predict the unlabeled data or information and feedback it as training data into the supervised learning method. This model can be used to predict the unseen information or data.

An important shortcoming of the supervised learning procedure is that a machine learning engineer or a data scientist considering the dataset has to undergo the procedure of hand-labeling. The procedure is costly while dealing with a large data set. The limitation of the application spectrum is an important weakness of the supervised method. To overcome these disadvantages, the introduction of semi-supervised learning was done. Characteristically, the combination of labeled and unlabeled data consists of a small quantity of labeled data and more of unlabeled data. The fundamental steps involved are initially the programmer will group alike data by means of an unsupervised learning algorithm and finally uses the present labeled data to label the remaining of the unlabeled data. The common property they share among themselves is that the attainment of unlabeled data with a comparatively cheap value with labeling the data is very costly.

Following are the data assumptions in semi-supervised algorithms.

In continuity assumption algorithm, it is assumed that the same output label is obtained for the points which are nearer to each other.

In cluster assumption algorithm, the data can be disconnected into discrete bunches, and facts in the same bunch are more likely to be part of an output label.

3.5 Binary Classification

There are two classes, crosses, and circles with two features, x_1 and x_2. To estimate the class where it belongs to in the model to find an association between the topographies of every data point and its specific class and to keep a boundary line in between so by providing the new data, it can evaluate the class where it fits (Figure 3.6).

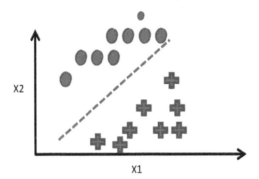

FIGURE 3.6
Binary classification.

In the above scenario, the fresh data come under the circle subspace, and hence, the model will forecast it in the class of circle.

3.5.1 Different Classes

It is significant to annotate that not all the classification models will be useful to separate properly different classes from a dataset. In some of the scenarios, the classes are unable to get distinguished by linear decision boundary as represented in Figure 3.7.

3.5.2 Classification in Preparation

In reality, it is suggested to attempt and associate diverse algorithm's concert, in order to select the maximum suitable to challenge the delinquent. This routine will be very prejudiced by the obtainable data, number of topographies and examples, the dissimilar classes, and they are linearly separable or not.

Next, we proceed to explore the dissimilar organization algorithms and to learn which one is more apt to perform each task.

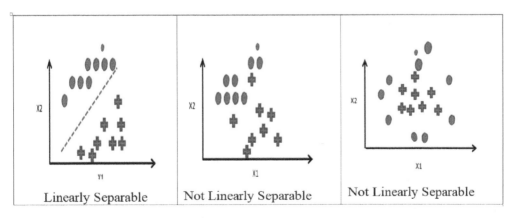

FIGURE 3.7
Different separability.

3.5.2.1 Logistic Regression Model

A classification problem occurs if the algorithm certainly not converges in the weight's appraising, while being qualified. When the linear separation is not possible, logistic regression comes into picture [32–34]. To solve binary classification problem, logistic regression is utilized. Linearly separable classes are appended to multiclass classification through the OvR technique.

3.5.2.2 Odds Ratio

The concept of logistic regression is better understood by odds ratio. The odds ratio is an important concept in order to understand the idea behind logistic regression. The probability of certain event that occurs is known by odds ratio. It can be written as follows:

$$\text{Odds Ratio} = \text{prp}/(1-\text{prp})$$

prp=probability of the positive event

3.5.2.3 Logit Function

$$\text{lfp} = \log(\text{prp}/1-\text{prp})$$

$$\text{lfp} = \log(\text{Odds Ratio})$$

Log-odds are logarithm of the odds ratio termed as logit function. This function takes the number from 0 to 1, and it converts theses binary range to real number range from $-\infty$ to $+\infty$. The relationship between log-odds and feature values is represented in a linear expression

$$\text{logit}\big(\text{prp}(y=1|x)\big) = w_0 x_0 + \ldots + w_m x_m = \text{sum}(w_i x_i) = w_t x$$

prp($y=1|x$) is conditional probability for a given feature x belonging to class 1.

3.5.2.4 The Sigmoid Function

The expression of the sigmoid function is

$$\phi(z) = \frac{1}{1+e^{-z}}$$

This expression is most often called sigmoid function which is the contrary of logit function. The net input is indicated as z [35–37]. The linear combination of sample features and weights are expressed as

$$z = w^t x = w_0 + w_1 x_1 + \ldots + w_m x_m$$

The graphical representation of z vs. $\Phi(z)$ is shown in Figure 3.8.

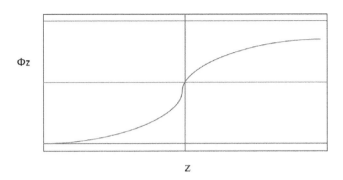

FIGURE 3.8
Plot of z versus Φ(z).

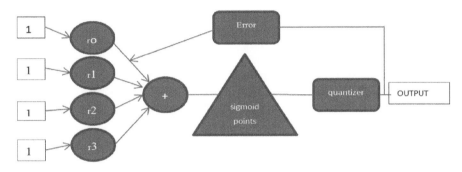

FIGURE 3.9
Net input function, sigmoid function, and quantizer [38,39].

$\varnothing(z)$ is varying from binary value 0 to 1 as the property z is varying from $-\infty$ to $+\infty$ (Figure 3.9).

In the logistic regression, the productivity of the sigmoid function is understood as the prospect of a definite example to fit in to class 1, assumed its features x limited by the w weight as

$$\varnothing(z) = P(y = 1 \mid x; w)$$

The predicted possibility can be rehabilitated into a binary product by unit step function as a quantizer

$$\widehat{y} = \begin{cases} 1 & \text{if } \phi(z) \geq 0.5 \\ 0 & \text{otherwise} \end{cases}$$

from the graph, the equivalence is

$$\widehat{y} = \begin{cases} 1 & \text{if } z \geq 0.5 \\ 0 & \text{otherwise} \end{cases}$$

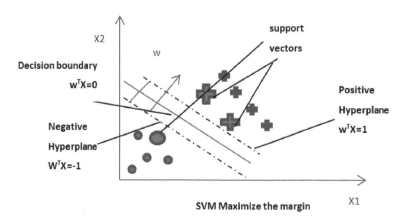

X2

Decision boundary
wᵀX=0

Negative
Hyperplane
WᵀX=-1

support
vectors

Positive
Hyperplane
wᵀX=1

SVM Maximize the margin

X1

FIGURE 3.10
SVM maximizing the margin.

3.5.2.5 Support Vector Machines

A SVM is considered to be the enhancement of the perceptron algorithm. The optimization objective is to set a decision line that splits the classes by increasing the merging between the line and the sample data that are nearby to the hyperplane as shown in Figure 3.10. These data points are expressed as support vectors [39–42].

3.5.2.6 Maximum Margin Lines

To set the extreme margins, two parallel lines (margins) are added, and the distance is maximized to the original decision line. The errors or misclassified points (errors), points between the margins and the line, are considered. Large margin decision lines incline to have a lower overview error. In other words, models having small margins incline to be less disposed to overfitting [43–58].

The calculation of maximization function is done as follows:

$$w_0 + w^T x_{\text{pos}} = 1$$

$$w_0 + w^T x_{\text{neg}} = -1$$

Subtraction of expressions leads to

$$\Rightarrow w^T \left(x_{\text{pos}} - x_{\text{neg}} \right) = 2$$

the vector length w,

$$\|w\| = \sqrt{\sum_{j=1}^{m} w^2{}_j}$$

The procedure leads to the margin error expression

$$\frac{w^T \left(x_{\text{pos}} - x_{\text{neg}} \right)}{\|w\|} = \frac{2}{\|w\|}$$

TABLE 3.1

Comparison of Supervised and Unsupervised Methods

Parameters	Supervised Learning Method	Unsupervised Learning Method
Process	In a supervised learning model, input and output variables are present	In unsupervised learning model, only input data are present
Input data	Training of algorithms using labeled data	Algorithms are used against data which are not labeled
Algorithms used	SV/VI, neural network, linear and logistics regression, random forest, and classification trees	Unsupervised algorithms can be divided into different categories: Cluster algorithms, K-means, hierarchical clustering, etc.
Computational complexity	Supervised learning is a simpler method	Unsupervised learning is computationally complex
Use of data	Supervised learning model uses training data to learn a link between the input and the outputs	Unsupervised learning does not use output data
Accuracy of results	Highly accurate and trustworthy method	Less accurate and trustworthy method
Real-time learning	Learning method takes place offline	Learning method takes place in real time
Number of classes	Number of classes is known	Number of classes is not known
Main drawback	Classifying big data can be a real challenge in supervised learning	You cannot get precise information regarding data sorting and the output as data used in unsupervised learning is labeled and not known

x_{pos} is the positive hyperplane, and x_{neg} is the negative hyperplane. In the above expression, the margin has improvised. In reality, solution to quadratic programming can be obtained by minimizing the reciprocal term

$$\text{Margin} = \frac{1}{2}\|w\|^2$$

Table 3.1 depicts the comparison of supervised and unsupervised learning methods.

3.6 Conclusion

In supervised learning, training of machine happens using labeled data. In an unsupervised machine learning technique, the model needs to be supervised. Supervised learning permits to gather data or yield an output data from the earlier experience. In unsupervised machine learning, every kind of unknown patterns is found in data. Weather condition, timing, and holiday are some of the criteria to be considered to reach back home. Another example is identifying unknown dogs using the past supervised learning method. Regression, classification, clustering, and association are the subcategories of learning techniques. Machines are trained to perform activities in various areas in order to make man work easier with less time consumption. If the amount of data is lesser, and if it consists of labeled data for training, then the choice is supervised learning. Better performance is obtained in unsupervised learning as it can accommodate new entries and results in large data sets. In conclusion, in the development of machine learning models of choice, there is a necessity of considering various IDEs, development languages, and platforms.

References

1. S. Theodoridis and K. Koutroumbas, *Pattern Recognition*, 4th Ed. (Academic Press, ISBN 978-1-59749-272-0, 2009).
2. S. Theodoridis and K. Koutroumbas, *Introduction to Pattern Recognition: A Matlab Approach.* (Academic Press, ISBN 978-0-12-374486-9, 2010).
3. K. P. Murphy, *Machine Learning: A Probabilistic Perspective.* (The MIT Press, ISBN 978-0-262-01802-9, 2012).
4. F. Hu and Q. Hao, *Intelligent Sensor Networks: The Integration of Sensor Networks, Signal Processing and Machine Learning.* (CRC Press, ISBN 978-1-4398-9282-4, 2013).
5. S. Gannot, E. Vincent, S. Markovich-Golan, and A. Ozerov, "A consolidated perspective on multimicrophone speech enhancement and source separation," *IEEE Trans. Audio Speech Lang. Process.* 25(4), 692–730 (2017).
6. E. Vincent, T. Virtanen, and S. Gannot, *Audio Source Separation and Speech Enhancement* (Wiley, New York, 2018).
7. D. K. Mellinger, M. A. Roch, E.-M. Nosal, and H. Klinck, "Signal processing," in *Listening in the Ocean*, edited by W. W. L. Au and M. O. Lammers (Springer, Berlin, 2016), Chap. 15, pp. 359–409.
8. K. L. Gemba, S. Nannuru, and P. Gerstoft, "Robust ocean acoustic localization with sparse Bayesian learning," *IEEE J. Sel. Top. Sign. Process.* 13(1), 49–60 (2019).
9. H. Niu, E. Reeves, and P. Gerstoft, "Source localization in an ocean waveguide using supervised machine learning," *J. Acoust. Soc. Am.* 142(3), 1176–1188 (2017).
10. P. Gerstoft and D. F. Gingras, "Parameter estimation using multifrequency range–dependent acoustic data in shallow water," *J. Acoust. Soc. Am.* 99(5), 2839–2850 (1996).
11. F. B. Jensen, W. A. Kuperman, M. B. Porter, and H. Schmidt, *Computational Ocean Acoustics.* (Springer Science & Business Media, New York, 2011).
12. J. Traer and J. H. McDermott, "Statistics of natural reverberation enable perceptual separation of sound and space," *Proc. Natl. Acad. Sci.* 113(48), E7856–E7865 (2016).
13. M. I. Jordan and T. M. Mitchell, "Machine learning: Trends, perspectives, and prospects," *Science* 349(6245), 255–260 (2015).
14. Y. LeCun, Y. Bengio, and G. E. Hinton, "Deep learning," *Nature* 521(7553), 436–444 (2015).
15. Q. Kong, D. T. Trugman, Z. E. Ross, M. J. Bianco, B. J. Meade, and P. Gerstoft, "Machine learning in seismology: Turning data into insights," *Seismol. Res. Lett.* 90(1), 3–14 (2018).
16. K. J. Bergen, P. A. Johnson, M. V. de Hoop, and G. C. Beroza, "Machine learning for data-driven discovery in solid earth geoscience," *Science* 363, eaau0323 (2019).
17. C. M. Bishop, *Pattern Recognition and Machine Learning.* (Springer, Berlin, 2006).
18. K. Murphy, *Machine Learning: A Probabilistic Perspective*, 1st ed. (MIT Press, Cambridge, MA, 2012).
19. Y. Bengio, A. Courville, and P. Vincent, "Representation learning: A review and new perspectives," *IEEE Trans. Pattern Anal. Mach. Intell.* 35(8), 1798–1828 (2013).
20. Y. B. Goodfellow, A. Courville, and Y. Bengio, *Deep Learning*, Vol. 1. (MIT Press, Cambridge, 2016).
21. R. A. Fisher, "The use of multiple measurements in taxonomic problems," *Ann. Eugen.* 7(2), 179–188 (1936).

22. J. G. Proakis and M. Salehi, *Communication Systems Engineering*. (Prentice-Hall, Englewood Cliffs, NJ, 1994).
23. B. Widrow and E. Walach, *Adaptive Inverse Control*. (Prentice-Hall, Upper Saddle River, NJ, 1996).
24. R. W. Lucky, "Techniques for adaptive equalization of digital communication systems," *Bell Sys. Tech. J.*, 45, 255–286 (1966).
25. D. E. Borth, I. A. Gerson, J. R. Haug, and C. D. Thompson, "A flexible adaptive FIR filter VLSI IC." *IEEE J. Sel. Areas Commun.*, 6(3), 494–503 (1988).
26. S. U. H. Qureshi, Adaptive equalization. *Proc. IEEE*, 73(9), 1349–1387 (1985).
27. K. Murano, S. Unagami, and F. Amano, "Echo cancellation and applications," *IEEE Commun. Mag.*, 28(1), 49–55 (1990).
28. M. El-Sharkawy, "Designing adaptive FIR filters and implementing them on the DSP56002 processor," in *Digital Signal Processing Applications with Motorola's DSP56002 Processor*, pp. 319–342. (Prentice-Hall, Upper Saddle River, NJ, 1996).
29. J. MacQueen, "Some methods for classification and analysis of multivariate observations," *Proceedings of the 5th Berkeley Symposium on Math, Statistics, and Probability*, Vol. 1, Issue 14, pp. 281–297 (1967).
30. F. Rosenblatt, *Principles of Neurodynamics. Perceptrons and the Theory of Brain Mechanisms*. (Cornell Aeronautical Lab, Inc., Buffalo, NY, 1961).
31. D. E. Rumelhart, G. E. Hinton, and R. J. Williams, "Learning representations by back-propagating errors," *Nature* 323, 533–536 (1986).
32. T. Hastie, R. Tibshirani, and J. Friedman, *The Elements of Statistical Learning: Data Mining, Inference and Prediction*, 2nd ed. (Springer, Berlin, 2009).
33. R. O. Duda, P. E. Hart, and D. G. Stork, *Pattern Classification*. (Wiley, New York, 2012).
34. I. Cohen, J. Benesty, and S. Gannot, *Speech Processing in Modern Communication: Challenges and Perspectives*, Vol. 3. (Springer Science & Business Media, New York, 2009).
35. M. Elad, *Sparse and Redundant Representations*. (Springer, New York, 2010).
36. J. Mairal, F. Bach, and J. Ponce, "Sparse modeling for image and vision processing," *Found. Trends Comput. Graph. Vis.* 8(2–3), 85–283 (2014).
37. D. H. Wolpert and W. G. Macready, "No free lunch theorems for optimization," *IEEE Trans. Evol. Comput.* 1(1), 67–82 (1997).
38. L. V. D. Maaten and G. Hinton, "Visualizing data using tSNE," *J. Mach. Learn. Res.* 9(Nov), 2579–2605 (2008).
39. I. Tošić and P. Frossard, "Dictionary learning," *IEEE Signal Process. Mag.* 28(2), 27–38 (2011).
40. R. Kohavi, "A study of cross-validation and bootstrap for accuracy estimation and model selection," *Proc. Int. Joint Conf. Artif. Intel.* 14(2), 1137–1145 (1995).
41. A. Chambolle, "An algorithm for total variation minimization and applications," *J. Math. Imag. Vision* 20(1–2), 89–97 (2004).
42. Z. Ghahramani, "Probabilistic machine learning and artificial intelligence," *Nature* 521(7553), 452–459 (2015).
43. Z.-H. Michalopoulou and P. Gerstoft, "Multipath broadband localization, bathymetry, and sediment inversion," *IEEE J. Oceanic Eng.* 45, 92–102 (2019).
44. K. L. Gemba, S. Nannuru, P. Gerstoft, and W. S. Hodgkiss, "Multi-frequency sparse Bayesian learning for robust matched field processing," *J. Acoust. Soc. Am.* 141(5), 3411–3420 (2017).
45. S. Nannuru, K. L. Gemba, P. Gerstoft, W. S. Hodgkiss, and C. F. Mecklenbr€auker, "Sparse Bayesian learning with multiple dictionaries," *Sign. Process.* 159, 159–170 (2019).
46. Gelman, H. S. Stern, J. B. Carlin, D. B. Dunson, A. Vehtari, and D. B. Rubin, *Bayesian Data Analysis*. (Chapman and Hall/CRC, New York, 2013).
47. R. C. Aster, B. Borchers, and C. H. Thurber, *Parameter Estimation and Inverse Problems*, 2nd ed. (Elsevier, San Diego, 2013).
48. P. Gerstoft, A. Xenaki, and C. F. Mecklenbr€auker, "Multiple and single snapshot compressive beamforming," *J. Acoust. Soc. Am.* 138(4), 2003–2014 (2015).

49. R. Tibshirani, "Regression shrinkage and selection via the lasso," *J. R. Stat. Soc., Ser. B* 58(1), 267–288 (1996).
50. E. Candes, "Compressive sampling," *Proc. Int. Cong. Math.* 3, 1433–1452 (2006).
51. P. Gerstoft, C. F. Mecklenbr€auker, W. Seong, and M. Bianco, "Introduction to compressive sensing in acoustics," *J. Acoust. Soc. Am.* 143(6), 3731–3736 (2018).
52. K. Hornik, "Approximation capabilities of multilayer feedforward networks," *Neural Netw.* 4(2), 251–257 (1991).
53. D. P. Kingma and J. L. Ba, "Adam: A method for stochastic optimization," *Proceedings of the 3rd International Conference for Learning Representations*, arXiv:1412.6980 (2014).
54. D. D. Lee and H. S. Seung, "Algorithms for non-negative matrix factorization," *Adv. Neural Inf. Process. Syst.* 13, 556–562 (2001).
55. J. Alzubi, A. Nayyar, and A. Kumar, "Machine learning from theory to algorithms: An overview," *Journal of Physics: Conference Series* 1142(1), 012012 (2018).
56. V. Anavangot, V. G. Menon, and A. Nayyar, "Distributed big data analytics in the Internet of signals," *2018 International Conference on System Modeling & Advancement in Research Trends (SMART)*. IEEE, Moradabad, India, pp. 73–77 (2018, November).
57. S. S. Maram, N. Kumar, J. J. P. C. Rodrigues, S. Tanwar, and A. Jain, "Images to signals, signals to highlights," *IEEE Global Communications Conference (GLOBECOM-2020)*, Taipei, Taiwan, 7–11 December 2020, pp. 1–6 (2020).
58. J. Vora, M. Patel, S. Tanwar, and S. Tyagi, "Image processing based analysis of cracks on vertical walls," *IEEE 3rd International Conference on Internet of Things: Smart Innovation and Usages (IoT-SIU 2018), BIAS*, Bhimtal, Nainital, Uttarakhand, India, 23–24 February, 2018, pp. 1–5 (2018).

4

Applications of Signal Processing

Anuj Kumar Singh and Ankit Garg

Amity University

CONTENTS

DOI: 10.1201/9781003107026-4

4.1 Introduction

Machine learning technology tends to make a machine learn by its own from the information stored previously and from the new circumstances. The aim of continuous learning is to improve the system to get better results. Machine learning algorithms can be categorized as supervised learning algorithms, unsupervised learning algorithms, and reinforcement learning algorithms. Supervised learning algorithms can be further categorized as classification and regression algorithms while clustering and association are the two subcategories of unsupervised learning [1]. Various modern computing systems generally perform some kind of signal processing for improving efficiency, quality, and transmission of a signal. Signal processing obtains, interprets, explains, and modifies the physical phenomena of a system. Probability, statistics, mathematics, and stochastic processes in signal processing are used to interpret and model the physical phenomena of a system for extracting critical information. Certainly, machine learning algorithms can improve the efficacy of this process due to its many advantages including easy pattern identification, no human intervention, continuous improvement, and capability to handle multidimensional multi-variety data. In this chapter, ten applications of signal processing that are now being used massively in different computing environments and are also utilizing machine learning approaches have been discussed. Specifically, applications of machine learning approaches in audio signal processing, audio compression, digital image processing, video compression, digital communications, healthcare, seismology, speech recognition, computer vision, and economic forecasting have been highlighted.

4.2 Audio Signal Processing

As a physical process, voice or sound can be described as vibrations of molecules which usually changes the pressure of certain area of some medium like air. The measurement of these vibrations is carried out by a device called microphone in which the diaphragm is forced to move due to the change in pressure. This movement of diaphragm is then converted into a voltage signal using a magnet and a voice coil. This voltage signal produced

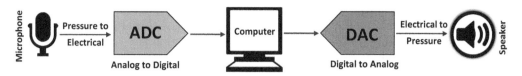

FIGURE 4.1
A typical audio processing system.

by the diaphragm is a continuous signal which takes some defined value at any moment of time [2]. The typical audio processing system is shown in Figure 4.1.

Due to the limited memory, a computer system can store finite values representing finite numbers. So, infinite quantity of numbers occurring infinitely times must be recorded, i.e., conversion of analog values to digital values must take place. In addition to this, reconstruction of analog signal from the digital one must also be feasible. This whole process consists of several phases which are known as sampling, quantization, and reconstruction. Analog to digital convertor (ADC) is a device which samples and quantizes the analog signal and produces the digital signal, whereas digital to analog convertor (ADC) performs reconstruction and produces analog signal from the digital signal.

4.2.1 Machine Learning in Audio Signal Processing

Development of machine learning models in audio signal processing requires the clear understanding of the features of audio signals. Features can be described as "measurable attributes and characteristics of a phenomenon." Features are of great importance because using features, a machine can comprehend the data, classify it into different categories, and can perform the prediction [3]. In this section, the features of audio which can be utilized in audio processing and machine learning have been discussed.

4.2.1.1 Spectrum and Cepstrum

Spectrum and cepstrum are the two significant attributes of audio signal processing. Mathematically speaking, a spectrum of an audio signal is obtained by computing its Fourier transform which converts a signal of time domain into the signal of frequency domain. In other words, using spectrum, the audio signal is represented in the frequency domain. In order to form the cepstrum first, the long magnitude of the spectrum is computed, and then the inverse Fourier transform of the long magnitude is calculated. This is the signal which is neither in the time domain nor in the frequency domain. The steps in creating the spectrum and cepstrum of the audio signal are shown in Figure 4.2.

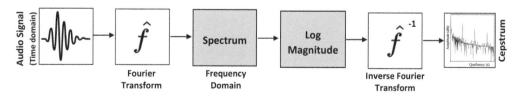

FIGURE 4.2
Steps in creating the spectrum and cepstrum of the audio signal.

The basic reasoning of why to consider the frequency of an audio signal is related to the biology of the hearing process by an ear. The cochlea is a part of the human ear that is filled with fluid, and it contains thousands of tiny hairs that have a connection to the nerves. The length of these hair is different, and the hair with shorter length resonates with higher frequencies while the hair with longer length resonates with lower frequencies. The time domain signal of air pressure is converted into a frequency spectrum, which is then processed by the brain. In this way, the human ear can be considered as a Fourier transform analyzer naturally.

4.2.1.2 Mel Frequency Cepstral Coefficients

It is a fact about hearing of sound by a human that the human ear gets less selective toward frequencies if the frequency of sound increases beyond 1 KHz. This resembles the Mel filter bank. Mel cepstrum can be produced by inputting the spectrum to the Mel filter bank and then taking the long magnitude of the result followed by discrete cosine transform (DCT). This process is demonstrated in Figure 4.3. The DCT obtains the significant information and peak values that are the summary of the audio. Generally, MFCCs are the very first thirteen coefficients obtained from the Mel cepstrum. MFCCs contain valuable information about the audio signal, and thus, they are utilized in training the machine learning models.

4.2.1.3 Gammatone Frequency Cepstral Coefficients

Gammatone filter bank is the another filter which is closely related to human hearing process. It provides simulation of cochlea which can be applied in different applications of audio processing. For producing GFCCs we must pass the spectrum throughn the Gammatone filter bank. After this, the result is downsampled/compressed which is followed by the computation of DCT. The GFCC feature consists of the very first twenty-two features. Speaker identification is one of the well known applications of GFCC. The process of producing GFCC is illustrated in Figure 4.4.

4.2.1.4 Building the Classifier

To build the classifier, special features of GFCC and MFCC can be utilized, in addition to this, a combination of both GFCC and MFCC can also be used. The very first step is to

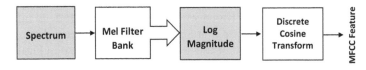

FIGURE 4.3
Process of producing MFCC.

FIGURE 4.4
Process of producing GFCC.

classify the input audio signals into different categories. For example, a system may classify the input audio as music, speech, animal, etc. In the next step, using a dataset and not performing any fine-tuning, we can estimate the capability of this classification model to detect the audio category. Then, special features like GFCC and MFCC can be applied for the appropriate genre classification. Some genres may be correct, while some can have possibilities of improvement. For appropriate genre classification, the following points must be considered.

- Checking the quality of data to ensure that it is sufficient for classification. Other features including transcription or text. Is it better to use a different classifier?
- Whether the study has been made to use neural networks for classification?

These features will certainly get significant information from the input audio signal, and a machine can learn better with these features and can extract appropriate information about the audio signal.

4.3 Audio Compression

Audio compression is a very important subfield of data compression. Storing audio on a computer system requires a large amount of memory, and therefore, the audio must be compressed before it is kept on a computer system. In addition to this, due to the compression of audio, cell phones are able to communicate with a better voice. Audio compression approaches are implemented as an audio codec in computer software. The applications of audio compression include digital TV, movies, DVDs, and many more. Optimal audio compression algorithms can be categorized as lossy algorithms and lossless algorithms. Lossy compression algorithms have a relatively greater compression rate and are generally used to compress real-time audio. The main aim of both lossy compression and lossless compression is to reduce the redundancy using different techniques like pattern recognition, coding, and prediction.

4.3.1 Modeling and Coding

The two foremost building blocks of the development of compression algorithms are modeling and coding. In the modeling stage, information about redundancy existing in the data is represented using a model. In the coding stage, the description of the model is encoded using binary symbols. Encoding can be done either in lossy format or lossless format. Encoding in lossless format is used to preserve the original quality of the media source. Minor degradations can be caused as a result of subsequent encoding using other lossless formats.

4.3.2 Lossless Compression

The approach considered by almost all the lossless compression algorithms is highlighted in Figure 4.5. In the very first step, some "prediction algorithm" is used to perform the

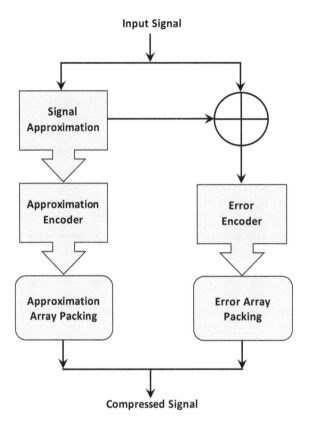

FIGURE 4.5
Approach for lossless compression.

signal approximation. The parameters of the "prediction algorithm" are selected in a way so that a waveform similar to the input wave is produced. However, the least number of bits as far as possible must be used to represent the difference between the real signal and the predicted waveform. For creating the correct value of a sample, the predicted signal is added to the error signal. To predict the subsequent sample, the prediction algorithm is executed again on the basis of past samples and new predicted samples [4]. In signal approximation, the signal is disintegrated into Gaussian functions which are normalized and linearly combined. This tends to focus the signal toward a smaller dimension because bandwidth and sampling step are data-adaptive. This approach can be useful in audio signal processing and many other applications of signal processing. To achieve standardization, security, reduced space, speed, and secrecy, approximation encoder is used. An approximation encoder is a circuit, device, software, algorithm, transducer, or person that transforms the information represented in one format or code into another. Error in audio compression means that the unknown format or unsupported codec has been represented. The error encoder takes the addition of signal approximation and input signal as input, and then from the output of the error encoder, it can be concluded whether the codec is supported or not. The combined result of error array packing and the approximation array packing produces the compressed signal.

4.3.3 Lossy Compression

In lossy compression, the decompressed signal is not identical as the original signal. There is some loss of information, and the signal may get distorted. In lossy compression, the compression rate is better than the lossless compression. For achieving the lossy compression, the approach is to maintain the quality of reconstruction to a certain limit. And similarly, the differences and distortion with the original signal are permitted within a limit. For lossy compression algorithms, some methods must be used to measure the quality of reconstruction. Due to diverse areas of application, a number of approaches are being used. For measuring the quality of reconstruction of a sound, Advanced Audio Coding (AAC), Adaptive Transform Acoustic Coding (ATRC), and Windows Media Audio (WMA) can be used.

4.3.4 Compressed Audio with Machine Learning Applications

In machine learning applications, for evaluating the model accurately, one must know what is happening inside the audio data. Without having appropriate information about the data, one cannot confirm that what the model is learning. Understanding of the audio data has many facets, and one of the prominent facets is the codec used in representing the compressed audio signal. On analyzing the various audio contents available from any source like YouTube, one can easily understand that this content is coded using various codecs and at varied quality levels. For utilizing this audio database, one must obtain information about how the codecs are implemented with the original audio signal and what will be the implications of this over the model [5]. Only then the validation results of machine learning and training methods can be correctly interpreted.

While testing the machine learning model with codec, there are the following three ways that can be used to increase the quality of classification.

- Restore or de-noise the original audio signal.
- Extend the training data used with the despoiled audio.
- Design and develop the attributes which are most robust with the despoiled audio.

Many software organizations are working hard for last many years for developing codecs which improve the best quality of sound. It will be relatively easier for the researchers and professionals if they use high-quality nonparametric codec in their machine learning models, and they must also ensure to augment their training data sets.

4.4 Digital Image Processing

An image can be defined as a function $F(x, y)$ in two dimensions. Here, function $F(x, y)$ represents the amplitude over x and y which are spatial coordinates. The amplitude F is also known as the intensity of the image at point (x, y). The image is called a digital image when F, x, and y are finite. In other words, an image can be represented as rows and columns or two-dimensional array. An image is composed of a finite number of small elements called pixels. Digital image processing is an area of digital signal processing in which a digital computer processes the images using specific algorithms. Digital image processing tends to reduce distortion and noise which are major problems in analog image processing. Digital image processing takes the image as an input and processes the image using various steps and algorithms to produce the output image relevant to the user. Today, with the exponential increase in the usage of smartphones, the applications of digital image processing have become very popular.

4.4.1 Fields Overlapping with Image Processing

With the evolution of digital image processing, other areas have become more significant for professionals and researchers. These include computer vision, computer graphics, and artificial intelligence [6]. The relationship of these fields with digital image processing is demonstrated in Figure 4.6. If the input and output are both images, then it is known as digital image processing. If the input is an image and the output is some description, knowledge, or information, then this subfield is computer vision. On the other hand, if the input is some kind of description or information, but the output is an image, then this subfield is computer graphics. And if both the input and output are some code, description, or knowledge, then it is artificial intelligence.

4.4.2 Digital Image Processing System

A typical digital image processing system shown in Figure 4.7 comprises six stages. The very first stage is image acquisition in which a device captures the input image [7]. This device can be a camera or a sensor depending upon the application. The second stage is preprocessing which is concerned with image reconstruction, image restoring, and brightness perception. Image restoring estimates the original image from a degraded image. The feature extraction stage identifies and extracts the features and then uses them to reduce the data. The observation is mapped to the feature space domain for reducing the dimensions at the same time holding the necessary information. In the next stage, associative memories which are high-speed content addressable memories are used to store the associative pairs of patterns. The objective of the knowledge-based stage is to classify the

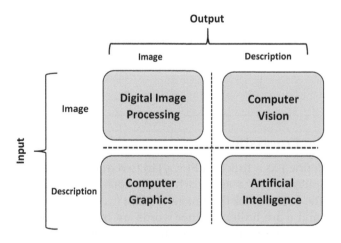

FIGURE 4.6
Fields overlapping with image processing.

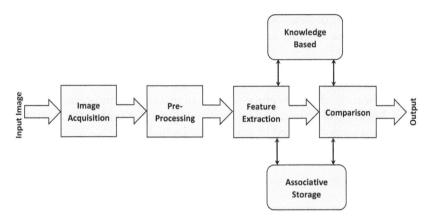

FIGURE 4.7
Typical digital image processing system.

information using different techniques. The classification rules are used in the knowledge base stage. The last stage is the comparison stage in which the data produced after feature extraction is compared with what is learned from the data [8]. This stage is utilized for image classification and neural network training.

4.4.3 Machine Learning with Digital Image Processing

In today's scenario, computer systems are not only able to classify images, but they are also able to give a description of different elements of a photograph. Moreover, the computers have become smart so that they can summarize the picture by writing a textual description of each segment. This has become possible with the evolution of the deep learning network which is capable to learn about the patterns which naturally exist in the images [9]. One of the largest databases which is used for training Convolutional Neural Networks (CNNs) is "Imagenet." The training is done through GPU-accelerated deep learning frameworks like Tensor Flow, Chainer, Caffe2, Pytorch, and many more. Using the multi-level structures, deep learning models are very significant in obtaining critical information about the images. CNN is the other model that harnesses the GPU to reduce the computational time in image processing by a huge amount. Deep learning in image data processing requires image classification, data labeling, and location detection.

4.4.3.1 Image Classification

Using image classification, the images are put into different categories. Utilizing CNN for image classification has been found most effective since CNN increases the accuracy of this process. For image classification, the critical input parameters that must be provided to CNN are the number of images, dimensions of the image, levels in a pixel, and the number of channels.

4.4.3.2 Data Labelling

The main objective of data labeling is the identification of the actual objects embedded in the image like text or other symbols. It will be much better to perform data labeling manually so that predictions can be made by the learning algorithms on their own. Some of the tools used for data labeling are SuperAnnotate, ImageTagger, VoTT, etc.

4.4.3.3 Location Detection

Detection of the location of objects embedded in an image is an important aspect that must be carried out. Location of objects can be detected using region-based CNN (RCNN) easily. Now RCNN has been advanced to mask RCNN which can achieve cognition of images up to the level of humans.

4.5 Video Compression

In the current computing world, videos play an important role in transmitting real-time information. With the growing popularity of social media, enormous video content is generated and shared on the web. Moreover, videos play a crucial role when it comes to surveillance and security since the high resolution and less space consumption are the priorities for this kind of transmitting real-time information. There is a trade-off between the resolution of the video and the memory required, and due to this reason, video compression is required.

Video can be understood as an array of image frames where every image frame possesses some information represented in terms of pixels. The resolution of a video is defined by these pixels. A comparison of the memory requirement and the resolution of various video formats has been presented in Table 4.1. The capture rate for all the formats in Table 4.1 is 30 frames per second for a color video stream [10].

By analyzing Table 4.1, it can be easily observed that for representing even a low-resolution small video, a big amount of storage is required. And due to this reason, video compression is a vital component for the applications involving videos.

4.5.1 Video Compression Model

A typical video compression model has two primary components; first is a video encoder, and the other is a video decoder. The video encoder is responsible for converting the video frames into a block of bits. At the receiving side, this block of bits is decoded by the video decoder to reconstruct the video frame. The block diagram of a typical video compression model is shown in Figure 4.8. The functioning of the video encoder has been divided into predictor, transform coding, and encoder. On the other hand, the functioning of the

TABLE 4.1

Comparison of the Memory Requirement and the Resolution of Various Video Formats

Video Format	Memory Requirement (Mbps)	Resolution
HDTV (High-Definition Television)	632.81	1280×720
NTSC (National Television System Committee)	237.3	720×480
PAL (Phase Alternating Line)	284.77	720×576
CIF (Common Intermediate Format)	69.61	352×288
QCIF (Quarter Common Intermediate Format)	17.4	176×144

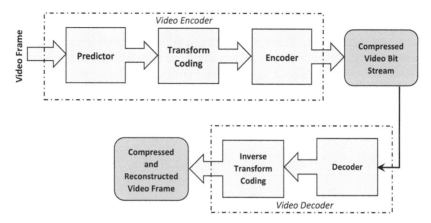

FIGURE 4.8
Typical video compression model.

decoder has been broken into inverse transform coding and decoder. The predictor identifies different redundant elements existing in the video frame. After identification of redundancy, transform coefficients are obtained by applying suitable transform coding. And finally, the encoder eliminates those coefficients that represent different redundancies. The decoder decodes the incoming video stream and obtains the transform coefficients of the compressed video frames. After doing this, inverse transform coding is applied at the receiving side to obtain the compressed and reconstructed video frame [11].

4.5.2 Machine Learning in Video Compression

Machine learning algorithms are now being applied in artificial intelligence-based video compression systems. The use of deep learning methods has also been started by researchers and professionals for improving artificial intelligence-based video compression. In the process of video encoding and video compression, supervised algorithms are used. In machine learning, supervised learning acts as a function that is used to map an input to an output. In modern video compression tools, the functions to implement attributes and features of artificial intelligence have been included. These solutions take advantage of machine learning algorithms and techniques that tend to automate the formatting and compression of video content. Moreover, the machine learning-based video compression approaches enable to perform compression during the uploading of video content [12]. These approaches are also able to compress the video upon uploading before they are downloaded by the users. Machine learning methods for video compression saves a huge amount of time, skill, and efforts as compared to the traditional video compression approaches, by automating the tasks and processes. The two important benefits of applying machine learning in video compression are listed below.

4.5.2.1 Development Savings

Video compression and video codecs are two different areas. Algorithms for video codecs are quite complex, and their development may take huge time and effort. Machine learning approach-based software reduces the effort and time because in this, the system learns on its own to adapt itself with little or no human interference.

4.5.2.2 *Improving Encoder Density*

Many machine learning algorithms are executed in a graphical processing unit (GPU), while others are executed in a central processing unit (CPU). The number of logical cores in GPU are less in number than CPU, and this enables the system to execute simple computations concurrently.

Autoencoders are also becoming popular in video compression. Autoencoders are artificial neural networks (ANNs) that are trained to learn the compressed input, but they can perform reconstruction without any kind of supervision.

4.6 Digital Communications

Digital communication has become an extremely important component of daily life. When a computer interacts with another computer irrespective of their locations and distance between them, the communication is essentially digital. With the rapid growth of cellular users and with the evolution of IoT, the role of digital communication has become more critical. Besides transmitting the analog data including video, picture, and audio between the devices, another important application of digital communication is to store a large amount of data over optical and magnetic media. The elements of a digital communication system are shown in Figure 4.9. The source generally generates the message which is first passed to the transducer at the transmitting side which converts it into electrical signals followed by analog to digital conversion [13]. The source encoder eliminates redundant bits and compresses the digital signal. The channel encoder adds some additional bits in the digital signal for performing error detection and correction. Then the digital modulator transforms the digital signal again back to the analog signal so that it can be transmitted over the communication channel.

At the receiving side, the received signal from the channel is demodulated and converted into a digital signal. The channel decoder decodes the digital sequence and checks

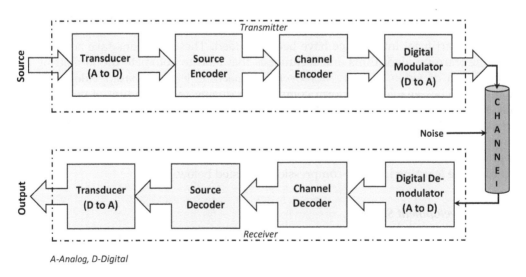

A-Analog, D-Digital

FIGURE 4.9
Elements of digital communication.

the same for any potential errors. If the sequence is erroneous, then the channel decoder corrects the same by adding redundant bits [14]. The source decoder recreates the digital signal by performing sampling and quantization. The output transducer transforms the digital signal to the original message.

4.6.1 Machine Learning in Digital Communications

A huge amount of data is being generated by the users using different platforms. Due to the usage of smart cell phones, the data are generated at the network level and also at the user level. These data consist of the information about the location of the user, call pattern of the user, and mobility which is valuable for many organizations. The network service providers tend to sell this information about the users to other organizations that are willing to use the same for optimizing their business profits. For achieving this, the primary requirement is to develop and implement appropriate machine learning approaches that can deal with big data in the digital communication world. The main aim is to extract critical information from the network and user data and then leverage the same for the potential growth of the business. The major areas of applications of machine learning include communication networks, wireless communication, smart infrastructure and IoT, multimedia communication, security, and privacy [15].

4.6.1.1 Communication Networks

In communication networks, machine learning algorithms can be used for predicting the traffic and throughput. This is highly significant because controlling throughput and analyzing traffic in advance can accomplish the quality of service (QoS) requirements. The other aspects of communication networks where machine learning can be utilized are routing and inference control.

4.6.1.2 Wireless Communication

In wireless networks, for attaining high efficiency to ensure desired QoS, it is necessary to adjust different attributes of MIMO-OFDM systems. This adjusting of the attributes can be done using machine learning algorithms. One of the most essential aspects of OFDM-based wireless systems is reducing the peak-to-average power ratio which is commonly known as PAPR. Reduction of PAPR can also be done effectively by using machine learning. The cognitive radio, power control, positioning, localization, and channel estimation are also the fields of wireless communication where machine learning can be applied to get better results.

4.6.1.3 Smart Infrastructure and IoT

With the evolution of IoT, smart infrastructure and smart services are the focus of the industries. The growing usage of sensors, smart devices, and gadgets is continuously generating a huge amount of multi-model heterogeneous data [16]. The concept of smart homes, smart cities, smart grids, etc. has gained utmost consideration in the development of various infrastructures [17]. Anavangot et al. [18] highlighted that the data and information circulated in the IoT network are in the form of a control signal or a signal in time domain. The researchers are applying machine learning algorithms in different smart services and infrastructure along with emergency communications, resource management, fault prediction, scheduling, monitoring, forecasting, etc.

4.6.1.4 Security and Privacy

Machine learning algorithms are now playing a crucial role in dealing with the issues related to security and privacy. Machine learning-based approaches automatically detect unusual behavior and activities. The critical applications of security in communications where machine learning can be utilized are fraud detection, spam identification, intrusion identification, and privacy-preserving. Bodkhe and Tanwar [19] presented various concerns and possible future implications of the verification and validation methodologies in order to secure the data distribution in an IoT environment. Tanwar et al. [20] presented a detailed analysis on the adoption of machine learning algorithms to make blockchain-based smart applications more secure from various threats and attacks. Machine learning and deep learning-based approaches are also capable in identifying and mitigating known attacks as well as unknown attacks [21].

4.6.1.5 Multimedia Communication

Machine learning is now also being used in communicating the audio, video, and images over the network. Signal compression is one of the significant fields where use of machine learning is giving outstanding benefits. Neural networks, tracking and deep learning, are the well-known concepts of machine learning that are being used extensively in multimedia content streaming.

4.6.2 Healthcare

Healthcare is a very important aspect of human life, and in countries with a large population base, the demand for improved healthcare systems has elevated rapidly. In healthcare, it is very important to maintain and monitor the medical data and records of patients. In addition to this, medical science is seeking great help from the technologies like sensors, RFID tags, IoT, artificial intelligence, and machine learning. Machine learning in healthcare is now proving to be a magic rod in dealing with different problems. In the area of healthcare, machine learning enables efficient analysis of many data points, recommends outcomes, and helps in proper resource allocation and utilization [22]. With the help of machine learning, machine learning applications are going to analyze real-time data of patients from multiple countries and different medical systems for finding out new ways of treatments that were not available in the past. The major applications of machine learning in healthcare [23] are highlighted in Figure 4.10.

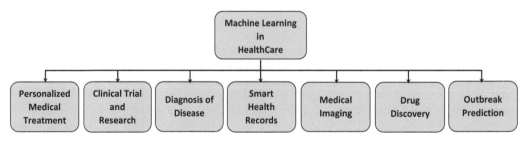

FIGURE 4.10
Universal applications of machine learning in healthcare.

4.6.2.1 Personalized Medical Treatment

In the present scenarios, generally, the physicians provide medical treatment on the basis of symptoms, pathological tests, and known genetic information. But using machine learning and predictive analysis along with the biosensors and sophisticated health measurement devices, better and multiple treatment options can be explored.

4.6.2.2 Clinical Research and Trial

The process of clinical trials and research in the area of pharmacy requires a lot of effort and time, and in few cases, it can take even many years. The application of machine learning-based predictive analysis for identifying an appropriate candidate for a clinical trial can be helpful to extract critical information from different data points like past medical consultancy, social media, etc.

4.6.2.3 Diagnosis of Disease

The most prominent application of machine learning in healthcare is to identify and diagnose the disease in patients which are generally presumed hard to diagnose. The diseases like initial stage cancer and genetic disorders which are difficult to diagnose manually can be identified at a fast pace using cognitive computing and genome-based sequencing.

4.6.2.4 Smart Health Records

In large medical systems, maintaining the data and medical records is an exhaustive process. The main aim of machine learning is to reduce the effort, money, and time so that the same can be utilized in other critical healthcare functioning. Document classification along with machine learning and vector machines and hand-writing recognition based on machine learning can be used to maintain medical records automatically in an efficient manner.

4.6.2.5 Medical Imaging

Computer vision has become possible due to machine learning and deep learning, and it can be used as an image diagnostic tool which is applied for recognizing the existing patterns in a medical image. Machine learning algorithms focus on extracting the features from the medical image which are primary for making the diagnosis and prediction. Then the system recognizes the best combinations of the extracted features for transforming the image into some metric.

4.6.2.6 Drug Discovery

One of the very significant applications of machine learning is in the process of early-stage drug discovery. Machine learning tools can be applied in various stages of the process of drug development including identification of drug, validation of drug, repurposing the drug, improving the efficacy of the drug, and analyzing biomedicine information. Precision medicine and next-generation sequencing can be effective in exploring alternate ways for drug discovery.

4.6.2.7 Outbreak Prediction

Artificial intelligence (AI)-based techniques are now being utilized to monitor the situation and predict upcoming epidemics. With the help of a huge amount of data available from different sources like real-time social media data, data from the web, information from satellites, etc., ANNs are able to predict various kinds of outbreaks like malaria, dengue, and other highly infectious diseases. This prediction of an outbreak is very important in developing nations that do not have sufficient and appropriate medical infrastructure.

4.6.3 Seismology

Seismology is the area of learning and scientifically studying about earthquake seismic waves that pass inside and around the earth. Seismic waves are energy waves that are created when a rock suddenly breaks inside the earth or due to some explosion inside the earth. These waves are logged using seismographs when there is a change in the energy level inside the earth. Seismology is an important area of study because seismic waves and earthquakes have other environmental side effects like tsunamis, volcanic eruptions, and oceanic storms, tectonic processes, and many more. Many of these side effects are life-threatening for human beings.

4.6.3.1 Interpreting Seismic Observations

Seismic observations are interpreted using a well-defined approach as illustrated in Figure 4.11. The very first stage in understanding seismic waves is the analysis of records in which the signal is detected in the background of noise. Then, the various parameters of the signal like amplitude, apparent period, polarization, and arrival time are measured which is followed by preliminary wave identification of a specific form. The second stage is the analysis of a source which tends to obtain source parameters like epicenter, mechanism, magnitude, energy, focal depth, and source dimensions [24]. With the help of these source parameters, the final identification of the wave is carried out. In the third stage, basic rules are constructed which include seismic wave kinematics, seismic wave dynamics, and statistical relations in seismicity. The fourth and final stage performs seismological

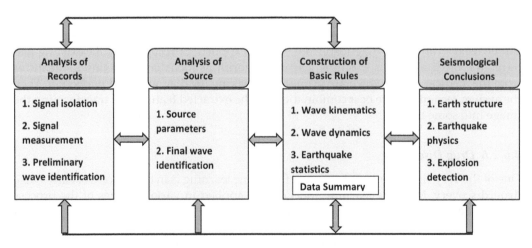

FIGURE 4.11
Stages in interpreting seismic observations.

conclusions about earth structure, earthquake physics, and source identification. Explosion detection is also done in this stage.

4.6.3.2 Machine Learning in Seismology

Seismologists are now utilizing machine learning algorithms along with high computationally capable machines, huge seismic data sets, and architecture for predicting the upcoming seismic events. Moreover, a machine learning-based approach can also be used to preserve past earthquake analog records. Deep neural networks are also being used by the researchers for learning the complex relationship between the past seismic data available and the predicted outcome. Because the media over which the huge amount of data is stored usually degrades, seismologists are trying hard to safeguard this critical information. Machine learning methods that are capable of identifying images are also potential candidates for preserving seismic data in a cost-effective way. Some of the researchers use machine learning to examine the seismic data for identifying the volcanic activity and earthquake aftershocks and to monitor the tectonic shock that signifies the distortion at the boundaries of the plate [25]. Few studies based on machine learning are also going on for locating earthquake origins and to differentiate the low-intensity earthquake from the seismic noise present in the surroundings. Techniques of machine learning like deep learning and CNNs can also be applied in the different stages of seismic observations highlighted in Figure 4.11. They may be utilized analyzing records, analyzing the source, construction of rules, and drawing important conclusions in an efficient and faster way.

4.6.4 Speech Recognition

Speech recognition is an integrated field of computational linguistics and computer science aimed to design and develop methods and techniques that are capable of recognizing and translating the oral language into textual form using digital computers. The two fundamentals behind speech recognition are acoustic modeling and language modeling. The relationship of linguistic components of speech and audio is represented by acoustic modeling while language modeling is used to match word sequence with sound for distinguishing the words that are similar in sound. For improving the accuracy of a speech recognition system, hidden Markov models are generally used for the identification of temporal patterns in speech [26]. On the other hand, natural language processing (NLP) performs speech recognition in an easy and time-efficient way. A general speech recognition system is shown in Figure 4.12.

Signal, acoustic, and language are the three important components of speech recognition. At signal level, different speech segments are extracted followed by feature extraction by MFCC or deep learning. At the acoustic level, classification of sound is done using machine learning approaches. Additional contextual information is also gathered at acoustic level. At the language level, sounds are translated into words, words are combined to form sentences, and deep learning methods are used to generate models. Machine learning approaches utilize sentence structure, grammar, and syntax along with the alignment of voice and audio signals for processing speech. Machine learning-based software learns continuously, and learning will increase as the usage increases, and due to this improved learning, it will be easier to understand the fundamentals like accents.

The machine learning approaches applied in automatic speech recognition (ASR) include generative learning, discriminative learning, supervised learning, semi-supervised learning, active learning, and deep learning. Machine learning paradigms in ASR and

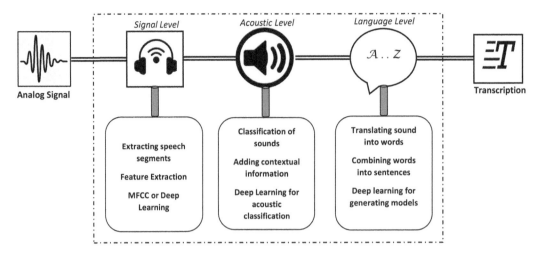

FIGURE 4.12
General speech recognition system.

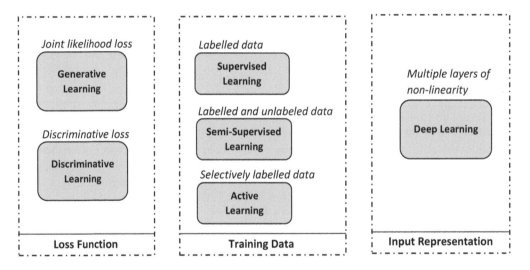

FIGURE 4.13
Paradigms of machine learning in speech recognition.

their key attributes are highlighted in Figure 4.13. On the basis of the loss function and the nature of decision function, machine learning paradigms have been categorized as generative learning and discriminative learning. The nature of the model and the core component in the objective of the train are the two major differences in generative learning and discriminative learning. Generative learning contains a generative model and adopts a training objective function that is based over joint likelihood loss. However, the paradigm of discriminative learning uses either a discriminative model or aims to apply discriminative training to the model [27]. Contingent upon the kind of training data available, supervised learning, semi-supervised learning, and active learning are the types of machine learning paradigms in ASR. In the supervised learning paradigm, the training data set contains different pairs of inputs and outputs obtained from a joint distribution. The major objective is to minimize empirical risk along with regularization. The minor difference in supervised and semi-supervised learning is that the latter one also deals with unlabeled data sets.

Active learning is slightly different from semi-supervised learning as it considers selectively labeled data sets. The main aim of active learning is to make the most informative data sets to be labeled for improving the classification performance. Subjected to the input representation, another kind of machine learning paradigm in ASR is deep learning. Deep learning is inherently related to the usage of multiple layers of nonlinear conversions for deriving speech features. ASR is now exploiting the power of machine learning paradigms due to the easy availability of huge training data sets.

4.6.5 Computer Vision

Computer vision is a field that aims to design and develop methods and techniques that enable a computer to see, analyze, and understand the digital content including images and videos. The data over the internet consist of both text and multimedia. For searching and indexing textual content, straightforward algorithms and tools can be used. But, for searching and indexing multimedia content like images and videos, algorithms must know what is contained by images and videos, i.e., computers must see the content inside the images [28]. Computer vision is closely related to artificial intelligence and machine learning. Computer vision has a big list of applications including machine inspection, medical imaging, automotive safety, motion capture, biometrics, and many more.

The well-known computer vision applications try to perform the following in images:

- **Object Classification**: To classify the broad category of the objects in the image.
- **Object Identification**: To identify the kind of object in the image.
- **Object Verification**: To check the presence of object in the image.
- **Object Detection**: To detect where the objects are in the image.
- **Object Landmark Detection**: To find out the key points of the object in the image.
- **Object Segmentation**: To identify the pixels belonging to the object.
- **Object Recognition**: To find out what object and where they are in the image.

Computer vision first acquires the image or large sets of photographs in real-time or videos, and then it applies machine learning or deep learning models to automate the process. Finally in the interpretive step, the machine learning or deep learning models are deployed to output the scores and decision. The basic steps followed in the process of multi-level computer vision for image are illustrated in Figure 4.14. First, image segmentation is carried out for the input image data, and then, feature extraction is done followed by object recognition. The image segmentation process is supported by segmentation parameter sets and genetic algorithm for parameter adaption. Learning new object features is done in synchronization with the feature extraction process. Object model acquisition and refinement are also carried out along with the object recognition process.

Machine learning-based approaches tend to improve computer vision for better recognition and tracking. They provide effective techniques for improving the acquisition of the image, processing the image, and focusing on the object which are primary components of computer vision [29]. For object recognition, the most common machine learning approach

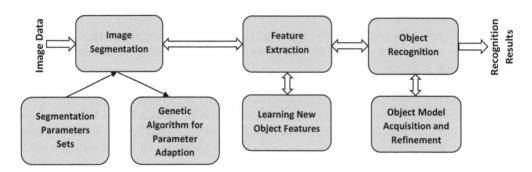

FIGURE 4.14
Computer vision process for image.

is scale-invariant feature transform (SIFT). SITF uses important attributes of the object and saves them in the database. In image categorization, these attributes of the object are checked by SITF and matched with the attributes saved in the database. The most common approach that deep learning uses for object recognition is CNN.

4.6.6 Economic Forecasting

Economic forecasting deals with making predictions of the various economical parameters that affect the economic condition of the nation. The parameters like inflation, fiscal deficit, GDP, employment rate, foreign exchange, etc. are predicted to make financial analysis in advance. Economic forecasting is a means to identify the key financial patterns existing in the economy of a nation [30]. The officials of the government and the business managers utilize the economic forecasts to plan financial policies and future economic activities. Machine learning-based methods are proving to be effective and less time consuming for the area of financial forecasting. The primary advantage of machine learning in financial forecasting is its capability to analyze both structured data and unstructured data. The sources of structured data include ERP data of the organization, internal audit reports, or warehousing system while unstructured data can be gathered from reviews of products and services of the company.

For adopting the machine learning approach in business, the very first phase is to determine the scope which will be the specific area of the business-like expenses and revenues. Data availability and quality checks are also performed in this phase. The scope must include the most impactful area of the organization. In the second phase, the hypothesis is developed to determine the drivers of the business. In the third phase, the appropriate machine learning model is built to test the hypothesis and considerations about the business drivers. In the last phase, various tools are integrated into the process of financial forecasting, and then, visualizations and reporting are performed. This process of adopting machine learning for financial forecasting is shown in Figure 4.15.

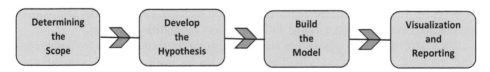

FIGURE 4.15
Roadmap for adopting machine learning in financial forecasting.

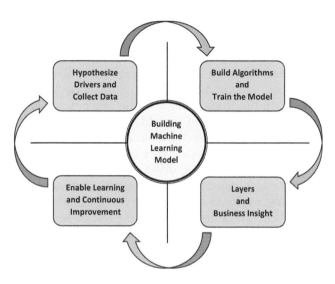

FIGURE 4.16
Process for building machine learning model in economic forecasting.

The most important component in implementing machine learning in economic forecasting is to build a machine learning model [31]. An iterative process for building a machine learning model in financial forecasting is shown in Figure 4.16. The first step toward the development of the model is to collect the data and hypothesize the parameters driving the business. While the hypothesis and the data are being tested the programmers can start developing the algorithms and training of the model in order to detect the existing patterns in the data, so that appropriate predictions can be made. The basic forecast produced in this step will enable the understanding the layer information and will also produce precise business insight. Upon the availability of the new drivers and new data sets, the model can be updated and improved continuously. It is very significant to ensure that during the model development, no mistakes are made by the machine in the learning process i.e., the model must be validated against the previously available data and the actual results [32].

4.7 Conclusion

Machine learning based solutions are going to be a very important part of computing in many real-life applications. There are many applications of signal processing in daily life that can be improved with the usage of machine learning techniques. This chapter has highlighted ten such applications where machine learning algorithms and techniques are being applied by the industry and the researchers to improve the results. This chapter has presented the application of machine learning to various areas including audio signal processing, audio compression, digital image processing, video compression, digital communication, healthcare, seismology, speech recognition, computer vision, and economic forecasting. Using machine learning in audio signal processing makes the feature extraction more effective. In audio and video compression machine learning is useful in developing more accurate models for codecs.

A CNN can be effectively combined with digital image processing to give better results. In the area of communication network, machine learning is proving to be very effective due to its ability to predict the network traffic and the behavior. The wide applicability of machine learning algorithms has been seen in the area of healthcare starting from personal medical treatment up to outbreak prediction. Deep neural networks can be used to predict seismic activities which are life threatening. On the other hand, NLP performs speech recognition in an easy and time-efficient way. Machine learning-based approaches tend to improve computer vision for better recognition and tracking. Machine learning-based predictive model can be utilized for making very accurate financial predictions. With the discussion of these applications, it can be deduced that machine learning is improving the efficiency of the processes incurred in these applications with reduced efforts and time. Since this chapter has explored only ten specific applications of machine learning, reconnoitering more applications of machine learning related to signal processing is open before the research community. The study presented in this chapter is highly significant for the people working in the field of applications of machine learning.

References

1. Alzubi, J., Nayyar, A. and Kumar, A., 2018, November. Machine learning from theory to algorithms: an overview. *Journal of Physics: Conference Series*, 1142(1), p. 012012.
2. Prasad, B. and Prasanna, S.M. eds., 2007. *Speech, Audio, Image and Biomedical Signal Processing Using Neural Networks* (Vol. 83). Springer, Heidelberg.
3. Singh, J. 2019. "Audio processing and ML using Python". *PyBay*. https://opensource.com/article/19/9/audio-processing-machine-learning-python
4. Kumbhar, P.Y. and Krishnan, S., 2011. Sound data compression using different methods. In *International Conference on Computing and Communication Systems* (pp. 100–108). Springer, Berlin, Heidelberg.
5. Oates, C., 2020. Intelligent audio engineering for emotion recognition personal analysis & scene detection. https://www.audeering.com. Last accessed 23 December 2020.
6. Gonzalez, R.C., and Woods, R.E., 2017. *Digital Image Processing*. Pearson, New York.
7. Vora, J., Patel, M., Tanwar, S. and Tyagi, S., 2018, February. Image processing based analysis of cracks on vertical walls. In *2018 3rd International Conference on Internet of Things: Smart Innovation and Usages (IoT-SIU)* (pp. 1–5). IEEE, Bhimtal, India.
8. Maram, S.S., Kumar, N., Joel, J.P.C., Rodrigues, T.S. and Jain, A., 2020. Images to signals, signals to highlights. In *IEEE Global Communications Conference (GLOBECOM-2020)* (pp. 1–6). IEEE, Taipei, Taiwan.
9. Lézoray, O., Charrier, C., Cardot, H. and Lefèvre, S., 2008. Machine learning in image processing. *EURASIP Journal on Advances in Signal Processing*, 2008(1), pp. 927–950.
10. Bhojani, D.R., Dwivedi, V.J. and Thanki, R.M., 2020. Introduction to video compression. In Bhojani, D.R., Dwivedi, V.J. and Thanki, R.M. (Eds.), *Hybrid Video Compression Standard* (pp. 1–14). Springer, Singapore.
11. Furht, B., Greenberg, J. and Westwater, R., 2012. *Motion Estimation Algorithms for Video Compression* (Vol. 379). Springer, Berlin.
12. Knop, M., Cierniak, R. and Shah, N., 2014, June. Video compression algorithm based on neural network structures. In *International Conference on Artificial Intelligence and Soft Computing* (pp. 715–724). Springer, Cham.
13. Barry, J.R., Lee, E.A. and Messerschmitt, D.G., 2012. *Digital communication*. Springer Science & Business Media, New York.

14. Meinel, C. and Sack, H., 2013. Network access layer (1): Wired LAN technologies. In *Internetworking* (pp. 131–259). Springer, Berlin, Heidelberg.

15. Samek, W., Stanczak, S. and Wiegand, T., 2017. The convergence of machine learning and communications. arXiv preprint arXiv:1708.08299.

16. Tanwar, S. ed., 2020. *Fog Data Analytics for IoT Applications: Next Generation Process Model with State of the Art Technologies* (Vol. 76). Springer Nature, Singapore.

17. Tanwar, S., Tyagi, S. and Kumar, N. eds., 2019. *Multimedia Big Data Computing for IoT Applications: CONCEPTS, Paradigms and Solutions* (Vol. 163). Springer, Singapore.

18. Anavangot, V., Menon, V.G. and Nayyar, A., 2018, November. Distributed big data analytics in the internet of signals. In *2018 International Conference on System Modeling & Advancement in Research Trends (SMART)* (pp. 73–77). IEEE, Moradabad, India.

19. Bodkhe, U. and Tanwar, S., 2020. Taxonomy of secure data dissemination techniques for IoT environment. *IET Software*, 14, pp. 563–571.

20. Tanwar, S., Bhatia, Q., Patel, P., Kumari, A., Singh, P.K. and Hong, W.C., 2019. Machine learning adoption in blockchain-based smart applications: The challenges, and a way forward. *IEEE Access*, 8, pp. 474–488.

21. Gupta, R., Tanwar, S., Tyagi, S. and Kumar, N., 2020. Machine learning models for secure data analytics: A taxonomy and threat model. *Computer Communications*, 153, pp. 406–440.

22. Gupta, S. and Sedamkar, R.R., 2020. Machine learning for healthcare: Introduction. In Jain, V. and Chatterjee, J. M. (Eds.), *Machine Learning with Health Care Perspective* (pp. 1–25). Springer, Cham.

23. Shailaja, K., Seetharamulu, B. and Jabbar, M.A., 2018, March. Machine learning in healthcare: A review. In *2018 Second International Conference on Electronics, Communication and Aerospace Technology (ICECA)* (pp. 910–914). IEEE, Coimbatore, India.

24. Borok, V.I.K. 1992. Introduction seismology and logic. In Keilis-Borok, V. I. (Ed.), *Computational Seismology*, Springer, US (pp. 1–9).

25. Bergen, K.J., Chen, T. and Li, Z., 2019. Preface to the focus section on machine learning in seismology. *Seismological Research Letters*, 90(2A), pp. 477–480.

26. Benesty, J., Sondhi, M.M. and Huang, Y.A., 2008. Introduction to speech processing. In Benesty, J., Sondhi, M.M. and Huang, Y. (Eds.), *Springer Handbook of Speech Processing* (pp. 1–4). Springer, Berlin, Heidelberg.

27. Deng, L. and Li, X., 2013. Machine learning paradigms for speech recognition: An overview. *IEEE Transactions on Audio, Speech, and Language Processing*, 21(5), pp. 1060–1089.

28. Klette, R., 2014. *Concise Computer Vision*. Springer, London.

29. Sebe, N., Cohen, I., Garg, A. and Huang, T.S., 2005. *Machine Learning in Computer Vision* (Vol. 29). Springer Science & Business Media, New York.

30. Guerard Jr., J.B., 2013. *Introduction to Financial Forecasting in Investment Analysis*. Springer Science & Business Media, New York.

31. Soofi, A.S. and Cao, L. eds., 2012. *Modelling and Forecasting Financial Data: Techniques of Nonlinear Dynamics* (Vol. 2). Springer Science & Business Media, New York.

32. Degiannakis, S. and Floros, C., 2016. *Modelling and Forecasting High Frequency Financial Data*. Springer, Berlin.

5

Dive in Deep Learning: Computer Vision, Natural Language Processing, and Signal Processing

V. Ajantha Devi

AP3 Solutions

Mohd Naved

Jagannath University

CONTENTS

DOI: 10.1201/9781003107026-5

5.1 Deep Learning: Introduction

Deep learning [1] is a subset of machine learning that centers around learning huge highlights from the info information, particularly in situations where the information is perplexing. This is pretty much a swap for a commonplace component extractor that was worked to be interesting to complex information types, for example, images, videos, audio, etc. Customary or rudimentary machine learning strategies were initially being used for image processing [2,3], natural language processing (NLP) [4–6], and audio processing [7,8].

In situations where an image had a similar item with an alternate brightening or point, the distance measure for all intents and purposes fizzled. Also, with the conventional direct classifier procedure [9], every pixel estimation of the info picture is surveyed and labeled in the event that it very well may be a boundary for coordinating. Regularly, a weighted normal estimation of the pixel is taken for correlation, which is the reason all the difficult regions of pictures, [10] (for example, enlightenments, various points or picture perspectives, commotion, foundation mess, and numerous assortments of the same items) cause the calculation to neglect to coordinate the info picture.

In NLP, deep learning strategies are ordinarily founded on neural network and depend on continuous word vector portrayals referred to as word embeddings. This segment initially presents the idea of word embeddings just as various unaided methods to create such portrayals. NLP applications exploiting words embeddings are depicted toward the finish of the part. Conventional NLP assignments, [4] for example, part-of-speech (POS) labeling or semantic role labeling (SRL) comprises labeling each word in a sentence with a tag. Another class of issues, for example, named entity recognition (NER) or shallow parsing (piecing) comprises recognizing and naming expressions (for example, gatherings of words) with predefined labels. Such undertakings can be communicated as word arrangement issues by distinguishing the expression limits rather than straightforwardly recognizing the entire expressions.

In the field of audio analysis [7], low-level highlights that characterize audio data fall under the classes of tone and worldly highlights. Tone is related with the recurrence area and characterizes highlights, for example, existing frequencies in a soundtrack [8], just as distinguishing common and consonant frequencies. Worldly highlights are characterized throughout the time space. Numerous strategies for extricating highlights from sound signs have been investigated for sound substance examination.

These expertly characterized techniques for removing sound data have had many recorded triumphs and have improved execution of sound examination across different issue areas. Notwithstanding, these strategies were not intended for melodic information. They were intended for discourse sound, which is just a solitary commitment to a melodic track, and research directed with these strategies for highlight extraction has demonstrated that they do separate some important data from music sound.

5.2 Past, Present, and Future of Deep-Learning

Throughout the long term, deep learning has advanced causing a monstrous interruption into ventures and business spaces. Deep learning is a part of machine learning that sends algorithms for information handling and copies the reasoning cycle and even creates reflections. Deep learning utilizes layers of algorithms for information handling, comprehends human speech, and recognizes object visually.

Year	Inventor	Description
1943	William McCulloch and Walter Pitts	A logical calculus of the ideas immanent in nervous activity in which they sketched out the principal computational model of a neural organization
1949	Donald Hebb	The organization of behavior, which contended that the associations between neurons reinforced with use. This idea demonstrated key to understanding human learning and how to prepare ANNs
1954	Belmont Farley and Wesley Clark	The principal PC reproductions of a fake neural organization (up to 128 neurons)
1957	Frank Rosenblatt	A sort of neural network called the perceptron and had the option to apply the preparation technique
1959	Bernard Widrow and Marcian Hoff	ADALINE short for adaptive linear elements, a multilayer neural organization called MADALINE, dispensed with echoes on calls and is supposed to be the principal down to earth use of an ANN
1960	Henry J. Kelley	"Gradient Theory of Optimal Flight Paths" shows the first ever versions of continuous backpropagation model
1962	Stuart Dreyfus	"The numerical solution of variation problems" shows a backpropagation model that uses simple derivative chain rule, instead of dynamic programming which earlier backpropagation models were using
1965	Alexey Grigoryevich Ivakhnenko and Valentin Grigor'evich Lapa	Created hierarchical representation of neural network that uses polynomial activation function and is trained using Group Method of Data Handling (GMDH)
1969	Marvin Minsky and Seymour Papert	"Perceptrons" in which they show that Rosenblatt's perceptron cannot solve complicated functions like XOR. For such function, perceptrons should be placed in multiple hidden layers which compromises perceptron learning algorithm
1970	Seppo Linnainmaa	General method for automatic differentiation for backpropagation and also implements backpropagation in computer code
1971	Alexey Grigoryevich	Neural networks. He creates 8-layer deep neural network using GMDH
1980	Kunihiko Fukushima	Neocognitron, the first convolutional neural network (CNN) architecture which could recognize visual patterns such as handwritten characters.
1982	John Hopfield	Hopfield network, which is nothing but a recurrent neural network. It serves as a content-addressable memory system, and would be instrumental for further RNN models of modern deep learning era
1982	Paul Werbos	The use of backpropagation for propagating errors during the training of neural networks.
1985	David H. Ackley, Geoffrey Hinton and Terrence Sejnowski create	Boltzman machine that is a stochastic recurrent neural network. This neural network has only input layer and hidden layer but no output layer

(Continued)

Year	Inventor	Description
1986	Terry Sejnowski	NeTalk, a neural network which learns to pronounce written English text by being shown text as input and matching phonetic transcriptions for comparison
1986	Geoffrey Hinton, Rumelhar, and Williams	"Learning representations by backpropagating errors" show the successful implementation of backpropagation in the neural network. It opened gates for training complex deep neural network easily
1986	Paul Smolensky	A variation of Boltzmann machine where there is not intra-layer connection in input and hidden layer. It is known as restricted Boltzmann machine (RBM). It would become popular in years to come especially for building recommender systems
1989	Yann LeCun	Uses backpropagation to train CNN to recognize handwritten digits. This is a breakthrough moment as it layers the foundation of modern computer vision using deep learning
1989	George Cybenko	Universal approximation theorem in his paper "Approximation by superpositions of a sigmoidal function." He proves that feed forward neural network with single hidden layer containing a finite number of neurons can approximate any continuous function
1991	Sepp Hochreiter	Identifies the problem of vanishing gradient which can make the learning of deep neural network extremely slow and almost impractical
1997	Sepp Hochreiter and Jurgen Schmidhuber	"Long short-term memory" (LSTM). It is a type of recurrent neural network architecture
2006	Geoffrey Hinton, Ruslan Salakhutdinov, Osindero and Teh	"A fast-learning algorithm for deep belief nets" in which they stacked multiple RBMs together in layers and called them deep belief networks. The training process is much more efficient for a large amount of data
2008	Andrew NG's group	Use of GPUs for training deep neural networks to speed up the training time by many folds. This could bring practicality in the field of deep learning for training on huge volume of data efficiently
2009	Fei-Fei Li	ImageNet which is a database of 14 million labeled images. It would serve as a benchmark for the deep learning researchers who would participate in ImageNet competitions (ILSVRC) every year
2011	Yoshua Bengio, Antoine Bordes, Xavier Glorot	"Deep Sparse Rectifier Neural Networks" shows that ReLU activation function can avoid vanishing gradient problem. This means that now, apart from GPU, deep learning community has another tool to avoid issues of longer and impractical training times of deep neural network
2012	Alex Krizhevsky	AlexNet, a GPU implemented CNN model designed wins Imagenet's image classification contest with an accuracy of 84%. It is a huge jump over 75% accuracy that earlier models had achieved
2014	Ian Goodfellow	Generative Adversarial Neural Network also known as GAN. GANs open a whole new door of application of deep learning in fashion, art, and science due its ability to synthesize real-like data
2016	Deepmind	Deepmind's deep reinforcement learning model beats human champion in the complex game of Go. The game is much more complex than chess, so this feat captures the imagination of everyone and takes the promise of deep learning to a whole new level
2019	Yoshua Bengio, Geoffrey Hinton, and Yann LeCun	Wins Turing Award 2018 for their immense contribution in advancement in the area of deep learning and artificial intelligence

Beginning in, research resurged for a couple of years after Geoff Hinton distributed learning representations by back-proliferating errors, which depicts the backpropagation learning system. Notwithstanding, genuine resurgence didn't happen until the mid-2000s. Today, deep learning and AI are in deep sprout, and some would state overhyped as shown below [11–42].

5.3 Natural Language Processing

NLP [4–6] is also called computational linguistics with the interactions between computer language and human (natural language). The earliest research in NLP is generally considered to have started in the 1950s where the so-called Turing test was introduced, proposing a test in machine intelligence which to this day is widely known. The Turing test, developed by Alan Turing in 1950, is a test of a machine's ability to possess indistinguishable human behavior and to appear to have human-like intelligence and interaction. The test is based on a machine's ability to analyze, process, and contribute in an interaction based in a human language [43].

Up until the 1980s, as in Figure 5.1, the area of NLP relied on sets of complex handwritten rules in order to execute decision-making. In the late 1980s, however, probabilistic models were introduced with machine learning algorithms, often based on decision trees or hidden Markov models [44]. These models required a higher amount of computational power which were not available until then. Today, computers have orders of magnitudes stronger computing power with more and more natural language data being accumulated over time, especially with the global usage of internet in recent years.

In recent years, deep neural networks have got considerable performance as in Figure 5.2 among many NLP tasks like sentiment analysis [45–47], syntactic analysis [48,49], and

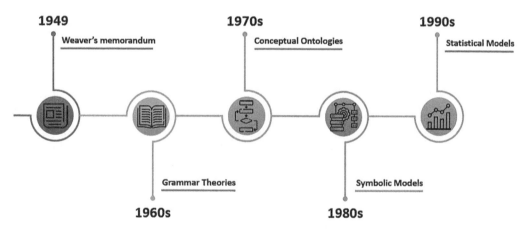

FIGURE 5.1
Stages of NLP before the deep learning era.

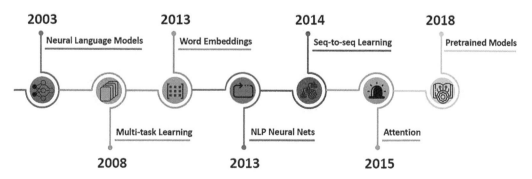

FIGURE 5.2
Stages of NLP in the deep learning era.

machine translation [50,51]. Different deep neural networks are applied for various tasks in the NLP field. For example, in tasks of dialogue system, Zhou et al. [52] used the LSTM encoder on the top of CNN for multi-turn human-computer conversation which takes utterance into consideration to catch utterance-level relations in the text. For POS tagging, Andor et al. [53] proposed a transition-based approach combined with feed-forward neural network, and Huang, Xu, and Yu [54] also used Bi-LSTM to predict POStags. Various deep models have become the new state-of-the-art methods in the NLP field.

5.3.1 Word Embeddings

In the most recent decade, word embeddings [48,49] have set up themselves as a center component of numerous NLP frameworks. Without a doubt, NLP techniques manage characteristic language, which frequently shows up as text. This content is itself made out of more modest units like words and characters, which are not straightforwardly justifiable by computer in any human sense. Subsequently, word embeddings are expected to mathematically speak to literary information which can be perused, perceived, and prepared by computer programs. This need was underlined with the new blast of deep realizing, which demonstrated to tackle a tremendous measure of issues in different fields.

NLP analysts [55] who needed to utilize promising deep learning models on content information needed to think of a mathematical method to speak to words. This brought about a broad examination for best speaking to printed information with the end goal that the portrayals catch both semantic and syntactic implications of words. Practically speaking, there are a few different ways to speak to a word by a vector. The easiest one is presumably one-hot encoding.

5.3.1.1 Word2vec

The Word2vec model was presented by Mikolov et al. [56]. The thought is to change a word into a ceaseless vector, which additionally speaks to the word's neighborhood setting. Embeddings of Word2vec don't have the inadequacy of one-hot encoded word vectors, which can just perceive if a word is actually the equivalent. Word2vec [57] makes these differentiations more particular by including a word's precursors and replacements.

The word portrayals incorporate semantic and syntactic data, which are recovered from the setting words. Figure 5.3 delineates the situation of word vectors with two measurements. The bolts show a numerical distance between two words. For instance, the cosine distance is an appropriate capacity for figuring the difference between word vectors. In an

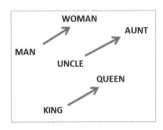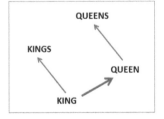

FIGURE 5.3
Arrows showing the distances between two-word embeddings in a two-dimensional space.

installing space, it is conceivable that equivalent relations between words can be spoken to by a comparative distance and heading. For instance, the English words "man" and "woman" do have a comparable distance to "king" and "queen." This implies that the logical difference among "man" and "woman" is equivalent to "king" and "queen." Words that relate to the male sexual orientation are utilized with regard to "man" and "king," though "woman" and "queen" are encircled by more female word structures. Along these lines, the language structure and semantic of a word is consolidated into a word portrayal. This is the genuine strength of word embeddings or Word2vec. It makes it simpler to find equivalents and concentrate a speaker's proposed meaning all the more without any problem.

The underlying paper of Word2vec proposes two different ways to deal with learn word vectors out of text corpora with the jargon of N. The first approach is the Continuous Bag-of-Words (CBOW), which predicts a word dependent on its unique situation. The subsequent methodology is called Skip-gram [58] and estimates a word's unique situation. The two endeavors limit computational intricacy and depend on FNNs, which are shown in Figure 5.4, portraying the two models in more detail.

To compute a word's vector portrayal, the neural network of CBOW takes the setting terms to one side $wt-2$, $wt-1$ and right $wt+1$, $wt+2$ of the word wt as info. This word window can be acclimated to increment or reduction of the size of the neighborhood setting related with the word inserting vt. Practically speaking, a setting window of 5 for CBOW and 10 for Skip-gram is favored1. CBOW takes the one-hot encoding of each information word and passes them to the organization to anticipate the one-hot-encoding of the objective word wt. The FNN models the spot of 1 in the yield vector, which can be viewed as a classification task.

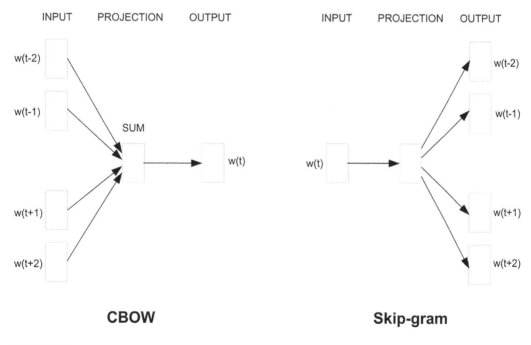

CBOW **Skip-gram**

FIGURE 5.4
FNN architecture of the CBOW and skip-gram model.

The organization that is utilized in Skip-gram trades the in-and yield. The objective word is presently the info, and the FNN predicts the word's unique situation. Skip-gram prompts better outcomes for little corpora, while CBOW is more efficient and recommendable for bigger content sets. For preparing the word vectors [57,58], the two methodologies utilize a multilayer perceptron with one shrouded layer. Consequently, the organization has two weight lattices. The first one W (1) is between the info layer and shrouded layer. W (2) is the subsequent network, which associates covered up and yield layer. The quantity of neurons in the shrouded layer is set to 300, and softmax initiation in the yield layer is utilized in the two methodologies.

5.3.2 Global Vectors for Word Representation

Global Vectors for Word Representation (GloVe) do have another methodology for building word vectors. They were at first proposed in Pennington et al. [59]; furthermore, they put their emphasis not exclusively on the word's neighborhood setting. The preparation of the GloVe vectors is done depending on a worldwide word-to-word co-event network Xij. This grid stores the recurrence with which two words wi and wj happen in a similar setting inside a corpus.

Accordingly, not just the neighborhood setting, which is dictated by the co-event network, is considered, yet additionally factual viewpoints from the corpus. To start with, the grid is developed in an introduction stage in which every content is seen once. Because the co-event architecture takes a portion of memory to parse down massive quantities of data, only word blends containing at least one co-event are saved.

5.3.3 Convolutional Neural Networks

CNNs were initially created for computer vision, for example, for picture investigation. Since 2011, they have gotten increasingly more famous in NLP [55]. Kim [47] and Kalchbrenner et al. [60] effectively utilized CNNs in NLP errands, for example, sentence arrangement and sentence displaying. Crafted by Kim's sentence, characterization will be examined further in this part, since it is an appropriate way to deal with breakdown writings regarding value forecast. From the outset, a short clarification of the fundamental thought behind a CNN will be given.

A CNN comprises convolutional and pooling layers. The info information is passed into a hanging of at least one convolutional layer, which is trailed by a pooling layer. This convolutional-pooling layer structure can be rehashed to make further designs that structure a deep CNN [1]. A convolutional layer applies a channel example to the information. This assists with planning the info information to a basic component map and to find nearby associations between them. The channel design decreases the quantity of loads in the organization by planning portions of the contribution to one element. Besides, the pooling layer shrivels the component map and combines semantically comparable highlights. A convolutional layer can comprise more than one channel design, which is shown by the stacked structure in Figure 5.5.

The creators apply various kinds of CNNs to different sentence order and question characterization assignments, for example, distinguishing positive or negative film surveys. Their methodology outflanks the cutting-edge strategy in four errands. They take a pretrained word2vec word inserting for each word in the sentence and build a network with the element of $n \, k$. Thus, $k = ED$ speaks to the component of the word installing, and n indicates the sentence's length. This network fills in as contribution for their CNN. They utilize the exaggerated digression as channel in the convolutional layer. A maximum

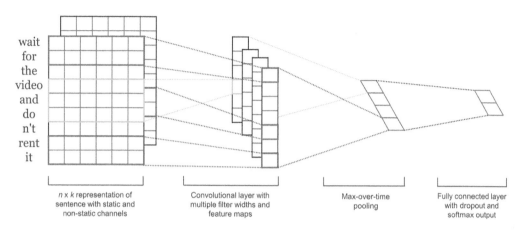

FIGURE 5.5
CNN that is used in sentence classification.

pooling layer is then applied to the separated element map. Their model joins a FNN with dropout utilized as the last layer to group the information sentence. Alterations of Kim's methodology [61] were effectively applied to anticipate classes in natural or clinical [62] science.

5.3.4 Feature Selection and Preprocessing

Highlight choice and preprocessing are significant undertakings in artificial intelligence and predominantly speak to the information arrangement. Particularly in NLP, this undertaking has a gigantic effect on the achievement of text analysis [63]. This is generally brought about by the unstructured and subjective nature of text information. Besides, machines need structure and mathematical information. Several methodologies for this change task, for example, word embeddings or the vector space model, exist.

This present area's degree lies on the hypothetical establishment of different preprocessing and include choice procedures. This part will be joined by the English expression "the best fox is running" as an illustration to delineate the use of preprocessing. It isn't generally the situation that a sensibly decent preprocessing strategy prompts better outcomes in each application [64].

5.3.4.1 Tokenization

For preparing composed characteristic language, it is inescapable to part messages into more modest units, which are called tokens. Computers need to recognize single substances of a book, and tokenization is utilized to make them. Normally, tokens speak to basic words, which are the littlest autonomous units of characteristic language. Besides, tokens can comprise colloquialisms or a hyphen, for example, "user-created." Tokenization breaks running writings into short content elements and is the very first task in any content preprocessing cycle. Other than the parcel of little units, entire sentences can likewise be the yield of a tokenizer. A basic word tokenizer [65] can be acknowledged in numerous dialects by parting the content at the events of room images. This basic benchmark approach has a few drawbacks, because of the absence of distinguishing words that semantically have a place together. In any case, a basic tokenizer separates the expression, which was presented above, into the accompanying five tokens as shown in Figure 5.6.

| the | best | fox | is | running |

FIGURE 5.6
Tokens.

By utilizing tokens, supposed n-grams can be made, which show a symbolic set with the length of n. "Gramma" is the Greek word for letter or token. When discussing a bunch of n letters in words, it is about character n grams.

5.3.4.2 Stop Word Removal

A significant way to deal with decreasing the colossal crude info space in NLP is stop word removal (SWR). Most dialects have specific words, which do show up more frequently than others or do exclude a lot of data about the substance of the content, for example, assistant action words or articles. Because of this, it frequently bodes well to prohibit this purported stop words in additional examination. In English, such words could be "the," "a," or "an," and in German, common stop words are the articles "der," "bite the dust," and "das." The disposal should be possible by checking the words against a normalized stop word list.

These rundowns are accessible in writing and are regularly executed in different programming bundles [66]. In our model, "the" and "is" are dispensed. SWR should be utilized with care, as shown in Figure 5.7 particularly in estimation examination, which endeavors to foresee a positive or negative aim of a book. The evacuation would reject words that can change an entire articulation, for example, "not" or "none."

5.3.4.3 Stemming

Other than stop word end, stemming is a valuable strategy to plan words to their promise stems and further diminish the info measurement. This assists with extricating the genuine importance of a book and improves the unstructured information available for a machine. The first stemming calculation dependent on erasing longest suffixes and spelling special cases was created in 1968. At this point, the watchman stemming calculation is a cutting-edge approach and strips suffixes from words to hold the word stem.

While this strategy performs well in English, there are a few downsides for the German language, because of the way that German words do not for the most part work by adding suffixes. Be that as it may, there is a German comparable dependent on Porter's thought and the string preparing language Snowball. By utilizing the English Porter Stemmer, the words "best," "fox," and "running" are allocated to the accompanying words as shown in Figure 5.8.

| ~~the~~ | best | fox | ~~is~~ | running |

FIGURE 5.7
Stop word removal.

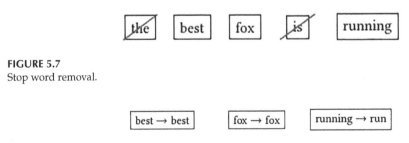

| best → best | fox → fox | running → run |

FIGURE 5.8
Cutting-edge stemmer.

5.3.4.4 Lemmatization

Lemmatization is the way toward planning each word in a book to its word reference type or expected beginning structure. Action words are changed to their infinite structure, a thing is reproduced to its solitary portrayal, and verb modifiers or descriptors envision their positive configuration. The strategy depends on morphological investigation and regularly utilizes a word reference, for instance WordNet, where the lemma of each modified word structure could be recovered. This preprocessing step is like stemming and decreases the information space, by planning different word structures to their normal portrayal. Since lemmatization is upheld by word reference sections, it can plan "best" to its lemma "good":

5.3.5 Named Entity Recognition

NER is a classic NLP task; it aims to find predefined categories for each word in the text, and these categories include names of persons, names of organizations, expressions of times, etc. The output of named entity tags could be used in many applications, such as finding relevant web pages in the search engine and posting ads according to identified texts. Most NER systems take a block of text without annotation, and outputs the annotated text, or the sequence consists of name entity tags.

NER is a challenging problem, not only because labeled data are not enough in every language, but also because there are a few constraints on which kind of words can be named entities. Most existing methods to solve this task are linear statistical models, like Hidden Markov Models (HMMs), Maximum Entropy Markov Models (MEMMs) [67], and CRF [68]. With the thrift of deep learning, CNN has been used to tackle NER problem [55], as well as RNN, like Graves and Schmidhuber [69]. Currently, the popular solution for NER is to use Bi-LSTM combined with CRF [54]. The Bi-LSTM layer could capture relations of texts from both directions of the text, and the CRF layer is able to create rules of output labels to avoid situations like 'B-PER' followed by 'B-ORG' (it is not possible that the beginning of an organization's name follows the beginning of a person's name).

NER can be evaluated with two methods, either with a token for token match or span-level evaluation. Token level evaluation looks at each token individually and is the simplest evaluation method. Span-level evaluation is stricter, requiring not only each individual token to be correct, but also the full length of the connecting classes. So, if an entity spans several words, all words within that subsequence need to be correct for the prediction to be considered correct. In general, the results are reported as harmonic mean or *F*1-score which is detailed further below in the method section. Current research is looking at ways of reducing the expensive annotation necessary to create good datasets [70] and increasing the performance across domains [71].

5.4 Image Processing

In deep learning [72] and Computer Vision, a CNN is a class of deep neural networks, most ordinarily applied to examining visual symbolism. From the outset, we will have a conversation about the means and layers in a CNN as in Figure 5.9. At that point, we will continue with making classes and strategies for a custom execution of CNN utilizing the Keras Library which highlights various channels that we can use for pictures.

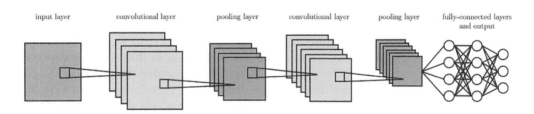

FIGURE 5.9
Convolutional neural network.

At that point, we will have a fast conversation about the CNN Design Best Practices and afterward will proceed with ShallowNet and the fundamental and straightforward CNN engineering. We will make the regular class for actualizing ShallowNet and later will prepare and assess the ShallowNet model utilizing the famous animals just as CIFAR 10 picture datasets. At that point, we will perceive how we can serialize or save the prepared model and afterward load it and use it. Despite an exceptionally shallow organization, we will attempt to do expectation for a picture we give utilizing ShallowNet for both the Animals and CIFAR 10 dataset.

After that, we will attempt the well-known CNN design called 'LeNet' for transcribed and machine-printed character acknowledgment. For LeNet additionally, will make the basic class and later will prepare, assess, and save the LeNet model utilizing the MNIST dataset. Later, we will attempt to do forecast for a manually written digit picture. At that point comes the strong VGGNet engineering. We will make the regular class and later will prepare, assess, and save the VGGNet model utilizing the CIFAR-10 dataset. Twilight of preparing, later we will attempt to do expectation for photographs of not many normal genuine articles falling in the CIFAR-10 classifications. While preparing deep organizations, it is useful to decrease the learning rate as the quantity of preparing ages increments.

5.4.1 Introduction to Image Processing and Computer Vision

Deep learning is currently universal in the field of computer vision. As an AI device, deep neural networks are powerful at comprehension high dimensional information, for example, images. Deep learning models were first utilized in computer vision for image recognition [73,74]. Nonetheless, the study of computer vision means to assemble machines which can see. This requires models which can extricate more extravagant data from image and video than recognition to different issues in computer vision.

5.4.1.1 Scene Understanding

Semantic pixel-wise segmentation requires a gauge of every pixel's semantic class as in Figure 5.10 [75]. It is a functioning subject of examination, fueled by testing datasets [76–81]. Prior to the appearance of Deep learning, the best performing techniques generally depended on available designed highlights grouping pixels autonomously.

Ordinarily, an image fix was taken care of into a classifier, for example, irregular woodlands [82,83] or boosting [84,85], to foresee the class probabilities of the middle pixel. Highlights dependent on appearance [83] or on the other hand movement and appearance [82,84,85] have been investigated. These per-pixel uproarious forecasts (regularly called unary terms) from the classifiers are then smoothed by utilizing pairwise (or higher request) contingent irregular fields (CRFs) [84,85] to improve the precision. Later methodologies

FIGURE 5.10
SegNet predictions on indoor and outdoor scene [see Ref. 75].

have intended to deliver excellent unaries by attempting to foresee the marks for all the pixels in a fix instead of just the middle pixel. This improves the consequences of arbitrary woodland based unaries [86] yet decreases execution on flimsy designs. Another methodology contends for the utilization of a blend of famous hand planned highlights and spatio-transient super-pixels to acquire higher precision [87].

The achievement of deep CNNs for object classification has all the more as of late prompted analysts to abuse their component learning capacities for organized expectation issues, for example, division. There have additionally been endeavors to apply networks intended for object classification to segmentation, especially by repeating the deepest layer highlights in squares to coordinate image measurements [88–91].

Another methodology utilizing recurrent neural networks [92] combines a few low-resolution forecasts to make input image resolution expectations. These procedures are now an improvement over hand-designed highlights [89]; in any case, their capacity to outline limits is poor. More up to date deep learning models [93–97] especially intended for division have progressed the best in class by figuring out how to disentangle or plan low goal picture portrayals to pixel-wise forecasts. These strategies depend on preprepared highlights from the huge ImageNet object classification dataset [98].

Multiscale deep learning designs are additionally being sought after [93,99–101]. The normal thought is to utilize feature extracted at various scales to give both local and global context [102].

5.4.2 Localization

Enormous scope localization exploration can be partitioned into two classes: place localization and metric localization. Place localization discretizes the world into

FIGURE 5.11
PoseNet.

various milestones and endeavors to recognize which spot is obvious in a given picture. Customarily, this has been demonstrated as an image retrieval issue [103–106] empowering the utilization of effective and adaptable retrieval approach [107,108], for example, Bag-of-Words (BoW) [109], VLAD [110,111], and Fisher vectors [112]. Deep learning models have additionally been demonstrated to be compelling for making productive descriptors. Numerous methodologies influence classification networks [113–116] and adjust them on localization datasets [117].

Conversely, metric localization methods gauge the measurement position and direction of the camera. Customarily, this has been drawn closer by figuring the posture from correspondences between two-dimensional (2-D) highlights in the question picture and three-dimensional (3-D) focuses in the model, which are resolved through descriptor coordinating [118–121]. This accepts that the scene is addressed by a 3-D construction from-movement model. The full six levels of opportunity posture of a question picture can be assessed absolutely [120]. Anyway, these techniques require a 3-D model with a huge data set of highlights and proficient recovery strategies. They are costly to process, regularly don't scale well, and are frequently not vigorous to changing ecological conditions [122].

Later work has stretched out PoseNet as in Figure 5.11 to utilize RGB-D information [123], learn relative personality movement [124], improve the setting of highlights [122], limit over video arrangements [125], and decipher relocalization vulnerability with Bayesian Neural Networks [126]. Furthermore, [122] shows PoseNet's adequacy on featureless indoor conditions, where they exhibit that SIFT-based design from movement strategies come up short in a similar climate. Despite the fact that PoseNet is adaptable and strong [127], it doesn't create adequately exact appraisals of pose contrasted with conventional techniques [128].

5.4.3 Smart Cities and Surveillance

Notwithstanding advanced mechanics, computer vision calculations are valuable to comprehend scenes from fixed cameras. One can envision brilliant city foundation, or web of things (IOT) gadgets which would profit by visual scene understanding. Semantic and occurrence video division are significant advancements. These could have applications for security checking, gathering conduct measurements, and giving examination of the world progressively.

5.4.4 Medical Imaging

Computer vision is demonstrating effective in cutting edge finding of clinical pictures [129]. Be that as it may, getting preparing information is troublesome, and it is regularly one-sided against uncommon conditions and sicknesses. Hence, it is essential to represent vulnerability when making a finding, with a considerable lot of the thoughts in this theory extremely helpful for this errand. Clinical imaging additionally frequently includes 3-D information with pictures acquired in voxels. Calculation may help deep neural networks to learn all the more productively and be more compelling in this area.

5.4.5 Object Representation

Applications may remember following specific individuals for a video for security purposes behind following planetary items from satellite information for cosmic investigations. An object of interest is characterized based on specific application which is available close by. An object of interest may rely upon the kind of utilization. For instance, in rush hour gridlock observation application, intrigued article might be human or vehicle, though for satellite application, intrigued item might be a planet, or for gaming application, it very well might be face of a specific individual.

5.4.6 Object Detection

The intrigued object with regard to either each casing of video or from that outline where the item first appears on record is identified. Of course, some item recognition framework makes usage of common data resister from the edge succession to diminish the measure of bogus location. For object recognition, there are not many customary article identification methods portrayed.

- **Point Locators:** One of the item recognition strategies is point identifier. These finders are by and large utilized to find intriguing point from the video outline which has an expressive surface in their specific territory. A charming nature of an intriguing point is its invariance to changes in edification and camera viewpoint. In writing, routinely used intriguing point indicators fuse Harris identifier, Moravec's finder, SIFT locator, and KLT identifier.

5.5 Audio Processing and Deep Learning

Technology has introduced some interesting tools and techniques that have improved the handling of signals, such as audio. Audio signals may be digital, binary, or simply a series of such a representation of messages or patterns that might be useful [130]. The signals are usually collected by digital devices with recording tools. The aims of these different devices might be different, such as speech recognition, record keeping, and medical purposes, among others. Picking and processing these signals is crucial for different applications, with the result depending on how the machines will apply the knowledge. Audio signals are waves of sound that vary in intensity and collectively contain variables such as bandwidth, frequency, and decibel levels, among others; the flow of audio processing is as shown in Figure 5.12.

One area that is being dug into is audio processing using deep learning. Deep learning is an artificial intelligence method that works in a similar way to the human brain [131].

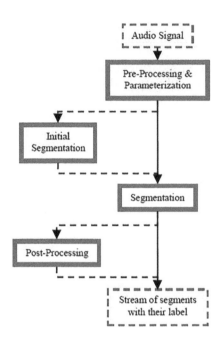

FIGURE 5.12
Flow of audio processing.

The technique builds nodes and interlinks them to handle different sections of information. Deep learning is helpful in solving difficult problems that are complex to handle in conventional means. Deep learning can also help in handling issues without the need for human input, which is crucial in handling large amounts of data.

The process of processing audio analysis takes several steps, such as collecting it, preparing it for analysis, and passing it through the analysis algorithms. Given that, audio signals have complicated data and are difficult for machines to understand, and teaching them to analyze it without supervision is the best way forward. Audio processing with deep learning techniques might need some guidance, whereby the experts train the algorithms and let the networks work their way through unknown data. Some types of neural networks apply a combination of processing nodes and filters, which helps get more refined results. These categories of deep learning are known as convolutional neural networks. CNNs can be applied by first converting the audio signal to an image, which the machine can analyze and check for variations. The accuracy levels of neural networks are quite high, given that enough data can allow the machines to figure out minor trends and build a knowledgebase.

Assessing the outcome of neural networks is also a critical step in deep learning. This helps determine if the technique has provided meaningful information [132]. In the setting of audio processing, evaluation is important in determining whether the audio signals represent the real message. The research on audio processing and deep learning is still ongoing, with successful applications being showing up in personal assistant devices.

5.5.1 Audio Data Handling Using Python

The Python programming language has proven time and again its usefulness in handling data and its understandability. The open-source nature of Python has also enabled its continued use in managing data. The learning curve is much better than other tools and languages, making it much preferable. It also has a large repository of modules that perform specific tasks, making it easy to pick the best one for handling unique instances like audio data handling. Python shines in audio data handling, as indicated in a study [133]. The study looks through one of the many audio processing libraries called Madmom, which handles the data in the low level. Other advanced processing methods use artificial intelligence methods such as neural networks to train the models in the best ways to handle the data. Other libraries possible to handle audio data include Librosa and PyAudio and provide extensive options to manipulate the data [134].

An advantage of Python for audio data is that it can be easily integrated into big data tools. These tools help handle the large volumes of data that are being generated daily. The shift in concentration on big audio processing is a fairly recent one but progresses steadily [135]. The paper indicates that valid use of the data handling is processing audio streaming services. More powerful machines are emerging to make it easy to use the flexibility of Python and still leaving room for the exponential expansion of the archives. It is possible for the research on audio data handling to provide new perspectives on big audio processing and build better tools for managing the information.

The data handling process covers the extraction of meaningful characteristics such as metadata, which contains embedded details of the track. Different audio file types have unique ways of storing the information [136], but all have similar data like the bitrate, length of the file, among others. The libraries to handle this information are easily available, with Python containing most of them in-built. These details go toward the larger audio signal processing of research. Identified possibilities of well-working tools and methods are endless, such as music analysis and recommendation, speech handling, and transformation of audio signals, among others. Other processing possibilities with audio are voice enhancing capabilities since the loss of quality is a frequent phenomenon in conversions. Compression of the audio signals also leads to irreversible changes in the quality, and the application of advanced Python models is expected to find solutions to these issues.

Feature extraction follows a more detailed process of applying analysis libraries such as pyAudioAnalysis [136]. The features are obtained from short clips ranging from two to four seconds of audio. The possible data to obtain and handle from the audio signals include signal energy, entropy, spectral data, frequency, and Chroma vector information. These details can uniquely identify an audio file and allow further handling methods such as classification. The data handling methods at this stage are much similar to other information processing models.

5.5.2 Spectrogram

Spectrograms help map the audio signals into visual formats. A spectrogram shows the frequency of the audio signal as it goes through time, with the frequency covering the vertical axis and the time covering the horizontal one. Spectrograms are useful in audio analysis and allow machines to observe the signal in detail. A study [137] indicates an interesting way a spectrogram can be used to identify audio. In this demonstration, the researchers show the similar-looking visual representations of someone pronouncing the same name at different times. The similarities in the results indicate that the audio is much similar. Another excellent demonstration of spectrograms in the audio analysis is by Ramalingam and Dhanalakshmi [138], in which the researcher applies a neural network to

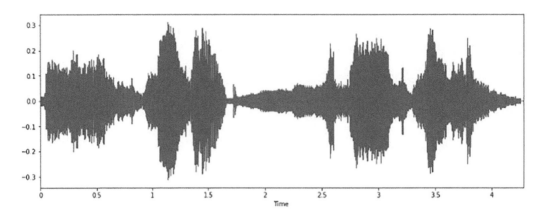

FIGURE 5.13
Audio frequency to the spectrogram images.

generate audio signals. The convolutional neural network, in this case, allows the transfer of the signals through the images, where they observe for the patterns and characteristics. The results indicate that spectrograms can keep more data than the conventional audio analysis processes. However, data loss is still present compared to raw audio files, which retain all information recorded.

Different modules existing in Python allow the analysis and mapping of audio frequency to the spectrogram images [139] as in Figure 5.13. The approach looks at different sections of music signals such as the beat, vocal, and instruments. These categories collectively make up the audio signal and are detectible through analysis of the signal data. Some modules like Librosa also provide the ability to separate the different characteristics of an audio signal, useful for translating the spectrogram in different ways. Advances in music recognition tools allow the tuning of different variables and parameters of audio signals to make the visual representations much more pronounced. Handling graphics and audio is also resource-intensive, which calls for better efficiency of tools that generate and interpret them. Some studies are concentrating on optimization frameworks that help balance between performance and accuracy.

Spectrogram analysis is merely a method with which audio signals can be processed and observed. The area benefits from research based on both audio and images, which implies that it will improve as better methods emerge. Spectrograms have also shown to be useful in genre recognition of music, an area that currently depends on human assistance. Significant differences in high accuracy graphics keep showing up, indicating that slight changes in the original audio files result in different visuals. However, common features are easily detected through the method [140], allowing the matching of signals at a higher level.

The major issue in spectrogram analysis is the noise in the audio signals [141]. The error rates marginally increase, proving difficult for applications like speech recognition tools to be accurate. Machine learning can help detect and reduce the noise, but the research on their perfection is still ongoing. The matching of human perception of audio signals is seemingly impossible, especially considered that the reduction of noise is totally voluntary. Spectrogram analysis has the potential of allowing the separation of speech and enhancing the resulting signal.

5.5.3 Wavelet-Based Feature Extraction

Pattern recognition in audio signals can apply feature extraction methods. The wavelet-based method can localize both time and frequencies of data, allowing easy recognition of useful patterns. In neural networks, the method can be combined with forwarding selection, whereby the variables of the data are added to the model one at a time. [142] indicates a way to apply this type of feature extraction using discrete wavelet transform (DWT). The requirements are to compute the subband codes of the signal. This approach proves to be much more efficient and faster. The acoustic features of the audio signal determine the method of getting the features. The features are applicable in classifying the audio signals, especially in music files. Mel frequency cepstral coefficients also make up important parameters of audio signals, with their success going toward speech recognition. Applying support vector machines on the transformed audio signals allows machine learning training, improving the result accuracy.

Short-term features on the frequency of the audio signals are applicable when refining the results of analysis [143]. The features include things like the entropy of the spectrum, energy entropy, energy, spread of the spectrum, and harmonic ratio, among others. Extracting such features has proven to introduce discrimination against certain sounds, which makes them inaccurate in determining the nature of the signal. Implementation in fingerprinting audio files shows success using the DWT process [144]. The researcher, in this case, combines statistics with audio signal processing to look for the unique features that define the signal. Despite different types of audio encoding losing some information, the process shows much promise in creating unique fingerprints each time. The reliability of the feature extraction technique is also much higher, but the results need boosting from further techniques such as applying filters, sampling the signals, and reducing the noise present. Compressing the audio files also has a limit, with reduced accuracy as the audio quality becomes less pronounced.

The perceptual wavelet packet process handles feature extraction as in Figure 5.14 by filtering the transformations upon segmenting the signal and calculating the necessary coefficients after extracting meaningful parameters [145]. High- and low-pass filters keep the necessary components for analysis. An algorithm based on this technique has been shown as much more effective than conventional comparisons. The technique is possible to handle successful noise reduction or recognition in noisy signals. The performance of

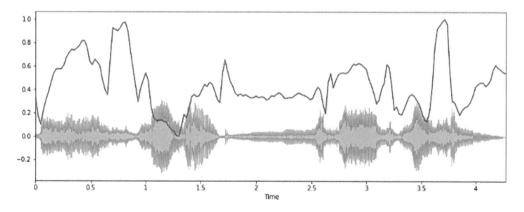

FIGURE 5.14
Feature extraction of wavelet.

the approach is much better and can possibly improve with tweaking of parameters. The tools to apply the wavelet-based feature extraction for audio analysis are increasing in number, with Python having access through available modules. The accuracy and performances of these modules differ, but the general results indicate a promising future for the technique. Polynomial kernels for support vector machines show much better accuracy in recognizing speech. It's indicative that activities dealing with audio and voice analysis are a long way from perfection, but the research on the area is steadily improving the results. Combination with self-learning algorithms and machine learning is creating better tools and techniques.

5.5.4 Current Methods

5.5.4.1 Audio Classification

Classifying audio files using deep learning methods has been recently applied by researchers. This process is possible through building classification models tailored for audio signals [146]. The process entails the use of CNN models, which require modification given that they were tailored for natural images. The time factor in audio images makes it difficult for conventional CNN models to work. The results of the trained ImageNet classification models show high accuracy, especially in performing training prior to using them for real audio. Further, fine-tuning shows better promise of more accurate results.

5.5.4.2 Audio Fingerprinting

Fingerprinting of audio as shown in Figure 5.15 is a process that provides a unique identity of a piece of an audio signal, depending on its nature. Fingerprinting audio files has shown excellent application for recognition and identification purposes. An example by [147] illustrates the process of fingerprinting, whereby different versions of similar audio files are compared.

The example derives its technique from convolution neural networks, which allow step by step encoding for the audio. The results of the traditional CNN for distorted audio files are still weak, making it hard to use them for uniquely identifying them. The process, though, can be improved by tuning it for general similarities and possible changes.

5.5.4.3 Feature Extraction

The features of an audio file contain meaningful characteristics that can distinguish different types, such as music, speech, and other sounds [148]. The study indicates the different

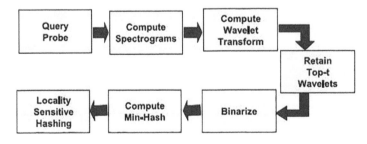

FIGURE 5.15
Fingerprinting of audio signal.

processes used in temporal, wavelets, frequency, time-frequency, cepstral, and domain features. Studies indicate that these areas have the best defining characteristics in what the different types of audios have. Audio types such as speech operate in a specific frequency range of between 100 Hz and 17 kHz. Other sounds like environmental sounds are also more continuous and permanent than created ones like music. The research indicates the importance of considering these factors, alongside the consideration of their magnitude.

5.5.4.4 Speech Classification

Classification of speech has been progressing in through years, with recent techniques being quite accurate in recognizing simple cases. The complex technological tools are powerful enough to process human speech with high accuracy rates [149]. Building an acoustic model for automatic speech recognition is a growing trend in audio processing. DNN models have been steadily improving acoustic models since they are in a better position to learn and fix the mistakes of prior models like the Gaussian mixture models. The advantages of DNNs are evident, especially in audio signals with noise, and work with higher efficiency rates.

5.5.4.5 Music Processing

Music also presents a good platform to perform audio processing with deep learning methods. Music files include a collection of different sounds that provide entertainment for people. Classifying music files requires creating spectrogram images of the audio signals and applying filters to distinguish the defining features of each one [150]. Using timbre to distinguish sound has shown to have excellent results, especially when considering time-constrained pieces like music. Other considerable factors include a variance of speech, loudness levels, differences in duration, and spatial differences. Deep learning models collect each music piece and consider the variables for creating unique signatures for the files.

5.5.4.6 Natural Sound Processing

Environmental sounds represent a large portion of audio recordings. Although the human mind has learned to ignore them and concentrate on the meaningful sound, machines still need to learn how to filter them out [151]. The current models have a hard time classifying and filtering out environmental sounds. Improving performance is possible by merging DNN with traditional GMM ones improving the accuracy by a high margin. Training the classification algorithms separately with different files and parameters also helps improve the overall performance of the technique. With such techniques, future research is possible to make it possible to filter out unnecessary noise and leave meaningful ones.

5.5.4.7 Technological Tools

TensorFlow is an open-source tool that helps in applying machine learning techniques to data. The tool was developed by Google and had widespread applications, one of which is audio processing. The tool shows much promise in effective audio processing since it is built with efficiency in mind [152]. TensorFlow is also adaptable to other tools and techniques, making it dynamic for meaningful results. The customization options for TensorFlow are also many, making it quite useful for audio processing. Previous research has revealed the importance of varying the variables of audio to understand the best ones to consider for different situations. TensorFlow provides the room for these variabilities.

Different programming languages also exist with considerations of built-in machine learning. For example, Python is a programming language that has excellent capabilities in handling large amounts of data evident in machine learning. Integrating Python with processing audio files is easy, given that there are many libraries built for this purpose. The study by Li et al. [151] shows the excellent use of Python to train the data and run the models. The possibilities of Python are endless, given that it is built specifically for handling data of different forms [153]. The tools compatible with Python are also many, with an example being TensorFlow.

5.6 Conclusion

The studies highlighted show that using deep learning has a huge potential for application in image processing, text processing, and audio processing. Deep neural networks are excellent in recognizing errors and mistakes and fixing themselves to handle them. The adaptability of the algorithms also indicates that they will keep improving, which means that the extracted knowledge will not go waste.

In NLP, change can be portrayed in two significant lines. The primary line is learning better portrayals through steadily improving neural language models. At present, self-consideration-based transformer language model is best in class, and learned portrayals are proficient to catch a blend of syntactic and semantic highlights and are context-dependent. The subsequent line is identified with neural network arrangements in various NLP undertakings. Despite the fact that LSTMs demonstrated valuable in catching long-term conditions in the idea of temporal information, the new pattern has been to move the preprepared language models' information into calibrated assignment explicit models. Self-consideration neural network component has become the predominant plan in pretrained language models. This exchange learning arrangement beats existing methodologies in a critical manner.

In the field of computer vision, CNNs are the best performing arrangements. There are profound CNN models that are calibrated, because of enormous measures of preparing information. The utilization of preprepared models in various vision assignments is a typical philosophy too. The application of audio processing is widespread, with early versions of personal assistants providing meaningful conveniences. Devices like Amazon's Alexa, Google's Assistant, and Apple's Siri are examples where audio analysis is successful. These tools help users to interact with other devices by providing audio commands. The commands, though, are still simple, initiated by set words which the devices constantly listen for. The technological movements are still not able to handle complex speeches or conversations, where humans combine contexts with words to communicate.

The research for creating tools and algorithms to understand speech is still ongoing, with more work still needed. Neural networks will allow the learning of integration of contexts to speech and will steadily improve the processing of audio files. The variety of different languages and cultures also presents new layers of complexity in audio processing, but the possibilities are getting better. The improvement of audio filtering is also good in determining how future audio signals will integrate with devices. Given that the brain has evolved to filter with high efficiency, the research on this area will be a tough feat, as the better analysis is still required. Neural network will provide the needed filters, and the applications will be endless in the real world. The studies also show the need to look for better ways of representing the audio. For instance, converting the signals into pictures and analyzing them is a tedious process that requires extra processing power.

References

1. LeCun, Y., Bengio, Y., & Hinton, G. (2015). Deep learning. *Nature* 521 (7553), 436–444.
2. Oquab, M., Bottou, L., Laptev, I., & Sivic, J. (2014). Learning and transferring mid-level image representations using convolutional neural networks. In *Proceedings of the IEEE Conference on Computer Vision and Pattern Recognition* (pp. 1717–1724). IEEE, Columbus, OH.
3. Liu, F., Shen, C., & Lin, G. (2015). Deep convolutional neural fields for depth estimation from a single image. In *Proceedings of the IEEE Conference on Computer Vision and Pattern Recognition* (pp. 5162–5170). IEEE, Boston, MA.
4. Jurafsky, D. (2000). *Speech & Language Processing*. Noida: Pearson Education India.
5. Socher, R., Lin, C. C. Y., Ng, A. Y., & Manning, C. D. (2011, January). Parsing natural scenes and natural language with recursive neural networks. In *ICML*, Bellevue, WA.
6. Kumar, A., Irsoy, O., Ondruska, P., Iyyer, M., Bradbury, J., Gulrajani, I.,,… & Socher, R. (2016, June). Ask me anything: Dynamic memory networks for natural language processing. In *International Conference on Machine Learning* (pp. 1378–1387). PMLR, New York.
7. Lee, H., Pham, P., Largman, Y., & Ng, A. (2009). Unsupervised feature learning for audio classification using convolutional deep belief networks. *Advances in Neural Information Processing Systems*, 22, 1096–1104.
8. Tzanetakis, G., & Cook, P. (2002). Musical genre classification of audio signals. *IEEE Transactions on Speech and Audio Processing*, 10(5), 293–302.
9. Krizhevsky, A., Sutskever, I., & Hinton, G. E. (2012). ImageNet classification with deep convolutional neural networks. *Advances in Neural Information Processing Systems*, 25, 1097–1105.
10. Zagoruyko, S., & Komodakis, N. (2015). Learning to compare image patches via convolutional neural networks. In *Proceedings of the IEEE Conference on Computer Vision and Pattern Recognition* (pp. 4353–4361). IEEE, Boston, MA.
11. https://news.cornell.edu/stories/ 2019/09/professors-perceptron-paved-way-ai-60-years-too-soon. Accessed on 8th Feb 2021.
12. http://www.cs.cmu.edu/~10701/slides/Perceptron_Reading_Material.pdf. Accessed on 8th Feb 2021.
13. http://alchessmist.blogspot.com/2009/06/stuart-dreyfus-on-mathematics-chess.html. Accessed on 8th Feb 2021.
14. Dreyfus, S. (1962). The numerical solution of variational problems. *Journal of Mathematical Analysis and Applications*, 5(1), 30–45. ISSN 0022-247X, doi:10.1016/0022-247X(62)90004-5.
15. Rojas, R. (1996). "The backpropagation algorithm". In R. Rojas (Ed.), *Neural Networks: A Systematic Introduction* (pp. 149–182). Berlin: Springer. ISBN 3-540-60505-3.
16. https://www.gwern.net/docs/statistics/decision/1960-kelley.pdf. Accessed on 5th Feb 2021.
17. http://beamandrew.github.io/deeplearning/2017/02/23/deep_learning_101_part1.html. Accessed on 4th Feb 2021.
18. https://mailman.srv.cs.cmu.edu/pipermail/connectionists/2014-July/027158.htm. Accessed on 5th Feb 2021.
19. Ivakhnenko, A. G. (1971). Polynomial theory of complex systems. *IEEE Transactions on Systems, Man, and Cybernetics*, 4, 364–378.
20. https://www.abebooks.com/Perceptrons-Introduction-Computational-Geometry-Marvin-Minsky/30050854532/bd. Accessed on 6th Feb 2021.

21. http://people.idsia.ch/~juergen/linnainmaa1970thesis.pdf. Accessed on 7th Feb 2021.

22. http://personalpage.flsi.or.jp/fukushima/index-e.html. Accessed on 8th Feb 2021.

23. LeCun, Y., Bottou, L., Bengio, Y., & Haffner, P. (1998). Gradient-based learning applied to document recognition. *Proceedings of the IEEE*, 86(11), 2278–2324.

24. Bhardwaj, A., Di, W., & Wei, J. (2018). *Deep Learning Essentials: Your Hands-on Guide to the Fundamentals of Deep Learning and Neural Network Modeling*. Birmingham: Packt Publishing Ltd.

25. Gu, J., Wang, Z., Kuen, J., Ma, L., Shahroudy, A., Shuai, B.,... & Chen, T. (2018). Recent advances in convolutional neural networks. *Pattern Recognition*, 77, 354–377.

26. Rumelhart, D. E., Hinton, G. E., & Williams, R. J. (1986). Learning representations by back-propagating errors. *Nature*, 323(6088), 533–536.

27. Kurenkov, A. (2015). A "Brief" history of neural nets and deep learning. *andreykurenkov.com*, December, 24.

28. Ackley, D. H., Hinton, G. E., & Sejnowski, T. J. (1985). A learning algorithm for Boltzmann machines. *Cognitive Science*, 9(1), 147–169.

29. Jones, A. T., Bagnall, J. J., & Nguyen, H. D. (2019). BoltzMM: an R package for maximum pseudo-likelihood estimation of fully-visible Boltzmann machines. Journal of Open Source Software, 4(34), 1193.

30. Abdollahi, B., & Nasraoui, O. (2016). Explainable restricted Boltzmann machines for collaborative filtering. arXiv preprint arXiv:1606.07129.

31. Cybenko, G. (1989). Mathematics of control. *Signals and Systems*, 2, 303.

32. Haykin, S., & Network, N. (2004). A comprehensive foundation. *Neural Networks*, 2(2004), 41.

33. Schmidhuber, J. (2014). Who invented backpropagation?. More in [DL2].

34. Beam, A. L. (2017). Deep learning 101-part 1: history and background. http://beamandrew.github.io/deeplearning/2017/02/23/deep_learning_101_part1.html. Accessed 3, 2018.

35. Chui, M. (2017). Artificial intelligence the next digital frontier. *McKinsey and Company Global Institute*, 47, 3–6.

36. https://slideslive.com/38906590/deep-learning-is-revolutionizing-artificial-intelligence?locale=cs. Accessed on 8th Jan 2021.

37. Hinton, G. E., Osindero, S., & Teh, Y. W. (2006). A fast learning algorithm for deep belief nets. *Neural Computation*, 18(7), 1527–1554. https://pubmed.ncbi.nlm.nih.gov/16764513/

38. Ng, A. (2011). Sparse autoencoder, CS294A lecture notes, pp. 1–19. http://web.stanford.edu/class/cs294a/sparseAutoencoder_2011new.pdf

39. Ng, A. (2016). What does Andrew Ng think about deep learning? *Quora*. https://quorasession-swithandrewng.quora.com/What-does-Andrew-Ng-think-about-Deep-Learning. Created: 03.02.2016. Retrieved: 25.01.2021.

40. Gershgorn, D. (2018). The inside story of how AI got good enough to dominate Silicon Valley. *Quartz*. https://qz.com/1307091/the-inside-story-of-how-ai-got-good-enough-to-dominate-silicon-valley/. Retrieved, 5.

41. Goodfellow, I. J., Pouget-Abadie, J., Mirza, M., Xu, B., Warde-Farley, D., Ozair, S.,... & Bengio, Y. (2014). Generative adversarial networks. arXiv preprint arXiv:1406.2661.

42. Glorot, X., Bordes, A., & Bengio, Y. (2011, June). Deep sparse rectifier neural networks. In *Proceedings of the Fourteenth International Conference on Artificial Intelligence and Statistics* (pp. 315–323). *JMLR Workshop and Conference Proceedings*.

43. https://www.turing.org.uk/scrapbook/test.html. Accessed on 26th Jan 2021.

44. Johnson, M. (2009, March). How the statistical revolution changes (computational) linguistics. In *Proceedings of the EACL 2009 Workshop on the Interaction between Linguistics and Computational Linguistics: Virtuous, Vicious or Vacuous?* (pp. 3–11).

45. Socher, R., Perelygin, A., Wu, J., Chuang, J., Manning, C. D., Ng, A. Y., & Potts pp., C. (2013, October). Recursive deep models for semantic compositionality over a sentiment treebank. In *Proceedings of the 2013 Conference on Empirical Methods in Natural Language Processing* (pp. 1631–1642).

46. Iyyer, M., Manjunatha, V., Boyd-Graber, J., & Daumé III, H. (2015, July). Deep unordered composition rivals syntactic methods for text classification. In *Proceedings of the 53rd Annual Meeting of the Association for Computational Linguistics and the 7th International Joint Conference on Natural Language Processing* (Volume 1: Long papers) (pp. 1681–1691).

47. Kim, Y. 2014. Convolutional neural networks for sentence classification. In *Proceedings of EMNLP.*

48. Chen, D., & Manning, C. D. (2014, October). A fast and accurate dependency parser using neural networks. In *Proceedings of the 2014 Conference on Empirical Methods in Natural Language Processing (EMNLP)* (pp. 740–750).

49. Collobert, R., & Weston, J. (2008, July). A unified architecture for natural language processing: deep neural networks with multitask learning. In *Proceedings of the 25th International Conference on Machine Learning* (pp. 160–167).

50. Bahdanau, D., Cho, K., & Bengio, Y. (2014). Neural machine translation by jointly learning to align and translate. arXiv preprint arXiv:1409.0473.

51. Devlin, J., Zbib, R., Huang, Z., Lamar, T., Schwartz, R., & Makhoul, J. (2014, June). Fast and robust neural network joint models for statistical machine translation. In *Proceedings of the 52nd Annual Meeting of the Association for Computational Linguistics (Volume 1: Long Papers)* (pp. 1370–1380).

52. Zhou, X., Dong, D., Wu, H., Zhao, S., Yu, D., Tian, H.,… & Yan, R. (2016, November). Multi-view response selection for human-computer conversation. In *Proceedings of the 2016 Conference on Empirical Methods in Natural Language Processing* (pp. 372–381).

53. Andor, D., Alberti, C., Weiss, D., Severyn, A., Presta, A., Ganchev, K.,… & Collins, M. (2016). Globally normalized transition-based neural networks. arXiv preprint arXiv:1603.06042.

54. Huang, Z., Xu, W., & Yu, K. (2015). Bidirectional LSTM-CRF models for sequence tagging. arXiv preprint arXiv:1508.01991.

55. Collobert, R., Weston, J., Bottou, L., Karlen, M., Kavukcuoglu, K., & Kuksa, P. (2011). Natural language processing (almost) from scratch. *Journal of Machine Learning Research*, 12, 2493–2537.

56. Mikolov, T., Chen, K., Corrado, G., & Dean, J. (2013). Efficient estimation of word representations in vector space. arXiv preprint arXiv:1301.3781.

57. Mikolov, T., Yih, W. T., & Zweig, G. (2013, June). Linguistic regularities in continuous space word representations. In *Proceedings of the 2013 Conference of the North American Chapter of the Association For Computational Linguistics: Human Language Technologies* (pp. 746–751).

58. Mikolov, T., Le, Q. V., & Sutskever, I. (2013). Exploiting similarities among languages for machine translation. arXiv preprint arXiv:1309.4168.

59. Pennington, J., Socher, R., & Manning, C. D. (2014, October). Glove: global vectors for word representation. In *Proceedings of the 2014 Conference on Empirical Methods in Natural Language Processing (EMNLP)* (pp. 1532–1543).

60. Kalchbrenner, N., Grefenstette, E., & Blunsom, P. (2014). A convolutional neural network for modelling sentences. arXiv preprint arXiv:1404.2188.

61. Rios, A., & Kavuluru, R. (2015, September). Convolutional neural networks for biomedical text classification: application in indexing biomedical articles. In *Proceedings of the 6th ACM Conference on Bioinformatics, Computational Biology and Health Informatics* (pp. 258–267).

62. Hughes, M., Li, I., Kotoulas, S., & Suzumura, T. (2017). Medical text classification using convolutional neural networks. *Studies in Health Technology and Informatics*, 235, 246–250.

63. Allahyari, M., Pouriyeh, S., Assefi, M., Safaei, S., Trippe, E. D., Gutierrez, J. B., & Kochut, K. (2017). A brief survey of text mining: classification, clustering and extraction techniques. arXiv preprint arXiv:1707.02919.

64. Greene, Z., Ceron, A., Schumacher, G., & Fazekas, Z. (2016). The nuts and bolts of automated text analysis. Comparing different document pre-processing techniques in four countries. doi:10.31219/osf.io/ghxj8.

65. See, A., Liu, P. J., & Manning, C. D. (2017). Get to the point: summarization with pointer-generator networks. arXiv preprint arXiv:1704.04368.

66. Denny, M., & Spirling, A. (2017, September 27). Text preprocessing for unsupervised learning: why it matters, when it misleads, and what to do about it. When it misleads, and what to do about it. *Political Analysis*, 26(2), 168–189.

67. McCallum, A., Freitag, D., & Pereira, F. C. (2000, June). Maximum entropy Markov models for information extraction and segmentation. In *ICML* (Vol. 17, No. 2000, pp. 591–598).

68. Lafferty, J., McCallum, A., & Pereira, F. C. (2001). Conditional random fields: probabilistic models for segmenting and labeling sequence data. https://repository.upenn.edu/cis_papers/159/

69. Graves, A., & Schmidhuber, J. (2005). Framewise phoneme classification with bidirectional LSTM and other neural network architectures. *Neural Networks*, 18(5–6), 602–610.

70. Lin, D., & Wu, X. (2009, August). Phrase clustering for discriminative learning. In *Proceedings of the Joint Conference of the 47th Annual Meeting of the ACL and the 4th International Joint Conference on Natural Language Processing of the AFNLP* (pp. 1030–1038).

71. Ratinov, L., & Roth, D. (2009, June). Design challenges and misconceptions in named entity recognition. In *Proceedings of the Thirteenth Conference on Computational Natural Language Learning (CoNLL-2009)* (pp. 147–155).

72. Goodfellow, I., Bengio, Y., Courville, A., & Bengio, Y. (2016). *Deep Learning* (Vol. 1, No. 2). Cambridge: MIT Press.

73. Krizhevsky, A., Sutskever, I., & Hinton, G. E. (2012). ImageNet classification with deep convolutional neural networks. *Advances in Neural Information Processing Systems*, 25, 1097–1105.

74. LeCun, Y., Touresky, D., Hinton, G., & Sejnowski, T. (1988, June). A theoretical framework for back-propagation. In *Proceedings of the 1988 Connectionist Models Summer School* (Vol. 1, pp. 21–28).

75. Badrinarayanan, V., Kendall, A., & Cipolla, R. (2017). Segnet: a deep convolutional encoder-decoder architecture for image segmentation. *IEEE Transactions on Pattern Analysis and Machine Intelligence*, 39(12), 2481–2495.

76. Brostow, G. J., Fauqueur, J., & Cipolla, R. (2009). Semantic object classes in video: a high-definition ground truth database. *Pattern Recognition Letters*, 30(2), 88–97.

77. Cordts, M., Omran, M., Ramos, S., Rehfeld, T., Enzweiler, M., Benenson, R.,… & Schiele, B. (2016). The cityscapes dataset for semantic urban scene understanding. In *Proceedings of the IEEE Conference on Computer Vision and Pattern Recognition* (pp. 3213–3223).

78. Everingham, M., Eslami, S. A., Van Gool, L., Williams, C. K., Winn, J., & Zisserman, A. (2015). The pascal visual object classes challenge: a retrospective. *International Journal of Computer Vision*, 111(1), 98–136.

79. Geiger, A., Lenz, P., & Urtasun, R. (2012, June). Are we ready for autonomous driving? the kitti vision benchmark suite. In *2012 IEEE Conference on Computer Vision and Pattern Recognition* (pp. 3354–3361). IEEE.

80. Silberman, N., Hoiem, D., Kohli, P., & Fergus, R. (2012, October). Indoor segmentation and support inference from rgbd images. In *European Conference on Computer Vision* (pp. 746–760). Springer, Berlin, Heidelberg.

81. Song, S., Lichtenberg, S. P., & Xiao, J. (2015). Sun rgb-d: a rgb-d scene understanding benchmark suite. In *Proceedings of the IEEE Conference on Computer Vision and Pattern Recognition* (pp. 567–576).

82. Brostow, G. J., Shotton, J., Fauqueur, J., & Cipolla, R. (2008, October). Segmentation and recognition using structure from motion point clouds. In *European Conference on Computer Vision* (pp. 44–57). Springer, Berlin, Heidelberg.

83. Shotton, J., Johnson, M., & Cipolla, R. (2008, June). Semantic texton forests for image categorization and segmentation. In *2008 IEEE Conference on Computer Vision and Pattern Recognition* (pp. 1–8). IEEE.

84. Ladický, Ľ., Sturgess, P., Alahari, K., Russell, C., & Torr, P. H. (2010, September). What, where and how many? Combining object detectors and CRFs. In *European Conference on Computer Vision* (pp. 424–437). Springer, Berlin, Heidelberg.

85. Sturgess, P., Alahari, K., Ladicky, L., & Torr, P. H. (2009, September). Combining appearance and structure from motion features for road scene understanding. In *BMVC-British Machine Vision Conference*. BMVA.

86. Kontschieder, P., Bulo, S. R., Bischof, H., & Pelillo, M. (2011, November). Structured class-labels in random forests for semantic image labelling. In *2011 International Conference on Computer Vision* (pp. 2190–2197). IEEE.

87. Tighe, J., & Lazebnik, S. (2013). Superparsing. *International Journal of Computer Vision*, 101(2), 329–349.

88. Farabet, C., Couprie, C., Najman, L., & LeCun, Y. (2012). Scene parsing with multiscale feature learning, purity trees, and optimal covers. arXiv preprint arXiv:1202.2160.

89. Farabet, C., Couprie, C., Najman, L., & LeCun, Y. (2012). Learning hierarchical features for scene labeling. *IEEE Transactions on Pattern Analysis and Machine Intelligence*, 35(8), 1915–1929.

90. Gatta, C., Romero, A., & van de Veijer, J. (2014). Unrolling loopy top-down semantic feedback in convolutional deep networks. In *Proceedings of the IEEE Conference on Computer Vision and Pattern Recognition Workshops* (pp. 498–505).

91. Grangier, D., Bottou, L., & Collobert, R. (2009, June). Deep convolutional networks for scene parsing. In *ICML 2009 Deep Learning Workshop* (Vol. 3, No. 6, p. 109).

92. Pinheiro, P., & Collobert, R. (2014, January). Recurrent convolutional neural networks for scene labeling. In *International Conference on Machine Learning* (pp. 82–90). PMLR.

93. Eigen, D., & Fergus, R. (2015). Predicting depth, surface normals and semantic labels with a common multi-scale convolutional architecture. In *Proceedings of the IEEE International Conference on Computer Vision* (pp. 2650–2658).

94. Hong, S., Noh, H., & Han, B. (2015). Decoupled deep neural network for semi-supervised semantic segmentation. arXiv preprint arXiv:1506.04924.

95. Long, J., Shelhamer, E., & Darrell, T. (2015). Fully convolutional networks for semantic segmentation. In *Proceedings of the IEEE Conference on Computer Vision and Pattern Recognition* (pp. 3431–3440).

96. Noh, H., Hong, S., & Han, B. (2015). Learning deconvolution network for semantic segmentation. In *Proceedings of the IEEE International Conference on Computer Vision* (pp. 1520–1528).

97. Zheng, S., Jayasumana, S., Romera-Paredes, B., Vineet, V., Su, Z., Du, D.,... & Torr, P. H. (2015). Conditional random fields as recurrent neural networks. In *Proceedings of the IEEE International Conference on Computer Vision* (pp. 1529–1537).

98. Deng, J., Dong, W., Socher, R., Li, L. J., Li, K., & Fei-Fei, L. (2009, June). ImageNet: A large-scale hierarchical image database. In *2009 IEEE Conference on Computer Vision and Pattern Recognition* (pp. 248–255). IEEE.

99. Hariharan, B., Arbeláez, P., Girshick, R., & Malik, J. (2015). Hypercolumns for object segmentation and fine-grained localization. In *Proceedings of the IEEE Conference on Computer Vision and Pattern Recognition* (pp. 447–456).

100. Lin, G., Shen, C., Van Den Hengel, A., & Reid, I. (2016). Efficient piecewise training of deep structured models for semantic segmentation. In *Proceedings of the IEEE Conference on Computer Vision and Pattern Recognition* (pp. 3194–3203).

101. Liu, W., Rabinovich, A., & Berg, A. C. (2015). ParseNet: Looking wider to see better. arXiv preprint arXiv:1506.04579.

102. Mostajabi, M., Yadollahpour, P., & Shakhnarovich, G. (2015). Feedforward semantic segmentation with zoom-out features. In *Proceedings of the IEEE Conference on Computer Vision and Pattern Recognition* (pp. 3376–3385).

103. Chen, A. Y., & Corso, J. J. (2011, January). Temporally consistent multi-class video-object segmentation with the video graph-shifts algorithm. In *2011 IEEE Workshop on Applications of Computer Vision (WACV)* (pp. 614–621). IEEE.

104. Cummins, M., & Newman, P. (2008). FAB-MAP: probabilistic localization and mapping in the space of appearance. *The International Journal of Robotics Research*, 27(6), 647–665.

105. Schindler, G., Brown, M., & Szeliski, R. (2007, June). City-scale location recognition. In *2007 IEEE Conference on Computer Vision and Pattern Recognition* (pp. 1–7). IEEE.

106. Torii, A., Sivic, J., Pajdla, T., & Okutomi, M. (2013). Visual place recognition with repetitive structures. In *Proceedings of the IEEE Conference on Computer Vision and Pattern Recognition* (pp. 883–890).

107. Nister, D., & Stewenius, H. (2006, June). Scalable recognition with a vocabulary tree. In *2006 IEEE Computer Society Conference on Computer Vision and Pattern Recognition (CVPR'06)* (Vol. 2, pp. 2161–2168). IEEE.

108. Philbin, J., Chum, O., Isard, M., Sivic, J., & Zisserman, A. (2007, June). Object retrieval with large vocabularies and fast spatial matching. In *2007 IEEE Conference on Computer Vision and Pattern Recognition* (pp. 1–8). IEEE.

109. Sivic, J., & Zisserman, A. (2003, October). Video Google: a text retrieval approach to object matching in videos. In *IEEE International Conference on Computer Vision* (Vol. 3, pp. 1470–1470). IEEE Computer Society.

110. Delhumeau, J., Gosselin, P. H., Jégou, H., & Pérez, P. (2013, October). Revisiting the VLAD image representation. In *Proceedings of the 21st ACM International Conference on Multimedia* (pp. 653–656).

111. Jégou, H., Douze, M., Schmid, C., & Pérez, P. (2010, June). Aggregating local descriptors into a compact image representation. In *2010 IEEE Computer Society Conference on Computer Vision and Pattern Recognition* (pp. 3304–3311). IEEE.

112. Jégou, H., Perronnin, F., Douze, M., Sánchez, J., Pérez, P., & Schmid, C. (2011). Aggregating local image descriptors into compact codes. *IEEE Transactions on Pattern Analysis and Machine Intelligence*, 34(9), 1704–1716.

113. Babenko, A., & Lempitsky, V. (2015). Aggregating deep convolutional features for image retrieval. arXiv preprint arXiv:1510.07493.

114. Gong, Y., Wang, L., Guo, R., & Lazebnik, S. (2014, September). Multi-scale orderless pooling of deep convolutional activation features. In *European Conference on Computer Vision* (pp. 392–407). Springer, Cham.

115. Razavian, A. S., Sullivan, J., Carlsson, S., & Maki, A. (2016). Visual instance retrieval with deep convolutional networks. *ITE Transactions on Media Technology and Applications*, 4(3), 251–258.

116. Tolias, G., Sicre, R., & Jégou, H. (2015). Particular object retrieval with integral max-pooling of CNN activations. arXiv preprint arXiv:1511.05879.

117. Stutz, D. (2014). Neural codes for image retrieval. In *Proceedings of the Computer Vision-ECCV* (pp. 584–599), Zurich, Switzerland.

118. Choudhary, S., & Narayanan, P. J. (2012, October). Visibility probability structure from SFM datasets and applications. In *European Conference on Computer Vision* (pp. 130–143). Springer, Berlin, Heidelberg.

119. Li, Y., Snavely, N., Huttenlocher, D., & Fua, P. (2012, October). Worldwide pose estimation using 3d point clouds. In *European Conference on Computer Vision* (pp. 15–29). Springer, Berlin, Heidelberg.

120. Sattler, T., Leibe, B., & Kobbelt, L. (2012, October). Improving image-based localization by active correspondence search. In *European Conference on Computer Vision* (pp. 752–765). Springer, Berlin, Heidelberg.

121. Svarm, L., Enqvist, O., Oskarsson, M., & Kahl, F. (2014). Accurate localization and pose estimation for large 3D models. In *Proceedings of the IEEE Conference on Computer Vision and Pattern Recognition* (pp. 532–539).

122. Walch, F., Hazirbas, C., Leal-Taixe, L., Sattler, T., Hilsenbeck, S., & Cremers, D. (2017). Image-based localization using LSTMS for structured feature correlation. In *Proceedings of the IEEE International Conference on Computer Vision* (pp. 627–637).

123. Li, R., Liu, Q., Gui, J., Gu, D., & Hu, H. (2017). Indoor relocalization in challenging environments with dual-stream convolutional neural networks. *IEEE Transactions on Automation Science and Engineering*, 15(2), 651–662.

124. Melekhov, I., Ylioinas, J., Kannala, J., & Rahtu, E. (2017, September). Relative camera pose estimation using convolutional neural networks. In *International Conference on Advanced Concepts for Intelligent Vision Systems* (pp. 675–687). Springer, Cham.

125. Clark, R., Wang, S., Markham, A., Trigoni, N., & Wen, H. (2017). VidLoc: a deep spatio-temporal model for 6-DoF video-clip relocalization. In *Proceedings of the IEEE Conference on Computer Vision and Pattern Recognition* (pp. 6856–6864).

126. Kendall, A., & Cipolla, R. (2016, May). Modelling uncertainty in deep learning for camera relocalization. In *2016 IEEE international conference on Robotics and Automation (ICRA)* (pp. 4762–4769). IEEE.

127. Kendall, A., Grimes, M., & Cipolla, R. (2015). PoseNet: a convolutional network for real-time 6-DoF camera relocalization. In *Proceedings of the IEEE International Conference on Computer Vision* (pp. 2938–2946).

128. Sattler, T., Sweeney, C., & Pollefeys, M. (2014, September). On sampling focal length values to solve the absolute pose problem. In *European Conference on Computer Vision* (pp. 828–843). Springer, Cham.

129. Ronneberger, O., Fischer, P., & Brox, T. (2015, October). U-Net: convolutional networks for biomedical image segmentation. In *International Conference on Medical Image Computing and Computer-Assisted Intervention* (pp. 234–241). Springer, Cham.

130. Qazi, K. A., Nawaz, T., Mehmood, Z., Rashid, M., & Habib, H. A. (2018). A hybrid technique for speech segregation and classification using a sophisticated deep neural network. *PLoS One*, 13(3), e0194151.

131. Kim, P. (2017). *Matlab Deep Learning. With Machine Learning, Neural Networks and Artificial Intelligence* (Vol. 130, p. 21). New York: Apress.

132. Wen, W., Wu, C., Wang, Y., Chen, Y., & Li, H. (2016). Learning structured sparsity in deep neural networks. arXiv preprint arXiv:1608.03665.

133. Böck, S., Korzeniowski, F., Schlüter, J., Krebs, F., & Widmer, G. (2016, October). Madmom: a new python audio and music signal processing library. In *Proceedings of the 24th ACM International Conference on Multimedia* (pp. 1174–1178).

134. Goel, S., Pangasa, R., Dawn, S., & Arora, A. (2018, August). Audio acoustic features based tagging and comparative analysis of its classifications. In *2018 Eleventh International Conference on Contemporary Computing (IC3)* (pp. 1–5). IEEE.

135. Helali, W., Hajaiej, Z., & Cherif, A. (2020). Real time speech recognition based on PWP thresholding and MFCC using SVM. *Engineering, Technology & Applied Science Research*, 10(5), 6204–6208.

136. Kamaladas, M. D., & Dialin, M. M. (2013, February). Fingerprint extraction of audio signal using wavelet transform. In *2013 International Conference on Signal Processing, Image Processing & Pattern Recognition* (pp. 308–312). IEEE.

137. McFee, B., Raffel, C., Liang, D., Ellis, D. P., McVicar, M., Battenberg, E., & Nieto, O. (2015, July). Librosa: audio and music signal analysis in python. In *Proceedings of the 14th Python in Science Conference* (Vol. 8, pp. 18–25).

138. Ramalingam, T., & Dhanalakshmi, P. (2014). Speech/music classification using wavelet based feature extraction techniques. *Journal of Computer Science*, 10(1), 34.

139. Sahal, R., Breslin, J. G., & Ali, M. I. (2020). Big data and stream processing platforms for Industry 4.0 requirements mapping for a predictive maintenance use case. *Journal of Manufacturing Systems*, 54, 138–151.

140. Too, J., Abdullah, A. R., Saad, N. M., Ali, N. M., & Zawawi, T. N. S. T. (2019). Exploring the relation between EMG pattern recognition and sampling rate using spectrogram. *Journal of Electrical Engineering & Technology*, 14(2), 947–953.

141. Vryzas, N., Tsipas, N., & Dimoulas, C. (2020). Web radio automation for audio stream management in the era of big data. *Information*, 11(4), 205.

142. Waldekar, S., & Saha, G. (2018, September). Wavelet transform based Mel-scaled features for acoustic scene classification. In *INTERSPEECH* (Vol. 2083, pp. 3323–3327).

143. Wyse, L. (2017). Audio spectrogram representations for processing with convolutional neural networks. arXiv preprint arXiv:1706.09559.
144. Zacarias-Morales, N., Pancardo, P., Hernández-Nolasco, J. A., & Garcia-Constantino, M. (2021). Attention-inspired artificial neural networks for speech processing: a systematic review. *Symmetry*, 13(2), 214.
145. Zanoni, M., Lusardi, S., Bestagini, P., Canclini, A., Sarti, A., & Tubaro, S. (2017, May). Efficient music identification approach based on local spectrogram image descriptors. In *Audio Engineering Society Convention 142*. Audio Engineering Society.
146. Palanisamy, K., Singhania, D., & Yao, A. (2020). Rethinking CNN models for audio classification. arXiv preprint arXiv:2007.11154.
147. Yu, Z., Du, X., Zhu, B., & Ma, Z. (2020). Contrastive unsupervised learning for audio fingerprinting. arXiv preprint arXiv:2010.13540.
148. Sharma, G., Umapathy, K., & Krishnan, S. (2020). Trends in audio signal feature extraction methods. *Applied Acoustics*, 158, 107020.
149. Deng, L., Hinton, G., & Kingsbury, B. (2013, May). New types of deep neural network learning for speech recognition and related applications: an overview. In *2013 IEEE International Conference on Acoustics, Speech and Signal Processing* (pp. 8599–8603). IEEE.
150. Pons, J., Slizovskaia, O., Gong, R., Gómez, E., & Serra, X. (2017, August). Timbre analysis of music audio signals with convolutional neural networks. In *2017 25th European Signal Processing Conference (EUSIPCO)* (pp. 2744–2748). IEEE.
151. Li, J., Dai, W., Metze, F., Qu, S., & Das, S. (2017, March). A comparison of deep learning methods for environmental sound detection. In *2017 IEEE International Conference on Acoustics, Speech and Signal Processing (ICASSP)* (pp. 126–130). IEEE.
152. Pouyanfar, S., Sadiq, S., Yan, Y., Tian, H., Tao, Y., Reyes, M. P.,… & Iyengar, S. S. (2018). A survey on deep learning: algorithms, techniques, and applications. *ACM Computing Surveys (CSUR)*, 51(5), 1–36.
153. Choi, K., Joo, D., & Kim, J. (2017). Kapre: on-GPU audio preprocessing layers for a quick implementation of deep neural network models with Keras. arXiv preprint arXiv:1706.05781.

6

Brain–Computer Interfacing

Paras Nath Singh
CMRIT

CONTENTS

DOI: 10.1201/9781003107026-6

6.1 Introduction to BCI and Its Components

The most complex organ in our human body is the brain with more than 100 billion nerves communicating trillions of synapses (connections between neurons and muscle cells). The time period of the brain–computer interface (BCI) presently utilized in the literature was first coined at the college of California, Los Angeles by Vidal and others between the years 1973 and 1977. BCI is a powerful subsystem between users and computing devices. BCIs detect brain signals, analyze them, and interpret neuronal information to the associated output device. Now, there are a number of invasive and noninvasive strategies for measuring the brain activity which include the electroencephalography (EEG), magnetoencephalography (MEG), functional magnetic resonance imaging (fMRI), functional near-infrared spectroscopy (fNIRS), and optical imaging.

Techniques in a BCI subsystem support an instantaneous exchange pathway between a brain and an external artificial device. The purpose of the BCI systems was to assist, increase, or restore human cognitive or sensory-motor characteristics. An electrode is a conductor in which electric currents pass (enter or leave). The BCIs make it possible to operate an artificial system primarily on the basis of the abilities acquired from voluntary electrical, magnetic, or various body manifestations of mind hobby acquired from the cortex or scalp epidural or subdural or intrusive electrophysiological means, i.e., brain signals captured with single or multiintracortical electrode arrays (MIEA). However, within the BCI network, the most efficient EEG monitoring and related techniques are used for technological, time decision, real-time, and price constraints.

More information on neuronal electrical activity is given by He et al. [73] and Abdulkader [115] with a broad band frequency, so brain signals are preprocessed, filtered, and de-noised to extract the relevant data, and finally, with the help of synchronous control or extra-correctly with the help of self-paced or asynchronous control, this statistic is decoded and commuted into tool commands so that you can reach whether or not a user is processing something or not. In addition to the control interface input, an uncooked brain signal acts as a stimulus for a few precise BCI responsibilities. Therefore, the promising future of researchers in this field motivated them to study the role of BCI in life through medical applications, and the scope is now extended to include nonmedical applications to improve the accuracy of human–computer interface (HCI) systems. There are two kinds of BCI systems in general, called endogenous and exogenous. Endogenous BCIs are based on unprompted activity, and control signal is internally generated that does not rely on external stimuli and can be regulated by focusing on particular mental tasks. On the other hand, exogenous BCIs are based on task reminders, which, depending on external stimuli, use brain signals.

BCI (Brain Machine Interface) innovation has since become a ground-breaking professional subsystem for users and computers. To provide orders and complete the collaboration [9], no external gadgets or muscle intercession is required. In order to improve the design of BCIs, a good method of signal processing is required. Many scholars have advocated reestablishing the improvement capacity for surely examined or secured clients and supplanting lost engine usefulness [2]. This chapter is prepared and written to present a compact guide of different techniques referring different signal processing ideas and their usage. The promising future anticipated for BCI has urged study networks to do not forget the contribution of BCI within the lifestyles of nonincapacitated humans via medical applications. So, some selected feature extraction and classifications are represented here in context to BCI systems/subsystems. Output feedback is provided in human applications by visualizing on the monitor or displaying actual brain response acoustics for cortical responses or other potentials. A BCI framework, therefore, provides a modern form of communication to directly relay messages and instructions from the brain to the outside world.

6.1.1 BCI Components

There are four fundamental components of BCI systems, as shown in Figure 6.1.

1. **Signal Acquisition:** The signal acquisition stage captures the electrophysiological signals mainly feeding to the BCI for signal enhancement and noise reduction. Sensory stimulation may be required depending on analyzed brain signals.

2. **Signal Preprocessing:** The need of signal preprocessing is to improve the SNR (signal-to-noise ratio). It may include artifact reduction strategies and to apply advanced signal processing methods.

3. **Feature Extraction:** In order to generate suitable representation of improved signal, feature extraction algorithms are necessary, reducing the scale of the statistics applied to the class factor. Extracted features of electrophysiological data simplify the detection of brain signal patterns. Examples of feature extraction methods are amplitude measures and family of auto-encoders for de-noising, variation, sparse, etc.

4. **Classification:** Produced features are translated by classifiers. Classifier components use the features produced by feature extractor to assign and categorize the brain patterns and to translate the produced functions into device instructions [2]. Single trial EEG data sets are detected by means of the threshold method.

6.2 Framework/Architecture of BCI

In BCI, individual imagery activities can be classified primarily based on the adjustments in μ and β rhythms and their spatial distributions. Model and taxonomy are considered a general framework for BCI system design. In BCI framework, error-related potentials (ErrPs) are studied to define whether the machine has selected to perform assignment or instruction given by the user. It is possible to subdivide this task into two separate phases. The first one is externally paced computer-driven cue-based synchronous BCI with a predefined time window, and the second one is internally paced user-driven non-cue-based asynchronous BCI. Most of known BCIs work like cue-based. The main difference in synchronous and asynchronous BCIs is that in asynchronous BCI, a self-paced system has to work independently, which may be in rest or idle state. The framework supports features of BCI shown in Figure 6.2. The proposed framework and basic architecture have been

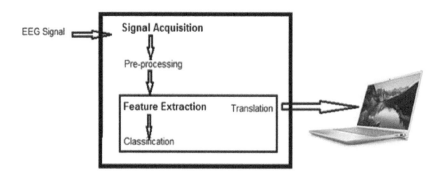

FIGURE 6.1
Fundamental BCI.

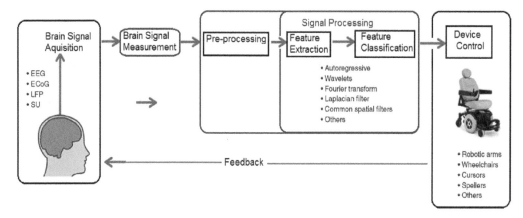

FIGURE 6.2
Basic BCI layout/framework.

created by going through existing BCI technologies. It should be compared with a TTD (thought translation device).

In particular, Figure 6.2 again reflects the BCI layout in which uncooked brain signal serves as stimulus as well as input from the management interface.

6.3 Functions of BCI

Most of the functions of BCI are related to the state of the user and enabling the user to communicate his ideas. BCI provides a nonmuscular communication channel that, depending on the case of the patient, can be used in healthcare to support a patient who has extremely impaired motor functions. Using invasive or noninvasive techniques, to complete the intended tasks, BCI systems record brain signals and send them to the computer system. To communicate an idea or regulate an entity, the transmitted waves are then used.

The main functions of BCI are correspondence and control and client state checking.

6.3.1 Correspondence and Control

BCI subsystems create links between the human brain and the outside environment to record, decode, and interpret the signals, and that shells out with the need for conveyance techniques for daily documents. They deal with transmitting the messages from human cerebrums and translating their quiet considerations. In this manner, they can help the disabled with peopling to inform and file their conclusions and mind by an assortment of strategies, for example, in spelling packages [4], semantic association [5], or quiet discourse correspondence.

BCIs just require fusing cerebrum signals to be able to achieve a whole lot of orders, and no muscle group mediation is required [2,6,7]. BCI-assistive robots can offer to assist for impaired clients in each day and expert lifestyles, increasing their collaboration in constructing their locale [8].

6.3.2 Client State Checking

Early BCI applications have centered on handicapped clients who have portability or speak troubles. Their point was to give an optional correspondence channel to those clients. Be that as it could, later on, BCI enters the universe of sound individuals also. It fills in as a physiological estimating instrument that recovers and makes use of statistics about someone's enthusiastic, highbrow, or profundity state. In what is referred to as passive BCI [1], the purpose of mind signal utilization has been expanded prior to controlling any article or providing a substitute for specific capacities. As indicated with the support of researchers in [10], the precise knowledge will affect to recognize the actual behavior linked with brain signals.

In HCIs, BCI individual nation looking at capability is regarded as a supporting hand and adjusts them as in line with the enthusiastic or intelligent country of the assessed customer [10].

It additionally gives the advancement of savvy conditions and emotions scheming applications [3]. Operating situations' appraisal and instructive techniques' assessment are instances of different fields that could earn by using estimating customer's cerebrum kingdom. The subsequent place features a few programs that journey cerebrum laptop interface.

- Acquires brain signals
- Analyzes them
- Translates those instructions
- Relay to output tool

BCIs allow the operation of a synthetic instrument on the basis of functions derived from voluntary electrical, magnetic, or other physical manifestations of mental interest derived from subdural cortex or scalp epilepsy or from invasive electrophysiological methods, i.e., mental signals captured intracortical with signal electrode or multielectrode arrays. In patients with subdural hematoma, posttraumatic epileptic seizures (PTS) are a severe complication (SDH).

This way, BCI functions focuses on supporting, augmenting, or repairing human cognitive or sensory-motor functions.

6.4 Applications of BCI

BCIs can also make hands-free packages simple and convenient for individuals who operate devices by mind. They only need signals integrating mind waves as a way to carry out multiple instructions, and there is no need for muscle intervention [2,6,7]. Robots that support BCI will assist technicians in daily and professional life for disabled people, extending their cooperation in developing their locale [8]. The area of BCIs has attracted in various fields of research and applications. Several applications of BCI are shown below and in Figure 6.3, and a few of them are discussed herewith.

- Health care field
- Neuroergonomics and smart environment
- Neuro-marketing
- Education
- Games
- Entertainment
- Security
- Authentication

6.4.1 Healthcare

The spectrum of BCI usage for healthcare field has a wide range of subsystems including neural prosthetics, wheelchairs, and humanoid robots. Epilepsy surgery can be a life-changing strategy in the subgroup of thousands of patients who are medically intractable. As BCI systems require a degree of knowledge about signal and computations, integration of most applications in practice will take little more time. In medical clinics and labs, operational treatment remains inspired by the original seizure recording procedures. The recording of seizures and localization of the seizure onset zone in the subset of surgical patients needing an intracranial EEG (icEEG) evaluation is the best available surrogate marker of *epileptogenic* tissue to date. Some risks and challenges are posed by icEEG, making it a frontier for those who benefit from optimization.

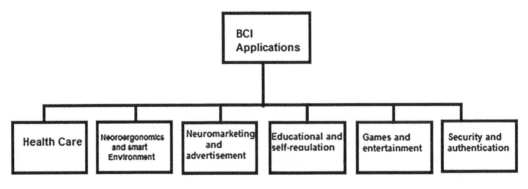

FIGURE 6.3
Applications of BCI.

In all related processes, including prevention, identification, diagnosis, recovery, and regeneration, healthcare packages may take advantage of brain signals. With the shortage of such systems like BCI, medical staff worldwide due to situations such as the COVID-19 pandemic, there is a growing interest for testing and to address the problem in development of vaccines. BCIs are designed to provide vulnerable people with a good alternative and allow for innovative and constructive practices between the purpose of the user and supporting resources. For the design of a competent BCI device, brain signals like motor imagery, steady-state visual evoked potential, error-related potential, motion-related potential, and P300 were used. The demand for time is to use neurotechnology to provide them with augmented cognition, senses, and behavior for effective diagnosis and treatment of BCI systems. Different phases of healthcare applications are shown in Figure 6.4.

6.4.1.1 Prevention

Many awareness level determination structures in conjunction with their brain-associated studies and research are being done. In multiple studies, the attentive effects of smoking and alcohol on brain waves have been explained. The significance of such research for clinical prevention lies in the potential loss of function and decrease in the degree of alertness due to smoking and/or consuming alcohol, though few have investigated the full response of mind components to alcoholism [13]. One of the major causes of unnatural death or such serious injuries is road accidents [14]. Analysis of these reasons for prevention has now become a situation for researchers in several fields. Drivers of the vehicles are studied for the concentration stage who is suffering from motion sickness. Motion sickness, which occurs due to the transmission to the brain of conflicting sensory facts produced from the frame, inner ear, and eye, typically occurs when transport media is transferred. It can cause accidents for vehicle driver as it reduces the ability of a person to control him/her self. Wei et al. [16] said that the forecasting of motion sickness can lead to the use of a collection of EEG power indicators in driver condition monitoring and alertness

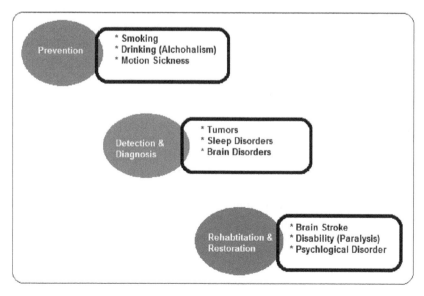

FIGURE 6.4
Phases of healthcare.

application gadgets. The following EEG signals from five separate areas of the brain were investigated in Ref. [15]. As part of the sensory records amassing process, the human hearing stage was assessed through the Auditory Evoked Potential (AEP) applications based on BCI by Paulraj et al. [17]. In another observation by Ko et al. [18] with a 32-channel EEG system and a joystick used in real-time experiments to record the motion sickness level (MSL), a motion sickness platform based on virtual reality has been proposed. Bagchi and Chattopadhyay [19] had discussed about the consciousness level of brain signals. They discussed about drivers with sick people staying alone.

6.4.1.2 Detection and Diagnosis

The control functions for the identification of consciousness in BCI systems have also benefited in the prediction and diagnosis of fitness issues, including abnormal mind structure (including abnormal cells in brain), seizure (periods of unusual behavior and sensation including epilepsy, sleep disorder such as narcolepsy, and *cerebral edema* consisting of encephalitis. The use of EEG for MRI and CT scan as a reasonably priced secondary choice can be found in tumors that are created from out-of-control self-division of cells. The primary concern of the research was EEG-based fully mental tumor detection structures in [20, 21], and even in [22] the use of EEG alerts was involved in identifying breast cancer.

Sharanreddy and Kulkarni [23] indicated that EEG anomalies associated with tumors of the mind and epilepsy seizures are known. Early diagnosis and monitoring of the effects of epilepsy seizures, one of the most unusual neurological disorders, are described in Ref. [24]. Fadzal et al. [25] described dyslexia, one of the mental issues, which can be recognized by means of measuring mind conduct. It affects the ability to assess and learn that its discovery at an early age protects young people from problems of self-esteem and self-confidence and helps them to benefit from their basic skills and know-how. Sleep problems, [26,27], can be established with BCI assistance. They demonstrate some strategies for the implementation of EEG indicators in the notification of sleep behavior disorder (iRBD) of idiopathic rapid eye movement (REM). A strong early predictor of Parkinson's disease has been found to be iRBD. Experimentally, the relationship between the human locomotion and EEG signals by the use of the plantar strain measurement system had been demonstrated by Abdulkader et al. [115].

6.4.1.3 Rehabilitation and Restoration

Many researchers of clinical studies have demonstrated the function recovery induced by the BCI system in patients after strokes. Mobility therapy is a process of changing body positions to help the patients to adapt their acquired disabilities in order to regain their lost functions and recover previous phases of mobility [28]. Assistive BCIs provide paralyzed patients with facilities for contact or control of external equipment by trained nursing personnel. Individuals suffering major injuries or incidents along with strokes may also be able to recover completely.

A stroke is a condition in which, due to the dearth of oxygen, brain cells all die at once. A blockage within the blood waft may trigger it. The person affected may not speak properly or lose memory, or one portion of the frame may become senseless. For some researchers who were interested in brain alert solutions, disorders and brain strokes were barriers. The mental processes linked with stroke can be reactivated, and the affected motor functions can be re-established by neuroplasticity [29,30].

To help locked-in people complete everyday lifestyle operations, mobile robots can be used [2]. BCI-based prosthetic limbs, also referred to as neuroprosthetic devices, can be used in patients who are unable to recover from previous movement or touch ranges to regain normal functioning [31–33].

Various truth techniques for BCI-primarily based rehabilitation education together with actual, digital, and augmented strategies have been provided. In addition to the decoded kinematic parameters, the actual rehabilitation technique exploits brain signals produced by healthy individuals [34]. It helps patients with strokes change their wonderful actions to resemble the recorded warnings and to retrain the brain's healthy regions to take over. Another technique of recovery includes virtual reality by monitoring and manipulating the movement of avatars created by the outgoing waves of the mind [35]. Augmented reality represents the third solution along with an augmented mirror box system within the truth-based BCI treatment, which seems like the creation of mirror box therapy (MBT). MBT uses vision to treat wounded individuals and people with amputated limbs through brain signals produced from symmetrical actions [36].

Motor imaging signals also lead to the poststroke motor therapy of neuro-feedback systems [37,38]. It is important to alter poststroke motor therapy to make it task-specific. Holler et al. [39] and Kang et al. [40] provided the description and evaluation of the effects of motor imagery and behavior.

6.4.2 Neuroergonomics and Smart Environment

The deployment of brain signals in the BCI system is as previously stated not special to the scientific field. In addition to security, luxury, and physiological exploitation of the day-to-day life of human beings, smart environments that involve smart homes, offices, workplaces, or transport could also take advantage of BCI. The application of neuroscience to ergonomics consists of neuroergonomics. A linear transformation algorithm is used by BCI to translate EEG spectral characteristics into system commands. Cooperation between the IoT and the BCI systems was defined by Domingo [41]. Researchers have proposed a cognitive control system known as the BCI-based smart living environmental auto-adjustment control system (BSLEACS) [42,43]. It scans the user's mental state and follows the encircling components accordingly. Smart environments have increased their capacity in modern systems with different applications. In different circumstances, through awareness of context, the environmental contribution to the improvement of BCI primarily dependent home applications has been considered. Navarro [3] proposed a subsystem that routinely modifies the user-accessible options available, depending on the time requirement. A current strategy has been seen in [44] combining healthcare, wellness, and smart home.

There are many ways to measure the mind activity in the BCI system. Brain signals additionally help in improving administrative center conditions by way of assessment of an operator's cognitive state. The effects on EEG functions of mental fatigue and work time are also analyzed [45]. Operating room as a candidate region is nicely defined for BCI smart workplace-primarily oriented application by Marquez et al. [62]. The device tests a medical professional's degree of stress and a signal associated with the form of reaction.

A widely encountered practice in everyday life is multitasking. The smart transportation sector has also benefited from the BCI function of cognitive state monitoring. In many studies, it has been examined in the conduct of the cognitive state of the driver that distraction and exhaustion are key resources for the inattention of the driver. These are considered a robust cause for the majority of traffic accidents [47]. Various forms of tests have helped to assess the cognitive condition of the driver [48–50]. The use of

EEG signals to detect exhaustion was extensively studied by Wang et al. [51], whereas Borghini et al. [52] proposed the use of the workload index to measure the mental state of the driver. Several models for detecting distracted drivers were tested by Wang et al. [53]. In order to predict concentration and strain, Kim et al. [54] offered multimodal context awareness for smart driving systems by analyzing each ECG and EEG signal and monitoring the vehicle's speed using brain signal concentration values. Drunken drivers can also be identified by the use of EEG signals as one of the reasons of road accidents, as observed by Murata et al. [55]. Some have warned that the simulated driving model uses unique tasks and discovers the neural dynamics produced, by using multiple stimulation strategies while managing drowsy drivers to increase their degree of attention [57]. Fan et al. [14] explored the possibility of using EEG signals from the driving force to stumble under emergency conditions, including the sudden arrival of a pedestrian.

6.4.3 Neuromarketing and Advertisement

We will be able to see ads of BCI apps that will let us surf the web (when this chapter will be published). The "BrainPort" technology is targeting to create substitute vision processing for individuals who lack their ability. Flipping the eye, the page will be flipped, and scrolling the eyelid, the pages will be scrolled. But doing the same thing only by brain signals will be the main task. It is time to convert WYSIWYG (What You See is What You Get) to WYTIWYG (What You Think is What You Get).

In addition, an interest in BCI research was also a marketing field subject. Neuromarketing is a growing field that links the cognitive and affective aspects of consumer behavior using neuroscience. The studies in Ref. [58] have established the advantages of using the EEG assessment for TV ads applicable to each market and policy area. By neuro-marketing study, the implicit customer responses are articulated. The generated attention accompanying the searching pastime [59] is fully evaluation-based BCI tests. The effect of another cognitive function was taken into account in neuromarketing subjects [60]. They analyzed the TV commercials to memorize, thereby offering other ads.

6.4.4 Pedagogical and Self-Regulating Oneself

A learner is the main element for good learning at present. Educational BCIs are expected to bring about potential shifts in academia. The main characteristics of educational BCIs using EEG will be specifics of assessment and evaluation of pedagogy. Neurofeedback is an efficient way of enhancing brain function by focusing on modulating the actions of the human mind. It invades academic systems which use electrical brain signals to evaluate the degree of clarity of the studied facts. Individual communication with each student and trainee is established based on the subsequent response encountered. In addition, learning by intrusive BCI to self-assess and rectify has been studied. It offers a forum for strengthening methods of cognitive recovery. The efficacy of fMRI for emotional law has been examined by a few forms of study. Zotev et al. [61] also advocated the use of hybrid real-time fMRI-EEG to combat depression through training sessions, in addition to other neuropsychiatric conditions. Furthermore, as tested by Marquez et al. [62], EEG-based emotional intelligence sports competitions to handle the accompanying pressure have been implemented. The BCI era has been developed into self-regulation and talent to learn about neurofeedback via fMRI [29].

6.4.5 Games and Entertainment

Good users now have more interest in BCI games by attracting them. A new marketplace for nonmedical brain machine interfaces has opened up for entertainment and gaming applications. Researchers, creators, and consumers have been found to agree on the value of the applicability of BCI games. Different games are provided where helicopters in a 2D or 3D virtual environment are rendered to navigate to certain variables. For many types of science, which includes [63], which usually appear to enjoy multibrain enjoyment, matching the characteristics of current games with brain control skills has been a challenge.

It can be difficult for BCI video games to distinguish fiction from fact. Technologies such as Synapse, a technology developed by NexeonMedSystems that is implanted in the chest and linked to wires that run through the brain, are on the intrusive side, as seen in Figure 6.5. It has also been used to treat disorders such as Parkinson's and was developed to activate precise parts of the brain with electricity when combined with a game.

The name of one video game is BrainArena. With the assistance of BCIs, players may engage in a collaborative or violent football game. By imagining left or appropriate hand gestures, they will score goals. In its structure, BCI forms a closed loop and contains five elements: "control paradigm," "measurement," "processing," "prediction," and "application." Neuroprosthetic rehabilitation involves either a new or a changed game concept.

6.4.6 Security and Authentication

This section reviews different security and authentication aspects depicted in the literature. If BCI operational phases are regarded as BCI cycle, we are to analyze the security attacks affecting those phases or BCI cycle. Know-how-oriented, object-oriented, and/or biometrics-based authentication is used in security systems. Also, to be addressed are the effects and countermeasures. Like simple vulnerable passwords, spying user with their devices surfing, theft abuse, and intentional and repeatable distortion of biometric features, they have proved to be liable for many drawbacks [64]. Cognitive biometrics or electrophysiology, in which the use of bio-signals is used as source of authenticated facts in the most realistic manner, provides a response to these vulnerabilities [65–66]. Most of the existing literature only considers the signal acquisition process, missing the stimulation of neurons.

FIGURE 6.5
Video game on BCI.

The inducement in the back of exploring the feasibility of electrophysiology is that bio-signals cannot be casually obtained by the way of external observers. Furthermore, they can be of extraordinary benefit to users of impaired patients who lack the corresponding physical characteristics. This makes it difficult to synthesize certain signals and thus increases biometric systems' resistance to spoofing attacks. With the exception of the electroencephalogram (EEG) [67], covert alert can be sent as a biometric modality when the legitimate user is, as applied, in external pressuring situations. The term protection, which refers to the prevention of unauthorized access, use, disclosure, disruption, modification, or destruction of information and information systems in order to ensure integrity, confidentiality, and accessibility, is stated here.

Numerous studies have considered the authentication of the EEG signal produced by the use of actions as part of intelligent driving systems [68–69]. To check driver identity on demand, a simulator for simplified driving with mental-tasked conditions was used by the researchers. The authentication of unconscious drivers was needed for analysis and discussion [70].

6.5 Signal Acquisition

Invasive and noninvasive methods for the monitoring of brain signals are available. One of the foremost additives in any BCI-based device is measuring brain-generated oscillations. It shows the voluntary neural moves produced by the current behavior of the user. Different techniques for signal acquisition were studied in [115]. It is the application of the BCI and the class of its intended users who settle on the correct method of obtaining the signal and its observable measured truth.

In Figure 6.6, with hierarchy and diagram, invasive and noninvasive classes of brain acquisition techniques are shown and detailed here.

6.5.1 Invasive Techniques

Underneath the scalp, intrusive recording methods insert electrodes. In the invasive technology, methods are implemented and examined by the *electrocorticography* (ECoG) as well

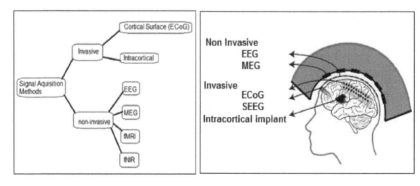

FIGURE 6.6
Signal acquisition.

as by intracortical recordings. Electrodes are neurosurgically implanted either inside the person's brain or over the surface of the brain. Neural activity of the brain either intracortical from the motor cortex or at the cortical surface can be ranked. Their primary advantage is that they have high temporal and spatial resolution, increasing the received outstanding signal and the signal-to-noise ratio.

With these methods, though, there are several problems. In addition to usability concerns resulting from the presence of surgical care, there have been problems relating to the output of the systems. The tiny size of the brain areas controlled by these implants is one of them. When added, they will not be transformed in any other field to a measure of mental activity. Secondly, medical complications can be triggered by the adaptation of the new body, which can also fail. Issues related to implant stability and protection from infection can also increase. The use of intrusive real-world documentation has therefore traditionally been limited to the BCI-based medical subsystems for a few disadvantageous people [72].

In the studies of BCI systems using monkeys, invasive systems have also been attempted, consistent with He et al. [73]. Implanted electrodes have been used by a few patients with *tetraplegia* (paralysis caused by injury). Information of invasive approaches is given here.

6.5.1.1 Intracortical

The most invasive technique demonstrated by Hochberg et al. [74] is the intracortical acquisition process. A surgical technique for implanting an electrode array into the brain requires intracortical stimulation using intracortical electrode arrays to assess brain electrical activity. Under the surface of the brain cortex, it is planted. As opposed to try only from the brain surface, the intracortical stimulation electrode goes further into the brain to activate the primary visual cortex more efficiently, which can cause an unwanted visual signal, discomfort, and even damage to the nervous tissue. A single electrode or series of electrodes can be used to perform it, measuring motion signals from individual neurons. Due to its particularly high spatial resolution, its use in source localization problems is extensively encouraged. Intracortical acquisition, however, should be accompanied by long-term signal variability. This may occur due to death of a cell or elevated tissue resistance. Furthermore, if a detectable change is needed by the device to trigger the handicapped leg or limb, this additional stimulation may also produce a major noise effect [73].

Self-regulation of slow cortical potentials (SCPs) was originally derived from animal experiments. In intracortical invasive acquisition, mostly rates and monkeys were extensively involved in BCI research studies. The records extracted have helped to estimate the intention to move and implement to train the algorithm for adaptive motion forecasting. Researchers got succeeded in helping to devour monkeys with a real robot arm [72].

Any seriously impaired individuals have been restricted by studies utilizing intrusive recording techniques for human subjects. A progressive neurodegenerative disease that affects nerve cells in the brain and the spinal cord is amyotrophic lateral sclerosis (ALS). Motor neurons reach from the brain to the spinal wire and from the spinal wire to the muscle tissue in the course of the picture. After a single electrode in the motor cortex is implanted, an affected person with ALS was able to shift a cursor on a computer screen to select the items presented [72]. Another examination conducted by Shan et al. [75] aimed to show that the precision of the classification improves as the number of electrodes grows slowly. Nonetheless, various experiments have taken place to reduce the selection of electrodes to reduce the size of the features or improve the acceptability of a consumer [76–78].

6.5.1.2 ECoG and Cortical Surface

ECoG is a type of recording that uses electrodes and offers a semi-invasive alternative while simultaneously retaining the advantages of the invasive process. ECoG subdural grid electrodes and strips consist of a series of flat electrode contacts placed on a thin silicon sheet that is located directly under the dura (thick membrane surrounds the brain and spinal and spinal cord) on the brain surface or is theoretically placed within a *sulcus* (a furrow/fissure or groove in cerebral cortex). It includes implanting electrode grids or strips via a surgical operation [79] shown in Figure 6.7 over the cortex surface. The electrical activity of neurons in the surrounding area is registered. The number of electrodes was considered by Muller and Kubler [72] as a calculation of the invasiveness level.

In the middle of invasive precision and the security of noninvasiveness, ECoG recording is located. It closes signal sources and gives better spatial decision-making than EEG. With better amplitude, it is much less affected by noise. This is the reason that ECoG is a smart alternative. As a consequence, epilepsy patients have used it before surgical treatment.

In order to anticipate kinematic claims for five-class finger flexion, Elghrabawy and Wahed [80] used ECoG signals, while Hill et al. [81] had prominent multiple motor-imagery task pairs for both. It was found that the method should have identified and interpreted nonparalyzed subjects' operations.

ECoG has also been very helpful, particularly in the development of tools for language and speech, where animals may not be helpful in assessing vocal activity-related brain signals and oral grammars. The possibility of decoding the meaning of words or phrases linked to different image categories was examined by Wang et al. [5]. They asked the subjects to apply specific tasks related to language-related tasks, including nomenclature on the given pictures.

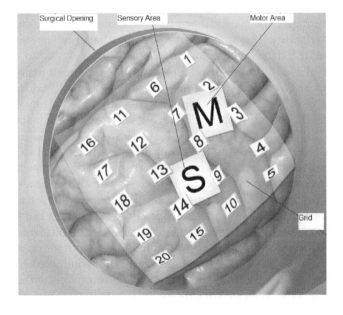

FIGURE 6.7
ECoG acquisition.

6.5.2 Noninvasive Techniques

These methods of documentation comply with a process that does not involve the implantation into the mind of the subject of external objects. Electrical potential charges are recorded by noninvasive technologies such as EEG and represent the common behavior of millions of neurons spreading over cortical tissues. The use of external sensors in noninvasive technology is assessed by brain activity. Unlike the EEG, ECoG is an integrated bioelectrical operation in a much smaller cortical region; it even represents the typical activity of several thousands of neurons. For that purpose, the surgical methods or stable accessories needed by intrusive acquisition are avoided. Several measurement techniques are provided here for various varieties of measured signals consisting of MEG, fMRI, fNIRS, and EEG.

6.5.2.1 Magneto-encephalography (MEG)

MEG is a noninvasive technique that tests magnetic fields that clearly exist inside the brain by using electrical currents. MEG is a practical neuro-imaging technique used by sensitive magnetometers to map brain activity. The SQUID (superconducting quantum interference) process is used for better results. Various signals may interact with MEG signals. This is used with specialized devices [82], as shown in Figure 6.8.

EEG records electrical activity, and MEG signals record magnetic activity. MEG is done using a protecting surface (for user's head) containing multiple sensor coils. He et al. [73] observed that it does not give better hike in both performance and training times over noninvasive electronic acquisition techniques.

6.5.2.2 fMRI (functional Magnetic Resonance Imaging)

Using the system shown in Figure 6.9, fMRI senses changes in blood flow that may be linked to neuronal activity within the brain. For this purpose, it helps to map operations to the corresponding fields of brain called problem of source localization [115]. It relies on the fact that more incoming blood flow is called for by the use of the brain portion. It uses the hemodynamic response responsive blood-oxygen-level-established (BOLD) contrast [83]. The strength of the bold evaluation represents the shifts in the concentration of *deoxy-hemoglobin* in brain tissue. Although the temporal judgment of fMRI is weak, it provides

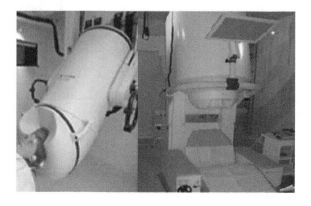

FIGURE 6.8
MEG acquisitions.

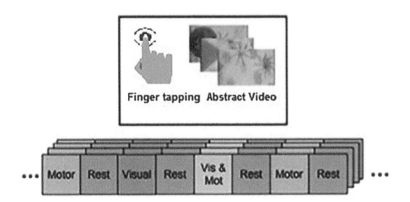

FIGURE 6.9
fMRI acquisition.

excessive spatial decision-making and gathers information that cannot be accrued from deep brain components by electrical or magnetic measurement [73].

6.5.2.3 fNIRS (functional Near-Infrared Spectroscopy)

In an attempt to classify the neuronal hobby, fNIRS is a noninvasive technique that tests blood dynamics within the brain. It uses light to assess blood flow within the close-to-infrared range. It has the benefit of supplying signals with high spatial resolution. However, the fNIRS recording is likely to be much less powerful in terms of temporal resolution than the one primarily based on electromagnetic signals. As shown in Figure 6.10, compared to fMRI, fNIRS is lightweight and much less costly, but has much lower capabilities for imaging. Its benefits include a viable alternative for science studies and, perhaps, realistic applications [73,115].

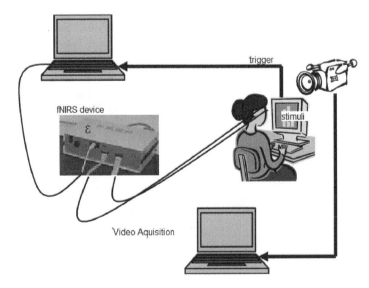

FIGURE 6.10
fNIRS acquisition.

6.5.2.4 EEG (Electroencephalogram)

EEG is a process of recording and evaluating of voltage shifts within the brain around the scalp. As shown in Figure 6.11, the electrodes are connected to a cap-like tool. Brain cells interact with each other through pulses to detect any issues of brain disorder. It is mostly recommended for commercial use to record brain cells activity. Measurement and report help to confirm about epilepsy, any head injury, brain tumor, sleep disorders, memory problems, etc.

It was warned that it was appropriate to increase the usage of electrodes to 256. In line with the assignment validated in Figure 6.12, it allows the distance between adjoining pairs of electrodes either 10% or 20% of the scalp diameter [2]. In general, this configuration has been used across unique EEG symbols

Researchers have tested sensors such as NeuroSky and Emotiv (brain data measurement systems) that permit less obtrusiveness and excessive portability options for large-scale consumer use [84]. A further EEG acquisition strategy is seen in Ref. [85]. The EEG test is painless and safe. In fixing electrode function, calming human, and robustness

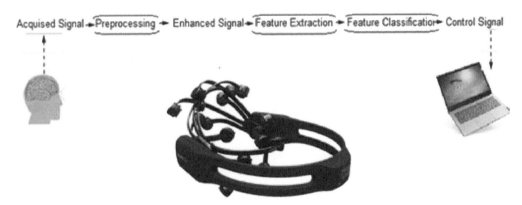

FIGURE 6.11
EEG acquisition block layout and a tool.

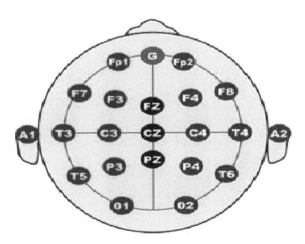

FIGURE 6.12
The 10–20 international positioning system.

TABLE 6.1

Summary of Brain Signal Acquisition Management

Modality	Invasiveness	Spatial resolution	Portability	Temporal Resolution	Recorded Signal
Cortical Surface	Invasive	High	Portable	High	Electrical
Intracortical	Highly Invasive	Very high	Portable	High	Electrical
EEG	Noninvasive	Low	Portable	Medium	Electrical
MEG	Noninvasive	Medium	Nonportable	Medium	Magnetic
fMRI	Noninvasive	High	Nonportable	Low	Metabolic
fNIRS	Noninvasive	Medium	Nonportable	Low	Metabolic

to electromagnetic interference, the advantage of this technique appears. The technician marks the spots on the scalp, scrubs with a special cream for high-quality reading, and puts 16–25 electrodes. There are many studies to reduce the number of electrodes maintaining signal-to-noise in BCIs. Motor actions are studied in Refs. [86,87] giving awareness about knee and ankle contractions, hand grasping is discussed in Refs. [88–89], and Refs. [90,91] discussed imagined writing. These are known to discriminate toward various behavioral modes.

Hill et al. [81] done analysis of classification effects using EEG and ECoG signals for of both paralyzed and nonparalyzed persons. In addition, within the classification of motor imagery, the function of speech has been studied, and it has been found that the presence of speech has no drastic impact on the results of precision. In accordance with their merits and drawbacks, Table 6.1 provides a description of brain signal acquisition methods [92].

6.6 Electrical Signal of BCI

We have understood that electrical signals from brain activity are observed by electrodes. There are two major approaches for detecting those signals as shown in Figure 6.13.

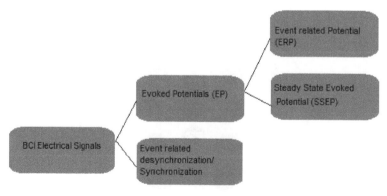

FIGURE 6.13
BCI electrical signal.

i. **Evoked Potential (EP):** Discovers the effect on them of various activating factors.

ii. **Brain Waves:** may not be linked with external stimulus, such as Event-Related De-synchronization and Synchronization reflecting decrease in brain oscillatory.

6.6.1 Evoked Potential (EP) or Evoked Response

EP is an electrical response that is recorded from the specific part of the nervous system after a stimulus is introduced. The Steady state evoked potential (SSEP) and event-dependent potential could be split similarly [93]. The components of the EP are known as exogenous or endogenous [94]. The physical characteristics of stimuli, including depth, modality, and rate of presentation, influence exogenous components. However, the endogenous elements are determined by the stimulus' psychological or cognitive meaning, i.e., the state of affairs' psychological or cognitive demands. They are not affected by the stimulus's physical characteristics. Endogenous components differ with techniques, perceptions, and other mental behaviors triggered by the occurrence in terms of amplitude, latency, and scalp distribution [95].

The SSEP study by Maye et al. [96] was evoked with the assistance of a stimulus modulated at a fixed frequency and occurs as an increase in stimulus frequency EEG behavior. The stimulus can be either visual, as in steady state visually evoked potentials, auditory, as in steady state auditory evoked potentials [97], or somatosensory (related to sensation), as in steady state somatosensory evoked potential [98].

A change in stimulus is elicited by event-related potential (ERP). After exposure to the spontaneous prevalence of the desired target case, it is the direct result of specific sensory, cognitive, or motor family. Sensory stimulation, a cognitive phenomenon, or the implementation of a motor response may be the case. Paulraj et al. [17] described ERPs. Visual evoked potentials, somatosensory evoked potential and AEP were discussed by Neela and Kahlon [99].

6.6.2 Event-Related Desynchronization and Synchronization

As a result of these practices, improvements were found to be capable of blocking or reducing the strength of the ongoing EEG signal. ERS (event-related synchronization) is hike in rhythmic activity. Event-related desynchronization shows a decrease in brain oscillatory activities. They are time-locked to the events, and averaging cannot be extracted.

The degree of synchrony of the neuronal populations underlying it can be related to this. The energy decrease is referred to as de-synchronization related to events or ERD, whereas the increased electricity is referred to as synchronization related to events (ERS) [100]. With the assistance of emerging mental duties, like motor visualization, mental mathematics, or mental rotation, they can be taken on.

6.7 Challenges of BCI and Proposed Solutions

The basic issues of the BCIs are difficulties in organizing the communication interface. Brain signals are prone to interference. It is possible to mark them as usability and technological challenges. The constraints affecting the degree of human acceptance [101] are defined by usability-demanding circumstances. The device boundaries, specifically those relating to EEG feature features, are concerned with technical issues.

6.7.1 Challenges of Usability

Legal and ethical concerns are also related to BCI applications. Brouwer et al. [9] discussed the issues of consumer appeals in BCI technology. They consist of issues relating to class discrimination related to the training process. One of the system evaluation metrics that combine each factor of success and acceptance is the information transfer rate (ITR).

- **User Training Process**: User training is either a time-inducing task to lead the customer through demonstration of processes and outcomes for different phases of recordings. This occurs in either the preliminary section or the classifier's calibration point. In addition to controlling the indicators of his/her mind remarks during the initial stage, the user is trained to deal with the system, even as the trained subject's signal was used during the calibration process to understand the methods and implementations used for the desired outcome.

  Common researched solutions to durability of time slots is the use of a single test, which is used to boost the signal-to-noise ratio [100], in contrast to multitrial evaluation, and to put the phase-wise training on subsequent BCI device additives to deal with. Numerous classifiers for adaptive and zero training were evaluated as solutions as referred to in Ref. [95].

- **Information Transfer Rate**: For command BCI systems, the widely used measurement metric is miles. There are two choices, correct target and mean time of a delivery. As a consequence, selective interest strategies obtain better ITR compared to imagery BCI as their delivered choices are broad.

6.7.2 Technical Issues

In technical challenges, there are some issues like nonlinearity, noise, nonstationarity, training units and size of the organization

- **Nonlinearity**: In humans, the brain is a particularly complex nonlinear system where neural ensembles can be observed in chaotic behavior. Consequently, nonlinear dynamic techniques can better describe EEG alarms than linear techniques.

- **Nonstationary and Noise**: Nonstationarity can be tough to predict due to trend, cycle, and random walks. A major problem in designing a BCI machine is the nonstationary function of electrophysiological brain signals [102]. This causes a nonstop alternation between or within the recording groups of the signals used over time. The intellectual and emotional heritage of the state through various sessions will contribute to the variability of the EEG signal. Some of the internal nonstationary components are often taken into account in terms of fatigue and awareness levels. Within the demanding situations going through the BCI generation and causing the nonstationary problem, noise is also a massive contributor. This involves unwanted signals due to changes in the positioning of electrodes and ambient noise [82].

- **Small Training Units**: As usability problems influence the training process, the training phases and sets are of smaller sizes. Although the subjects take time eating and distracting into account for heavy training times, they provide the consumer with the critical experience of addressing the system and learning how to monitor its neurophysiological signals. In the design of a BCI, therefore, an essential task is to balance the trade-off between the technical complexity of the user's brain signal perception and the amount of training needed for the hit interface operation [93].

- **Excessive Dimensionality Curse:** In BCI structures, to preserve excessive spatial precision, the indicators are reported from more than one channel. Different characteristic extraction strategies have been suggested because the amount of information needed to correctly identify separate indicators would increase exponentially with the dimensionality of the vectors. In recognition of distinguishing characteristics, they play a crucial function. Therefore, the overall efficiency of the classifier could be reached only by the limited broad range of one-of-a-kind patterns rather than the entire reported signals that could contain redundancy.

  In at least five to ten cases, it is generally encouraged to use as many training samples in accordance with the class as the number of dimensions [101]. However, since the BCI machine causes the growth of the dimensionality curse [103], this solution cannot be maintained in a surprisingly dimensionless setting.

6.7.3 Proposed Solutions

In order to confront and restrict the effect of the previously noted technological challenges, multiple solutions have been explored. Numerous BCI machine additives can be scattered over them. The following sections provide an overview of a few techniques used to enhance the performance of structures based on BCI.

6.7.3.1 Noise Removal

Preprocessing has contributed to the improvement of the signal in both spatial, time, and frequency domains, especially with the aid of external factors. Being positive, sometimes noise can improve the accuracy of BCIs. Decreasing the level of noise and improving SNR (Signal to Noise Ratio) are discussed in Ref. [104].

An unbiased independent component analysis (ICA) is a commonly used spatial filtering process [105]. ICA performs spatial filtering in unmanaged way of independent components. By separating the components of the project-associated EEG from the inappropriate EEG and the components of the assignment artifact, it aims to increase the SNR of EEG signals.

Electrooculography (EOG) measures the Corneo-retinal standing potential (CRSP) between front and back of the eye. Using eye motion recording electrodes, a linear combination of EEG signal polluted by the EOG, temporary-primarily-based preprocessing will lead to casting off artifacts [106] from the signal. Mixture variables are calculated using linear regression techniques. Due to the difficulty of positioning muscle detection electrodes, while it is the most common method for the removal of ocular objects from EEG indicators, it no longer satisfies the same satisfaction as the disposal of EMG signals.

Filtering of frequency bands allows disposing of noise and artifacts. In addition, it could provide valuable assistance in handling the internal nonstationary components. The task-related frequencies may be used in BCI systems for additional evaluation. For the eye or muscle movement to be placed, this form of filtering no longer involves larger electrodes. The benefit of the filtering implementation is its simplicity. A critical review was done by Neela and Kahlon [99].

6.7.3.2 Disconnectedness of Multiple Classes

To convert the intent of a consumer into a true desire, machine learning techniques are used. They discriminate and become conscious of the magnificence chosen. As a consequence, they are also striving to achieve improved efficiency and better ITR outcomes. Next, three different machines are briefed here, acquiring knowledge of algorithms like linear discriminant analysis (LDA), support vector machine (SVM), and k-nearest neighbor (KNN).

- **Linear Discriminant Analysis (LDA)**: A technique for minimizing dimensionality is LDA. In order to find linear combos of characteristic vectors representing the features of the corresponding signal, the LDA is deployed. Two or more types of objects of various classes are attempted by the LDA to distinguish. In a dataset, it decreases dimensions/variables while preserving as much data as possible. It makes use of hyper-planes to accomplish this mission. A hyper-plane is a plane of decision or space divided between groups of objects with distinct groups.

  The LDA steps are as follows:

  1. Calculate the scatter matrices inside and between classes.
  2. Calculate the eigen-vectors for the scatter matrices and the corresponding eigen-values.
  3. Sort the eigen-values and choose the top k value.
  4. Build a new matrix with eigenvectors mapping to the k eigen-values.
  5. Get the new features (i.e., LDA components) from phase 4 by taking the data dot product and the matrix.

  The LDA algorithm has a very low measurement requirement and is simple to implement. In various forms and multiclass of BCI systems, LDA has been used with satisfaction. But while, because of its immunity to the nonstationary problem, it generally gives desirable and good results, its linearity can motivate general performance degradation in a few circumstances with complex nonlinear EEG truth.

- **Support Vector Machine (SVM)**: SVM is one of the supervised machine learning algorithms that belong to a class of methods of classification that separate two distinctive classes of data using supervised learning. Data points that are closest to the hyper-plane are called support vectors. In SVM, the term margin is defined as the distance between two lines on the closest data points of various groups. Practically, the SVM algorithm is implemented with a kernel that converts and inputs the necessary type of data space. In order to interpret groups like LDA, it utilizes a discriminating hyper-plane.

  A support vector machine's objective is not only to draw hyper-plans and divide data points, but to draw the hyper-plane with the largest margin, or with the most space between the dividing line and any given data point, to separate data points. In the case of the SVM, however, the chosen hyper-plane is the only one maximizing the space from the nearest training points. The vectors that lie at the margin that could be known as guide vectors describe this ideal hyper-plane.

  The SVM algorithm has many benefits. It is considered to have correct generalization characteristics [107]. Eventually, SVM proposes specific performance results, but many data scientists comment about SVM as "black box method and inclined to over-fitting method."

6.7.3.2.1 KNN (K-Nearest Neighbors)

The KNN is recognized as the simplest machine learning algorithm based on supervised machine learning in which the function vector among k neighbors is assigned to its closest class by the nearest unattended neighbor classifiers. The KNN algorithm stores all available data and, on the basis of similarity, classifies a new data point. This means that it can be easily grouped into a well suite category as new data emerge.

Basic steps of KNN algorithm are as follows:

1. Pick the neighbors' number K.
2. Calculate the Euclidean distance from the number of neighbors of K.
3. Take the K nearest neighbors, as per the determined Euclidean distance.
4. Count the number of data points between these k neighbors and the group.
5. Assign the category for which the limit is the neighbor's number to new data points.
6. The model's readiness.

KNN is a nonparametric (does not take any inference of underlying data) algorithm and a lazy learner algorithm that does not automatically learn from the training set.

Simplicity is the main technical beauty of KNN algorithms. This machine learning algorithm owes an easy way of implementation and effectiveness. It can therefore give good results with successful algorithms for characteristic selection and reduction.

Table 6.2 gives a few examples (with their citations) of the use of these classifiers to progressively distinguish stimulation types in the BCI method, along with the techniques (with performance result) used for preprocessing and extraction of the functionality whose abbreviations are as follows:

- **BPF**: Band Pass Filtering
- **PLNF**: Power Line Notch Filter
- **LPF**: Low Pass Filtering
- **MPS**: Mean Power Spectrum
- **LPS**: Low Pass Spectrum
- **PSD**: Power Spectral Density
- **STTF**: Short Time Fourier Transform
- **ICA**: Independent Component Analysis
- **AF**: Asymmetric Features
- **ASP**: Asymmetrical Spatial Pattern
- **CSP**: Common Spatial Pattern
- **CSPP**: Common Spatial Pattern Patches
- **CCA**: Canonical Correlation Analysis
- **SPM**: Spectral Power Modulations
- **WT**: Wavelet Transform

TABLE 6.2

BCI with Some Deployed Preprocessing and Extraction of Functionality Techniques

Type of Stimulation/Application	Preprocessing and Extraction of Functionality			Citation	Classifier	Results (%)
Static sound P300 speller	BPF			[4]	SVM	62.90
	BPF				LDA	20.00
Moving sound P300 speller	BPF			[4]	SVM	71.40
	BPF				LDA	28.60
Detect emergency circumstances From the mental states of drivers	PLNF+BPF	MPS		[14]	LDA	70.00
Discrimination about motor and mental function	LPF	PSD		[86]	SVM	64.18
	LPF	PSD			LDA	52.76
Impact of type of image stimulus on smart TV neural control	BPF			[108]	SVM	95.10
	BPF				SVM	93.30
Impact of the video stimulus type on smart TV's neural control	BPF			[108]	SVM	93.30
Go/No-go Job Classification	BPF	WT	STFT	[109]	SVM	91.00
Acknowledge common objects		ICA		[110]	SVM	87.00
Detection of BCI arousal	BPF	ASP		[111]	KNN	82.25
	BPF	CSP			KNN	76.98
	BPF	AF			KNN	62.52
Detection of BCI arousal	BPF	ASP		[111]	SVM	82.03
	BPF	CSP			SVM	77.72
	BPF	AF			SVM	69.42
Detection of BCI valence	BPF	ASP		[111]	KNN	66.51
	BPF	AF			KNN	62.01
	BPF	CSP			KNN	58.23
Detection of BCI valence	BPF	ASP		[111]	SVM	65.39
	BPF	AF			SVM	61.89
	BPF	CSP			SVM	57.54
Task choice/no choice	BPF	CSP		[112]	LDA	80.00
Motor imagery classification	BPF	CSP+CSPP		[113]	LDA	70.00
Intended route for movement	ICA	CCA+EEG SPM		[114]	SVM	69.70
	ICA	CCA			SVM	65.60
	ICA, EEG SPM				SVM	65.40

6.8 Conclusion

Brain signals represent the behaviors discussed and are controlled by the activities of the mind or the influence of the data collected from various components of the body, both sensory and internal organs. A channeling facility between the brain and outside electronic devices is created by brain computer interfacing.

BCI represents a highly rising area in artificial intelligence and expert systems science. In the past 10 years, research papers on brain machine interface have been growing rapidly, as shown in Figure 6.14. More than one hundred articles and studies have been reviewed and cited in this chapter. They include healthcare, transportation, protection,

Articles on BCI

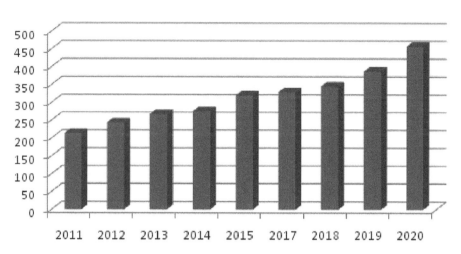

FIGURE 6.14
Peer-reviewed articles on BCI.

and authentication. It also displays the different subsystems used to take pictures of the markers of the brain.

In addition, understanding and designing more powerful BCI control systems with robot programming is a challenge for the coming generation. Technically, either by intracortical recordings or cortical potential adjustments through ECoG electrode grids, all BCI subsystems should be realizable.

References

1. G. Garcia-Molina, T. Tsoneva, A. Nijholt. Emotional brain-computer interfaces. *Int J Auton Adapt Commun Syst*, 6 (1) (2013), pp. 9–25.
2. L. Bi, X.-A. Fan, Y. Liu. EEG-based brain-controlled mobile robots: a survey. *IEEE Trans Human-Machine Syst*, 43 (2) (2013), pp. 161–176.
3. A.A. Navarro, L. Ceccaroni, F. Velickovski, S. Torrellas, F. Miralles, B.Z. Allison, R. R. Scherer, J. Faller. Context-awareness as an enhancement of brain-computer interfaces. In: *Ambient Assisted Living, IWAAL 2011*. Springer, Berlin; 2011.
4. Y. Lelievre, Y. Washizawa, T.M. Rutkowski. Single trial BCI classification accuracy improvement for the novel virtual sound movement-based spatial auditory paradigm. In: *2013 Asia-Pacific Signal and Information Processing Association Annual Summit and Conference (APSIPA)*. IEEE, Kaohsiung, Taiwan; 2013. pp. 1–6.
5. W. Wang, A.D. Degenhart, G.P. Sudre, D.A. Pomerleau, E.C. Tyler-Kabara. Decoding semantic information from human electrocorticographic (ECoG) signals. In: *2011 Annual International Conference of the IEEE Engineering in Medicine and Biology Society, EMBC*. IEEE, Boston, MA; 2011. pp. 6294–6298.
6. A. Vourvopoulos, F. Liarokapis. Robot navigation using brain-computer interfaces. In: *2012 IEEE 11th International Conference on Trust, Security and Privacy in Computing and Communications (TrustCom)*. IEEE, Liverpool, UK; 2012. pp. 1785–1792.

7. B. Van de Laar, H. Gurkok, D. Plass-Oude Bos, M. Poel, A. Nijholt. Experiencing BCI control in a popular computer game computational intelligence and AI in games. *IEEE Trans*, 5 (2) (2013), pp. 176–184

8. N. Prataksita, Y.-T. Lin, H.-C. Chou, C.-H. Kuo. Brain-robot control interface: Development and application. In: *2014 IEEE International Symposium on Bioelectronics and Bioinformatics (ISBB)*. IEEE, Chung Li, Taiwan; 2014. pp. 1–4.

9. A.-M. Brouwer, J. van Erp, D. Heylen, O. Jensen, M. Poel. Effortless passive BCIs for healthy users in Universal Access in Human-Computer Interaction Design Methods. In: *Tools and Interaction Techniques for eInclusion. UAHCI 2013*. Springer, Berlin; 2013.

10. J. van Erp, F. Lotte, M. Tangermann. Brain-computer interfaces: beyond medical applications. *Computer*, 45 (4) (2012), pp. 26–34.

11. Z. Eksi, A. Akgül, M. R. Bozkurt. The classification of EEG signals recorded in drunk and non-drunk people. *Int J Comput Appl*, 68 (2013), pp. 40–44.

12. T.K. Padmashri, N. Sriraam. EEG based detection of alcoholics using spectral entropy with neural network classifiers. In: *2012 International Conference on Biomedical Engineering (ICoBE)*. IEEE, Penang, Malaysia; 2012. pp. 89–93.

13. E. Malar. A novel approach for the detection of drunken driving using the power spectral density analysis of EEG. *Int J Comput Appl*, 21 (2011), pp. 10–14.

14. X. Fan, L. Bi, Z. Wang. Detecting emergency situations by monitoring drivers' states from EEG. In: *2012 ICME International Conference on Complex Medical Engineering (CME)*. IEEE, Kobe, Japan; 2012. pp. 245–248.

15. C.-T. Lin, S.-F. Tsai, L.-W. Ko. EEG-based learning system for online motion sickness level estimation in a dynamic vehicle environment. *IEEE Trans Neural Networks Learn Syst*, 24 (10) (2013), pp. 1689–1700.

16. C.-S. Wei, S.-W. Chuang, W.-R. Wang, L.-W. Ko, T.-P. Jung, C.-T. Lin. Implementation of a motion sickness evaluation system based on EEG spectrum analysis. In: *2011 IEEE International Symposium on Circuits and Systems (ISCAS)*. IEEE, Rio de Janeiro, Brazil; 2011. pp. 1081–1084.

17. M. Paulraj, S. Bin Yaccob, B. Adom, A. Hamid, C. Hema, K. Subramaniam. EEG based hearing perception level estimation for normal hearing persons. In: *2012 IEEE Conference on Control, Systems & Industrial Informatics (ICCSII)*. IEEE, Bandung, Indonesia; 2012. pp. 160–162.

18. L.-W. Ko, H.-C. Lee, S.-F. Tsai, T.-C. Shih, Y.-T. Chuang, H.-L. Huang, S.-Y. Ho, C.-T. Lin. EEG-based motion sickness classification system with genetic feature selection. In: *2013 IEEE Symposium on Computational Intelligence, Cognitive Algorithms, Mind, and Brain (CCMB)*. IEEE, Singapore; 2013. pp. 158–164.

19. S. Bagchi, M. Chattopadhyay. An easy-to-adopt approach for regular and routine monitoring of the consciousness level of human brain of stayed alone sick person. In: *2012 Sixth International Conference on Sensing Technology (ICST)*. IEEE, Kolkata, India; 2012. pp. 698–703.

20. V.S. Selvam, S. Shenbagadevi. Brain tumor detection using scalp EEG with modified wavelet-ICA and multi layer feed forward neural network. In: *2011 Annual International Conference of the IEEE Engineering in Medicine and Biology Society, EMBC*. IEEE, Boston, MA; 2011. pp. 6104–6109.

21. M. Sharanreddy, P. Kulkarni. Detection of primary brain tumor present in EEG signal using wavelet transform and neural network. *Int J Biol Med Res*, 4 (1) (2013), pp. 2855–2859.

22. M. Poulos, T. Felekis, A. Evangelou. Is it possible to extract a fingerprint for early breast cancer via EEG analysis?. *Med Hypotheses*, 78 (6) (2012), pp. 711–716.

23. M. Sharanreddy, P. Kulkarni. Automated EEG signal analysis for identification of epilepsy seizures and brain tumour. *J Med Eng Technol*, 37 (8) (2013), pp. 511–519.

24. K.H. Kulasuriya, M. Perera. Forecasting epileptic seizures using EEG signals, wavelet transform and artificial neural networks. In: *2011 International Symposium on IT in Medicine and Education (ITME)*, vol. 1. IEEE, Guangzhou, China; 2011. pp. 557–562.

25. C. Fadzal, W. Mansor, L. Khuan. Review of brain computer interface application in diagnosing dyslexia. In: *2011 IEEE Control and System Graduate Research Colloquium (ICSGRC)*. IEEE, Shah Alam, Malaysia; 2011. pp. 124–128.

26. H. Koch, J.A. Christensen, R. Frandsen, L. Arvastson, S.R. Christensen, H.B. Sorensen, P. Jennum. Classification of iRBD and Parkinson's patients using a general data-driven sleep staging model built on EEG. In: *2013 35th Annual International Conference of the IEEE Engineering in Medicine and Biology Society (EMBC)*. IEEE, Osaka, Japan; 2013. pp. 4275–4278.

27. I.H. Hansen, M. Marcussen, J.A. Christensen, P. Jennum, H.B. Sorensen. Detection of a sleep disorder predicting Parkinson's disease. In: *2013 35th Annual International Conference of the IEEE Engineering in Medicine and Biology Society (EMBC)*. IEEE, Osaka, Japan; 2013. pp. 5793–5796.

28. C.S. Ang, M. Sakel, M. Pepper, M. Phillips. Use of brain computer interfaces in neurological rehabilitation. *Brit J Neurosci Nurs*, 7 (3) (2011), pp. 523–528.

29. N. Birbaumer, S. Ruiz, R. Sitaram. Learned regulation of brain metabolism. *Trends Cognitive Sci*, 17 (6) (2013), pp. 295–302.

30. S. Ruiz, K. Buyukturkoglu, M. Rana, N. Birbaumer, R. Sitaram. Real-time fmri brain computer interfaces: self-regulation of single brain regions to networks. *Biol Psychol*, 95 (2014), pp. 4–20.

31. C.E. King, P.T. Wang, M. Mizuta, D.J. Reinkensmeyer, A.H. Do, S. Moromugi, Z. Nenadic. Noninvasive brain-computer interface driven hand orthosis. In: *2011 Annual International Conference of the IEEE Engineering in Medicine and Biology Society, EMBC*. IEEE, Boston, MA; 2011. pp. 5786–5789.

32. T. Meyer, J. Peters, D. Brtz, T.O. Zander, B. Scholkopf, S.R. Soekadar, M. Grosse-Wentrup. A brain–robot interface for studying motor learning after stroke. In: *2012 IEEE/RSJ International Conference on Intelligent Robots and Systems (IROS)*. IEEE, Vilamoura-Algarve, Portugal; 2012. p. 4078–4083.

33. C.L. Jones, F. Wang, R. Morrison, N. N.Sarkar, D.G. Kamper. Design and development of the cable actuated finger exoskeleton for hand rehabilitation following stroke. *IEEE Syst J* (2014), pp. 1–6.

34. A. Presacco, L. Forrester, J.L. Contreras-Vidal. Towards a non-invasive brain-machine interface system to restore gait function in humans. In: *2011 Annual International Conference of the IEEE Engineering in Medicine and Biology Society, EMBC*. IEEE, Boston, MA; 2011. pp. 4588–4591.

35. J.L. Contreras-Vidal, A. Presacco, H. Agashe, A. Paek. Restoration of whole body movement: toward a noninvasive brain–machine interface system. *IEEE Pulse*, 3 (1) (2012), pp. 34–37.

36. H. Regenbrecht, S. Hoermann, C. Ott, L. Muller, E. Franz. Manipulating the experience of reality for rehabilitation applications. *Proc IEEE*, 102 (2) (2014), pp. 170–184.

37. K.K. Ang, C. Guan, K.S. Phua, C. Wang, I. Teh, C.W. Chen, E. Chew. Transcranial direct current stimulation and EEG-based motor imagery BCI for upper limb stroke rehabilitation. In: *2012 Annual International Conference of the IEEE Engineering in Medicine and Biology Society (EMBC)*. IEEE, San Diego, CA; 2012. pp. 4128–4131.

38. S.W. Tung, C. Guan, K.K. Ang, K.S. Phua, C. Wang, L. Zhao, W.P. Teo, E. Chew. Motor imagery BCI for upper limb stroke rehabilitation: an evaluation of the EEG recordings using coherence analysis. In: *2013 35th Annual International Conference of the IEEE Engineering in Medicine and Biology Society (EMBC)*. IEEE, Osaka, Japan; 2013. pp. 261–264.

39. Y. Höller, J. Bergmann, M. Kronbichler, J.S. Crone, E.V. Schmid, A. Thomschewski, K. Butz, V. Schütze, P. Höller, E. Trinka. Real movement vs. motor imagery in healthy subjects. *Int J Psychophysiol*, 87 (1) (2013), pp. 35–41.

40. H. Kang, W. Park, J.-H. Kang, G.-H. Kwon, S.-P. Kim, L. Kim. A neural analysis on motor imagery and passive movement using a haptic device. In: *2012 12th International Conference on Control, Automation and Systems (ICCAS)*. IEEE, Jeju, Korea (South); 2012. pp. 1536–1541.

41. M.C. Domingo. An overview of the internet of things for people with disabilities. *J Netw Comput Appl*, 35 (2) (2012), pp. 584–596.

42. C.-T. Lin, B.-S. Lin, F.-C. Lin, C.-J. Chang. Brain computer interface-based smart living environmental auto-adjustment control system in UpnP home networking. *IEEE Syst J*, 8 (2012), pp. 363–370.

43. C.-Z. Ou, B.-S. Lin, C.-J. Chang, C.-T. Lin. Brain computer interface-based smart environmental control system. In: *2012 Eighth International Conference on Intelligent Information Hiding and Multimedia Signal Processing (IIH-MSP)*. IEEE, Piraeus-Athens, Greece; 2012. pp. 281–284.

44. Peng H, Hu B, Qi Y, Zhao Q, Ratcliffe M. An improved EEG de-noising approach in electroen-cephalogram (EEG) for home care. In: *2011 5th International Conference on Pervasive Computing Technologies for Healthcare (PervasiveHealth)*. IEEE, Dublin, Ireland; 2011. pp. 469–474.

45. R.N. Roy, S. Bonnet, S. Charbonnier, A. Campagne. Mental fatigue and working memory load estimation: Interaction and implications for EEG-based passive BCI. In: *2013 35th Annual International Conference of the IEEE Engineering in Medicine and Biology Society (EMBC)*. IEEE, Osaka, Japan; 2013. pp. 6607–6610.

46. D.G. Duru, A. Deniz Duru, D.E. Barkana, O. Sanli, M. Ozkan. Assessment of surgeon's stress level and alertness using EEG during laparoscopic simple nephrectomy. In: *2013 6th International IEEE/EMBS Conference on Neural Engineering (NER)*. IEEE, San Diego, CA; 2013. pp. 452–455.

47. Y. Dong, Z. Hu, K. Uchimura, N. Murayama. Driver inattention monitoring system for intel-ligent vehicles: a review. *IEEE Trans Intell Transport Syst*, 12 (2) (2011), pp. 596–614.

48. R. Coetzer, G. Hancke. Driver fatigue detection: a survey. In: *AFRICON, 2009. AFRICON'09*. IEEE, Dalian, China; 2009. pp. 1–6.

49. S. Pritchett, E. Zilberg, Z.M. Xu, M. Karrar, D. Burton, S. Lal. Comparing accuracy of two algo-rithms for detecting driver drowsiness—single source (EEG) and hybrid (EEG and body move-ment). In: 2011 6th International Conference on Broadband and Biomedical Communications (IB2Com). IEEE, Melbourne, VIC, Australia; 2011. pp. 179–184.

50. N. Dahal, N. Nandagopal, A. Nafalski, Z. Nedic. Modeling of cognition using EEG: a review and a new approach. In: *TENCON 2011–2011 IEEE Region 10 Conference*. IEEE, Bali, Indonesia; 2011. pp. 1045–1049, just the hierarchy of a model with no serious results but good abstract introduction for BCI.

51. Q. Wang, H. Wang, C. Zhao, J. Yang. Driver fatigue detection technology in active safety systems. In: *2011 International Conference on Remote Sensing, Environment and Transportation Engineering (RSETE)*. IEEE, Nanjing, China; 2011. pp. 3097–3100.

52. G. Borghini, G. Vecchiato, J. Toppi, L. Astolfi, A. Maglione, R. Isabella, C. Caltagirone, W. Kong, D. Wei, Z. Zhou et al. Assessment of mental fatigue during car driving by using high reso-lution EEG activity and neurophysiologic indices. In: *2012 Annual International Conference of the IEEE Engineering in Medicine and Biology Society (EMBC)*. IEEE, San Diego, CA; 2012. pp. 6442–6445.

53. Y.-K. Wang, S.-A. Chen, C.-T. Lin. An EEG-based brain-computer interface for dual task driv-ing detection. *Neurocomputing* (2013), pp. 85–93.

54. T. Kim, S. Kim, D. Shin, D. Shin. Design and implementation of smart driving system using context recognition system. In: *2011 IEEE Symposium on Computers & Informatics (ISCI)*. IEEE, Kuala Lumpur, Malaysia; 2011. pp. 84–89.

55. K. Murata, E. Fujita, S. Kojima, S. Maeda, Y. Ogura, T. Kamei, T. Tsuji, S. Kaneko, M. Yoshizumi, N. Suzuki. Noninvasive biological sensor system for detection of drunk driving. *IEEE Trans Inform Technol Biomed*, 15 (1) (2011), pp. 19–25.

56. C.-T. Lin, S.-A. Chen, L.-W. Ko, Y.-K. Wang. EEG-based brain dynamics of driving distraction. In: *The 2011 International Joint Conference on Neural Networks (IJCNN)*. IEEE, San Jose, CA; 2011. pp. 1497–1500.

57. R. Kawamura, M.S. Bhuiyan, H. Kawanaka, K. Oguri. Simultaneous stimuli of vibration and audio for in-vehicle driver activation. In: *2011 14th International IEEE Conference on Intelligent Transportation Systems (ITSC)*. IEEE, Washington, DC; 2011. pp. 1710–1715.

58. G. Vecchiato, L. Astolfi, F. De Vico Fallani, S. Salinari, F. Cincotti, F. Aloise, D. Mattia, M.G. Marciani, L. Bianchi, R. Soranzo et al. The study of brain activity during the observation of commercial advertising by using high resolution EEG techniques. In: *Annual International Conference of the IEEE Engineering in Medicine and Biology Society, 2009. EMBC 2009*. IEEE, Minneapolis, MN; 2009. pp. 57–60.

59. M. Yoshioka, T. Inoue, J. Ozawa. Brain signal pattern of engrossed subjects using near infrared spectroscopy (NIRS) and its application to TV commercial evaluation. In: *The 2012 International Joint Conference on Neural Networks (IJCNN)*. IEEE, Brisbane, QLD, Australia; 2012. pp. 1–6.

60. G. Vecchiato, F. Babiloni, L. Astolfi, J. Toppi, P. Cherubino, J. Dai, W. Kong, D. Wei. Enhance of theta EEG spectral activity related to the memorization of commercial advertisings in Chinese and Italian subjects. In: *2011 4th International Conference on Biomedical Engineering and Informatics (BMEI)*, vol. 3. IEEE, Shanghai, China; 2011. pp. 1491–1494.

61. V. Zotev, R. Phillips, H. Yuan, M. Misaki, J. Bodurka. Self-regulation of human brain activity using simultaneous real-time FMRI and EEG neurofeedback. *NeuroImage*, 85 (2014), pp. 985–995.

62. B.Y. Marquez, A. Alanis, M.A. Lopez, J.S. Magdaleno-Palencia. Sport education based technology: stress measurement in competence. In: *2012 International Conference on e-Learning and e-Technologies in Education (ICEEE)*. IEEE, Lodz, Poland; 2012. pp. 247–252.

63. L. Bonnet, F. Lotte, A. Lécuyer. Two brains one game: design and evaluation of a multi-user BCI video game based on motor imagery. *IEEE Trans Comput Intell AI Games*, 5 (2013), pp. 185–198.

64. W. Khalifa, A. Salem, M. Roushdy, K. Revett. A survey of EEG based user authentication schemes. In: *2012 8th International Conference on Informatics and Systems (INFOS)*. IEEE, Giza, Egypt; 2012. p. BIO-55.

65. D.T. Karthikeyan, B. Sabarigiri. Enhancement of multi-modal biometric authentication based on iris and brain neuro image coding. *Int J Biometrics Bioinform (IJBB)*, 5 (5) (2011), pp. 249–256.

66. I. Svogor, T. Kisasondi. Two factor authentication using EEG augmented passwords. In: *Proceedings of the ITI 2012 34th International Conference on Information Technology Interfaces (ITI)*. IEEE, Cavtat, Croatia; 2012. pp. 373–378.

67. F. Su, H. Zhou, Z. Feng, J. Ma. A biometric-based covert warning system using EEG. In: *2012 5th IAPR International Conference on Biometrics (ICB)*. IEEE, New Delhi, India; 2012. pp. 342–347.

68. I. Nakanishi, S. Baba, S. Li. Evaluation of brain waves as biometrics for driver authentication using simplified driving simulator. In: *2011 International Conference on Biometrics and Kansei Engineering (ICBAKE)*. IEEE, Takamatsu, Japan; 2011. pp. 71–76.

69. I. Nakanishi, S. Baba, K. Ozaki, S. Li. Using brain waves as transparent biometrics for on-demand driver authentication. *Int J Biometrics*, 5 (3) (2013), pp. 288–305.

70. I. Nakanishi, K. Ozaki, S. Li. Evaluation of the brain wave as biometrics in a simulated driving environment. In: *2012 BIOSIG-Proceedings of the International Conference of the Biometrics Special Interest Group (BIOSIG)*. IEEE, Darmstadt, Germany; 2012. pp. 1–5.

71. J. Thorpe, P. Van Oorschot, A. Somayaji. Pass-thoughts: authenticating with our minds. In: *New Security Paradigms Workshop: Proceedings of the 2005 workshop on New Security Paradigms*, UCLA Conference Center, Southern California, USA vol. 20, No. 23; 2005. pp. 45–56.

72. K.-R. Muller, A. Kubler. *Toward Brain Computer Interfacing*. Massachusetts Institute of Technology, Cambridge (2007), pp. 1–25.

73. B. He, S. Gao, H. Yuan, J.R. Wolpaw. *Brain-Computer Interfaces, Neural Engineering*. Springer, Boston, MA (2013).

74. L.R. Hochberg, M.D. Serruya, G.M. Friehs, J.A. Mukand, M. Saleh, A.H. Caplan, A. Branner, D. Chen, R.D. Penn, J.P. Donoghue. Neuronal ensemble control of prosthetic devices by a human with tetraplegia. *Nature*, 442 (7099) (2006), pp. 164–171.

75. H. Shan, H. Yuan, S. Zhu, B. He. EEG-based motor imagery classification accuracy improves with gradually increased channel number. In: *2012 Annual International Conference of the IEEE Engineering in Medicine and Biology Society (EMBC)*. IEEE, San Diego, CA; 2012. pp. 1695–1698.

76. M. Mikhail, K. El-Ayat, J.A. Coan, J.J. Allen. Using minimal number of electrodes for emotion detection using brain signals produced from a new elicitation technique. *Int J Auton Adapt Commun Syst*, 6 (1) (2013), pp. 80–97.

77. N. Jatupaiboon, S. Pan-ngum, P. Israsena. Emotion classification using minimal EEG channels and frequency bands. In: *2013 10th International Joint Conference on Computer Science and Software Engineering (JCSSE)*. IEEE, Khon Kaen, Thailand; 2013. pp. 21–24.

78. Q. Wei, Y. Wang, Z. Lu. Channel reduction by cultural-based multi-objective particle swarm optimization based on filter bank in brain-computer interfaces. In: *Unifying Electrical Engineering and Electronics Engineering*. Springer (2014). DOI:10.1007/978-1-4614-4981-2_146, Corpus ID: 60426360.

79. J.L. Roland, C.D. Hacker, J.D. Breshears, C.M. Gaona, R.E. Hogan, H. Burton, M. Corbetta, E.C. Leuthardt. Brain mapping in a patient with congenital blindness–a case for multimodal approaches. *Front Human Neurosci*, 7 (2013), p. 431.

80. A. Elghrabawy, M.A. Wahed. Prediction of five-class finger flexion using ECoG signals. In: *2012 Cairo International Biomedical Engineering Conference (CIBEC)*. IEEE, Giza, Egypt; 2012. pp. 1–5.

81. N.J. Hill, T.N. Lal, M. Schroder, T. Hinterberger, B. Wilhelm, F. Nijboer, U. Mochty, G. Widman, C. Elger, B. Scholkopf et al. Classifying EEG and ECoG signals without subject training for fast BCI implementation: comparison of nonparalyzed and completely paralyzed subjects. *IEEE Trans Neural Syst Rehabil Eng*, 14 (2) (2006), pp. 183–186.

82. O.P. Sosa, Y. Quijano, M. Doniz, J. Chong-Quero. BCI: a historical analysis and technology comparison. In: *2011 Pan American Health Care Exchanges (PAHCE)*. IEEE, Rio de Janeiro, Brazil; 2011. pp. 205–209.

83. H. Ayaz, P.A. Shewokis, S. Bunce, B. Onaral. An optical brain computer interface for environmental control. In: *2011 Annual International Conference of the IEEE Engineering in Medicine and Biology Society, EMBC*. IEEE, Boston, MA; 2011. pp. 6327–6330.

84. C. Hondrou, G. Caridakis. Affective. Natural interaction using EEG: sensors, application and future directions. In: *Artificial Intelligence: Theories and Applications*. Lamia, Greece; 2012. p. 331–338.

85. D. Looney, P. Kidmose, C. Park, M. Ungstrup, M.L. Rank, K. Rosenkranz, D.P. Mandic. The in-the-ear recording concept: user-centered and wearable brain monitoring. *IEEE Pulse*, 3 (6) (2012), pp. 32–42.

86. N. Ozmen, L. Ktu. Discrimination between mental and motor tasks of EEG signals using different classification methods. In: *2011 International Symposium on Innovations in Intelligent Systems and Applications (INISTA)*. IEEE, Istanbul, Turkey; 2011. pp. 143–147.

87. J.T. Gwin, D. Ferris. High-density EEG and independent component analysis mixture models distinguish knee contractions from ankle contractions. In: *2011 Annual International Conference of the IEEE Engineering in Medicine and Biology Society, EMBC*. IEEE, Boston, MA; 2011. pp. 4195–41198.

88. W. Park, W. Jeong, G.-H. Kwon, Y.-H. Kim, L. Kim. A rehabilitation device to improve the hand grasp function of stroke patients using a patient-driven approach. In: *2013 IEEE International Conference on Rehabilitation Robotics (ICORR)*. IEEE, Seattle, WA; 2013. pp. 1–4.

89. C.C.W. Fadzal, W. Mansor, L. Khuan. An analysis of EEG signal generated from grasping and writing. In: *2011 IEEE International Conference on Computer Applications and Industrial Electronics (ICCAIE)*. IEEE, Penang, Malaysia; 2011. pp. 535–537.

90. K. Ismail, W. Mansor, L. Khuan, C.C.W. Fadzal. Spectral analysis of EEG signals generated from imagined writing. In: *2012 IEEE 8th International Colloquium on Signal Processing and Its Applications (CSPA)*. IEEE, Bandung, Indonesia; 2012. pp. 510–513.

91. A. Zabidi, W. Mansor, Y. Lee, C.C.W. Fadzal. Short-time Fourier Transform analysis of EEG signal generated during imagined writing. In: *2012 International Conference on System Engineering and Technology (ICSET)*. IEEE, Bandung, Indonesia; 2012. pp. 1–4.

92. L.F. Nicolas-Alonso, J. Gomez-Gil. Brain computer interfaces, a review. *Sensors*, 12 (2) (2012), pp. 1211–1279.

93. B.Z. Allison, S. Dunne, R. Leeb. *Towards Practical Brain-Computer Interfaces: Bridging the Gap from Research to Real-World Applications*. Springer, Berlin (2012).

94. C.N. Gupta, R. Palaniappan, R. Paramesran. Exploiting the p300 paradigm for cognitive biometrics. *Int J Cognitive Biometrics*, 1 (1) (2012), pp. 26–38.

95. S. Gao, Y. Wang, X. Gao, B. Hong. Visual and auditory brain-computer interfaces. *IEEE Trans Biomed Eng*, 61 (2014), pp. 1436–1447.

96. A. Maye, D. Zhang, Y. Wang, S. Gao, A.K. Engel. Multimodal brain-computer interfaces. *Tsinghua Sci Technol*, 16 (2) (2011), pp. 133–139.

97. S.H. Fairclough, K. Gilleade. *Advances in Physiological Computing*. Springer, New York (2014).

98. G. Muller-Putz, R. Scherer, C. Neuper, G. Pfurtscheller. Steady-state somatosensory evoked potentials: suitable brain signals for brain-computer interfaces. *IEEE Trans Neural Syst Rehabilitation Eng*, 14 (1) (2006), pp. 30–37.

99. T.K. Neela, K.S. Kahlon. A framework for authentication using fingerprint and electroencephalogram as biometrics modalities. *Int J Comput Sci Manage Res*, 1 (1) (2012), pp. 56–62.

100. G. Pfurtscheller, F.H. Lopes da Silva. Event-related EEG/MEG synchronization and desynchronization: basic principles. *Clin Neurophysiol*, 110 (11) (1999), pp. 1842–1857.

101. F. Lotte, M. Congedo, A. Lécuyer, F. Lamarche, B. Arnaldi et al. A review of classification algorithms for EEG-based brain-computer interfaces. *J Neural Eng*, 4 (2007), pp. R1–R13.

102. W. Samek, K.-R. Muller, M. Kawanabe, C. Vidaurre. Brain-computer interfacing in discriminative and stationary subspaces. In: *2012 Annual International Conference of the IEEE Engineering in Medicine and Biology Society (EMBC)*. IEEE, San Diego, CA; 2012. pp. 2873–2876.

103. A. Soria-Frisch. A critical review on the usage of ensembles for BCI. In: B. Allison, S. Dunne, R. Leeb, R. Del, J. Millán, A. Nijholt (eds.), *Towards Practical Brain–Computer Interfaces* (pp. 41–65). Springer, Berlin (2013).

104. S. Xing, R. McCardle, S. Xie. Reading the mind: the potential of electroencephalography in brain computer interfaces. In: *2012 19th International Conference on Mechatronics and Machine Vision in Practice (M2VIP)*. IEEE, Auckland, New Zealand; 2012. pp. 275–280.

105. Y. Wang, T.-P. Jung. Improving brain-computer interfaces using independent component analysis. In: B. Allison, S. Dunne, R. Leeb, R. Del, J. Millán, A. Nijholt (eds.), *Towards Practical Brain–Computer Interfaces* (pp. 67–83). Springer, Berlin (2013).

106. S. Makeig, C. Kothe, T. Mullen, N. Bigdely-Shamlo, Z. Zhang, K. Kreutz-Delgado. Evolving signal processing for brain-computer interfaces. *Proc IEEE*, 100 (13) (2012), pp. 1567–1584.

107. W. Wu, X. Gao, B. Hong, S. Gao. Classifying single-trial EEG during motor imagery by iterative spatio-spectral patterns learning (ISSPL). *IEEE Trans Biomed Eng*, 55 (6) (2008), pp. 1733–1743.

108. J.J. Kim, T. Hwang, M. Kim, E. Oh, M. Hwangbo, M.-K. Kim, S.-P. Kim. The effect of stimulus type and distance on neural control of a smart TV. In: *2013 6th International IEEE/EMBS Conference on Neural Engineering (NER)*. IEEE, San Diego, CA; 2013. pp. 1343–1345.

109. A. Ahmadi, R. Jafari, J. Hart. Light-weight single trial EEG signal processing algorithms: computational profiling for low power design. In: *2011 Annual International Conference of the IEEE Engineering in Medicine and Biology Society, EMBC*. IEEE, Boston, MA; 2011. pp. 4426–4430.

110. A.X. Stewart, A. Nuthmann, G. Sanguinetti. Single-trial classification of EEG in a visual object task using ICA and machine learning. *J Neurosci Meth*, 228 (2014), pp. 1–14.

111. D. Huang, C. Guan, K.K. Ang, H. Zhang, Y. Pan. Asymmetric spatial pattern for EEG-based emotion detection. In: *The 2012 International Joint Conference on Neural Networks (IJCNN)*. IEEE, Brisbane, QLD, Australia; 2012. pp. 1–7.

112. A. Jain, I. Kim, B.J. Gluckman. Low cost electroencephalographic acquisition amplifier to serve as teaching and research tool. In: *2011 Annual International Conference of the IEEE Engineering in Medicine and Biology Society, EMBC*. IEEE, Boston, MA; 2011. pp. 1888–1891.

113. C. Sannelli, C. Vidaurre, K.-R. Muller, B. Blankertz. Common spatial pattern patches: online evaluation on BCI-naive users. In: *2012 Annual International Conference of the IEEE Engineering in Medicine and Biology Society (EMBC)*. IEEE, San Diego, CA; 2012. pp. 4744–4747.

114. J. Li, Y. Wang, L. Zhang, T.-P. Jung. Combining ERPs and EEG spectral features for decoding intended movement direction. In: *2012 Annual International Conference of the IEEE Engineering in Medicine and Biology Society (EMBC)*. IEEE, San Diego, CA; 2012. pp. 1769–1772.

115. S.N. Abdulkader, A. Atia, M.-S.M. Mostafa. Brain computer interfacing. *Egyptian Informatics Journal* 16 (2015), pp. 213–230.

7

Adaptive Filters and Neural Net

Sowmya K. B., Chandana G., and Anjana Mahaveer Daigond
RV College of Engineering

CONTENTS

DOI: 10.1201/9781003107026-7

7.1 Introduction

A filter is a system that is used to extract useful information from noisy input data. There are varieties of sources from which noise may arise. For example, data collected by means of sensors or noise that gets added to useful signal component by transmitting it through a communication channel. Linear and nonlinear filters are two classes of filters. If the filtered output is a linear function of input data, then filter is said to be linear. Otherwise, filter is said to be nonlinear. Prior information about the statistical nature (i.e., mean, variance) of useful information and unwanted additive noise is required to design a linear filter. Linear filter can be optimized to reduce the mean square value (MSE) of the unwanted additive noise. The resulting linear filter which is optimized in mean square sense is Wiener filter. Wiener filter cannot deal with the situations in which signal and/or noise has nonstationary nature. In such situations, Kalman filter (time-varying form of linear filter) can be used. Linear filter is most efficient when the characteristics of the input observations are the same or nearly the same as prior information which was used to design the filter. Whenever this condition becomes false, it is difficult to design efficient Wiener filter. The "estimate and plug" approach can be used in such situations. It is a two-step process. Firstly, filter "estimates" statistical parameters of the useful signal and then "plugs" the obtained results into a non-iterative formula for calculating required parameters. For real-time applications, this process requires excessively elaborate and costly hardware. Another solution is to use an adaptive filter.

The adjective "adaptive" refers to a system that tries to adjust itself such that it will be able to understand and respond to some phenomenon that is happening in its surrounding environment. The system tries to adjust its parameters to meet specific objectives that depend on the state of the system and the state of system environment. This is called as adaptation. Moreover, "adaptation" can be achieved using many algorithms. Adaptation is achieved using a recursive or iterative algorithm, which helps for the filter to operate efficiently in an environment where absolute information of the relevant parameters is not available. This algorithm starts with some predetermined set of initial values, representing whatever is already known. In reality, adaptive filter is a nonlinear device (because filter parameters are data-dependent), which means it does not follow the principle of superposition. Adaptive filters can be classified into linear and nonlinear filters. If the value of the required quantity is calculated adaptively as a linear function of samples applied as input of filter, then it is said to be linear.

The advantages of using iterative algorithm for achieving adaptation are as follows:

1. Direct calculation of the statistical properties and their usage for calculating the other quantities of interest (filter coefficients) can be done only by adding a large number of input observations. Iterative solutions do not require accumulation of a large number of observations, thereby reducing memory usage.

2. In non-iterative solutions, accumulation of signal samples and post processing to produce the filter output result in a significant delay in computation of filter output. This is not acceptable in many real-time applications. Recursive solutions, on the other hand, do not add any considerable amount of delay in computation of the filter output.

3. The use of iterative algorithms gives in adaptation with tracking capability. That is, if the signal characteristics are changing with time, adaptive filter will be able

to adapt and change filter output according to the new statistics provided that the rate of change is less.

4. It is very easier to code iterative algorithms in software or implement in hardware when compared to non-iterative algorithms.

There are wide varieties of iterative algorithms which have been proposed and completely developed for the implementation of linear adaptive filters. The choice of one algorithm for any application is decided by considering the following factors:

1. **Maladjustment**: This parameter is calculated as the difference between the final value of MSE, averaged over a number of adaptive filters and the minimum MSE that is generated by the Wiener filter. It gives the amount of deviation from the expected behavior.

2. **Rate of Convergence**: It is defined as the number of iterations required for the considered algorithm to converge close enough to the efficient Wiener solution in a stationary environment.

3. **Tracking**: There should be some form of tracking in nonstationary environment to track statistical variations in the input observations. The tracking efficiency of the algorithm depends on two opposite factors: (i) steady-state fluctuation due to noise and (ii) rate of convergence.

4. **Computational Requirements**: Number and type of operations in each iteration and memory usage are major issues to be considered here. The investment required to implement the algorithm is also a major concern.

5. **Robustness**: Whenever small variations in input statistical properties result in small estimation changes in computed values, then adaptive filter is said to be robust.

6. **Structure**: The manner in which adaptive filter is implemented in hardware form is determined by the structure.

The above factors should also be considered while designing a nonlinear adaptive filter, except that there is no well-defined frame of reference as Wiener filters.

7.1.1 Adaptive Filtering Problem

Adaptive filter is defined by the following basic aspects:

- Characteristics of the signals that are being processed by the filter.
- Filter structure which defines how the output response of the filter is calculated from the corresponding input data.
- The parameters within the filter structure that can be recursively changed to modify the filter's input-output relationship.
- The adaptive algorithm which demonstrates how the filter structure parameters are updated.

Selection of the filter structure and adaptation algorithm plays a very important role in designing optimum adaptive filter. The selected adaptation algorithm should minimize

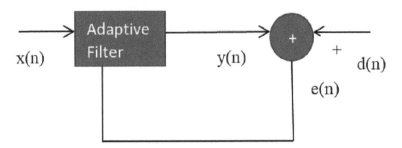

FIGURE 7.1
Adaptive filtering problem.

the error parameter in order for the filter to work optimally. Lattice structure, direct form, etc. are linear filter structures which can be used when the relationship between input signal and desired response is linear. Volterra and bilinear filters are two nonlinear filter structures. The selection of a particular filter structure depends on the input-output relationship and computational complexity.

Figure 7.1 shows the block diagram of adaptive filter where $x(n)$ is the input signal, $y(n)$ is output signal, and $d(n)$ is the desired response signal. The output signal is compared with desired response. The difference signal which can be computed as

$$e(n) = d(n) - y(n) \tag{7.1}$$

is called error signal. The error signal is given as input to an algorithm which modifies the filter structure with the objective to minimize MSE. In Figure 7.1, the oblique arrow that pierces into adaptive filter block is the process of adaptation. As the adaptation proceeds, the output signal becomes a better match to the $d(n)$. The following sections of this chapter give complete information about linear adaptive filters and Volterra-based nonlinear adaptive filters. Various limitations and reasons for moving to different adaptation algorithms are also explained.

7.2 Linear Adaptive Filter Implementation

The adaptive filter functions in two steps:

1. Filtering process, which is expected to produce an output in response to the input observations.
2. Adaptive process, which allows adaptive control of quantities of interest used in the filtering process.

These two processes are highly interconnected and work in accordance with each other. Transversal filter, lattice predictor, and systolic array structure are different types of linear filter structures. The choice of structure for implementation of filter has much impact on working of algorithm as a whole. There are two different approaches to derive iterative algorithms for the operation of linear adaptive filters.

7.2.1 Stochastic Gradient Approach

In this approach, a transversal or tapped-delay filter can be used as a structural basis for implementing the linear adaptive filter. In stationary environment, the cost function (i.e., index of performance) is calculated as the difference between expected response and transversal filter output (i.e., mean-square error). A second-order function of the tap weights in the tapped-delay filter is cost function. The dependence of the MSE on the unknown tap weights may be treated as a multidimensional paraboloid having a uniquely defined minimum point. This paraboloid is called the error-performance surface. Optimum Wiener solution can be obtained by considering tap weights corresponding to the minimum point of the surface.

There are two steps in developing an iterative algorithm for estimating unknown tap weights of the adaptive tapped-delay filter. First, use the method of steepest descent, a well-known procedure in optimization theory, to change the system of Wiener-Hopf equations which is the matrix equation defining the optimum Wiener solution. This change has to be done using a gradient vector. The value of gradient vector depends on two parameters: the auto-correlation matrix of the tap inputs and the cross-correlation vector between expected response and the same tap inputs. Next, use the obtained results to get an estimate for the gradient vector. The resulting algorithm is popularly known as the least-mean-square (LMS) algorithm, which can be described in words as follows for the case of a tapped-delay structure working on real-time data:

$$(\text{updated value}) = (\text{old value}) + (\text{tap input vector}) * (\text{learning rate}) * (\text{error signal})$$

The error signal is the difference between some expected response and the obtained response of the tapped-delay filter. The LMS algorithm is simple, but it has the capability to achieve satisfactory results under the right conditions. Major issues of concern in LMS algorithm are high sensitivity to changes in the correlation matrix of the tap inputs and a relatively slow rate of convergence. LMS algorithm is highly popular and widely used in many applications. In a nonstationary environment, the LMS algorithm should also track the bottom of the error-performance surface provided that rate of change of input data is relatively slow when compared to the adaptation rate of the LMS algorithm.

Lattice structure can also be used to develop the stochastic gradient approach which results in the gradient adaptive lattice (GAL) algorithm. The GAL and LMS algorithms are two types of filters belonging to the stochastic gradient family. So far, the LMS algorithm is the most popular and widely used member of the stochastic gradient family.

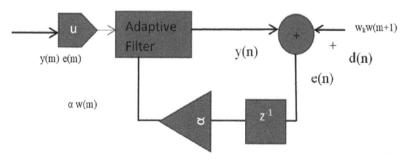

FIGURE 7.2
Computation of coefficients in LMS filter.

The computation of coefficients with LMS filter is shown in Figure 7.2. Pure LMS algorithm is very much sensitive to scaling of its input $x(n)$ which makes it very complicated to choose learning rate. Normalized LMS filters solve this problem by normalizing the power of input.

7.2.2 Least Square Estimation

In this second approach, a cost function is minimized. Cost function is computed by accumulating weighted error squares. The method of least squares can be implemented using block estimation or iterative estimation. Block estimation works in two steps. First, the input data observations are organized as blocks of equal length (duration), and then, filtering of input samples proceeds by considering one block at a time. On the contrary, in recursive estimation, the quantities of interest (e.g., tap weights of a transversal filter) are calculated and updated by processing each sample at a time. However, recursive estimator is mostly used in practice because it consumes less storage than a block estimator. Recursive least-squares (RLS) estimation can be thought as a special case of Kalman filtering. A special feature of the Kalman filter is the notion of state, which provides statistical properties of all the inputs applied to the filter up to a particular instant of time. Thus, recursion is used at the heart of the Kalman filtering algorithm which may be described in words as follows:

$$(\text{updated value}) = (\text{old value}) + (\text{Kalman gain}) * (\text{innovation vector}),$$

where new information fed to the filtering process at the time of the processing is treated as the innovation vector. It can be said that there is indeed a one-to-one correspondence between the RLS and Kalman variables. This correspondence means that the vast literature on Kalman filters can be used for designing least square estimation-based linear adaptive filters. Moreover, depending on the approach taken, the recursive RLS family of linear adaptive filters can be classified into three types:

1. Standard RLS algorithm uses a tapped-delay filter as the structural basis for implementing the linear adaptive filter. Standard RLS algorithm is derived completely based on the result of matrix inversion lemma. Standard RLS algorithm has advantages and limitations (lack of numerical robustness and more computational complexity) as the standard Kalman filtering algorithm. Indeed, these limitations have prompted the development of the other variations of RLS algorithms.

2. Square-root RLS algorithms, which are based on QR-decomposition of the incoming data stream. The Householder transformation and the Givens rotation are two well-known techniques used for performing this decomposition. RLS algorithms developed based on the Householder transformation or Given's rotation result in computationally stable and robust adaptive filters which are called square-root adaptive filters.

3. Fast RLS Algorithms, which are modified RLS algorithms. Standard RLS algorithm and square-root RLS algorithms are $O(M^2)$ algorithms where computational complexity is directly proportional to the square of M, where M is the number of adjustable weights. $O()$ denotes "order of." On the other hand, the LMS algorithm has less computational complexity in which computational complexity increases linearly with M. So, LMS algorithm is called $O(M)$ algorithm. When M is large, the computational complexity of $O(M^2)$ algorithms is not tolerable from a hardware implementation point of view. Therefore, it is very much necessary to modify the implementation of the RLS algorithm in such a way that it can be referred as $O(M)$ algorithm. This objective can be achieved by exploring the redundancy in

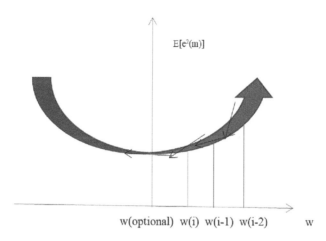

FIGURE 7.3
MSE surface for the minimum error point.

the Toeplitz structure of the input data matrix in both the forward and backward directions. The resulting algorithms are collectively known as fast RLS algorithms. The MSE surface for the minimum error point is specified in Figure 7.3. There are two types of fast RLS algorithms depending on the filtering structure used:

- **Order-recursive adaptive filters:** These filters use lattice structure for performing linear forward and backward predictions.
- **Fast transversal filters:** These filters use separate transversal filters to perform the linear predictions in both forward and backward directions.

In practical applications, fast traversal filters require some form of stabilization to compensate their numerical stability issue. However, few implementations of order-recursive adaptive filters are known to be computationally stable.

Figure 7.4 shows that elapsed time for LMS filter varies randomly, whereas for NLMS, elapsed time varies gradually for a smaller number of iterations. RLS filter has larger elapsed time due to complex matrix inversion lemma.

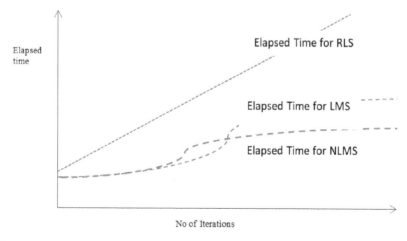

FIGURE 7.4
Performance comparison of LMS, NLMS, and RLS algorithms in terms of time taken.

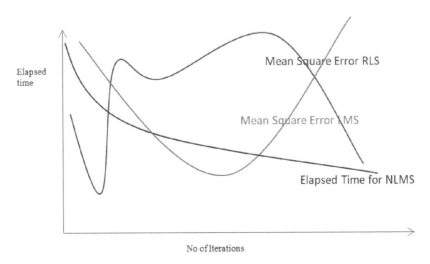

FIGURE 7.5
MSE vs. number of iterations for LMS, NLMS, and RLS algorithms.

In Figure 7.5, performance of different algorithms is compared based on MSE. MSE of LMS and RLS filters vary randomly, whereas MSE of NLMS filter decreases gradually. So, NLMS filters are preferred.

7.3 Nonlinear Adaptive Filters

The implementation of optimum linear filters is purely based on the MSE criterion. The optimum Wiener filter, which is developed to get minimum MSE, and which is treated as a frame of reference for linear adaptive filters working in a stationary environment, considers until second order statistics of the input data stream but not higher. This is the major limitation due to which a linear adaptive filter can't be used to extract useful information from input data stream in a nonstationary environment. In many signal processing applications, nonstationary processes are encountered quite often in practice. This limitation can be overcome by making the adaptive filter nonlinear to use in a nonstationary environment. Wiener filter is no longer a frame of reference, and mathematical analysis also gets complicated. Improved learning efficiency is the main advantage because of which nonlinear adaptive filters can be used in broad application areas.

7.3.1 Volterra-Based Nonlinear Adaptive Filter

This type of nonlinear adaptive filter is based on the use of a Volterra series that provides an efficient method for deriving the input-output relationship of a nonlinear system. Nonlinearity is added at the front end of the filter.

Let the series x_n denote the input samples/observations of a nonlinear system. Then, accumulate all input data observations to define a set of Volterra kernels as follows:

$$H_0 = \text{zero order } (dc) \text{ term}$$

$$H_1 \left(x_n \right) = \text{first-order term} = \sum_i h_i x_i$$

$$H_2 \left(x_n \right) = \text{second-order term} = \sum_i \sum_j h_{ij} x_i x_j$$

$$H_3 \left(x_n \right) = \text{third-order term} = \sum_i \sum_j \sum_k h_{ijk} x_i x_j x_k$$

where

hs are nonlinear model coefficients and are fixed by analytical methods.

Higher-order terms can be defined in the same way as shown above. Two important parts of nonlinear adaptive filter are as follows:

- A nonlinear Volterra stair expander, which accumulates the set of input samples $x_1, \ldots x_n$ to produce a larger set of outputs $u_0, \ldots u_n$. For example, the extension vector for a (3, 2) system can be written as

$$u = \left\{ 1, \, x_1, \, x_2, \, x_0^2, \, x_0 x_1, \, x_0 x_2, \, x_1 x_0, \, x_1^2, \, x_1 x_2, \, x_2 x_0, \, x_2 x_1, \, x_2^2 \right\}$$

- A linear FIR adaptive filter, which works on the u_k as inputs to produce an estimate d_n, where d_n is treated as desired response (Figure 7.6).

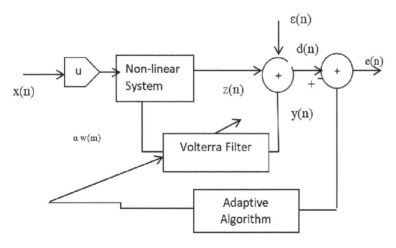

FIGURE 7.6
Volterra-based nonlinear adaptive filter.

7.4 Applications of Adaptive Filter

7.4.1 Biomedical Applications

7.4.1.1 ECG Power-Line Interference Removal

An ECG signal distorted by the PLI can be given by $d(n)=x(n)+N(n)$; $d(n)$ is noisy ECG signal samples, $x(n)$ is the useful part of noisy ECG signal, and $N(n)$ is the noise having sinusoidal nature with the frequency 50 Hz.

The block diagram in Figure 7.7 shows that if approximation of $N(n)$ signal is computed and later subtracted from noisy signal $d(n)$, original signal $x(n)$ can be obtained. If $N'(n)$ is nearly same as $N(n)$, then the gauged desired signal $x'(n)$ considerably matches with $x(n)$. Mathematical equations of output can be written as follows:

$$e(n) = x(n) + N - y \tag{7.2}$$

The power of signal is calculated by squaring equation (7.2),

$$e^2 = x^2 + (N-y)^2 + 2x(N-y) \tag{7.3}$$

Taking statistical mean on both sides of the above equation,

$$E(e^2) = E(x^2) + E(N-y)^2 \tag{7.4}$$

Decreasing the error using adaptive LMS filter does not have any impact on signal power. So, minimum error is

$$E(e^2)_{min} = E(x^2) + E(N-y)^2_{min} \tag{7.5}$$

The LMS algorithm delivers the least mean squared error signal by modifying filter weight coefficient, and the coefficient equation is

$$W_{k+1} = W_k + 2\mu e_k x_k \tag{7.6}$$

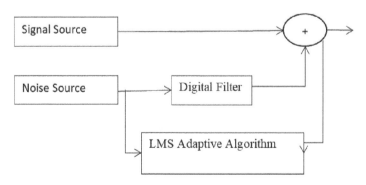

FIGURE 7.7
Block diagram of LMS adaptive filter denoising.

where

μ is a step size to be selected in a domain $0 < \mu < 2$ input signal power.

The adaption rate varies linearly with step size.

7.4.1.2 Maternal-Fetal ECG Separation

Another measurement MMECG(n) from maternal electrode is used as a reference signal, that is correlated with maternal signal and uncorrelated with desired fetal ECG signal. MMECG can be used to estimate the noise $r(n)$ by minimizing MSE. Figure 7.8 below shows the block diagram for processing of fetal ECG signal.

An adaptive filter uses measured maternal ECG (MMECG) to estimate the maternal components present in MFECG. Then, adaptive filtered fetal ECG (AFECG) is obtained by taking the difference between obtained signal samples and MFECG. This subtraction is performed to suppress maternal components. Other sources of noise, such as muscular activity from maternal body and fetal movement, will introduce baseline wandering in the MFECG.

7.4.2 Speech Processing

7.4.2.1 Noise Cancelation

Noise cancellation is necessary to remove intense background noise which affects the actual information. It is extremely necessary in mobile phones and radio communications because these devices are used in the environment which has high background noise. An adaptive noise cancellation system is shown in Figure 7.9.

The cancellation system makes use of a directional microphone to record and determine the instantaneous amplitude of the ambient noise s_1, and another microphone is used to get the speech signal which is corrupted by the surrounding noise $s + n_0$. The adaptive filter makes the recorded ambient noise equal to the noise in the speech signal by processing s_1

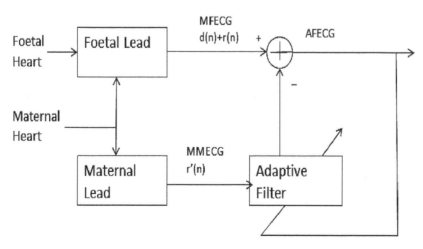

FIGURE 7.8
Block diagram of maternal-fetal ECG separation.

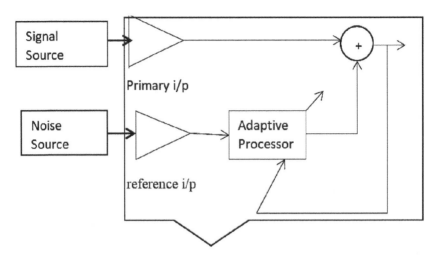

FIGURE 7.9
Adaptive noise canceller system.

and then subtracts it from recorded speech signal to suppress the noise present in desired signal. The cancellation system is most efficient when ambient noise is highly correlated with the additive noise signal in the speech signal. If the instantaneous value of the contaminating signal can't be accessed, the noise cannot be cancelled out, but it can be suppressed using statistics of the desired signal and the additive noise signal. The output of noise canceller is the error signal obtained by removing undesired frequency components.

Another application is active headphones which cancel out low-frequency noise from the surroundings which has achieved a widespread success commercially. The active headphones contain microphones outside the ear cups which measures the ambient noise surrounding the headphones. This ambient noise will be then cancelled by sending the corresponding "anti-noise" to headphone speakers. In feed-forward active noise cancellers, the headphones also include a microphone which is inside each ear cup which monitors the error part of the signal that has not been cancelled by the speakers. Active headphones play an essential role for pilots working in noisy helicopters and propeller-powered airplanes.

7.4.3 Communication Systems

7.4.3.1 Channel Equalization in Data Transmission Systems

In telecommunication, equalization is a reverse effect of distortion incurred by a signal transmitted through a channel. Equalizers are used to give frequency response. When a channel is equalized, the frequency domain attributes of the signal at input are faithfully reproduced at output. To prepare the data signals for transmission, telephones, DSL lines, and television cables use equalizers. Equalizers are very critical to the successful operation of electronic systems such as analog broadcast television. In this application, actual waveform of the transmitted signal must be preserved, along with its frequency content. Equalizing filters must cancel out any group delay and phase delay between different frequency components. Channel equalization is one of the most widely explored topics in the field of adaptive filters [1–3].

One of the various adaptive algorithms can be applied to channel equalizers. However, while selecting an adaptive algorithm, one should also take care of the following points:

- Depending on channel impulse response, the power spectral density of the input to an equalizer varies vastly. Hence, the performance of the LMS algorithm in channel equalization is highly dependent on channel and will vary significantly from channel to channel.

- On the other hand, the RLS algorithm performs independently irrespective of the channel characteristics. But it has higher computational complexity and numerical stability problem, especially for poorly conditioned channels, that is, cases where the eigenvalue spread of the underlying correlation matrix is large.

- The algorithms affine projection algorithm and LMS-Newton algorithm are good, compromised choices for adaptation of channel equalizers.

- The input signal to the equalizer is oversampled above its Nyquist rate, which makes that power spectral density of input signal over higher portion of its frequency band zero. This shows the fact that underlying correlation matrix is poorly conditioned. Hence, problems mentioned in the first two points above may be more relevant in the case of fractionally spaced equalizers. So, these points have to be taken care for fractionally spaced equalizers.

7.4.3.2 *Multiple Access Interference Mitigation in CDMA*

In a CDMA system, all users share same frequency band, and they are distinguished by (quasi)-orthogonal spreading codes. However, on dispersive broadband channels, orthogonality among codes is disrupted, and multi-user access interference (MAI) is present on received signal. But interference among the symbols and chips of the same user arises. One of the most common solutions to suppress the MAI is use of an adaptive filter. A single user receiver, based on a linear filter, minimizes the square of the difference between the output and the transmitted symbols of the user. In multi-user communication systems, for example, code division multiple access (CDMA) systems, the dominant source of impairment is co-channel interference coming from simultaneous active user signals occupying the same frequency band. Significant efforts have been made on developing multi-user detection techniques for reducing interference [4,5].

We can use LMS algorithm-based adaptive filter in a direct-sequence code-division multiple-access (DSCDMA) dispreading application. The filter can extract useful information from noisy data by correlating input chips with PN sequence of the desired user. Interference from other users as well as any multipath effects are all treated as noise in this system (Figure 7.10).

7.4.4 Adaptive Feedback Cancellation in Hearing Aids

The hearing-aid processor basically amplifies the input signal to larger amplitude in order to help the people with hearing loss. The system tends to become unstable when the amplification factor of the processor is larger than the attenuation of the feedback path which results in feedback whistling, this limits the efficiency of the system.

Acoustic feedback in a hearing aid is the acoustical coupling between receiver and microphone. The hearing aid produces a severe distortion of the useful signal and an annoying sound when the gain is more, due to this feedback.

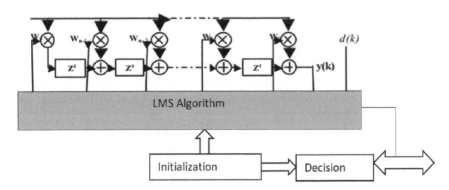

FIGURE 7.10
Structure of LMS algorithm-based adaptive filter.

The system environment is not stable, due to which feedback transfer function is not known directly, and thus, it cannot be implemented using required hardware. Some possible sources of this problem are hugs or objects like a telephone coming in close proximity to ear.

The feedforward suppression and many other feedback cancellation techniques can be used to reduce negative effects caused by acoustic feedback. In feedforward suppression techniques, the regular signal processing part of hearing aid is changed such that it is stable in conjunction with acoustic feedback path. The most common technique is to use a notch filter. In a notch filter, gain is less in a narrow frequency band around the cut off frequencies whenever feedback occurs. However, the feedforward suppression technique compromises with the basic frequency response of the hearing aid. Thus, it may seriously affect sound quality. Hence, a more promising solution for the problem is use of a feedback cancellation system.

Figure 7.11 shows an adaptive feedback canceller which produces an estimate $z(n)$ of the feedback signal $v(n)$ and eliminates this estimate $z(n)$ from the microphone signal, so

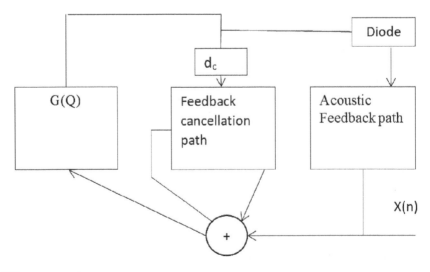

FIGURE 7.11
Adaptive feedback canceller.

ideally, only desired signal is preserved at the input of the forward path. The feedback canceller should be adaptive since there are many chances of significant variations in acoustic path between the loudspeaker and the microphone.

7.5 Neural Network

Neural network is a computational system that is inspired by the structure and functioning of human brain. An artificial neuron network (ANN), commonly known as NN, is a computational system based on the structure and functioning of biological neural networks. It is similar to an artificial human nervous system which receives, processes, and transmits information. It has been developed by using biological NN as a reference. The human brain processes information in an entirely different way from the existing digital computer. The human brain is a highly complex, nonlinear, and parallel information-processing system. It has the capability to arrange and use its structural components, known as neurons, in order to achieve specific goals (e.g., pattern recognition, perception, and motor control) in a much faster way than the existing fastest digital computer [5–7].

In general, a NN is a system that is implemented to operate the way in which the brain performs a particular task. The NN is usually designed by using electronic components or is simulated using software on a digital computer. The complexity of ANN is much lesser when compared to the complexity of the brain. But there are two key similarities between ANN and biological NN. First, building blocks of both the networks are computational devices called neurons, which are highly interconnected. Interneuron connection strengths (called as synaptic weights) are used to keep a record of acquired information. Second, knowledge is acquired by both the networks from its environment through a learning process. Learning algorithm (i.e., procedure used for the learning process) modifies the synaptic weights of the inter-connected network in a required manner to achieve a required design objective [8–10]. The modification of synaptic weights is the traditional method for the design of ANN. Such an approach is similar to adaptive filter theory, which is already well developed and successfully applied in many fields. NN are also called connectionist networks, neurocomputers, parallel distributed processors, etc.

Any NN consists of the following basic layers:

1. **Input Layer**: It is made up of artificial neurons which take input from the physical world based on which the NN will learn about or process the information to produce desired results.
2. **Hidden Layer**: It comes in between input layer and output layer. There can be more than one hidden layer to process the input data received from the input layer.
3. **Output Layer**: The data after processing in hidden layer is made available at the output layer. The output layer comes in between input and hidden layers (Figure 7.12).

ANN can also be represented as weighted directed graphs in which artificial neurons correspond to nodes, and interconnections between nodes in different layers correspond to directed edges with weights. The ANN gets information from the external world in

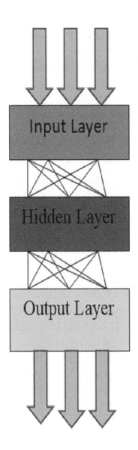

FIGURE 7.12
Architecture of neural network.

the form of pattern, stream, and image in vector form. Each input gets multiplied by its corresponding weights. Typically, weight represents the strength of the interconnection between artificial neurons inside the NN and is used by the NN to meet the desired objective. The weighted inputs are all accumulated in the computing unit. Bias is added to make the output nonzero or to scale up the system response if the weighted sum is zero. Bias has the weight and input always equal to "1." The sum can be any value between 0 and ∞ [10–14].

To get the desired output, the activation function is set to the transfer function. Activation function can be linear or nonlinear. Some of the commonly used activation functions are binary, sigmoidal (linear), and tan hyperbolic sigmoidal functions (nonlinear) (Figure 7.13).

Commonly known training algorithms of ANN are as follows:

- Hebbian Learning Rule
- Self-Organizing Kohonen Rule
- Hopfield Network Law
- LMS (Least Mean Square) Algorithm
- Competitive Learning

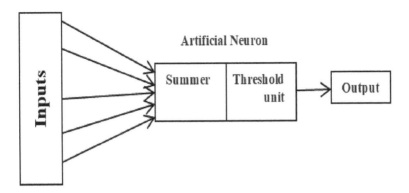

FIGURE 7.13
Working model of ANN.

7.5.1 Learning Techniques in ANN

- **Supervised Learning**: In supervised learning, the training data is fed as input to the network for which the expected output is already known. Weights are updated until the algorithm produces the required value.

- **Unsupervised Learning**: This type of learning is done without supervision which means that there is no feedback from the environment indicating what is the required output and whether it is correct or not.

- **Offline Learning**: The weight vector and threshold are adjusted only after all the training set is fed to the NN. It is also called batch learning.

- **Online Learning**: The weight vector and threshold are adjusted after feeding each training sample to the NN.

- **Reinforcement Learning**: The value of the output is unknown, but the NN provides feedback to help in checking whether the output is correct or not. It is also called semi-supervised learning.

7.6 Single and Multilayer Neural Net

Single and multilayer neural networks are two classes of network architectures. The manner in which NN is organized is directly linked with the learning method used to train the NN.

7.6.1 Single-Layer Neural Networks

It is the simplest form of NN which contains only one layer of input nodes that forward weighted inputs to the next layer of receiving nodes. Perceptron and single-layer binary linear classifier are early examples of a single-layer neural network. In single-layer NN, information moves in only the direction from inputs to outputs. So, single-layer neural network can also be treated as a part of feedforward neural networks (Figure 7.14).

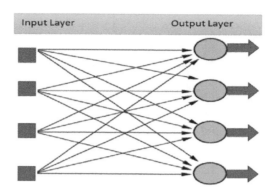

FIGURE 7.14
Single-layer neural network.

7.6.2 Multilayer Neural Net

Multilayer neural networks use hidden layers in between input and output layer to work on nonlinear set of inputs. Geometrically, additional hidden layers are referred to as additional hyper-planes to increase the computation capability of the neural network. Figure 7.15 shows the typical multilayer network architecture.

A multilayer neural network is also called a "multilayer perceptron" (MLP) which is a typical example of a feedforward artificial neural network. Multilayer neural networks are trained using back propagation algorithm. Each artificial neuron present in a particular layer is connected to all neurons in the subsequent layer. The weight coefficient assigned to a link shows the importance of that connection in the working of neural network.

The multilayer neural networks in two modes: training and prediction mode. In the training set, expected output is known and test set are two data sets that are necessary for the training of multilayer NN and for the prediction using the multilayer neural network. At the starting of training, random values are assigned to weights of connections. Then, multilayer NN proceeds recursively. Each iteration of the complete training set is called an

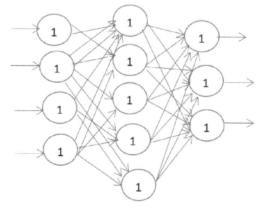

FIGURE 7.15
Multilayer neural network architecture.

epoch. The goal of each epoch is to reduce the error. As the recursive process of adjustment of weights proceeds, the weights slowly converge to an optimal set of values. For a given training set, it requires many epochs for the training to be completed. Back-propagation algorithm is used for updating weights [15–20].

For a given training set, back-propagation learning algorithm may operate in one of two basic ways: pattern mode and batch mode. In the pattern mode, weights are updated after the processing of each training pattern. In the batch mode, weight updating is done after the processing of all the training sets (i.e., after the whole epoch). Pattern mode consumes less memory when compared to batch mode of updating weights. Usually, the patterns are fed to the network in a random manner. The use of pattern mode of updating weights makes the search in weight space more complex, which makes it difficult for the back-propagation algorithm to converge to a local minimum. On the other hand, the use of batch mode of weight updating provides a more exact estimate of the gradient vector.

A network is considered to be efficient when the input-output data relationship generated by neural network match with expected result for data streams never used in the learning process of the NN. There are chances that the neural network may memorize the training data and therefore be less able to generalize between similar input-output patterns when the learning process is repeated for too many training sets. Then NN is said to be over trained NN or over fitted NN because of which NN produces a nearly perfect outcome for examples from the training set but fails for examples from the test set.

Use of multilayer NN for any application has the following advantages:

1. **Learning**: Adaptive ability of the ANN.

2. **Nonlinearity**: A neural network is a nonlinear system because neurons are nonlinear elements. Nonlinearity property plays a very important role when the system has to deal with nonlinear data.

3. **Input-Output Mapping**: The NN learns from the training set by constructing an input-output mapping for the presented problem. An example picked from the training set is fed to the network, and the weight coefficients are adjusted with the aim to minimize the difference between the expected output and the actual response of the network. The training of the network is repeated for different training sets until the network reaches the stable state.

4. **Robustness**: Multilayer neural networks are very robust, i.e., their performance degrades considerably in the presence of a significant amount of noise.

7.7 Applications of Neural Networks

7.7.1 ECG Classification

The ECG waveform is a graphical representation of electrical activity of the heart. In this application, our main focus is on five important features of ECG signal, i.e., P, Q, R, S, T. This is achieved by extracting various features and P-wave, PR segment, PR interval, QRS complex, ST segment, T-wave, ST- interval, QT and QRS voltage segments of different ECG waveforms.

7.7.1.1 Methodology

The block diagram in Figure 7.16 explains the overall methodology for detection and classification of arrhythmias. The overall block diagram shown in Figure 7.16 consists of signal preprocessing, QRS peak detection, feature extraction, and ANN signal classification blocks.

Different ECG signals with different abnormalities are recorded. In signal preprocessing, the ECG signal is usually filtered to remove noise, and the signal is presented to the QRS detection block. The second step is QRS detection which corresponds to the period of ventricular contraction or depolarization which is done for determining the heart rate. The third step is to find the smallest set of features by processing the ECG signal that facilitate in maximizing the performance of the classification step. The last step is classification, and MLP neural network is known to be the best for this classification. Each ECG waveform can be either used as a training set or data set. First, a set of ECG signals with known abnormalities are used for training the NN. Then, the data set is presented to the NN to find the abnormality present in ECG signal based on feature extraction and classification.

7.7.2 Speech Recognition

Speech is the most efficient way of communication used by human beings. This, being the best mode of communication, could also be used as a protocol to interact with high-end machines. Therefore, the popularity of automatic speech recognition systems has been greatly increased. Hidden Markov model (HMM), dynamic time warping (DTW), vector quantization (VQ), etc. are different approaches to speech recognition. This section provides an insight about the use of ANN in speech recognition [20–24] (Figure 7.17).

7.7.2.1 Methodology

Speech is a vocalized form of human interactions. Often, background noise or room reverberation sounds will get added to speech which makes it noisy. Noise may get added to speech even during transmission through noisy channels. Therefore, we go for speech preprocessing. This plays an important role in eliminating noise from speech signal to improve efficiency and accuracy of speech recognition. The speech preprocessing step generally involves processes like noise filtering, smoothing, framing, windowing, reverberation cancelling and echo removing, etc. Theoretically, a system should be able to recognize speech from the digitized waveform. But due to large variations in speech signal, there is a need to extract useful features to reduce those variations. Mel frequency cepstrum coefficient (MFCC) is the most prominent method used in the process of feature extraction in speech recognition. A tool which is most widely used for medium or low bit rate coder is linear predictive coding (LPC).

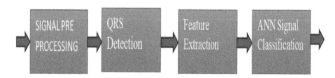

FIGURE 7.16
Block diagram of ECG classification.

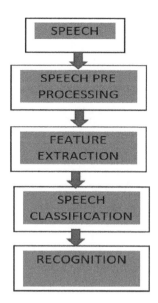

FIGURE 7.17
Process of speech recognition.

- **ANN from the Viewpoint of Speech Recognition**: In applications like speech recognition, there is a requirement to turn physical world inputs into discrete values. ANN that simply performs accumulation of input samples and thereby smooth input data is not capable of achieving desired objectives in such applications. In software packages, artificial neurons used for these applications are called processing elements and have many more capabilities than basic ANN. Some of the examples are feed-forward neural network, recurrent neural network, modular NN, and Kohonen self-organizing maps.

7.7.3 Communication Systems

7.7.3.1 Mobile Station Location Identification Using ANN

In [25,26], ANN-based mobile station, a location identification system is designed. The authors have proposed a method that uses time of arrival (TOA) records and angle of arrival (AOA) data to locate MS when three base stations (BSs) are available. The proposed method uses the intersections of three TOA circles (and the AOA line), based on various NN, to find MS location in non-line-of-sight (NLOS) environments when MS is heard by three base stations. Location-based services in the wireless communication networks are mostly provided by the mobile positioning technique. E-911 wireless emergency services, location-based billing, fleet management, and the intelligent transportation system (ITS) are different applications of wireless location services. The ANN model proposed helps find the location of the mobile station. If the TOA measurements are available, then the location of the BS is estimated by the intersection of the circles as given in Figure 7.18 [27–29].

The true location of MS is in the intersection region of the circles denoted by U, V and W. From this input, output parameters for the training of the ANN model are extracted. The input parameters taken are the values of intersection, i.e., U, V, and W, and at the output

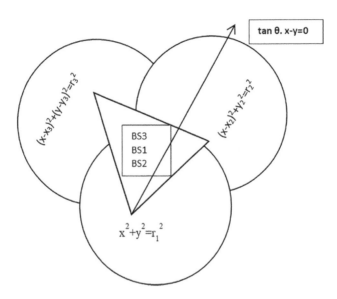

FIGURE 7.18
Geometrical layout of three circles.

of the ANN model, the position of the MS is predicted. Further, the ANN model was enhanced by considering the AOA measurement and the three TOA measurements. The intersection of three TOA and one AOA information gives the alignment of the MS with respect to the BS.

The single AOA measurement helps find angle between the serving BS and the MS. So, intersection between three TOA and the AOA are given as input to the ANN and the location of the MS is estimated. These parameters are given as input to ANN model and were found by the authors that the proposed algorithm can reduce NLOS errors and obtain a more accurate MS location estimate.

7.7.3.2 ANN-Based Call Handoff Management Scheme for Mobile Cellular Network

In [30–34], ANN-based handoff algorithm is proposed which has the capability to give more accurate results. A handoff process is basically changing of the controlling base station when the mobile station moves from one cell to other. So, in order to make the call continuous, a handoff process is required. The handoff has to be initiated in such a manner that there is no unnecessary handoff, or there is no call termination. Handoff is dependent on the velocity characteristics and path loss which further depends on the distance between the transmitting base station and the mobile station, path loss exponent, and the velocity of the MS. So based on these factors, an algorithm is developed in this paper.

Signal strength from serving and target base stations and traffic intensities of the serving and target base stations are considered. A three-layered ANN model is chosen in the design. Signal strengths from serving and target base stations are estimated using the least square estimation method incorporating Rayleigh fading. The input parameters to the ANN model are signal strength of mobile from the serving base station and the transmitted base station, traffic intensity of the serving, and target base station. Depending on these parameters, ANN model will decide whether a hand off is required. So, the handoff process is initiated at a proper state of network.

7.7.3.3 A Hybrid Path Loss Prediction Model based on Artificial Neural Networks

In [38], the authors presented a hybrid, error correction-based NN model to predict path loss for suburban areas at 800 and 2,600 MHz, ECC-33, Ericsson 9999, Okumura Hata, and 3GPP's TR 36.942. Feedforward ANN model is designed by combining empirical propagation models. The efficiency and accuracy of hybrid model were compared against common types of the empirical models, and a simple NN fed with input data commonly used in related works. At the end, the hybrid NN obtained the lowest RMSE indexes, besides almost equalizing the distribution of simulated and experimental data, indicating greater similarity with measurements. Prediction data are calculated by models Ericsson 9999, Free Space, ECC-33, and TR 36.942.

The experiment was set in suburban areas, at frequencies of 800 and 2,600 MHz. ECC-33 model was employed in 2,600 MHz, while Free Space model was employed in the frequency of 800 MHz; Ericsson and TR 36.942 covered both bands. An error correction-based ANN model, using empirical models, is used for prediction of path loss. The ANN is trained to learn the deviation from expected values. The error is obtained by taking the difference between predicted and expected path loss. $E = PL_{\text{measured}} - PL_{\text{predicted}}$. The output of ANN is the corrected path loss. A feedforward multilayer perceptron type with two inputs, one output and one hidden layer, is used. The input data stream consists of two vectors with 455 elements each (in the 2,600 MHz scenario, while in 800 MHz case, it consists in 450 elements). The transfer functions used for hidden and output layers were tangent-sigmoid and linear, respectively, while the algorithm chosen to train the network was the Levenberg-Marquardt backpropagation [35–39].

7.7.3.4 Classification of Primary Radio Signals

A new technique, automatic modulation classification (AMC) proposed in Ref. [40–43] developed a primary modulation technique in the cognitive radio environment. The objective of the ANN training is to identify primary signal's modulation technique. So, AMC here tries to distinguish 2ASK, 4ASK, BPSK QPSK, and 2FSK from each other. Power spectral density, standard deviation of absolute value of the nonlinear components of the instantaneous phase, standard deviation of the direct value of nonlinear component of direct instantaneous phase, and standard deviation of the absolute value of the normalized instantaneous amplitude values of different modulation techniques are applied as input to the ANN system. The NN is trained with these four characteristics of the signal at the input to identify the modulation technique used. 2,500 training data sets with four inputs and five outputs is used to make the NN learn to identify and distinguish the modulated signals. The structure of ANN has seven neurons in the hidden layer and five neurons in the output layer [45]. The ANN system precisely identifies the modulation technique [46] (Figure 7.19).

7.7.3.5 Channel Capacity Estimation Using ANN

The radio spectrum has become a scarce resource because of evolving technology and the increased demand for spectrum. Most relevant technology under development that enables one to utilize the available spectrum more efficiently [17] is the cognitive radio (CR). The cognitive radio tries to identify which frequency bands are free and which are occupied with a primary user. An ANN system is designed to estimate the channel capacity of received signal. This obtained information is analyzed theoretically which is subsequently verified by a suitable simulation scheme for identifying possible white space in

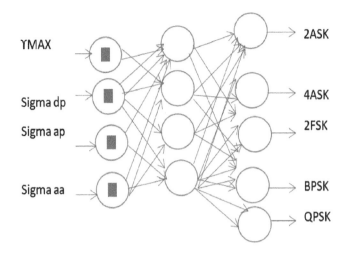

FIGURE 7.19
Multilayer feed-forward network.

a given band. The channel information here is channel capacity which is predicted from the SNR of the channel scanned and the distance between the transmitting and the receiving system. A QPSK transmission and the reception system over an AWGN channel are assumed. Bandwidth of the channel is taken as 5 KHz. This channel state information is analyzed by determining bandwidth efficiency and mutual information for identifying spectrum holes. We observe that channel capacity predicted by the ANN model can be considered as a decision-making parameter to declare the channel occupancy status as it provides a measure of bandwidth efficiency, entropy (H), and mutual information (I) over the channel.

In this section, we have discussed how ANN can be applied in the various communication systems for increasing the QoS of the system. ANN can be applied to make communication system learn and adapt to the environment [47–49]. As ANN is being applied in various optimization aspects of a communication system, it makes these systems more adaptive and intelligent.

7.8 Conclusion

In this chapter, we have presented an overview of adaptive filters and neural net, emphasizing the applications and basic algorithm that have already proven them to be useful in practice. Despite the many contribution in respective fields, research efforts continue at a strong pace, and are likely that new applications will be developed in future. The field of neural networks encompasses many other types of network structures and learning algorithms. Indeed, they have been established as an interdisciplinary subject with deep roots in the neurosciences, psychology, mathematics, and the physical sciences, and engineering. Needless to say, they have a major impact on adaptive signal processing, particularly in those applications that require the use of nonlinearity.

References

1. V. Kober, M. Mozerov, I. A. Ovseevich, "Adaptive Correlation Filters for Pattern Recognition", *Pattern Recognition and Image Analysis* 16(3), 425–431, ISSN 1054-6618, 2006.
2. J. Gerardo Avalos, J. C. Sanchez, J. Velazquez, *Applications of Adaptive Filtering*, National Polytechnic Institute Mexico, Mexico, 2011.
3. M. M. Daffalla, A. A. Babiker, *Adaptive Coding, Modulation and Filtering of Radar Signals*, Institute of Space Research and Aerospace (ISRA), Khartoum, 2000.
4. C.-F. Westin, H. Knutsso, R. Kikinis, "Adaptive Image Filtering", In *Handbook of Medical Imaging*, editor I. Bankman, Academic Press, Orlando, FL, pp. 19–31, 2000.
5. B. Farhang-Boroujeny, *Adaptive Filter Theory and Applications*, University of Utah, Salt Lake City, 2013.
6. M. Lavanya, A. Kalaiselvi, "High speed FIR adaptive filter for Radar applications", *IEEE WiSPNET 2016 Conference*, Chennai, India, 2016.
7. S. Haykin, *Neural Networks*, 2nd edition, Mc Master University Hamilton, Ontario, Canada.
8. R. Govil, "Neural Networks in Signal Processing", In *Fuzzy Systems and Soft Computing in Nuclear Engineering*, editor D. Ruan, Springer, Hiedelberg, pp. 235–257, 2000.
9. B. C. Kamble, "Speech Recognition Using Artificial Neural Network", *International Journal of Computing, Communications & Instrumentation Engineering* 3, 61–64, 2016.
10. A. Patnaik, D. E Anagnostou, R. K. Mishra, C. G. Christodoulou, J. C. Lyke, "Applications of Neural Networks in Wireless Communications", *IEEE Antennas and Propagation Magazine* 46, 130–137, 2004.
11. C.-S. Chen, "Artificial Neural Network for Location Estimation in Wireless Communication Systems", *Sensors* 12, 2798–2817, 2012. doi:10.3390/s120302798.
12. P. P. Bhattacharya, A. Sarkar, I. Sarkar, S. Chatterjee, "An ANN Based Call Handoff Management Scheme for Mobile Cellular Network", *International Journal of Wireless & Mobile Networks (IJWMN)* 5(6), 2013. doi:10.5121/ijwmn.2013.5610.
13. B. J. Cavalcanti, G. A. Cavalcante, L. M. de Mendonça, G. M. Cantanhede, M. M. de Oliveira, A. G. D'Assunção, "A Hybrid Path Loss Prediction Model Based on Artificial Neural Networks Using Empirical Models for LTE And LTE-A at 800 MHz and 2600 MHz", *Journal of Microwaves, Optoelectronics and Electromagnetic Applications* 16(3), 708–722, 2017.
14. J. J Popoola, R. V. Olst, "Application of Neural Network for Sensing Primary Radio Signals in a Cognitive Radio Environment", *AFRICON*, pp. 1–6, Victoria falls, Zambia, September 2011.
15. E. E. Azzouz, A. K. Nandi, *Automatic Modulation Recognition of Communication Signals*, Kluwer Academic Publishers, Boston, MA, pp. 46–47, 1996.
16. J. Mitola III, "Cognitive Radio: An Integrated Agent Architecture for Software Defined Radio", Ph.D. Dissertation Royal Institute of Technology, Sweden, May 2000.
17. M. Bellanger, *Adaptive Digital Filters*, Second edition, Marcel Dekker, New York, ISBN 978-0-8247-0563-7, 2001.
18. W. Chen, T. Nemoto, T. Kobayashi, T. Saito, E. Kasuya, Y. Honda, "ECG and Heart Rate Detection of Prenatal Cattle Fœtus Using Adaptive Digital Filtering", *Proceedings of the 22nd Annual International Conference of the IEEE*, Vol. 2, Chicago, IL, USA, 2000.
19. P. Diniz, *Adaptive Filtering, Algorithms and Practical Implementation*, Third edition, Springer, Boston, MA, ISBN 978-0-387-31274-3, 2008.
20. P. He, G. Wilson, C. Rusell, "Removal of Ocular Artifacts from Electroencephalogram by Adaptive Filtering", *Medical & Biological Engineering & Computing* 42(3), 407–412, 2004.
21. S. Kuo, B. Lee, W. Tian, *Real Time Digital Signal Processing*, Second edition, John Wiley & Sons Ltd, West Sussex, ISBN 978-0-470-01495-4, 2006.
22. G. Ma, F. Gran, F. Jocobsen, F. Agerkvist, "Adaptive Feedback Cancellation with Band-Limited LPC Vocoder in Digital Hearing Aids", *IEEE Transactions on Audio, Speech, and Language Processing* 19, 677–687, 2010.

23. A. Spriet, G. Rombouts, M. Moonen, J. Wouters, "Adaptive Feedback Cancellation in Hearing Aids", *Journal of the Franklin Institute* 343(6), 545–573, 2006.

24. A. Shoval, D. Johns, W. Snelgrove, "Comparison of DC Offset Effects in Four LMS Adaptive Algorithms", *IEEE Transactions on Circuits and Systems-II: Analog and Digital Signal Processing* 42(3), 176–185, 1995.

25. S. Vaseghi, *Advanced Digital Signal Processing and Noise Reduction*, Third edition, John Wiley & Sons Ltd, West Sussex, ISBN 978-0-470-09494-X, 2006.

26. P. S. Wright, P. Clarkson, M. J. Hall, "Application of Adaptive Noise Cancelling Filters in AC Electrical Measurements", *Conference on Precision Electromagnetic Measurements (CPEM)*, Daejeon, ISBN 978-1-4244-6795-2, 2010.

27. M. D. Rohan, A. J. Patil, "Layered Approach for ECG betas Classification Utilizing Neural Network Functions", *International Journal of Engineering Research and Applications (IJREA)* 2(6), 1495–1500, ISSN: 2248-9622, 2012.

28. J. J. Hannah, S. S. Priyadharsini, "Patient Adaptive ECG Beat Classifier Using Repetition Detection Approach Enhanced by Neural Networks", *International Conference on Computing and Research and Control Engineering (ICCCE 2012)*, Vols. 12 & 13, ISBN: 978-1-4675-2248-9, Chennai, India, 2012.

29. K. O. Gupta and P. N. Chatur, "ECG Signal Analysis and Classification using Data Mining and Artificial Neural Networks", *International Journal of Emerging Technology Advanced Engineering*, 2(1), 56–60, ISSN: 2250-2459, 2012.

30. S. Haykin, *Neural Networks: A Comprehensive Foundation*, Prentice-Hall, Upper Saddle River, NJ, 1999.

31. S. Rajasekaran, G. A. V. Pai, *Neural Network, Fuzzy and GA Algorithms: Synthesis and Applications*, PHI, New Delhi, 2013.

32. W. H. Tranter et al., "A Survey of Artificial Intelligence for Cognitive Radio", *IEEE Transactions on Vehicular Technology*, 59(4), 1578–1592, 2010.

33. C.-S. Chen, "Artificial Neural Network for Location Estimation in Wireless Communication Systems", *Sensors* 12, 2798–2817, 2012.

34. P. P. Bhattacharya, A. Sarkar, I. Sarkar, S. Chatterjee, "An ANN Based Call Handoff Management Scheme for Mobile Cellular Network", *International Journal of Wireless & Mobile Networks (IJWMN)* 5(6), 2013. doi:10.5121/ijwmn.2013.5610.

35. S. Pattanayak, R Nandi, "Identification of Spectrum Holes using ANN Model for Cognitive Radio Applications", *IEEE EUROCON*, 2013.

36. V. Anvangot, V. G. Menon, A. Nayyar, "Distributed Big Data Analytics in the Internet of Signals", *SMART*, IEEE, 2018.

37. S. Kuo, C. Chen, "Implementation of Adaptive Filters with the TMS320C25 or the TMS320C30", In *Digital Signal Processing Applications with the TMS320 Family*, editor P. Papamichalis, Prentice-Hall, Englewood Cliffs, NJ, pp. 191–271, 1991.

38. Analog Devices, Adaptive Filters, in ADSP-21000 Family Application Handbook, Vol. 1, Analog Devices, 1994, pp. 157–203.

39. J. G. Proakis, M. Salehi, *Communication Systems Engineering*, Prentice-Hall, Englewood Cliffs, NJ, 1994.

40. R.W. Lucky, "|Techniques for Adaptive Equalization of Digital Communication Systems", *Bell Labs Technical Journal* 45, 255–286, 1966.

41. D. E. Borth, I. A. Gerson, J. R. Haug, C. D. Thompson, "A Flexible Adaptive FIR Filter VLSI IC", *IEEE Journal on Selected Areas in Communications* 6(3), 494–503, 1988.

42. S. U. H. Qureshi, "Adaptive Equalization," *Proceedings of the IEEE* 73(9), 1349–1387, 1985.

43. K. Murano, S. Unagami, F. Amano, "Echo Cancellation and Applications", *IEEE Communications Magazine* 28(1), 49–55, 1990.

44. M. El-Sharkawy, "Designing Adaptive FIR Filters and Implementing Them on the DSP56002 Processor", In *Digital Signal Processing Applications with Motorola's DSP56002 Processor*, Prentice-Hall, Upper Saddle River, NJ, pp. 319–342, 1996.

8

Adaptive Decision Feedback Equalizer Based on Wavelet Neural Network

Saikat Majumder

National Institute of Technology

CONTENTS

8.1 Introduction

Equalizers are one of the important building blocks of wireless communication receivers for compensating the effects of inter-symbol interference (ISI) resulting from dispersive channels. Equalizers are also utilized for removing distortion in received signal affected by nonlinearities in transmitter and receiver hardware. Equalization aids in combating multipath and noise effect of channel resulting in enhancement of performance and spectral efficiency. Moreover, due to widespread access of internet through mobile devices and increasing requirement of high data rate, more and more bits are required to be transmitted in a small duration. As a consequence, interference between symbols (i.e., ISI) will continue to increase many folds in future and will demand significant improvement in equalizer performance.

Linear equalizers were first introduced by Robert W. Lucky in 1965 to eliminate the distortion caused by the transmission channel (Lucky 2006). The original form of the equalizer utilized the conventional gradient descent method to train the weights of the tapped delay line. Various adaptive equalizers were proposed since then, which are based on gradient descent algorithms and minimize MSE of the output to achieve the desired objective of removing ISI from the received signal (Haykin 2008). However, the performance of these linear equalizers with gradient descent learning is severely constrained in channels with deep spectral nulls in their magnitude response or has severe nonlinear distortions. Numerous research studies have shown that the performance of nonlinear equalizers is far superior compared to their linear counterpart in such cases. Decision feedback equalizers (DFEs) are one such category of nonlinear equalizers which is more robust to ISI and nonlinear effects in channel compared to linear equalizers. DFEs also show excellent capabilities for tracking changes in time-varying channels (Ling and Proakis 1985).

In recent times, neural networks have been applied to numerous engineering problems successfully (Abiodun et al. 2018). Artificial neural networks (ANNs) can learn complex mapping functions and can perform decision between regions with nonlinear boundaries. In the literature, several innovative applications of ANNs have been proposed recently. Jay et al. proposed multilayer perceptron and long-term short-term memory-based models for predictions of cryptocurrency price (Jay et al. 2020). A cancer disease diagnosis system was proposed by Al-Zubi et al. by utilizing ANN and ensemble classification technique (Al-Zubi et al. 2019). The resulting algorithm can classify attributes of cancer patients with higher accuracy and lesser false alarm rate. In a study by Farsad and Goldsmith (2018), the authors show that symbols transmitted through wireless channel can be detected without the knowledge of underlying communication channel model using neural networks. They evaluated the proposed model for data transmitted over the molecular communication platform.

Due to the ability of ANNs in efficiently modeling arbitrary nonlinearities, different neural network architectures and training algorithms were proposed for channel equalization. One of the first instances of application of ANN for digital communication channel equalization was proposed in Siu et al. (1990) and Chen et al. (1990), where multilayer perceptron (MLP) architecture is used. In their work, authors show that MLP equalizers perform better in general and overcome some of the limitations of equalizer based on LMS algorithm. Recently, radial basis function (RBF) neural network was proposed for equalization in coherent optical orthogonal frequency division multiplexing (OFDM) system (Ahmad and Kumar 2016). RBF neural networks are single hidden layer networks with significantly reduced complexity compared to MLP neural networks. Zhao et al. proposed a DFE using functional link neural network with LMS learning algorithm (Zhao et al. 2011). The novelty of the work lies in utilizing a finite impulse response (FIR) filter along with FLNN to accommodate for linear channels. The authors showed that this scheme results in improvement of convergence speed without further increase in steady-state error. A block LMS algorithm operating on fast Fourier transform (FFT) of the received signal and subsequent equalization using FLNN was proposed in a study by Sahoo and Mohanty (2016). The proposed equalizer is also based on decision feedback principle and is evaluated in terms of eye diagram and BER. An extreme learning machine (ELM)-based model was proposed for channel prediction and equalization for the OFDM system in a study by Liu et al. (2019). ELM is a variety of ANN in which only the weights at the output layer are trained and have significantly reduced training time requirement. In a study by Jarajreh (2019), an ANN design is proposed to compensate the nonlinearities introduced by the optical fiber channel. It was shown by those authors that the application of ANN equalizers enables extension of transmission reach compared to the existing techniques.

Some of the recent developments on recurrent neural networks (RNNs) have also benefited channel equalization research. RNNs are a kind of neural network with feedback. They are typically used for modeling dynamical systems in which output is not just dependent on the present input, but also on the previous states also. RNN are capable of outperforming both MLP and RBF neural networks, despite the large training complexity. Several computationally efficient equalizer designs based on RNN were proposed in literature (Zhao et al. 2011; Li et al. 2017). Li et al. (2017) leverage shift-invariance properties of convolutional neural network to learn matched filters. Learnt matched filters are then fed into RNN with long-short term memory (LSTM) memory cells for temporal modeling of the channel. In general, popular training methods for RNNs are computationally expensive and often have extremely slow convergence. Reservoir computing (RC) techniques are often proposed as a substitute for RNN. An echo state network (ESN)-based MIMO-OFDM equalization and detection technique was proposed by Mosleh et al. (2017). ESN neural networks belong to the broad class of RC techniques which can be trained without the complexity of RNN. In studies by Bauduin et al. (2015) and Majumder (2020a), ESN was applied for equalization of nonlinear satellite and wireless communication channels. Deep neural networks (DNNs) are also increasingly finding application in the field of channel equalization. Generally, DNNs are neural networks having a large number of hidden layers and have feature learning ability. In Ye et al. (2017), DNN is trained for channel estimation and signal detection for OFDM network. A variational autoencoder-based blind channel equalizer and decoder was proposed in (Caciularu and Burshtein 2020), in which the authors consider detection of symbols transmitted over ISI channels. They demonstrate significant and consistent improvement in error rate compared to existing techniques like constant modulus algorithm (CMA) equalizers. A DNN-based equalizer was proposed for equalization and detection of multilayer magnetic recording in a study by Aboutaleb et al. (2020). In this work, a convolutional neural network is utilized for equalization and separation of signals from each other. Finally, detection is performed by multilayer magnetic recording Viterbi detection algorithm.

Wavelet neural network (WNN) is an important tool in time series analysis. Similar to RBF neural networks, they are a single hidden layer network consisting of multiple neurons, which are linearly added at the output node. But unlike RBF neural networks, neurons in the hidden layer of WNN utilize wavelets functions for activation (Yang and Hu 2016). Though ANNs can be used to model any nonlinear dynamical system, classical sigmoidal networks have a series of drawbacks. With sigmoidal activation function, there is significant chance that training algorithm will converge to local minima. Moreover, random weight initialization in conventional neural network results in extended training times. WNN allows for constructive procedures for efficient initialization of the parameters of the network, resulting in reduced training time (Alexandridis and Zapranis 2013). WNN have been used in a variety of prediction applications, like load forecasting (Ribeiro et al. 2019), wind speed prediction (Zhang et al. 2019), distributed cooperative learning (Xie et al. 2019), and channel equalization (Majumder 2020b; Majumder and Giri 2020). Pradhan et al. proposed one of the first algorithms for WNN-based equalization of linear and nonlinear channels (Pradhan et al. 2006). They proposed a scheme to train WNN using extended Kalman filter based recursive algorithm and demonstrated its superiority over MLP and RBF neural network. Recently, Nanda et al. developed equalizers based on WNN trained by symbiotic organism's search (SOS) algorithm (Nanda and Jonwal 2017). They optimized the output weights of the WNN to achieve desired performance, leaving the translation and dilation parameters unchanged.

In recent times, swarm intelligence algorithms have attracted a lot of attention in problem solving in various fields (Nayyar et al. 2018; Nayyar and Nguyen 2018). Swarm intelligence refers to the field of artificial intelligence in which an intelligent multiagent system is designed by taking inspiration from the collective behavior of animals or insects in nature for problem solving (Beni 2020). In a study by Lipa et al. (2015), a bio-inspired time synchronization protocol was proposed for cognitive radio networks. The protocol is inspired by the synchronization observed in fireflies in which they seem to glow or dim together. This algorithm allows cognitive radio nodes to synchronize in a decentralized manner. Sutantyo and Levi proposed an algorithm inspired by firefly and frog for facilitating scheduling within robotic swarm (Sutantyo and Levi 2015). They have shown through simulations and experiments that the proposed swarm-based model is robust and viable for underwater swarm robots. Swarm intelligence was applied for wind energy potential and prediction of wind speed in the study by Zhao et al. (2019), which can be beneficial for wind farm management.

Various optimization algorithms based on swarm intelligence have been proposed in recent times. Ant colony optimization and particle swarm optimization are the best examples of such optimization algorithms and have been immensely popular (Mavrovouniotis et al. 2017). Inspired by the swarm behavior of a grasshopper, an optimization algorithm called grasshopper search optimization (GOA) was proposed to find the optimal shape of bar truss and cantilever beams (Saremi et al. 2017). An optimization algorithm called salp swarm optimization (SSA) was proposed by Mirjalili et al. based on the swarming behavior of salps when moving and foraging in oceans (Mirjalili et al. 2017). Besides swarm intelligence algorithms, another class of nature inspired algorithms is evolutionary algorithms. Instead of swarm behavior, they derive their capability from the theory of evolution and how species develop over multiple generations. Some optimization algorithms in this class are genetic algorithm (Mirjalili 2019), differential evolution (DE) (Opara and Arabas 2019), and biogeography-based optimization (BBO) (Ma et al. 2017).

Recently, metaheuristic techniques applied to equalization problems have shown significant improvement over conventional algorithms. Unlike conventional gradient-based optimization algorithms, nature-inspired or metaheuristic learning techniques can avoid getting trapped in local optima. Particle swarm optimization (PSO) is one such heuristic algorithm which was applied for optimization of weights in channel equalizers (Al-Awami et al. 2011; Al-Shaikhi et al. 2019; Iqbal et al. 2014). A modification to the PSO algorithm which resulted in improved performance of adaptive equalizer compared to other similar schemes was presented by Al-Awami et al. (2011). Al-Shaikhi et al. (2019) proposed a modification to PSO the algorithm, called hybrid PSO (HPSO) for improvement in equalizer performance. HPSO includes randomization and assignment of inertia weights to the particles so that they do not get trapped in local minima. In the study by Iqbal et al. (2014), a PSO trained equalizer for single carrier frequency division multiple access (SC-FDMA) system is proposed, where the authors demonstrate its robustness in high Doppler scenario. Decision feedback equalizers (DFEs) are known to outperform linear FIR equalizers in terms of performance. A DFE equalizer for multiple-input multiple output (MIMO) system was proposed for channels with high eigenvalue spread in the study by Iqbal et al. (2015). In it, the authors presented a hybrid of PSO and least mean square (LMS) algorithm to demonstrate improved performance over equalizer utilizing only PSO. Equalizer structures with FIR and infinite impulse response (IIR) filters optimized by moth flame optimization (MFO) was proposed by Nanda and Garg (2019). While the proposed FIR equalizer is an adaptive equalizer, the IIR equalizer is a blind adaptive equalizer for IIR channel.

Due to the ability of ANN in accurately modeling the nonlinearities present in wireless channel, several neural networks, which are optimized by nature inspired algorithm, were proposed in the literature. A neural network equalizer trained by the PSO algorithm was proposed for recovery of signal transmitted over ISI and nonlinear channels (Das et al. 2014). Panda et al. proposed a training algorithm based on directed search optimization (DSO) for neural network for equalization over nonlinear channel (Panda et al. 2015). Subsequently, the authors also proposed a neural network equalizer trained by shuffled frog leaping algorithm (SFLA) in Panda et al. (2014). A radial basis function neural network was introduced for equalization of wireless communication channel in the study by Sahu et al. (2018), where the authors proposed to train the RBF-NN with SFLA. In their study, Ingle and Jatoth (2020) enhanced the JAYA optimization algorithm with Levy search to mitigate its shortcoming due to lack of diversity of population and weak exploration capability. The proposed optimization algorithm was then utilized for training a FLNN equalizer. A quantum behaved PSO algorithm was proposed for training ANN based equalizer in Das et al. (2018). In this work, besides training the network weights, the authors also optimize the ANN topology using quantum PSO algorithm.

Through extensive literature survey, it has been observed that neural network-based equalizers are more suited for equalization over nonlinear channels compared to adaptive equalizers with the FIR structure. Moreover, decision feedback equalizers provide better BER performance in channels with deep spectral nulls and time-varying channel. Though there are some recent works on simple DFE equalizers trained by nature inspired algorithm (Iqbal et al. 2015), the literature on DFE based on neural networks and their training by metaheuristic algorithm is scant. Inspired by the WNN-based equalizer and its training by SOS algorithm (Nanda and Jonwal 2017), we propose a WNN decision feedback equalizer (WNN DFE) for communication channel suffering from ISI and nonlinearity. Significant contributions of this work are as follows:

1. New equalizer architecture based on WNN and decision feedback principle is proposed. The proposed structure allows equalization of symbols transmitted through time-varying channels and channels with deep spectral nulls.

2. In this work, we develop a new training method for WNN using cuckoo search optimization (CSO). To the best of our survey of existing literature, there is no existing scheme on training of WNN DFE equalizer with CSO.

3. In contrast to WNN equalizer proposed in Nanda and Jonwal (2017), in which only outer layer weights are modified in the process of training, proposed WNN DFE trains all the weights of the network, including translation and dilation parameters. This is especially challenging considering the involvement of a large number of parameters but results in significantly improved performance.

The rest of this chapter is organized as follows. System model for the study and some basic principles of equalization are introduced in Section 8.2. Principles of wavelet and the architecture of wavelet neural networks are described in Section 8.3. Section 8.4 introduces the CSO algorithm and presents the proposed architecture of WNN DFE. CSO-based training algorithm for WNN DFE is also given in this section. Simulation results are presented and discussed in Section 8.5. Finally, this chapter concludes in Section 8.6 with some scope of future work discussed.

8.2 System Model

8.2.1 Channel Equalization

The system model for the proposed equalizer is shown in Fig. 8.1. In it, the channel is modeled as FIR filter with impulse response $\mathbf{h} = [h_1, \dots h_i, \dots, h_{N_h}]$, where N_h is the length of the response. The impulse response $\mathbf{h}$ reflects the combined effect of channel response, transmit, and receive filters. In this work, we consider baseband equivalent model, and the channel is excited by binary phase shift keying (BPSK) symbols $u(n) \in \{+1, -1\}$ at time n. The output of the channel in response to input $u(n)$ is

$$v(n) = \sum_{i=1}^{N_h} h_i u(n-i) \tag{8.1}$$

While going through power amplifier stage of the transmitter, nonlinear effects are introduced into the signal in the form of function $\Phi(.)$. Signal received is further corrupted by additive white Gaussian noise $w(n)$ of mean $E[w(n)] = 0$ and variance σ^2. Thus, input to the adaptive equalizer is given as

$$x(n) = \Phi(v(n)) + w(n), \quad n = 1, \dots, N \tag{8.2}$$

where

N is the number of received symbols.

The purpose of the equalization is to mitigate the ISI effects caused by the FIR channel as well as neutralize the nonlinear distortions caused by the transmit/receive hardware. It is to be noted that in a typical communication receiver, equalizer operates in baseband and is placed after matched filter cum sampler stage. Equalizer reconstructs the transmitted sequence $u(n)$ or its delayed version $y(n) = u(n-d)$, where d is the propagation delay. An equalizer is trained with pair of training dataset $\{x(n), y(n)\}$, $n = 1, \dots, N$, with the objective to minimize the expected value of squared error $E[e^2(n)] = E\left[|\hat{y}(n) - y(n)|^2\right]$, where $\hat{y}(n)$ is the actual output of the equalizer corresponding to the input $x(n)$. After training is completed, the weights are frozen, and subsequent symbols are detected based on these weights. The last stage consists of decision device which maps the continuous signal to discrete symbol set (Figure 8.1). For BPSK transmission, the output of the decision device is given as

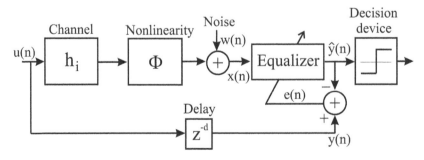

FIGURE 8.1
Transmitter and receiver system consisting of an equalizer in a wireless communication setup.

$$\hat{u}(n) = \text{sign}\{\hat{y}(n)\} = \begin{cases} 1, & \hat{y}(n) \geq 0 \\ -1, & \text{otherwise.} \end{cases} \tag{8.3}$$

8.2.2 Decision Feedback Equalization

Linear equalizer model as described in Section 8.2.1 is effective on simple channels like wireline telephony, where the problem of ISI is not too severe. The severity of an ISI channel is dependent on the spectral characteristics of the channel and is measured in terms of eigenvalue ratio (EVR) (Haykin 2008). Channels with larger EVR have a higher degree of spectral null, and linear equalizers will need to produce higher gains to compensate it. This will result in increased noise gain and significantly poorer equalizer performance. Nonlinear equalizers like DFE are not limited by such constraints and are suitable for both nonlinear channels and channels with high EVR. A DFE operates by utilizing the previous outputs of the equalizer to cancel out the ISI from the present symbol.

A simplified block diagram of a conventional DFE is shown in Figure 8.2, consisting of three main units: feed forward filter, decision device, and feedback filter. The input to the equalizer is noisy and distorted signal $x(n)$, while the output is an estimate $\hat{u}(n)$ of the transmitted symbol. If the feed-forward filter and feedback filters are of length N_f and N_b, respectively, the states of these filters at time n are given as

$$\mathbf{x}(n) = \left[x(n), \ldots, x(n - N_f + 1) \right] \tag{8.4}$$

$$\mathbf{u}(n) = \begin{cases} \left[y(n-1), \ldots y(n-N_b) \right], & \text{in training mode} \\ \left[\hat{u}(n-d-1), \ldots, \hat{u}(n-d-N_b) \right], & \text{in decision directed mode} \end{cases} \tag{8.5}$$

Input to the decision device is then obtained as

$$\hat{y}(n) = \sum_{i=1}^{N_f} x(n-i+1) h_i^f - \sum_{j=1}^{N_b} \hat{u}(n-d-j) h_j^b \tag{8.6}$$

where

$\left[h_1^f, \ldots, h_{N_f}^f \right]$ and $\left[h_1^b, \ldots, h_{N_b}^b \right]$ are filter coefficients of the feedforward and feedback filters, respectively.

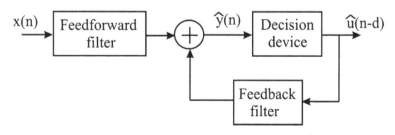

FIGURE 8.2
Simple block diagram of a DFE.

In the training mode, symbols $\left[\hat{u}(n-d-1),\ldots,\hat{u}(n-d-N_b)\right]$ in Equation (8.6) are replaced by the known target vector $\left[y(n-1),\ldots y(n-N_b)\right]$. The error signal is given as

$$e(n) = \begin{cases} y(n)-\hat{y}(n), & \text{in training mode} \\ \hat{u}(n-d)-\hat{y}(n), & \text{in decision directed mode} \end{cases} \tag{8.7}$$

The objective of training algorithm is to minimize the MSE given by $E\left[\left|e(n)\right|^2\right]$ which is achieved by adjusting the weights of feedforward and feedback filters.

8.3 Wavelet Neural Network

Wavelets were first introduced in the field of multiresolution analysis and have since been applied to numerous areas including signal processing (Goswami and Chan 2011). WNN, on the other hand, is usually a three-layer neural network consisting of input, hidden and output layer. Contrary to ANN, the hidden layer in WNN consists of wavelet bases as activation function instead of sigmoid function. The idea of WNN is to iteratively update the parameter of wavelet basis suitable for the training data. In this section, the fundamental concepts of wavelet analysis and WNN are explained.

8.3.1 Wavelet Analysis

The ability of wavelet transforms which distinguishes it from Fourier transform is its ability to efficiently represent an arbitrary signal in both time and frequency domain. It allows us to identify the time at which specific frequency components appear, exist or vanish. This is possible due to *compact support* feature of wavelet basis functions. Compact support of wavelet basis function allows the wavelet transform to efficiently represent abrupt changes or localized features in the signal.

Wavelet basis is generated from translation and dilation of *mother wavelet* ψ. The mother wavelet is a short duration oscillatory signal whose average value is zero, i.e.,

$$\int \psi(t)\,dt = 0 \tag{8.8}$$

besides fulfilling other requirements like admissibility condition (Goswami and Chan 2011). Translated and dilated versions of mother wavelet are given as

$$\psi_{a,b}(t) = \frac{1}{\sqrt{a}}\psi\left(\frac{t-b}{a}\right) \tag{8.9}$$

where
$a > 0$ is the scale or dilation factor, and
b is the position or translation factor. Let us consider an arbitrary function $x(t)$.

The continuous wavelet transform (CWT) of $x(t)$ is given as

$$W(a,b) = \int_{-\infty}^{\infty} x(t) \psi_{a,b}(t) dt \tag{8.10}$$

where
$a \neq 0$.

Wavelet transform $W(a,b)$ can be considered as "strength" or "amplitude" of corresponding basis function $\psi_{a,b}(t)$ component in the signal $x(t)$. Inverse wavelet transform (IWT) allows reconstruction of original signal back from wavelet coefficients $W(a,b)$:

$$x(t) = \frac{1}{C_\psi} \int_{-\infty}^{\infty} \int_{-\infty}^{\infty} \frac{1}{a^2} W(a,b) \psi_{a,b}(t) da \; db \tag{8.11}$$

where

$$C_\psi = \int_{-\infty}^{\infty} \frac{|\psi(\omega)|^2}{\omega} d\omega.$$

Discrete wavelet transform (DWT) is more used in practice due to high computational complexity associated with CWT. But in DWT, instead of discretizing the time, the translation and dilation parameters are taken to be discrete values. If in Equation (8.10), a and b are respectively substituted with 2^{-j} and $k2^{-j}$, where $j, k \in \mathbb{Z}$, DWT of a function $x(t) \in L^2$ is given as

$$W_\psi x(j,k) = 2^{j/2} \int_{-\infty}^{\infty} x(t) \psi(2^j t - k) dt \tag{8.12}$$

To study the reconstruction of a function from wavelet coefficients and the idea behind WNN, multiresolution analysis (MRA) plays an important role. MRA views a function at various levels of approximations or scales. Decomposition of a function $x(t)$ into various scales begins by projecting it into a sufficiently high-resolution subspace $\mathbf{C}_M$, i.e.

$$x_M = \sum_k c_{M,k} \phi(2^M t - k) \in \mathbf{C}_M \tag{8.13}$$

Thus, subspace $\mathbf{C}_\infty$ is the space of original analog (continuous-time) signal $x(t)$, and $x_M \in \mathbf{C}_M \subseteq \mathbf{C}_\infty$ is its lower resolution version. Subspace $\mathbf{C}_j$ at each level is itself composed of coarser approximation subspace $\mathbf{C}_{j-1}$ and a wavelet subspace $\mathbf{W}_{j-1}$. Since the subspaces are nested, we can write

$$\mathbf{C}_M = \mathbf{W}_{M-1} + \mathbf{C}_{M-1}$$

$$= \sum_{i=1}^{l} \mathbf{W}_{M-i} + \mathbf{C}_{M-l} \tag{8.14}$$

where
l is the number of levels of subspace or wavelet decomposition.

The signals in the corresponding subspaces are related as

$$x_M(t) = \sum_{i=1}^{l} y_{M-i}(t) + x_{M-l}(t) \tag{8.15}$$

where

$x_{M-l}(t)$ is the coarsest approximation of x_M, and

$$x_j(t) = \sum_k c_{j,k} \phi(2^j t - k) \in \mathbf{C}_j \tag{8.16}$$

$$y_j(t) = \sum_k w_{j,k} \psi(2^j t - k) \in \mathbf{W}_j \tag{8.17}$$

8.3.2 Wavelet Neural Network

WNN combines the principles of wavelet and neural network into one. From Equation (8.15), it can be concluded that an arbitrary function can be approximated using basis functions from wavelet and approximation subspaces. This idea has led to the development of WNN where scale and position factors are iteratively adapted to approximate a target function.

The simplest form of WNN consists of only one hidden neuron as shown in Figure 8.3. It consists of input x, wavelet function translated by τ and dilated by factor δ. The output of the function is y and computed as follows:

$$y = \psi_{\delta,\tau}(x) = \psi\left(\frac{x-\tau}{\delta}\right) \tag{8.18}$$

The output y of such a neuron is nonzero only when the input lies within the support of the function $\psi_{\delta,\tau}(x)$. Several such single "wavelet neurons" or "wavelons" form a hidden layer of WNN and their output are linearly combined to approximate a given function.

Wavelet neural networks are mainly of two types based on their architecture. The first on is based on relation (8.16) in which a given function is approximated using scaling function ϕ only. In this variety of WNN, wavelet analysis and neural network operations are performed separately (Veitch 2005). Such networks are called *wavenet*, in which signal input to the network is decomposed using different wavelet basis in the hidden layer and then combined at the output layer. In the architecture of wavenets, translation and dilation factors are fixed initially and are not changed during learning process of neural network.

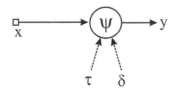

FIGURE 8.3
A single wavelon.

Only weights w_i from hidden layer to the output nodes are modified. The output of such a network is given as

$$y = \sum_{i=1}^{N_\phi} w_i \phi_{\delta,\tau}(x) \qquad (8.19)$$

where

N_ϕ is the number of hidden layer units required to cover the domain of the function to be analyzed, and $\phi_{\delta,\tau}$ is a scaling function.

Wavenets are limited by their fixed set of basis functions and are not suitable for modeling channels with time-varying response. The architecture of wavelet networks in which translation and dilation parameters of the hidden units are also modified, along with output weights of the network, is in the process of training. In prevalent nomenclature, such networks are referred to as *wavelet networks* and are considered in this work. In all the subsequent discussions, we shall mean WNN to be wavelet networks only. Figure 8.4 shows the architecture of a one-dimensional WNN. In contrast to multidimensional WNN discussed in the next section, input x to this network is a scalar or a one-dimensional sequence. Wavelons in this network are shown as $\psi_1, \ldots, \psi_{N_\psi}$ with corresponding values of translation parameters $\tau_1, \ldots, \tau_{N_\psi}$ and dilation parameters $\delta_1, \ldots, \delta_{N_\psi}$. Output y is obtained by weighted sum as

$$y = \sum_{i=1}^{N_\psi} c_i \psi_i(x) + a_0 \qquad (8.20)$$

where

$c_1, \ldots, c_{N_\psi}$ are output layer weights.

The term a_0 in Equation (8.20) is the bias parameter and is required for approximating functions whose mean is not zero.

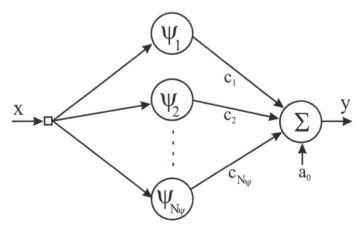

FIGURE 8.4
One-dimensional wavelet neural network.

8.4 Multidimensional Wavelet Neural Network

Based on the WNN model in Alexandridis and Zapranis (2013), a multidimensional wavelet network is constructed in which different inputs are interconnected with multiple hidden units. Outputs of the hidden units $\psi_j(\mathbf{x})$, as well as direct inputs x_i, are then linearly combined, to obtain the final output $\hat{y}$. Fig. 8.5 shows the structure of single hidden-layer multidimensional WNN. For N_I input wavelet network with N_ψ hidden units or wavelons, input-output relation is given as

$$\hat{y} = f(\mathbf{x}) = \sum_{j=1}^{N_\psi} c_j \psi_j(\mathbf{x}) + \sum_{i=1}^{N_I} a_i x_i + a_0 \tag{8.21}$$

where

c_j are weights from wavelons to output,

a_i are weights from input layer to the output, and

a_0 is the bias at the output layer.

In the expression (8.21), $\psi_j(\mathbf{x})$ is a multidimensional wavelet given as

$$\psi_j(\mathbf{x}) = \prod_{i=1}^{N_I} \psi(z_{ij}) \tag{8.22}$$

where

$z_{ij} = (x_i - \tau_{ij})/\delta_{ij}$.

The weights τ_{ij} correspond to translation and δ_{ij} correspond to dilation factors.

For performance evaluation of the proposed equalizer, Mexican hat function is considered for mother wavelet and is given as

$$\psi(z) = (1 - z^2) e^{-z^2/2} \tag{8.23}$$

A WNN with N_I inputs and scalar output $\hat{y}$ is considered, which is trained using a set of N examples $\{\mathbf{x}(n), y(n)\}$, where $\mathbf{x}(n) = [x_1(n), \ldots, x_{N_I}(n)]^T$ is the input vector for training example n. The objective of the training is to minimize mean-square error (MSE) $E\left[|y - \hat{y}|^2\right]$ between target output $y(n)$ and actual network output $\hat{y}(n)$. The WNN can be represented in the form of a parametrized nonlinear model (Figure 8.5):

$$\hat{y}(n) = f(\mathbf{x}(n), \mathbf{w}) \tag{8.24}$$

where the set of adjustable parameters of the WNN is $\mathbf{w} = \{a_0, a_i, c_j, \tau_{ij}, \delta_{ij}\}$ with $i = 1, \ldots, N_I$ and $j = 1, \ldots, N_\psi$.

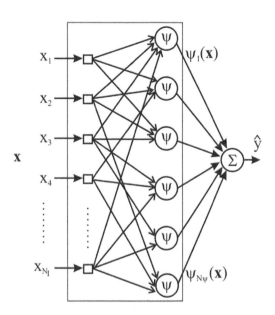

FIGURE 8.5
Architecture of a multidimensional wavelet neural network.

8.5 Proposed WNN DFE Architecture

8.5.1 Equalizer Architecture

Block diagram of the proposed WNN DFE is shown in Fig. 8.6. The equalizer consists of three subsections: N_ψ wavelet basis functions which map the input to vector $[\psi_1(\mathbf{x}), \ldots, \psi_1(\mathbf{x})]$, a feedback finite impulse response (FIR) filter with coefficients $b_1, \ldots, b_{N_B}$ and a feedforward FIR filter with coefficients $a_1, \ldots, a_{N_I}$ connecting inputs to the output $\hat{y}(n)$. The input to the equalizer $\mathbf{x}(n)$ is composed of vector of length N_I, which is applied to N_ψ wavelons or wavelet basis functions and feed-forward FIR filter. Input to the feedback filter part is delayed hard decision outputs $[\hat{u}(n-1), \ldots, \hat{u}(n-N_B)]$ of the equalizer. Output $\hat{y}(n)$ is obtained by adding signals from these three subsections.

$$\hat{y}(n) = \sum_{j=1}^{N_\psi} c_j \psi_j(\mathbf{x}(n)) + \sum_{i=1}^{N_I} a_i x_i(n) + \sum_{k=1}^{N_B} b_k \hat{u}(n-k) + a_0 \qquad (8.25)$$

In Equation (8.25), c_j, $j = 1, \ldots, N_\psi$ are weights of the connections from the output of multidimensional wavelets $\psi_j(\mathbf{x}(n))$ to the output adder. For binary transmission, the estimate of transmitted symbol is obtained at the receiver as (Figure 8.6)

$$\hat{u}(n) = \text{sign}\{\hat{y}(n)\} \qquad (8.26)$$

where

$\quad$ sign$\{\hat{y}\}$ returns the sign of $\hat{y}$.

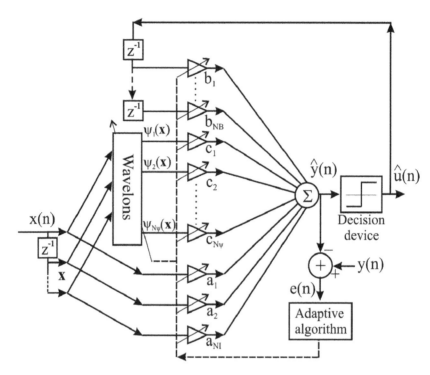

FIGURE 8.6
Wavelet neural network-based decision feedback equalizer.

Parameters of the equalizer are:

$$\mathbf{w} = \left\{ a_0, a_i, c_j, \tau_{ij}, \delta_{ij}, b_k \right\} \tag{8.27}$$

where

$i = 1, \dots, N_I$, $j = 1, \dots, N_\psi$ and $k = 1, \dots, N_B$.

The basic idea of training the equalizer is to adjust parameter vector $\mathbf{w}$ so as to minimize MSE given by

$$\mathcal{M}(\mathbf{w}) = \frac{1}{2N} \sum_{n=1}^{N} \left| y(n) - \hat{y}(n) \right|^2 \tag{8.28}$$

Argument in MSE cost function $\mathcal{M}(\mathbf{w})$ indicates that its value is dependent on network weight vector $\mathbf{w}$. Conventional techniques of training the WNN involve algorithms like BP, EKF LMS, which follow the hill-climbing approach to achieve optimality. However, these techniques are limited by slow rate of convergence and get easily trapped in local optima. In this work, $\mathcal{M}$ is minimized iteratively with the CSO algorithm.

8.5.2 Cuckoo Search Optimization

CSO is an optimization algorithm which mimics the breeding behavior of cuckoo birds (Yang and Deb 2014). Cuckoo birds are known for their aggressive breeding strategy. To increase the probability of survival of their offspring, they practice various types of brood parasitism. Birds of many cuckoo species, like European common cuckoo, lay their eggs in the nests of host species. Generally, eggs of cuckoo birds hatch earlier than the eggs of host bird, and cuckoo chicks can escape before detection. Moreover, shells of cuckoo eggs are stronger than the host bird so that they are not easily damaged. But the cost incurred by the brood parasitism is high on the host species, and it makes all attempt to identify and remove the cuckoo eggs. Thus, there is an evolutionary "arms race" where cuckoos try to fool the host species into making them raise their chicks and host birds trying to prevent it. This competitive behavior is utilized in CSO for finding the optimal solution.

Levy flights are random or quasi-random walks which model the search of food by insects, birds, and animals. It was shown that some fruit flies explore landscape by flying along a straight flight followed by sudden 90-degree turn. Similarly, in some hunter gatherer tribes of human, hunting is done by exploring the landscape in a series of straight paths and then taking a sudden turn. Time series representation of Levy flight is characterized by short burst of activity throughout the time series, resulting in a "heavy tailed" distribution. That is, it has high concentration of short steps and low concentration of large steps, though the concentration of large steps is higher than usual random walk. A distinguishing feature of Levy flight which gives it an edge over normal random walks for exploring wider search space is that its variance increases faster than normal random walks. This reduces the required number of iterations by approximately four orders compared to normal random walk (Mareli and Twala 2018).

In CSO, potential solutions are associated with cuckoo eggs. Cuckoo birds lay their eggs in the nest of other birds with the expectation that their offspring will be raised by the proxy parents. If some of them are identified by the host bird, they are removed from the nest. Based on these ideas, CSO is developed based on the following rules (Abdelaziz and Ali 2015):

- Each cuckoo lays an egg and randomly places it in any one of the nests.
- The nest having good quality of eggs (or solutions) will be permitted to carry over to the next generation.
- In a fixed fraction $p_a \in [0,1]$ of nests, the host bird will be able to identify parasitic eggs. In such cases, these eggs are either dropped, or the host bird completely abandons the nest.

Based on these three rules, the CSO algorithm is summarized in Algorithm 1. In the implementation, initially P random solutions $\mathbf{w}_p^{(0)}$, $p = 1,\ldots, P$ are generated. New solution $\mathbf{w}_p^{(l+1)}$ at $(l+1)$-th generation for p-th cuckoo is generated as

$$\mathbf{w}_p^{(l+1)} = \mathbf{w}_p^{(l)} + \alpha L(\beta) \tag{8.29}$$

where

$0 < \beta \le 2$ is Levy flight parameter and

$\alpha > 0$ is step-size scaling factor.

$L(\beta)$ are random numbers drawn from Levy distribution.

In practice, Levy flights are generated using Mantegna's algorithm as (Yang 2010):

$$L(\beta) = s\left(\mathbf{w}_p^{(l)} - \mathbf{w}_{min}\right) \otimes \mathbf{r} \tag{8.30}$$

where

   $\mathbf{w}_{min}$ is the best nest (with least cost),

   $\mathbf{r} = [r_1, \ldots, r_D]^T$ with $r_i \sim \mathcal{N}(0, 1)$ and $\otimes$ indicates element-wise multiplication of vectors.

In Equation (8.30), step length s is computed as

$$s = \frac{u}{|v|^{1/\beta}} \tag{8.31}$$

where

   $u \sim \mathcal{N}(0, \sigma_u^2)$ and

   $v \sim \mathcal{N}(0, \sigma_v^2)$ are Gaussian random variables with standard deviation.

$$\sigma_u = \left(\frac{\Gamma(1+\beta)\sin\left(\dfrac{\pi\beta}{2}\right)}{\Gamma\left[\dfrac{(1+\beta)}{2}\right] \beta\, 2^{(\beta-1)/2}} \right)^{1/\beta} \tag{8.32}$$

$$\sigma_v = 1 \tag{8.33}$$

However, to accommodate exploration capability of the algorithm, some fraction p_a of new solutions are generated as given below (Abdelaziz and Ali 2015):

$$\mathbf{w}_p^{(l+1)} = \mathbf{w}_p^{(l)} + \alpha\delta \otimes H(p_a - \acute{o}) \otimes \left(\mathbf{w}_i^{(l)} - \mathbf{w}_j^{(l)} \right) \tag{8.34}$$

where

   δ is step size,

   H is Heaviside function,

   $\acute{o}$ is a uniformly distributed random number.

- **Algorithm 1 Cuckoo Search Optimization (CSO)**

Input: Objective function $\mathcal{M}(\mathbf{w})$ with $\mathbf{w} = [w_1, \ldots, w_D]^T$
Initialize: Generate a population of P nests $\mathbf{w}_p^{(0)}$, $p = 1, \ldots, P$.
Evaluate cost of each nest as $\mathcal{M}_p^{(0)}$, with $\mathbf{w}_{min}$ having minimum cost $\mathcal{M}_{min}$.
while ($l < MaxGeneration$) or (stop criteria) **do**
       Generate new solutions $\mathbf{w}_p^{(l)}$ using $\mathbf{w}_{min}$ and Equation (8.29) for $p = 1, \ldots, P$.
       Evaluate its cost as $\mathcal{M}_p^{(l)}$, $p = 1, \ldots, P$.

   if $\mathcal{M}_p^{(l)} > \mathcal{M}_p^{(l-1)}$ **then**

              Replace $\mathbf{w}_p^{(l)}$ by older solution $\mathbf{w}_p^{(l-1)}$.
       end
       Replace a fraction p_a of the worse nests with new ones generated via (8.34).
       Evaluate the nests.
       Based on $\mathcal{M}_p^{(l)}$, find the current best nest as $\mathbf{w}_{min}$.
end

8.5.3 CSO-Based Training of WNN DFE

The proposed algorithm for channel equalization uses CSO for training weights in DFE WNN. The flowchart of the training algorithm is shown in Figure 8.7. While weights in artificial neural network can be initialized randomly, initialization of parameters in WNN needs careful attention. Since wavelet bases are time-shifted oscillatory waveforms of limited duration having an average value of zero, random initialization of τ_{ij} and δ_{ij} may lead to wavelons with zero value (Alexandridis and Zapranis, 2013). It was reported that training algorithms for WNN like gradient descent are severely sensitive to initial values of parameter **w,** and various techniques of initialization were proposed to improve network

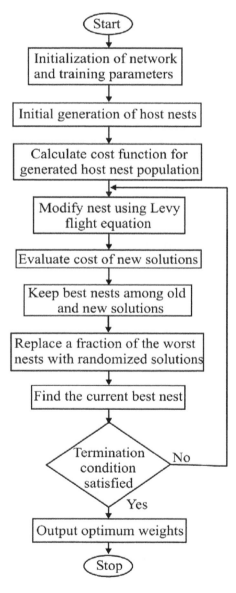

FIGURE 8.7
Flow chart of training WNN DFE with cuckoo search optimization.

performance. In this work, where network parameters are learnt through CSO, we did not find significant difference in performance for different initialization techniques. We adopt a simple technique for initialization of translation and dilation parameters (Alexandridis and Zapranis, 2013):

$$\tau_{ij} = \frac{m_i + M_i}{2} \tag{8.35}$$

$$\delta_{ij} = \frac{M_i - m_i}{5} \tag{8.36}$$

where

m_i and M_i are minimum and maximum value of input x_i, respectively.

All other weights are initialized to a small random number in the range $\left[a_{max}, a_{min} \right]$, where a_{max}, a_{min} are selected through experiments.

Steps involved in the training and testing of the proposed WNN DFE are as follows:

1. **Selection of Network and Optimization Parameters**: Algorithm begins with initialization of network parameters like number of inputs N_I, number of wavelons N_ψ, size of feedback filter N_B, and range of translation and dilation parameters. In addition, channel parameters like type of channel and its EVR, training SNR, and order of the channel filter are specified.

2. **Initialization**: In the next step, elements of vector **w**, which consists of $D = 1 + N_I + N_\psi + N_B + 2N_I N_\psi$ elements, are mapped to a host nest $\mathbf{w}_p = \left[w_{p1}, \dots, w_{pD} \right]$. P vectors of initial population $\mathbf{W} = \left[\mathbf{w}_1, \dots, \mathbf{w}_P \right]^T$ are generated as:

$$\mathbf{W} = \begin{bmatrix} w_{11} & \cdots & w_{1D} \\ \vdots & \ddots & \vdots \\ w_{P1} & \cdots & w_{PD} \end{bmatrix} \tag{8.37}$$

   While the weights corresponding to translation and dilation parameters are initialized according to Equations (8.35) and (8.36), other weights can be initialized uniformly in the range $\left[a_{max}, a_{min} \right]$, where $a_{max} = -a_{min}$.

3. Evaluate the cost of each nest as $\mathcal{M}_p^{(0)}$ using cost function given by (8.28) and find the nest $\mathbf{w}_{min}$ with minimum cost $\mathcal{M}_{min}$.

4. Generate new solutions $\mathbf{w}_p^{(l)}$ using $\mathbf{w}_{min}$ and Equation (8.29) for $p = 1, \dots, P$ and evaluate their costs as $\mathcal{M}_p^{(l)}, p = 1, \dots, P$.

5. Select only those nests $\mathbf{w}_p^{(l)}$ in the present generation for which there is a reduction in cost compared to the previous generation. Otherwise, carryover nests from $(l-1)$-th generation to l-th generation for which cost has not decreased.

6. Replace a fraction p_a of the worse nests with new ones generated via Equation (8.34) and evaluate their costs to find the best nest $\mathbf{w}_{min}$.

7. **Stopping Criteria**: Check if there is no significant change in minimum cost through few generations or maximum number of iterations is attained. If no, go to step 4.

8. **Testing**: Operate the equalizer in decision directed mode by removing the training input $y(n)$ and freezing the weights $\mathbf{w}_{min}$. Compute the testing error as given in Equation (8.7).

8.5.4 Simulation Results and Discussion

To evaluate the effectiveness of the proposed CSO-based training algorithm for WNN DFE, MSE and BER are used as performance measure. The proposed equalizer is compared with some of the recently introduced equalization algorithms based on machine learning and optimization, namely, ANN trained by PSO (Das et al. 2014), ANN trained by SFLA (Panda et al. 2014), WNN trained by SOS (Nanda and Jonwal 2017), FIR equalizer trained by PSO (Al-Shaikhi et al. 2019), and FIR DFE trained by PSO (Iqbal et al. 2015). While the network and simulation parameters for the proposed technique are given in Table 8.1, parameters of all the compared techniques are taken from the respective references. The abbreviated names of the equalization algorithms under consideration are given in Tables 8.2 and 8.3.

TABLE 8.1

Simulation Parameter of the Proposed Equalizer and CSO Algorithm

Network Parameters		CSO Parameters	
Number of inputs N_I	4	Number of nests	25
Number of wavelons N_ψ	8	Discovery rate of alien eggs p_a	0.15
Feedback filter length N_B	2	Levy flight parameter β	1.5
		Maximum number of iterations	500

TABLE 8.2

MSE Performance with Linear Channels Ch 1 or Ch 2 at 20 dB SNR

	Ch 1		Ch 2	
Algorithm	Training	Testing	Training	Testing
ANN PSO (Das et al. 2014)	0.0850	0.0892	0.0557	0.1217
ANN SFLA (Panda et al. 2014)	0.0830	0.0882	0.0429	0.0917
WNN SOS (Nanda and Jonwal 2017)	0.2044	0.2082	0.1879	0.2190
FIR PSO (Al-Shaikhi et al. 2019)	0.2027	0.2044	0.1859	0.2191
FIR DFE (Iqbal et al. 2015)	0.0331	0.0350	0.0353	0.0367
WNN DFE (Proposed)	0.0260	0.0292	0.0310	0.0321

TABLE 8.3

Channel 1 with Nonlinearity (NL 1 or NL 2) at 20 dB SNR

	NL 1		NL 2	
Algorithm	Training	Testing	Training	Testing
ANN PSO (Das et al. 2014)	0.0736	0.0707	0.1048	0.1101
ANN SFLA (Panda et al. 2014)	0.0453	0.0511	0.0894	0.0967
WNN SOS (Nanda and Jonwal 2017)	0.1875	0.1967	0.2166	0.2420
FIR PSO (Al-Shaikhi et al. 2019)	0.1556	0.1649	0.2306	0.2322
FIR DFE (Iqbal et al. 2015)	0.0652	0.0665	0.1750	0.1951
WNN DFE (Proposed)	0.0309	0.0332	0.0517	0.0548

8.5.4.1 *MSE Performance*

In the first set of experiments, the performance of the proposed WNN DFE equalizer is compared with other schemes in the literature. Simulation is performed on two reference channels from Iqbal et al. (2015), whose transfer function are given as

$$\text{Ch 1:}\quad H(z) = 0.408 + 0.816z^{-1} + 0.408z^{-2} \tag{8.38}$$

$$\text{Ch 2:}\quad H(z) = 1 - 1.9114z^{-1} + 0.95z^{-2} \tag{8.39}$$

Further, either of these linear channels is cascaded with one of the three types of nonlinear functions given below (Nanda and Jonwal 2017):

$$\text{NL 0:}\quad y = x \tag{8.40}$$

$$\text{NL 1:}\quad y = \tanh x \tag{8.41}$$

$$\text{NL 2:}\quad y = x + 0.2x^2 - 0.1x^3 \tag{8.42}$$

Obviously, NL 0 is a linear function (linear functions are subclass of nonlinear functions), while other two relations represent different degrees of nonlinearity.

In Table 8.2, the settled value of training and testing MSE for linear channels Ch 1 and Ch 2 are reported. While in this experiment, the nonlinearity model considered is NL 0, training and testing is done for 20 dB SNR. It is observed that the proposed WNN DFE trained by the CSO algorithm provides the lowest MSE among all the considered techniques. Moreover, second to the proposed algorithm, FIR DFE optimized by PSO provides the most competitive performance. Between both the channels, all the considered algorithms show relatively better performance in Ch 1. Further, it can be observed that in the absence of linear mapping in ANN-based models; their performance is worse compared to FIR DFE and the proposed scheme.

In Table 8.3, the effect of nonlinearity on the MSE performance is reported. In this experiment, the simulation setup consists of linear channel Ch 1 in cascade with either NL 1 or NL 2. The received signal SNR is again maintained at 20 dB for all the schemes. In this scenario also, the proposed equalization scheme shows the best performance for both NL 1 and NL 2. Different from the linear channel scenario given earlier, the ANN SFLA algorithm is the second best performing in case of nonlinear channels at 20 dB. This shows that neural network-based equalizers are better in approximating nonlinear functions compared to simple FIR DFE structure of Iqbal et al. (2015).

8.5.4.2 *Effect of EVR*

In the next set of simulations, we study the effect of eigenvalue ratio (EVR) of the channel on the BER performance of the proposed equalizer and compare it with other schemes in the literature. EVR is defined as $\lambda_{max}/\lambda_{min}$, where λ_{max} and λ_{min} are the largest and smallest eigenvalues of received signal correlation matrix $R = E[\mathbf{xx}^T]$, respectively (Haykin 2008). If the EVR of the channel is high, the receiver input signal is more concentrated in the direction of eigenvector corresponding to the largest eigenvalue. The transmitted signal is usually uncorrelated, but on passing through a channel with large EVR, it develops strong correlation resulting in severe ISI. On the other hand, if the EVR of the channel is low, the transmitted signal is less impacted by the channel, and ISI is small. In general, larger EVR results in more distortion and requires more complex equalizer.

To study the effect of EVR, we consider the following raised cosine channel of length $N_h = 3$ (Haykin 2008):

$$h_i = \begin{cases} \frac{1}{2}\left[1+\cos\left(2\pi(i-2)/\Lambda\right)\right], & i = 1,2,3 \\ 0, & \text{otherwise} \end{cases} \quad (8.43)$$

where

parameter Λ controls the EVR of channel.

For instance, EVR of Ch 1 in Equation (8.38) and Ch 2 in Equation (8.39) is 200 and 635, respectively (Iqbal et al. 2015).

The effects of variation of EVR on different channels are shown in Figures 8.8–8.10. In Figure 8.8, the effect of EVR is compared for different equalizers at SNR of 15 dB when the transmitted signal is passed through linear channel specified by Equation (8.43). Figures 8.9 and 8.10 show the simulation results when the signal is transmitted through a cascade of linear channel in Equation (8.43) with nonlinear functions NL 1 and NL 2, respectively. In all the figures, BER increases with increase in EVR and introduction of nonlinearity. In all these results, the proposed equalizer shows significantly better performance compared to all the schemes under consideration.

In the case of linear channel in Figure 8.8, it can be observed that the increase in BER is less severe with increase in EVR for both DFE equalizers. The effect of increase in EVR is more prominent, even for DFE equalizers, in case of nonlinear channels in Figures 8.9 and 8.10. For the channel with NL 2 (in Figure 8.10), the performance of FIR DFE is not much different from other linear and neural network-based equalizers, but the proposed WNN DFE equalizer stands out for exhibiting significantly improved performance.

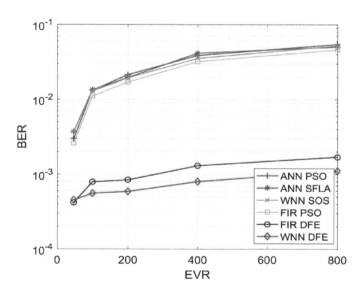

FIGURE 8.8
Effect of EVR for linear channel at SNR of 15 dB.

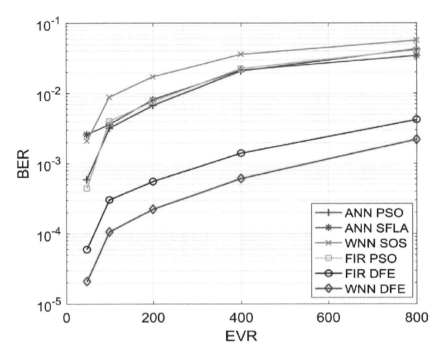

FIGURE 8.9
Effect of EVR with nonlinearity NL 1 at SNR of 15 dB.

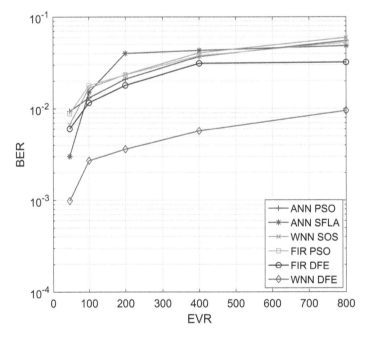

FIGURE 8.10
Effect of EVR on with nonlinearity NL 2 at SNR of 15 dB.

8.5.4.3 Effect of Time-Varying Channel

The transfer function of the channel in Equation (8.43) can be represented as $H(z) = h_1 + h_2 z^{-1} + h_3 z^{-2}$ for a given value of Λ. If we assume the channel to be time-varying with channel coefficients $h_i(n)$, the linear part of the channel is given as follows (Zhao et al. 2011):

$$H_n(z) = h_1(n) + h_2(n) z^{-1} + h_3(n) z^{-2} \tag{8.44}$$

Time variation in channel filter coefficients is generated as $h_i(n) = h_i + f_{LPF}(\rho w(n))$, where f_{LPF} is low-pass filter (LPF) with a normalized cutoff frequency of 0.1. $w(n)$ is white Gaussian noise, and its standard deviation ρ is taken to be 0.1. Simulation results in Figure 8.11 show that the performance of the proposed equalizer is worse compared to the FIR DFE equalizer for lower EVR values, but for EVR higher than 400, the proposed technique exhibits significantly improved BER performance. BER performances of all other equalizers are far inferior compared to the proposed equalizer.

8.5.4.4 BER Performance Evaluation

We now evaluate the BER performance of the proposed equalizer for different values of SNR and compare it with the FIR DFE algorithm. Figure 8.12 shows the comparison when symbols are transmitted over linear channels Ch 1 or Ch 2 with receiver SNR variation from 0 to 20 dB. It can be observed that the proposed equalizer results in lower BER compared to the FIR DFE technique. At SNR of 20 dB, the proposed technique achieves a BER of 10^{-6} and 6×10^{-5} with Ch 1 and Ch 2, respectively. For higher values of SNR (> 20 dB), it hits error floor and there is no significant increase in performance. BER plots are compared in Figure 8.13 when the transmitted signal is passed through a cascade of channel Ch 1 and either of the nonlinear functions. In this scenario also, we find that the proposed equalizer performs significantly better than the FIR DFE technique.

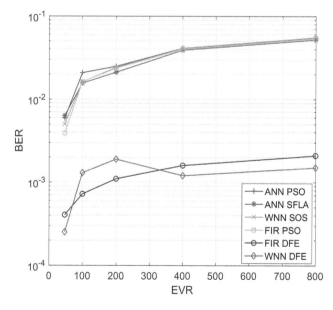

FIGURE 8.11
BER performance as a function of EVR for time varying channel at an average SNR of 15 dB.

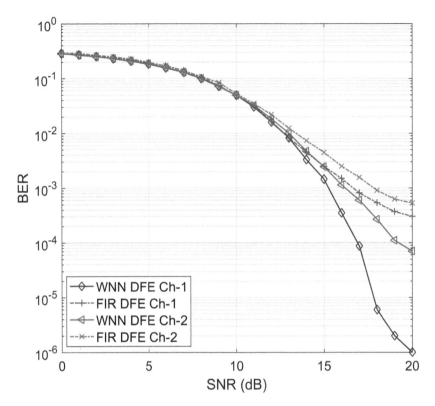

FIGURE 8.12
BER performance comparison over linear channels Ch 1 and Ch 2.

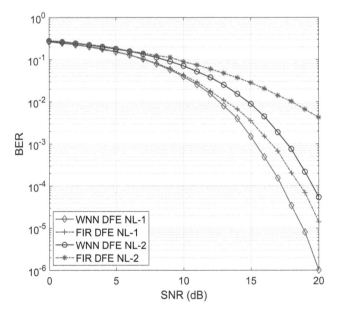

FIGURE 8.13
BER performance over linear channel Ch 1 in cascade with NL 1 or NL 2.

8.6 Conclusion

In this chapter, a wavelet neural network-based decision feedback equalizer for noisy and nonlinear ISI channels was proposed. The equalizer consists of a wavelet neural network and FIR filter in the forward path and a FIR filter for the backward path. While wavelet network helps in dealing with channels with high EVR and nonlinear functions, a forward FIR filter is suitable for channels with linear characteristics. To alleviate the problem of conventional wavelet network training methods where solutions get trapped in local minima, a WNN training algorithm based on CSO was proposed. Finally, simulation studies were carried out on benchmark linear and nonlinear channels to evaluate the performance of the equalizer in terms of mean square error and bit error rate. Simulations also evaluate the performance of the equalizer for a varying degree of EVR parameter and SNR of the channel. The results show that the performance of the proposed scheme is significantly improved compared to existing schemes in the literature.

Some possible future extensions of this work are as follows:

1. The number of parameters to be optimized in WNN is very large. It is observed that only a few of the translation and dilation parameters change during the process of learning. As a future work, a DFE with wavenet architecture can be explored, and various parameter initialization techniques may be compared.

2. The literature on neural network equalizers with decision feedback architecture is scarce. Moreover, very few authors have explored training ANN-based DFE with metaheuristic optimization algorithms. As a future study, design of the swarm optimization-based training algorithm for DFE with other neural network architectures like RBF and FLNN can be explored.

References

Abdelaziz, A.Y. and Ali, E.S. 2015. Cuckoo search algorithm based load frequency controller design for nonlinear interconnected power system. *International Journal of Electrical Power & Energy Systems 73*:632–643. doi:10.1016/j.ijepes.2015.05.050.

Abiodun, O.I., Jantan, A., Omolara, A. E., Dada, K.V., Mohamed, N. A. and Arshad, H. 2018. State-of-the-art in artificial neural network applications: A survey. *Heliyon 4*, no. 11. doi:10.1016/j.heliyon.2018.e00938.

Aboutaleb, A., Sayyafan, A., Sivakumar, K., Belzer, B., Greaves, S., Chan, K. S. and Wood, R. 2020. Deep neural network-based detection and partial response equalization for multilayer magnetic recording. *IEEE Transactions on Magnetics 57*, no. 3. doi:10.1109/TMAG.2020.3038435.

Ahmad, S. T. and Kumar, K. P. 2016. Radial basis function neural network nonlinear equalizer for 16-QAM coherent optical OFDM. *IEEE Photonics Technology Letters 28*, no. 22:2507–2510. doi:10.1109/LPT.2016.2601901.

Al-Awami, A. T., Zerguine, A., Cheded, L., Zidouri, A. and Saif, W. 2011. A new modified particle swarm optimization algorithm for adaptive equalization. *Digital Signal Processing 21*, no. 2:195–207. doi:10.1016/j.dsp.2010.05.001.

Alexandridis, A. K. and Zapranis, A. D. 2013. Wavelet neural networks: A practical guide. *Neural Networks 42*, 1–27. doi:10.1016/j.neunet.2013.01.008.

Al-Shaikhi, A. A., Khan, A. H., Al-Awami, A. T. and Zerguine, A. 2019. A hybrid particle Swarm optimization technique for adaptive equalization. *Arabian Journal for Science and Engineering* 44, no. 3:2177–2184. doi:10.1007/s13369-018-3387-8.

Al-Zubi, J. A., Bharathikannan, B., Tanwar, S., Manikandan, R., Khanna, A. and Thaventhiran, C. 2019. Boosted neural network ensemble classification for lung cancer disease diagnosis. *Applied Soft Computing* 80:579–591. doi:10.1016/j.asoc.2019.04.031.

Bauduin, M., Smerieri, A., Massar, S. and Horlin, F. 2015, May. Equalization of the non-linear satellite communication channel with an echo state network. In *2015 IEEE 81st Vehicular Technology Conference (VTC Spring)*. IEEE. doi:10.1109/VTCSpring.2015.7145827.

Beni, G. 2020. Swarm intelligence. In *Complex Social and Behavioral Systems: Game Theory and Agent-Based Models*, 791–818. Springer, New York, NY. doi:10.1007/978-1-0716-0368-0_530.

Caciularu, A. and Burshtein, D. 2020. Unsupervised linear and nonlinear channel equalization and decoding using variational autoencoders. *IEEE Transactions on Cognitive Communications and Networking* 6, no. 3:1003–1018. doi:10.1109/TCCN.2020.2990773.

Chen, S., Gibson, G. J., Cowan, C. F. N. and Grant, P. M. 1990. Adaptive equalization of finite non-linear channels using multilayer perceptrons. *Signal Processing* 20, no. 2:107–119. doi:10.1016/0165-1684(90)90122-F.

Das, G., Panda, S. and Padhy, S. K. 2018. Quantum particle swarm optimization tuned artificial neural network equalizer. In *Soft Computing: Theories and Applications*, 579–585. Springer, Singapore. doi:10.1007/978-981-10-5687-1_52.

Das, G., Pattnaik, P. K. and Padhy, S.K. 2014. Artificial neural network trained by particle swarm optimization for non-linear channel equalization. *Expert Systems with Applications* 41, no. 7:3491–3496. doi:10.1016/j.eswa.2013.10.053.

Farsad, N. and Goldsmith, A. 2018. Neural network detection of data sequences in communication systems. *IEEE Transactions on Signal Processing* 66, no. 21:5663–5678. doi:10.1109/TSP.2018.2868322.

Goswami, J. C. and Chan, A. K. 2011. *Fundamentals of Wavelets: Theory, Algorithms, and Applications* (Vol. 233). John Wiley & Sons, Hoboken, NJ.

Haykin, S. 2008. *Adaptive Filter Theory*. Pearson Education India, New Delhi.

Ingle, K. K. and Jatoth, R. K., 2020. An efficient JAYA algorithm with lévy flight for non-linear channel equalization. *Expert Systems with Applications*, 145, 112970. doi:10.1016/j.eswa.2019.112970.

Iqbal, N., Zerguine, A. and Al-Dhahir, N. 2014. Adaptive equalisation using particle swarm optimisation for uplink SC-FDMA. *Electronics Letters* 50, no. 6:469–471. doi:10.1049/el.2013.4091.

Iqbal, N., Zerguine, A. and Al-Dhahir, N. 2015. Decision feedback equalization using particle swarm optimization. *Signal Processing* 108, 1–12. doi:10.1016/j.sigpro.2014.07.030.

Jarajreh, M. 2019. Reduced-complexity artificial neural network equalization for ultra-high-spectral-efficient optical fast-OFDM signals. *Applied Sciences* 9, no. 19. doi:10.3390/app9194038.

Jay, P., Kalariya, V., Parmar, P., Tanwar, S., Kumar, N. and Alazab, M. 2020. Stochastic neural networks for cryptocurrency price prediction. *IEEE Access* 8, 82804–82818. doi:10.1109/ACCESS.2020.2990659.

Li, Y., Chen, M., Yang, Y., Zhou, M. T. and Wang, C. 2017, December. Convolutional recurrent neural network-based channel equalization: An experimental study. In *2017 23rd Asia-Pacific Conference on Communications (APCC)*. IEEE. doi:10.23919/APCC.2017.8304090.

Ling, F. and Proakis, J. 1985. Adaptive lattice decision-feedback equalizers-their performance and application to time-variant multipath channels. *IEEE Transactions on Communications 33*, no. 4:348–356. doi:10.1109/TCOM.1985.1096300.

Lipa, N., Mannes, E., Santos, A. and Nogueira, M. 2015. Firefly-inspired and robust time synchronization for cognitive radio ad hoc networks. *Computer Communications* 66:36–44. doi:10.1016/j.comcom.2015.04.005.

Liu, J., Mei, K., Zhang, X., Ma, D. and Wei, J. 2019. Online extreme learning machine-based channel estimation and equalization for OFDM systems. *IEEE Communications Letters* 23, no. 7:1276–1279. doi:10.1109/LCOMM.2019.2916797.

Lucky, R. W. 2006. The adaptive equalizer. *IEEE Signal Processing Magazine 23*, no.3:104–107.

Ma, H., Simon, D., Siarry, P., Yang, Z. and Fei, M. 2017. Biogeography-based optimization: A 10-year review. *IEEE Transactions on Emerging Topics in Computational Intelligence 1*, no. 5:391–407. doi.:10.1109/TETCI.2017.2739124.

Majumder, S., 2020a. Echo state network based nonlinear channel equalization in wireless communication system. In *Applications of Machine Learning*, 125–139. Springer, Singapore. doi:10.1007/978-981-15-3357-0_9.

Majumder, S. 2020b. Wavelet neural networks and equalization of nonlinear satellite communication channel. In *Applications of Artificial Neural Networks for Nonlinear Data*, 207–226. IGI Global. doi:10.4018/978-1-7998-4042-8.ch009.

Majumder, S. and Giri, M. K., 2020. Nonlinear channel equalization using wavelet neural network trained using PSO. In *Advances in Electronics, Electrical & Computational Intelligence (ICAEEC) 2019*. https://ssrn.com/abstract=3572806.

Mareli, M. and Twala, B., 2018. An adaptive Cuckoo search algorithm for optimisation. *Applied Computing and Informatics, 14*, no. 2:107–115. doi.10.1016/j.aci.2017.09.001.

Mavrovouniotis, M., Li, C. and Yang, S. 2017. A survey of swarm intelligence for dynamic optimization: Algorithms and applications. *Swarm and Evolutionary Computation 33*, 1–17. doi:10.1016/j.swevo.2016.12.005.

Mirjalili, S. 2019. Genetic algorithm. In *Evolutionary Algorithms and Neural Networks*, 43–55. Springer, Cham. doi:10.1007/978-3-319-93025-1_4.

Mirjalili, S., Gandomi, A. H., Mirjalili, S. Z., Saremi, S., Faris, H. and Mirjalili, S. M. 2017. Salp Swarm Algorithm: A bio-inspired optimizer for engineering design problems. *Advances in Engineering Software 114*, 163–191. doi:10.1016/j.advengsoft.2017.07.002.

Mosleh, S., Liu, L., Sahin, C., Zheng, Y.R. and Yi, Y. 2017. Brain-inspired wireless communications: Where reservoir computing meets MIMO-OFDM. *IEEE Transactions on Neural Networks and Learning Systems 29*, no. 10:4694–4708. doi:10.1109/TNNLS.2017.2766162.

Nanda, S. J. and Jonwal, N. 2017. Robust nonlinear channel equalization using WNN trained by symbiotic organism search algorithm. *Applied Soft Computing 57*:197–209. doi:10.1016/j.asoc.2017.03.029.

Nanda, S. J. and Garg, S. 2019. Design of supervised and blind channel equalizer based on moth-flame optimization. *Journal of the Institution of Engineers (India): Series B 100*, no. 2:105–115. doi:10.1007/s40031-018-0361-5.

Nayyar, A., Le, D. N. and Nguyen, N. G. eds. 2018. *Advances in Swarm Intelligence for Optimizing Problems in Computer Science*. CRC Press, Boca Raton, FL.

Nayyar, A. and Nguyen, N. G. 2018. Introduction to swarm intelligence. In Nayyar, A., Le, D. N. and Nguyen, N. G. eds. *Advances in Swarm Intelligence for Optimizing Problems in Computer Science*, 53–78. CRC Press, Boca Raton, FL.

Opara, K. R. and Arabas, J. 2019. Differential evolution: A survey of theoretical analyses. *Swarm and Evolutionary Computation 44*, 546–558. doi:10.1016/j.swevo.2018.06.010.

Panda, S., Mohapatra, P. K. and Panigrahi, S. P. 2015. A new training scheme for neural networks and application in non-linear channel equalization. *Applied Soft Computing 27*:47–52. doi:10.1016/j.asoc.2014.10.040.

Panda, S., Sarangi, A. and Panigrahi, S. P. 2014. A new training strategy for neural network using shuffled frog-leaping algorithm and application to channel equalization. *AEU-International Journal of Electronics and Communications 68*, no. 11:1031–1036. doi:10.1016/j.aeue.2014.05.005.

Pradhan, A. K., Meher, S. K. and Routray, A. 2006. Communication channel equalization using wavelet network. *Digital Signal Processing 16*, no. 4:445–452. doi:10.1016/j.dsp.2005.06.001.

Ribeiro, G. T., Mariani, V. C. and dos Santos Coelho, L. 2019. Enhanced ensemble structures using wavelet neural networks applied to short-term load forecasting. *Engineering Applications of Artificial Intelligence 82*:272–281. doi:10.1016/j.engappai.2019.03.012.

Sahoo, H. K. and Mohanty, B. 2016, December. Adaptive decision feedback equalizer for SISO communication channel using combined FIR-neural network and fast block LMS algorithm. In *2016 IEEE Annual India Conference (INDICON)*. IEEE. doi:10.1109/INDICON.2016.7839048.

Sahu, P. C., Panda, S., Panigrahi, S. P. and Rarvathi, K. 2018. RBFNN equalizer using shuffled frog-leaping algorithm. In *Soft Computing: Theories and Applications*, 549–558. Springer, Singapore. doi:10.1007/978-981-10-5687-1_49.

Saremi, S., Mirjalili, S. and Lewis, A. 2017. Grasshopper optimisation algorithm: Theory and application. *Advances in Engineering Software 105*:30–47. doi:10.1016/j.advengsoft.2017.01.004.

Siu, S., Gibson, G. J. and Cowan, C. F. N. 1990. Decision feedback equalisation using neural network structures and performance comparison with standard architecture. *IEE Proceedings I-Communications, Speech and Vision 137*, no. 4:221–225. doi:10.1049/ip-i-2.1990.0031.

Sutantyo, D. and Levi, P. 2015. Decentralized underwater multi-robot communication using bio-inspired approaches. *Artificial Life and Robotics 20*, no. 2:152–158. doi:10.1007/s10015-015-0201-5.

Veitch, D. 2005. *Wavelet Neural Networks and Their Application in the Study of Dynamical Systems.* Department of Mathematics university of York UK.

Xie, J., Chen, W. and Dai, H. 2019. Distributed cooperative learning algorithms using wavelet neural network. *Neural Computing and Applications 31*, no. 4:1007–1021. doi:10.1007/s00521-017-3134-1.

Yang, H. J. and Hu, X. 2016. Wavelet neural network with improved genetic algorithm for traffic flow time series prediction. *Optik 127*, no. 19:8103–8110. doi:10.1016/j.ijleo.2016.06.017.

Yang, X. S. 2010. *Nature-Inspired Metaheuristic Algorithms.* Luniver Press, Bristol.

Yang, X. S. and Deb, S. 2014. Cuckoo search: Recent advances and applications. *Neural Computing and Applications*, 24, no. 1:169–174. doi:10.1007/s00521-013-1367-1.

Ye, H., Li, G.Y. and Juang, B. H. 2017. Power of deep learning for channel estimation and signal detection in OFDM systems. *IEEE Wireless Communications Letters 7*, no. 1:114–117. doi:10.1109/LWC.2017.2757490.

Zhang, Y., Yang, S., Guo, Z., Guo, Y. and Zhao, J. 2019. Wind speed forecasting based on wavelet decomposition and wavelet neural networks optimized by the Cuckoo search algorithm. *Atmospheric and Oceanic Science Letters 12*, no. 2:107–115. doi:10.1080/16742834.2019.1569455.

Zhao, H., Zeng, X., Zhang, J., Li, T., Liu, Y. and Ruan, D. 2011. Pipelined functional link artificial recurrent neural network with the decision feedback structure for nonlinear channel equalization. *Information Sciences 181*, no. 17:3677–3692. doi:10.1016/j.ins.2011.04.033.

Zhao, H., Zeng, X., Zhang, X., Zhang, J., Liu, Y. and Wei, T. 2011. An adaptive decision feedback equalizer based on the combination of the FIR and FLNN. *Digital Signal Processing 21*, no. 6:679–689. doi:10.1016/j.dsp.2011.05.004.

Zhao, X., Wang, C., Su, J. and Wang, J. 2019. Research and application based on the swarm intelligence algorithm and artificial intelligence for wind farm decision system. *Renewable Energy 134*:681–697. doi:10.1016/j.renene.2018.11.061.

9

Intelligent Video Surveillance Systems Using Deep Learning Methods

Anjanadevi Bondalapati

MVGR College of Engineering

Manjaiah D. H.

Mangalore University

CONTENTS

DOI: 10.1201/9781003107026-9

9.1 Introduction

In computer vision, video surveillance is the emerging research area for the academicians, researchers, and industrialists. In recent days, the video surveillance system has become most popular and widely used in almost all places which in turn produces a huge amount of data from all the needed surveillance places. Therefore, it is highly essential to utilize a powerful computational tool for processing huge data in less time. It is also important to know the activities happening in different scenarios like identifying a movement of person in the screen, observing traffic in highways, monitoring the activities in offices, pedestrian detection in walking areas, monitoring gaming activities, and also monitoring people in shopping malls, hospitals, tourism locations, and parking places to prevent and reduce the chances of unusual or criminal activities. The video surveillance system is also playing a prominent role as evidence in identifying the criminals in shopping locations at crime scenes, hit and run accidents, etc.

The video surveillance system needs various tools to identify the people, objects, unusual activities, etc. For these tools, to find the given activities accurately, highly sophisticated and sensible models have to be developed. In video surveillance applications, manually observing the activities in video recordings takes more time to identify the object, motion and places, and events happening in various situations..

In recent days, the video surveillance system is used in many application areas such as academic institutions, government organizations, private sector companies, industries, hospitals, public areas, highway transportation system, automatic teller machines, medical imaging, and shopping malls. In these application areas, all the needful activities are recorded by using surveillance cameras. Patel et al. [1] proposed a Kafka-based model for fast live video streaming and also AWS S3 for distributed storage to accommodate a huge set of video frames. In this chapter, the proposed deep learning models are accurately performed in image classification using lightweight deep convolutional neural networks (LW-DCNN) model and unified model-based moving object detection.

9.1.1 Deep Learning

Profound learning is at the cutting edge of what machines can do. Deep learning is a subset of AI that dominates in perceiving objects in pictures as it's actualized utilizing at least three layers of counterfeit neural organizations where each layer is answerable for extricating at least one component of the picture. Late advances in profound learning made errands, for example, image and discourse acknowledgment, conceivable. Deep learning allows machines to solve complex problems even when using a dataset that is very diverse, unstructured, and inter-connected. The deeper learning algorithms learn the better they perform. It also powers some of the most interesting applications in the world, like autonomous vehicles and real-time translation. Deep learning models are more useful in data analytics. Kumari et al. [2] presented deep learning based data analytics framework which obtains the best results with less computation time. In recent days, deep learning models are popular and also achieve great power and flexibility by learning to represent the world as nested hierarchy of concepts, and each concept is related to a simple concept. The major difference between deep learning and machine learning is that the performance of deep learning increases as the scale of data increases. Deep learning algorithms work efficiently even on large amount of data. Deep learning algorithms try to learn high-level features from data, which reduces the task of developing feature extractor for new problems. In this chapter, the proposed customized deep learning model accurately detected moving objects in the agricultural domain.

9.1.2 Deep Learning – Past, Present, and Future

Through deep learning usage of techniques and algorithms, a model can learn from data in multiple levels of abstraction and representation. Mainly, deep learning (DL) algorithms outperform in various application areas. DL is a class of machine learning techniques and base on artificial neural networks. DL algorithms process data by using various numbers of layers. The first and last layer of the network layer are called input layer and out layer. The in-between layers are called hidden layers. Mainly, deep learning concepts are not new; they are revealed from the developments of huge dataset availability, new algorithms, and high computation power. McCulloch and Walter [3] proposed a neural network model where every neuron is postulated as being in binary state, which is in on or off condition in an initial stage of deep learning evolution. Rosenblatt [4] proposed a concept of perceptron which learns from data as similar to biological neurons. Hubel and Weisel [5] implemented receptive field-based neurons for detection of local features for a cat's visual system. Fukushima [6] proposed convolutional neural network for recognition of visual patterns for resembles the organization of animal visual cortex. Lecun [7] developed convolutional neural network-based backpropagation for zip code recognition. Later, Lecun [8] implemented LeNet for document recognition for gradient-based learning. Deep convolutional neural network (DCNN) is a base model for various applications like image classification, object detection, tracking, etc.

Hinton [9] proposed a method which converted high dimensional data to low dimensional code with multilayer network for reduction of dimensionality of data. Mainly, they have used restricted Boltzmann machines instead of random weight initialization. Alex and Stskever [10] developed deep convolutional neural networks for ImageNet classification on 1,000 different classes. In older days, region-based convolutional neural networks (RCNNs) are used for object classification and detection. From last four years usage of you only look once (yolo) method and single shot detectors for localization detection of objects with bounding boxes. From past 50 years handling huge data and the find the hidden patterns from underlying layers is a challenging task. From the twenty-first century, the current research majorly focused on deep learning to resolve this issue. The focused applications are object detection, social media analytics, spam detection, etc.

In a few years, deep learning will become a part of many software applications to embed the capabilities into devices which improves customer experience. These deep learning-based systems are very useful in understanding and processing simple human languages using natural language processing.

9.1.3 Recent Methodologies

Mohanty et al. [11] proposed convolution neural network on plant village dataset. This method obtained an accuracy of 85.3%. This method obtained more time to train the data and also constrained to the classification of single leaves on a homogeneous background. When they tested on a set of images which has taken under various conditions which they used for training, then automatically the model accuracy substantially reduced. Fuentes et al. [12] used combined meta-architectures like R-CNN and SSD with deep feature extractors. Here, the challenged part of this approach is to consider a small set of samples in which some classes with high pattern variation tend to be confused with others, resulting in false positives or lower average precision. Ferentinos [13] proposed the CNN approach, the main drawback of which was that the entire photographic material included solely images in experimental setups but not in real conditions in the cultivation field. Another important issue that should be noted and should be resolved is that the tested dataset used for the assessment of the models and part of the same database that constituted the trainset. Bhatt et al. [14] applied a model which has been used small set of images to train and evaluate the models are with different resolutions like quality, focus and brightness as they are captured with mobile phones having different cameras through a participatory sensing approach. They used the application of single shot detection in tea leaves that helps in reduced detection time of disease and pest through automation. From these results, it can also be realized that only classification cannot reliably help when there are occurrences of multiple pets and also disease conditions in a single image. Anandakrishnan and Hanson [15] proposed deep learning-based CNN approach with dataset images of apple leaf disease which consists of the images taken under field conditions and also dataset of laboratory images. Through this method, the obtained accuracy is limited to 78.80. Durmuş et al. [16] applied a method to improve the accuracy and to reduce the parameters on GoogLeNet and cifar-10 models to detect the plant diseases. In this method, the activation function used over here is ReLU. The GoogLeNet achieves an accuracy of 98.9, and the cifar model achieves an average accuracy of 98.9. They used the dataset with less existing images along with augmented dataset with rotation and flip operations. In this method, they used a dataset of 3,060 images in which 80% were used for training and 20% were used for testing. This method used pooling, an operation which leads to an increased accuracy by 5%.

Liu et al. [17] proposed a deep learning model to detect plant diseases. In this method, plant village dataset was used for accurate disease detection. In this approach, two different deep learning architectures are used namely AlexNet and SqueezeNet. Ten different classes along with the healthy images are used for training. In their work, AlexNet performed with accuracy 0.9722, when they trained from scratch, the images were segmented with 80% for training and 20% for testing and also the models are trained and tested on GPU systems for accurate results. Based on the results they concluded that AlexNet performed slightly better than SqueezeNet because the SqueezeNet is smaller than the AlexNet. Jiang et al. [18] developed single neural network for object detection. During predictions, the network generated the scores. In SSD the size of the images is (300×300) and (512×512). For the image of size (300×300) the SSD achieves 74.3 mAP and for (512×512) it achieves 76.9 mAP. The method produces good accuracy than other single-stage detectors. Khan and Narvekar [19] proposed a deep learning-based approach that helps in classifying the tomato leaf diseases. They have considered the category of diseases which are early blight, downy mildew, and powdery mildew. The dataset consists of the images taken from the nursery, plant village, and farm. The training and testing were implemented in the Torch7 machine learning framework. They have proven that the model will provide accuracy with minimum computational effort. Saleem et al. [20] used deep convolutional neural network. They have used the dataset which consists of 30,880 training images and 2,589 validation images which are taken from various internet resources. After the 100th training of iteration, they have achieved the accuracy of 96.3. The drawback of this methodology is more time consumption during training. Lu et al. [21] used a method for rice plant disease identification based on the deep convolutional neural network technique. They have been used the dataset which consists of both Healthy and diseased leaves. The total number of images presented in that dataset is 500. Proposed CNN method is effectively trained and identifies the diseases. The CNN has achieved an accuracy of 95.48. This model has high convergence rate along with better recognition of diseases. But only the drawback they have encountered is that the images in the dataset are very less.

9.1.4 Concepts Used in Deep Learning

9.1.4.1 Convolutional Neural Networks (CNN)

Convolutional neural organization is a class of profound discovering that has demonstrated to be fruitful in distinguishing and arranging objects. The principle preferred position of convolution networks for some such errands is that the whole framework is prepared start to finish, from crude pixels to extreme classes. Perceiving the classification of the predominant item in a picture is an errand to convolutional networks whether the articles were transcribed characters, house numbers, surface less toys, traffic signs, and so on. CNNs are incredible picture preparing, computerized reasoning (AI) that utilization profound figuring out how to perform both generative and unmistakable assignments, frequently utilizing machine vison that incorporates picture and video acknowledgment, alongside recommender frameworks and common language handling. The layers of a CNN comprise an information layer, a yield layer, and a concealed layer that incorporates different convolutional layers, pooling layers, completely associated layers, and standardization layers. The evacuation of restrictions and expansion in proficiency for picture handling brings about a framework that is unmistakably more viable, more straightforward to trains, restricted for picture preparing, and normal language handling. Over the most recent couple of years profound Convolutional neural organizations have been seeing a blast in writing and on the web. They contrast from customary organizations by making the express supposition that the information is a picture. This permits convolutional networks draw another motivation from nature – open fields of vision. CNNs can zero in on particular pieces of the picture utilizing convolutions. CNNs comprise of convolutional layers – which go about as open fields, trailed by pooling layers – which decline the quantity of highlights and pixels the following convolutional and pooling layers can zero in on. Convolutional and pooling layers are stacked commonly until at long last associated with an old-style neural organization (named completely associated in profound learning writing) with some concealed layers and afterward at last the yield layer as the classifier. Hypothetically unmistakable highlights should be near one another – this permit to make CNN open fields utilizing completely associated neural organizations in which the principal neuron layer is associated with each and every pixel of the picture. This will bring about a conceivably higher distinct capacity of the organization at the cost enormously expanded intricacy. The drawback of completely associated NNs is that they don't abuse the region of related highlights as CNNs do (highlights far away from one another are not liable to be connected). CNN is now the go-to model on every image-related problem. In terms of accuracy, they blow competition out of the water. It is also successfully applied to recommender systems, natural language processing, and more. The main advantage of CNN compared to its predecessors is that it automatically detects the important features without any human supervision. Anjanadevi et al. [22] proposed CNN based model for effective brain tumor classification. Patel et al. [23] proposed deep learning based crypto currency price detection. Bhattacharya et al. [24] implemented block chain integrated deep learning service useful in current health care applications. Further section focused on natural language processing tasks using deep learning algorithms.

9.2 Natural Language Processing Using Deep Learning

9.2.1 Introduction to Natural Language Processing (NLP)

Natural language refers to the language spoken by people, e.g., English, Hindi, etc. as opposed to artificial languages, like C++, Java, etc. Natural language processing (NLP) is a field of computer science, artificial intelligence, and linguistics concerned with the interactions between computers and human (natural) languages like human–computer interaction. The ultimate goal is to build computer systems which performs well at usage natural language as humans do (making computers as intelligent as people) and also build computer systems that can process text and speech more intelligently those are enable human-machine communication, improving human-human communication, processing of text or speech. In natural language understanding, we can enable computers to derive meaning from human or natural language input.

- **Applications of Natural Language Processing:** Need of NLP is more if machines could process our emails, translate languages accurately, help us manage, summarize, and aggregate information, understand phone conversation, and talk to us/listen to us. The following section provides a list of applications of natural language processing.
  - **Speech recognition:** The process of transforming one spoken language to machine readable format. These are essential in virtual assists like Alexa and Google assistant.
  - **Natural language generation (NLG):** Natural language generation system is like a translator that converts a computer-based representation into a natural language representation. NLG may be viewed as the opposite of natural language understanding: whereas in natural language understanding the system needs to disambiguate the input sentence to produce the machine

representation language, in NLG the system needs to make decisions about how to put a concept into words.

- **Machine translation:** The process of translating the text to other language is called machine translation. Automated translation is very useful in business applications to facilitate the effective communication and also helps to reach broader audiences.

- **Text classification:** To analyze the huge number of responses of the open survey we need to perform the analysis with understanding, processing, and classification of unstructured text.

- **Word counters:** In NLP, with the usage of word counters, we can perform frequency of each word in the given text after tokenization so that one can easily find the most common word occurring in the given text.

- **Spell checkers:** The most commonly used spell checkers are Norvig Sweeting, Symmetric Delete, and Context Spellchecker. In nlp, spell checkers are majorly useful when deep learning model is customized with context words into considerations so that spell correction also takes place to improve the accuracy.

NLG system is like a translator that converts a computer-based representation into a natural language representation. Natural Language Generation (NLG) may be viewed as the opposite of natural language understanding: whereas in natural language understanding, the system needs to disambiguate the input sentence to produce the machine representation language, in NLG, the system needs to make decisions about how to put a concept into words.

9.2.2 Word-Vector Representations (Simple Word, Multiword Prototypes, and Global Contexts)

9.2.2.1 Word Vector Representation

This predicts the surrounding words of every word. If both are quite similar, see faster and can easily incorporate a new sentence/document or add a word to the vocabulary. It predicts surrounding words in a window of length m of every word.

- **Objective Function:** Maximize the log probability of any context word given the current center word using the following equation

$$J(\theta) = \frac{1}{T} \sum_{t=1}^{T} \sum_{-m \leq j \leq m, j \neq 0} \log p\left(w_{t+j} | w_t\right) \tag{9.1}$$

where
μ represents all variables being optimized

Predict surrounding words in a window of length m of every word. For $p(w_t+j|w_t)$, the simplest first formulation is

$$p\left(o|c\right) = \frac{\exp\left(u_o^T v_c\right)}{\sum\limits_{w=1}^{W} \exp\left(u_w^T v_c\right)} \tag{9.2}$$

where

> o is the outside (or output) word id,

> c is the center word id,

> u and v are "center" and "outside" vectors of o and c.

Every word has two vectors. This is essentially "dynamic" logistic regression. We will optimize through minimizing or maximizing the cost function. For now: minimize -> gradient descent

9.2.2.2 Simple Word2VectorRepresentation

To minimize the main cost function (J) for reduction in error:

By using Equation 9.1 and Equation 9.2,

We derived the gradient for the internal vectors v_c, calculating all gradients

- We went through gradients for each center vector v in a window
- We also need gradients for outside vectors, hence derive all gradients

9.2.2.3 *Learning Representation through Backpropagation*

Taking more deeper derivatives of back propagation, we have all the basic tools in place to learn about more complex models.

9.2.2.3.1 Training with Backpropagation

$$J = \max\left(0,\ 1 - s + s_c\right) \tag{9.3}$$

where

$$s_c = U^T f\left(Wx_c + b\right) \tag{9.4}$$

$$s = U^T f\left(W_x + b\right) \tag{9.5}$$

Assuming cost J is >0, it is simple to see that we can compute the derivatives of s and s_c w.r.t all the involved variables: U, W, b, x.

$$\frac{\partial s}{\partial U} = \frac{\partial}{\partial U} U^T a \qquad \frac{\partial s}{\partial U} = a \tag{9.6}$$

9.2.2.3.2 Training with Back propagation (Backprop)

- Let's consider the derivative of a single weight W_{ij}

$$\frac{\partial s}{\partial W} = \frac{\partial}{\partial W} U^T a = \frac{\partial}{\partial W} U^T f(z) = \frac{\partial}{\partial W} U^T f\left(Wx + b\right) \tag{9.7}$$

Take the derivative of score with respect to single word vector (for simplicity, a 1D (dimension) vector, but the same if it was longer) Now, we cannot just take into consideration one a_i because each x_j is connected to all the neurons above, and hence, x_j influences the overall score through all of these; hence,

$$\frac{\partial}{\partial x_j} = \sum_{i=1}^{2} \frac{\partial s}{\partial a_i} \frac{\partial a_i}{\partial x_j}$$

$$= \sum_{i=1}^{2} \frac{\partial U^T a}{\partial a_i} \frac{\partial a_i}{\partial x_j} \tag{9.8}$$

$$= \sum_{i=1}^{2} U_i \frac{\partial f(W_i x + b)}{\partial x_j}$$

$$\text{Reused as part of previous derivative} = \sum_{i=1}^{2} U_i f'(W_i \cdot x + b) \underbrace{\frac{\partial W_i \cdot x}{\partial x_j}}$$

9.2.2.4 Natural Language Tasks for Text Classification

- **Process Steps**
  - Initialize with pretrained word vectors (**word2vec or Glove**)
  - Start with two copies
  - Backprop into only one set, keep the other "static"
  - Both channels are added to c_i before max-pooling
  - Classification after one CNN layer
  - First one convolution, followed by one max-pooling
  - To obtain final feature vector: (assuming m filters w)

$$y = \text{softmax}\left(W^{(S)} z + b\right) \tag{9.9}$$

  - Simple final softmax layer for better performance
  - Idea: randomly mask/dropout/set to 0 some of the feature weights
  - Create masking vector r of Bernoulli random variables with probability p (a hyper parameter) of being 1
  - Delete features during training

$$y = \text{softmax}\left(W^{(S)}\left(r \circ z\right) + b\right) \tag{9.10}$$

  - **Reasoning**: Prevents co-adaptation (overfitting to seeing specific feature constellations)
  - With the usage of Equation 9.10
  - At training time, gradients are back propagated only through those elements of z vector for which $r_i = 1$

- At test time, there is no dropout, so feature vectors, z, are larger.
- Hence, we scale the final vector by Bernoulli probability p

$$\widehat{W}^{(S)} = pW^{(S)}$$

- Model with improved accuracy and ability to use very large networks without overfitting.

9.2.2.5 Natural Language Tasks for Image Description Generation

A snappy look at a picture is adequate for a human to call attention to and portray an enormous measure of insights regarding the visual scene. Be that as it may, this noteworthy capacity has demonstrated to be a subtle undertaking for our visual acknowledgment models. Most of past work in visual acknowledgment has zeroed in on marking pictures with a fixed arrangement of visual classes, and extraordinary advancement has been accomplished in these endeavors. Notwithstanding, while shut vocabularies of visual ideas comprise an advantageous demonstrating suspicion, they are tremendously prohibitive when contrasted with the colossal measure of rich depictions that a human can make. In this work, we endeavor to make a stride toward the objective of creating thick depictions of pictures. The essential test toward this objective is in the plan of a model that is sufficiently rich to at the same time reason about substance of pictures and their portrayal in the space of common language.

9.2.2.5.1 Bidirectional RNN Model (BRNN Model)

- **Overview**: A definitive objective of our model is to produce portrayals of picture areas. During preparing, the contribution to our model is a bunch of pictures and their comparing sentence depictions (shown below). Presented model adjusts sentence scraps to the visual districts that they portray through a multimodal installing. We at that point treat these correspondences as preparing information for a second, multimodular recurrent Neural Network model that figures out how to create the bits.

9.3 Machine Translation Using Gated Recurrent Neural Networks (GRNN) and Long Short-Term Memory (LSTM)

9.3.1 Gated Recurrent Units (GRUs)

Mainly, the gated recurrent units are used to keep around memories to capture long distance dependencies and allow error messages to flow at different strengths depending on the inputs.

Standard RNN computes hidden layer at the next time step directly.

$$h_t = f\left(W^{hh}h_{t-1} + W^{)hx}x_t\right) \tag{9.11}$$

GRU first computes an update gate (another layer) based on current input word vector and hidden state using Equation 9.11

Compute reset gate similarly but with different weights

$$z_t = \sigma\left(W^{(z)}x_t + U^{(z)}h_{t-1}\right) \tag{9.12}$$

Update gate

$$r_t = \sigma\left(W^{(r)}x_t + U^{(r)}h_{t-1}\right)$$

Reset gate
  Using update gate equation, we can reset gate unit.
  New memory content
  If reset gate unit is ~0, then this ignores previous memory and only stores the new word information

$$\tilde{h}_t = \tanh\left(Wx_t + t_t \circ Uh_{t-1}\right) \tag{9.13}$$

Final memory at time step combines current and previous time steps

$$h_t = z_t \circ h_{t-1} + (1 - z_t) \circ \tilde{h}_t \tag{9.14}$$

9.3.2 Long Short-Term Memory (LSTM)

In deep learning, long short-Term memory (LSTM) is well suited for image processing, classification, and prediction from time series data. LSTM model is popular Envogue default model for most sequence labeling tasks. It is very powerful, especially when stacked and made even deeper (each hidden layer is already computed by a deep internal network). Most useful if you have lots and lots of data. LSTM is an efficient recurrent neural network (RNN) architecture to retrieve the restored state information to make the units even more complex Allow each time step to modify.
  Input gate (current cell matters)

$$i_t = \sigma\left(W^{(i)}x_t + U^{(i)}h_{t-1}\right) \tag{9.15}$$

Forget (gate0, forget past)

$$f_t = \sigma\left(W^{(f)}x_t + U^{(f)}h_{t-1}\right) \tag{9.16}$$

Output (how much cell is exposed)

$$o_t = \sigma\left(W^{(o)}x_t + U^{(o)}h_{t-1}\right) \tag{9.17}$$

New memory cell

$$\tilde{c}_t = \tanh\left(W^{(c)}x_t + U^{(c)}h_{t-1}\right)$$

Final memory cell $c_t = f_t \circ c_{t-1} + i_t \circ \tilde{c}_t$

Final hidden state $h_t = o_t \circ \tanh(c_t)$ \hfill (9.18)

The below section describes the advantages of the LSTM model.

- **Pros**
  - Envogue default model for most sequence labeling tasks
  - Very powerful, especially when stacked and made even deeper (each hidden layer is already computed by a deep internal network)
  - Most useful if you have lots and lots of data

9.3.3 Results Analysis

To start with, full BRNN beats who prepared with a comparable misfortune yet utilized a solitary picture portrayal and a Recursive Neural Network over the sentence. A comparative misfortune was embraced by Kiros that LSTM is used to encode sentences. We list their exhibition with a CNN that is identical in force to the one utilized in this work; however, they beat our model with an all the more remarkable CNN. Since we utilize distinctive word vectors, dropout for regularization and diverse cross-approval ranges, and bigger installing sizes, we re-actualized their misfortune for a reasonable examination contrasted with other work that utilizes AlexNets, and our full model shows steady improvement.

Our simpler cost function improves performance. We endeavor to all the more likely comprehend the wellspring of our presentation. To begin with, we eliminated the RNN and utilized reliance tree relations precisely as depicted. The main distinction between this model and "reimplementation of DeFrag" is that it is new as well as reduces cost with less work complexity.

- **BRNN Outperforms Dependency Tree Relations**: Furthermore, when we supplant the reliance tree relations with the BRNN, we notice extra execution improvements. Since the reliance relations appeared to work in a way that is better than single words and bigrams, this recommends that the BRNN is exploiting settings longer than two words. Besides, our strategy doesn't depend on separating a dependency tree and rather utilizes the crude words straightforwardly.

- **MSCOCO Results for Future Comparisons**: We don't think about other conveyed situating results on MSCOCO. In a like manner, we report results on a subset of 1,000 pictures and the full game plan of 5,000 test pictures for future connections. Note that the 5,000 picture numbers are lower in cerecal@kisacomponent of test set size. For every test image above, we retrieve the most compatible test sentence and visualize the highest-scoring region for each word (before MRF smoothing described) and the associated scores (v_T s_t). We shroud the arrangements of low-scoring words to decrease mess. We allot every district discretionary shading. We assessed its performance on both full frame and level wise analysis and demonstrated that in the two cases on the multimodal RNN outer-structures with recover baselines.

9.4 Image Processing Using Deep Learning Algorithms

9.4.1 Introduction to Image Processing and Computer Vision

Nowadays, video surveillance cameras play a major role in identifying and detecting the events in all the places. Most common applications using surveillance cameras are shopping malls, parking lots, educational institutions, government offices, etc. Deep learning algorithms are getting popular in computer vision applications with the advent of big data and high computational power.

9.4.2 Data Preparation for Image Processing Tasks

It includes several steps such as image acquisition, image preprocessing, feature extraction, and classification. It works as follows:

- **Image Acquisition**: The underlying cycle is to gather the information from the public vault. It accepts the picture as a contribution for additional handling. We have taken most well-known picture areas with the goal that we can take any arrangements like .bmp, .jpg, .gif as contribution to our cycle.
- **Image Preprocessing**: As the images are acquired from the real field, they may contain dust, spores, and water spots as noise. The purpose of data preprocessing is to eliminate the noise in the image, so as to adjust the pixel values. It enhances the quality of the image. In this model, we trained the plant leaf images of tomato, potato, and corn with diseases of 38 classes samples are (Figure 9.1):
- **Image Segmentation**: Image segmentation is the third step in our proposed method. The segmented images are categorized into color and area affected of leaf.
- **Feature Extraction**: Feature extraction is the important part to gracefully predict the infected region. Here, shape and textural feature extraction is done. The shape-oriented features of extraction like area, color axis length, eccentricity, solidity, and perimeter are calculated. Similarly, the texture-oriented features of extraction like contrast, correlation, energy, homogeneity, and mean are calculated. Leaf image is captured and processed to determine the health of each plan. The initial process is to select the image. By using the image preprocessing technique, the leaf has to be diagnosed whether it was affected or unaffected. Then, the image has to be segmented, and the name of the disease has to be identified. This project provides a solution to overcome from the leaf diseases, and it also analyzes the overall percentage of the affected leaf and its surrounding region.

The below section describes the most common preprocessing operations used for accurate tumor classification

Methods	Range
Flip horizontally	0.5
Flip vertically	0.5
Rotation	15°
Shift	0.05 (in horizontal & vertical direction)
Shear	0.05 (in horizontal direction)

(a)   (b)   (c)

FIGURE 9.1
(a) SquashMildew, (b) Corn_blight, and (c) PotatoEarly disease category images.

9.4.3 Classification Algorithms with Applications

Deep learning-based classification algorithms are very useful in health care domain. Anjanadevi B and N S Akhil [22] proposed a model in health care domain which describes the techniques in classification to build a CNN model that would classify the tumor and nontumor images. This model is effective and accurate in classifying if the images are tumor type or not. Patel et al. presented a deep learning-based price prediction model for cryptocurrency. This model obtains high accuracy in the prediction of cryptocurrency price. Bondalapati et al. [25] proposed an effective unified moving object detection model in real-time video surveillance systems which handles challenging conditions such as camera jitter, dynamic background, and shadow appearance of images. This project is the combination of classification and segmentation. Mainly, VGG16 and Mobile Net are recent methodologies used to categorize the insulator images which are captured through drone cameras, Anjanadevi et al. [26] proposed a lightweight deep learning-based classification model to classify the insulators' working condition weather they are working good or not. This model consumes less time compared to the brain tumor classification model found in Anjanadevi et al. which classified the tumor (yes) and nontumor (No) images, and later segmentation is applied on the tumor (yes) images. We implemented a classification model with eight convolution layers and five pooling layers with three fully convolution layers as a base model. Furthermore, to improve the accuracy along with base model, we proposed the transfer learning technique with one dropout layer with 0.5 value and extended to dense layer with sigmoid function. This model achieves high accuracy in classifying images having tumor or not. The following section describes about various deep learning models.

9.5 Lightweight Deep Convolution Neural Network Architecture (LW-DCNN)

9.5.1 Introduction

Deep convolution neural networks (DCNNs) have a good breakthrough in processing images while reducing computational cost and increasing accuracy. The proposed approach focuses on object detection using classification with the DCNN model. This model uses feature map for preprocessing the images, and convolution layers help to minimize the processing using deep learning perceptrons. After that, the proposed approach uses the lightweight deep convolution neural network (LW_DCNN) model which includes a smaller number of convolution layers, max pooling layers with relevant parameters, and dense, flattened layers to train the data using Leaky ReLU function for improving accuracy. The proposed methodology LW_DCNN is highly efficient compared to traditional classification techniques and present simple and powerful model for object detection in video surveillance systems.

- **Algorithm (Lightweight DCNN Classification Model (LW_DCNN)):** Input images considered in target size 251 * 250 * 3 hold raw pixel values of the image (width, height, and channels) as (251, 250, 3).

FIGURE 9.2
Proposed LW_DCNN model.

The applied Convolution2D with kernel (3×3) and 64 filters are used to compute the feature map with local regions in the input image, and ReLu activation function is used with a dot product between their weights, and local regions that are connected to input volume produce the output shape (118, 118, 32).

Max pooling with pool size 2×2 with padding=1 produces output shape (59, 59, 32).

Convolution 2D with 32 filters with ReLU produces (57,57,32), and max pooling with same padding produces (28, 28, 32).

Repeating step 4 and applying layers produce output shape (13, 13, 32).

Finally, flattened and dense layers used in the network for handling data into vectors achieved an accuracy of 0.8154. Figure 9.2 describes the overall system process step by step. This customized algorithm effectively classifies the working condition of insulators on electric polls. This algorithm is emerging in usage in current real-time surveillance systems. Through drone cameras or surveillance cameras, we can collect the large set of images of insulators from electric polls, and through this, we can automatically classify the working condition (either good or bad) of insulators without manual check.

9.5.2 Architecture

The proposed network is trained for object classification which is used for monitoring the working condition of pin insulators which are equipped in overhead power lines. Periodical checking of insulator work condition (good or bad) is the most important requirement in current scenarios. Therefore, working on this problem and giving efficient results is challenging. Here, we considered data of 720 images in which 320 are good working insulators, and 360 insulators are not working (bad conditioned). In the training stage, the network is trained using a dataset of 60% and tested on 40% data. By using deep convolutional neural network (DCNN), in less computational time, we can process more data, because here, overhead power polls insulator data generation is more in less time. By traditional image processing techniques, it takes more time to process this much of data. Therefore, the custom DCNN model gives better results in this area. The proposed customized DCNN model (LW_DCNN) uses convolution plus max pooling plus leaky ReLU function along with flattened and dense layers. It performs automatic feature extraction with weight assignments. Here the weights are assigned in a random fashion. In the first convolution layer, the activation function is used with stride and padding on the input image, and then batch normalization is performed on the data which are passed through the first convolution layer. Then the max pooling layer is applied on convolved shape, so that closure features are extracted, and conv+max pool is continued to classify the objects of suitable condition type (working or not). The LW-DCNN algorithm presents in detail about all the core layers of the model are convolution, max_polling, dense layers, and flattened layers. The functionality of these layers is as follows.

9.5.3 Results

9.5.3.1 Comparison Analysis

The graphs in below section provide the progress of accuracy in each epoch (Figure 9.3). The obtained results are more accurate in classification of insulator images. Figures 9.4 and 9.5 display the results of test images in each epoch. It is clearly identifying that the proposed algorithm is useful in automatic identification of working condition of each insulator on electric polls. The graph in Figures 9.4 and 9.5 shows the accuracy results

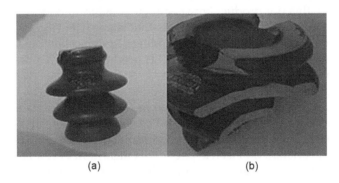

(a)   (b)

FIGURE 9.3
(a) Test image (in working condition). (b) Test image (in not working condition).

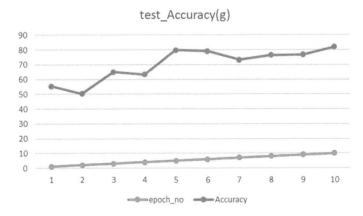

FIGURE 9.4
LW_DCNN-based accuracy graph (when insulator is good conditioned).

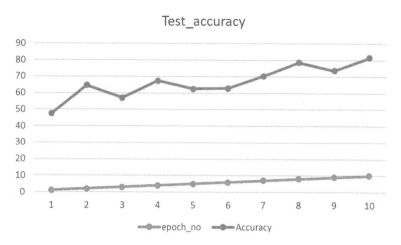

FIGURE 9.5
Accuracy graph (insulator is in not working condition).

which are obtained after testing the network on the insulator dataset. The dataset contains images of insulators which belong to two classes based on the working condition.

The below section provides a sample dataset of images to obtain the features on pin insulators which are captured from electric polls.

9.6 Improved Unified Model for Moving Object Detection

9.6.1 Introduction

Deep convolutional neural networks (DCNNs) are urgently improved for confinement, recognizable proof, and recognition of articles. Plant sicknesses influence the development of their individual species; thus, early recognizable proof is significant. Many machine learning (ML) models have been utilized for the location and arrangement of plant illnesses; however, after the progressions in a subset of ML, that is, deep learning (DL), this zone of examination seems to have incredible potential as far as expanded precision. Many created/changed DL models are executed alongside a few representation strategies to recognize and characterize the side effects of plant illnesses.

We performed writing survey and gave an exhaustive clarification of DL models used to envision different plant infections. Furthermore, some examination holes are recognized from which to acquire more noteworthy straightforwardness for identifying illnesses in plants, even before their indications show up obviously.

We have focused on plant data images in agricultural field. Agriculture is one of the major living sources in India. To increase the yield, preventing diseases and detection of diseases play a major role in the agriculture domain. We used improved DCNN model in the agricultural domain with plant doc and plant village datasets. We mainly focused on tomato, corn, and potato plants for model training and testing. We have experimented on plant image dataset of tomato leaves, both healthy and diseased ones. Experimental results are compared with state of the architectures like Mobile Net, Dark Net-19, and ResNet-101, and the proposed model outperforms in location and detection of plant diseases and obtains the best results in computation and accuracy.

Algorithm Steps

Firstly, we have taken an image of input size 416×416 with convolution filter size of 3×3 and stride 2. Then, the obtained result will be of 208×208×64.

In the second step, we have used a residual block which will help to reduce the complexity of architecture, and along with that, the convolutional filters with size 3×3 and with stride 2 are used which results in the formation of an image with size 104×104×128.

In this step, we have used the filters of size 3×3 along with stride=2 which produced the reshape of size 52×52×256.

In this step, we have used the same parameters as above and obtained the result with the shape 26×26×512.

The concatenation is done here for the result obtained in the above step and the result obtained after upsampling the image.

Now, in this step, we have concatenated the filters of size 3×3 and 1×1, and then, we have obtained the size of 52×52×256.

Finally, we have obtained the result of detected object with bounding boxes.

9.6.2 Object Detection Architecture

In this model, we have considered an input image 416×416 in video surveillance data set from change detection (CD NET 2014) with 75 layers of unified model with residual blocks (Figure 9.6). One special feature in this is that it uses darknet-53 network which is having 53 convolutional layers. It uses nine anchor boxes which are generated by clustering

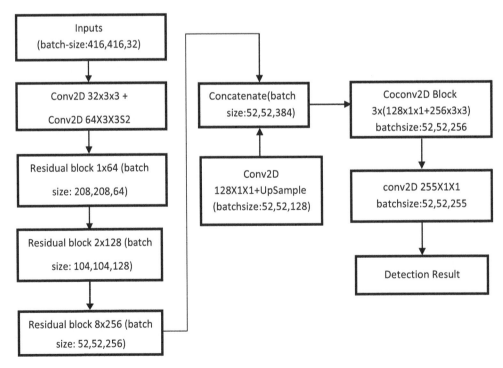

FIGURE 9.6

Customized deep learning architecture for plant disease detection.

TABLE 9.1

The Experimental Evaluation on Bad Weather Images

Image Category	Image Resolution	Overall Accuracy
Blizzard	720×480	74.545
Snow Fall	720×480	89.66
Wet Snow	720×540	88.23

FIGURE 9.7
Bad weather challenge conditioned Blizzard video frame with input and outputs of the existing method and proposed method.

algorithms. The process will be done in three levels. In the first level, the image is down sampled, which results in the reduction in the size of image from 416×416×32 to 13×13×255. In the next step, the feature map from one layer is connected to another convolutional layer, and then, it is upsampled. In the third step, the obtained one is passed through the 1×1 convolutional layer, and at this, the obtained feature map is used for detection.

The proposed unified model method and existing method were analyzed in the Bad Weather image, as shown in Table 9.1. The proposed unified model method has the accuracy of 94.545%, and the existing method has 73.58% accuracy.

The bad weather images were analyzed in the existing and proposed method for moving object detection, as shown in Figure 9.7. The developed method has a higher efficiency in the bad weather region than the existing method. Detailed analysis is presented by Bondalapati et al.

9.6.3 Results

The proposed model was experimented and tested in agricultural data set to detect the plant diseases where data were collected from the plantdoc dataset. When a diseased leaf image is supplied as an input to our approach, it will show the output as below with some accuracy value. The output images are displayed in Figures 9.8–9.16.

9.6.4 Comparison Analysis

The results of the improve object detection model are compared with state-of-the-art methods using accuracy and inference time. The proposed model is more accurate in detection of plant diseases. We have used DarkNet-53 as it produced the results with higher accuracy in various types of plant diseases. We have presented proposed results in the below section.

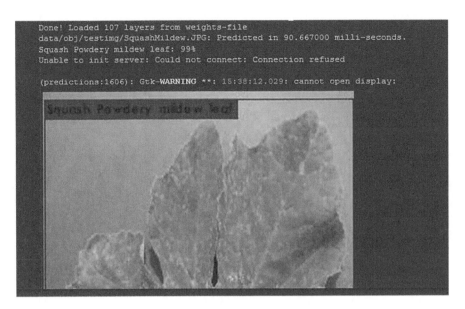

FIGURE 9.8
Output image of squash powdery mildew potato leaf blight.

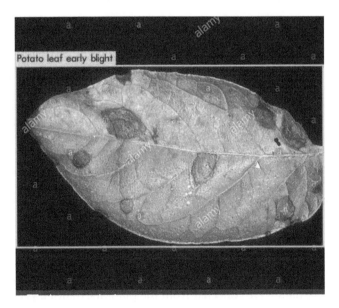

FIGURE 9.9
Output image of potato leaf blight.

In this, we have evaluated the accuracy of backbone networks for classification of different health conditions of a plant. The proposed model uses darknet-53 which will produce high accuracy in various conditions. In the above table, mean average precision (mAP) means it is used to decide whether the predicted object is correct or not. By the graph, we can say that the proposed model is more accurate in classification as well as localization.

FIGURE 9.10
Output image of grape leaf black rot.

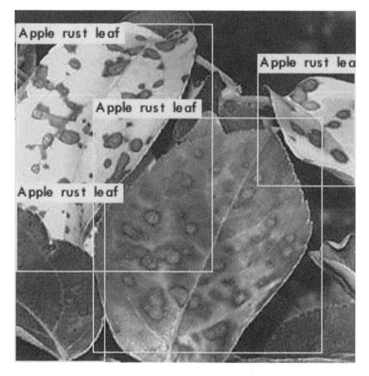

FIGURE 9.11
Output image of apple rust leaf.

We have considered the tomato, corn, and potato plants. The diseases and accuracy of detection for these plants are as follows: tomato leaf late blight (81%), tomato Septoria leaf spot (89%), potato leaf early blight (83%), squash powdery mildew leaf (88%), apple scab leaf (99%), corn rust leaf (96%), and corn leaf blight (99%). We have plotted a graph below

FIGURE 9.12
Output image squash powdery mildew leaf.

FIGURE 9.13
Output image of corn rust leaf.

FIGURE 9.14
Output image of tomato leaf late blight.

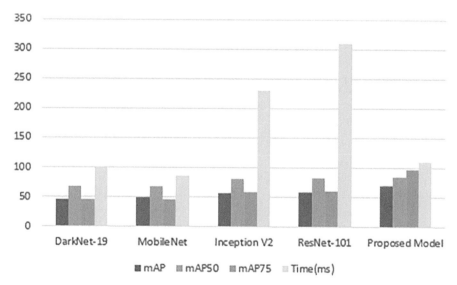

FIGURE 9.15
Accuracy and inference time graph.

for showing the accuracy of detection of diseases. By that graph, we can clearly say that by using DarkNet-53, results with higher accuracy can be obtained (Table 9.3).

The below section shows the accuracy of different diseases' detection, and the proposed model obtains good results in detection of corn rust leaf with 98% and corn leaf blight with 99%. Also, the model detects tomato diseases with good accuracy values.

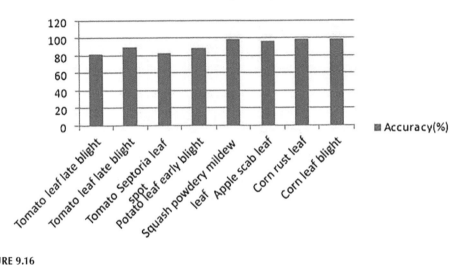

FIGURE 9.16
Accuracy results for disease detection.

TABLE 9.2

Accuracy and Inference Time

Model	mAP	mAP50	mAP75	Time (ms)
DarkNet-19	46.6	68.4	46.4	102
MobileNet	48.9	68.4	45.6	87
Inception V2	56.7	81.6	58.3	230
ResNet-101	58.4	82.7	61.1	310
Proposed model	69.3	84.1	98.5	110

TABLE 9.3

Plant Disease Names and Proposed Model Accuracy

Disease Name	Accuracy (%)
Tomato leaf late blight	81
Tomato leaf late blight	89
Tomato septoria leaf spot	83
Potato leaf early blight	88
Squash powdery mildew leaf	99
Apple scab leaf	96
Corn rust leaf	98
Corn leaf blight	99

9.6.5 Applications to Human Action Recognition

The convolution RNN method considers various convolution features to recognize the emotion in wild using 1-min gradual dataset samples. Bhatt et al. proposed a method for training done on large (aff-wild) datasets. Using task-variant framework, it fetches all the features from high to low and computes prediction with their mean values. Efficiency is improved by fusing of various networks and leads to accurate results. It receives the third rank in 1 min emotion challenge, mainly in technologies. Mainly, this method obtains the second rank in the technologies used category. This method produces accurate results than state-of-the-art methods for visual modality. The proposed approach is further extended to improvement in arousal estimation results.

In computer vision field, Ananda Krishnan and Hanson [15] proposed many developments which are implemented using large standard datasets. Mainly, in machine learning technology, having large sets of open-source libraries for implementation and also less expensive hardware is possible to obtain better results in novel methodologies. By using Image net, we can use large datasets for image processing mainly in image understanding. In video classification, there is no barrier for datasets because of CCTV utilization in many places in which we need to monitor activities.

A model presents a user-independent deep learning-based approach for online human activity classification. Convolutional neural networks are used for local feature extraction together with simple statistical features that preserve information about the global form of time series. Furthermore, the impact of time series length on the recognition accuracy is investigated and limit it up to 1 s that makes possible continuous real-time activity classification. The accuracy of the proposed approach is evaluated on two commonly used WISDM and UCI datasets that contain labelled accelerometer data from 36 and 30 users, respectively, and in cross-dataset experiment. The results show that the proposed model demonstrates state-of-the-art performance while requiring low computational cost and no manual feature engineering.

Recurrent neural network (RNN) and DCNN (deep convolution neural network) are used to train with available data and also other information retrieved from various networks which is similar in nature with suitable databases. To minimize loss, extra information is included in terms of its features, and also, performance is increased with various datasets without losing the knowledge which is learned from the dataset of images. It is tested, in identifying facial expression and emotion recognition for better performance. The results are reasonably good with comparison of state-of-the-art methods (Jiang et al.).

9.7 Wavelet-Based Feature Extraction Methods and Application to Audio Signals

Malignant growth arrangement by specialists and radiologists depended on morphological and clinical highlights and had restricted symptomatic capacity in former times. The ongoing appearance of DNA microarray innovation has prompted the simultaneous observation of thousands of quality articulations in a solitary chip which animates the advancement in malignancy order. In this work, we have proposed a half breed approach for microarray information characterization dependent on closest neighbor (KNN), innocent Bayes, and backing vector machine (SVMs). Highlight choice before arrangement assumes an indispensable job and an element determination procedure which consolidates discrete wavelet change (DWT) and moving window strategy (MWT) are utilized. The exhibition of the proposed strategy and the ordinary classifiers like help vector machine, closest neighbor, and credulous Bayes is contrasted. Examinations have been led on both genuine and benchmark datasets, and the outcomes demonstrate that the outfit approach produces higher arrangement precision than traditional classifiers.

9.7.1 Introduction to Discrete Wavelet Transform Techniques

The proposed framework has the ability to recognize typical and unusual instances of various tumors dependent on discrete wavelet change. Highlight determination before grouping is a basic assignment. Highlight choice strategies presented in He and Lin [27] also eliminate super fluous and excess highlights to improve characterization precision. Numerous change strategies, for example, free part investigation presented in Huang and Zheng [28] and wavelet examination in Liu [29] applied a method to lessen the element of the before. Li et al. [30] proposed a feature extraction strategy dependent on discrete wavelet change (DWT). The estimate coefficients of DWT along with some helpful highlights from the high recurrence coefficients chose by the greatest modulus strategy are utilized as highlights. A tale approach to consider microarray information is as a sign set. The quantity of qualities is the length of signs and henceforth signals preparing strategies, for example, wavelet change can be utilized to perform microarray information investigation.

9.7.2 Wavelet-Based Feature Selection Methods

This work considers the order of specific microarray information into ordinary or anomalous dependent on discrete wavelet change (DWT). DWT is a significant multiresolution investigation apparatus that has been regularly applied to flag handling, picture examination, and different order frameworks proposed in Nanni and Lumini [31]. A tale moving window strategy (MWT) is applied for include extraction and half and half classifier dependent on closest neighbor (NN), naive Bayes, and backing vector machine (SVM) classifier is utilized for order reason. The obtained results are compared with state-of-the-art methods.

9.7.3 Hybrid Feature Extraction Method for Classification

The two different stages involved in the proposed classification system are feature extraction and classification.

- **Feature extraction:** The process consists simplified amount of resources which are used to describe the large amount of data in effective manner. Mainly, discrete wavelet transform (DWT) can be used to analyze high dimensional data such as image processing and image data analysis. Proposed approach is used to analyze the data with appropriate threshold to the wavelet coefficient using DWT and also applying the inverse function to transformed data after that compute the appropriate value of the data. So that, after ranking of wavelet coefficients inside the window, high-ranked wavelet coefficient is selected as a more dominant feature of that window. Similar process is applied to all the windows placed in the microarray data and also stores the top-ranked coefficients in database for classification.

- **Classification:** Order of microarray information into normal and anomalous is finished by planning crossover classifier dependent on NN, innocent Bayes, and SVM. In the order stage, similar sorts of highlights are extricated and contrasted, and the references are acquired in the preparation stage. Cross-approval is utilized to assess how an AI calculation will perform when confronted with new information. It is expected to lessen blunder related with one of the pitfalls of AI where a theory is framed on similar information to test it. In K-overlay cross-approval, the information is haphazardly separated into K parcels. Information in one segment is utilized to test, and the leftover allotments are utilized to prepare. This implies

TABLE 9.4

Level-wise Accuracy Values

Method	Window Size	Accuracy					
		Level 1	Level 2	Level 3	Level 4	Level 5	Level 6
SVM	64	91.35	87.31	92.8	0	0	0
KNN	256	68.57	62.52	74.06	81.56	94.25	0
Bayes	64	92.8	91.35	84.46	0	0	0
Hybrid	512	93.06	95.83	93.06	79.17	100	97.22

that the preparation information should be determined K occasions as each segment gets tried. To assess the strength of the proposed framework, triple cross-approval is utilized. Each overlay is utilized to test the exactness by utilizing one classifier each. The characterization precision got from every one of classifiers is considered as the heaviness of the equivalent while the classifiers are hybridized.

9.7.4 Results

In this part, the trial results and their suggestions are talked about. Here, the exhibition of the proposed arrangement of malignant microarray information dependent on DWT and half and half classifier is clarified. To assess the presentation of the proposed framework, PC recreations and tests with microarray information are performed. The framework is executed in MATLAB® edition 2016. The preparation and testing are run on a cutting-edge standard PC 2.40 GHz Intel processor, 8 GB of RAM running under Windows10. The measurement used to examine the exhibition of the proposed framework is arrangement precision. In this examination, four datasets having enormous number of qualities and one dataset with least number of qualities are thought of (Table 9.4).

The above table shows the window sizes and the different levels in which the greatest precision is accomplished for the proposed framework with different datasets.

The characterization of microarray information is dependent on DWT. The multiresolutional portrayal of microarray information is accomplished by DWT inside a window of predefined size as test design. The presentation of the proposed framework is evaluated by methods for broad computational tests concerning the order of five malignant growth microarray datasets: bosom, colon, ovarian, CNS, and leukemia. Test results show that the proposed technique is fruitful in characterizing the microarray information and the effective grouping rate is 100% for every one of the five microarray datasets. It is seen from the outcomes that DWT arises as a conceivably predominant aspect extraction strategy for microarray information grouping.

9.7.5 Various Applications of Audio Signals

The following section presents various applications of audio signals:

- **Speech Recognition**: The speech recognition applies on translation of speech from verbal format to text format which enables the human speech to written text format.
- **Speaker Identification**: This process is applied on to identify the speaker from all the registered list of speakers to determine the given utterance comes.

- **Machine Translation**: Machine translation is a subfield of computer linguistics which translates speech from one language to another
- **Sound Recognition**: Sound recognition technology is based on audio signal analysis and pattern recognition approaches where it performs feature extraction and classification methods.

9.8 Conclusion

This chapter focuses on deep learning algorithms used in computer vision. Firstly, we presented a detailed description of past, present, and future aspects of deep learning. Extension is made on natural language processing techniques based on deep learning algorithms. Further, the proposed model is focused on deep learning-based image classification approaches, and the developed lightweight deep learning-based object classification model performs in real-time environment. The proposed model LW_DCNN method effectively classified the objects in real time environment. This architecture is very useful in real time monitoring of working condition of the insulators on overhead power polls, which in turn reduces a lot of time for finding the working condition instead of manual check. This method obtained good accuracy with less computation time while compared to existing models. Further scope is extended to focus LW-DCNN method to collect the data using drone thermal cameras and performance evaluation with finetuned parameters. Later, an application from the agricultural domain (customized plant disease detection model) is presented. Next, extension is made on human action recognition applications and discrete wavelet-based feature extraction methods in computer vision. In this chapter, all the sections are presented with the results with comparison analysis of various methods with proposed approaches. The obtained results proved that the presented deep learning algorithms outperformed in computer vision field. Future enhancement is open for a model which works in real time data set of images captured under challenging environments like camera jitter, dynamic background, pan-tilt-zoom (PTZ) images, and intermittent object motion.

References

1. U. Patel, S. Tanwar, A. Nair, "Performance Analysis of Video On-demand and Live Video Streaming Using Cloud based services", *Scalable Computing: Practices and Experience*, Volume 21, No. 3, 2020, pp. 479–496.
2. A. Kumari, D. Vekaria, R. Gupta, S. Tanwar, "Redills: Deep Learning-Based Secure Data Analytic Framework for Smart Grid Systems", *IEEE Conference on Communications (IEEE ICC-2020)*, Dublin, Ireland, 07–11th June, 2020, pp. 1–6.
3. W. McCulloch, P. Walter. "A Logical Calculus of the Ideas Immanent in Nervous Activity", *Bulletin of Mathematical Biophysics*, Volume 5, pp. 115–133.
4. F. Rosenblatt. *The Perceptron – A Perceiving and Recognizing Automaton Project Para.* Cornell Aeronautical Laboratory Inc, Buffalo, NY, 1957.
5. D. H. Hubel, T. N. Wiesel. "Receptive Fields of Single Neurones in the Cat's Striate Cortex", *Journal of Physiology*, Volume 148, 1959, pp. 574–591.

6. K Fukushima, "Neocognitron: A Self-Organizing Neural Network Model for a Mechanism of Pattern Recognition Unaffected by Shift in Position", *Biological Cybernetics*, Volume 36, 1980, pp.193–202.

7. Y. Lecun, "Backpropagation Applied to Handwritten Zip Code Recognition", *Neural Computation*, Volume 1, 1989, pp. 541–551.

8. Y. Lecun, L. Bottou, Y. Bengio, P. Haffner, "Gradient-Based Learning Applied to Document Recognition", *Proceedings of the IEEE*, Volume 86, No. 11, pp. 2278–2324, 1998.

9. G. E. Hinton. "Reducing the Dimensionality of Data with Neural Networks", *Materials and Methods*, Volume 313, No. 5786, pp. 504–507, 2006, Sciencemag.com.

10. K. Alex, I. Stskever. "ImageNet Classification with Deep Convolutional Neural Networks", *Advances in Neural Information Processing Systems*, Volume 25, pp. 1097–1105, 2012.

11. S. P. Mohanty, Hughes, D. P., & Salathe, M. "Using deep learning for image-based plant disease detection." *Frontiers in plant science*, 7, 1419, 2016.

12. A. Fuentes, S. Yoon, S. C. Kim, D. S. Park. "A Robust Deep-Learning-Based Detector for Real-Time Tomato Plant Diseases and Pests Recognition", *Sensors*, Volume 17, No. 9, p. 2022, 2017.

13. K. P. Ferentinos. "Deep Learning Models for Plant Disease Detection and Diagnosis", *Computers and Electronics in Agriculture*, Volume 145, pp. 311–318, 2018.

14. P. V. Bhatt, S. Sarangi, S. Pappula. "Detection of Diseases and Pests on Images Captured in Uncontrolled Conditions from Tea Plantations", *Autonomous Air and Ground Sensing Systems for Agricultural Optimization and Phenotyping IV*, International Society for Optics and Photonics, United States, 14 May 2019, Volume 11008.

15. M. G. Anandakrishnan, J. Hanson, "Plant Leaf Disease Detection Using Deep Learning and Convolutional Neural Network", *International Journal of Engineering Science and Computing*, Volume 7, March, 2017, pp. 5325–5328.

16. H. Durmuş, E. O. Güneş, M. Kırcı, "Disease Detection on the Leaves of the Tomato Plants by Using Deep Learning", *2017 6th International Conference on Agro-Geoinformatics*, Fairfax, VA, USA 2017, pp. 1–5.

17. W. Liu, D. Anguelov, D. Erhan, C. Szegedy, S. Reed, C. Y. Fu, & A. C. Berg. " SSD: Single shot multibox detector." In *European Conference on Computer Vision* (pp. 21–37). Springer, Cham. October, 2016.

18. P. Jiang, Y. Chen, B. Liu, D. He, C. Liang, "Real-Time Detection of Apple Leaf Diseases Using Deep Learning Approach Based on Improved Convolutional Neural Networks", *IEEE Access*, Volume 7, pp. 59069–59080, 2019, doi: 10.1109/ACCESS.2019.2914929.

19. S. Khan, M. Narvekar. "Disorder Detection in Tomato Plant Using Deep Learning", In: H. Vasudevan, A. Michalas, N. Shekokar, M. Narvekar (eds) *Advanced Computing Technologies and Applications. Algorithms for Intelligent Systems*. Springer, Singapore, pp. 187–197, 2020.

20. M. H. Saleem, J. Potgieter, K. M. Arif. "Plant Disease Detection and Classification by Deep Learning", *Plants*, Volume 8, No. 11, p. 468, 2019.

21. Y. Lu, S. Yi, N. Zeng, Y. Liu, Y. Zhang. "Identification of Rice Diseases Using Deep Convolutional Neural Networks", *Neurocomputing*, Volume 267, pp. 378–384, 2017.

22. B. Anjanadevi, V. Hima Bindu ,S. Nitish , M. Yunesha. "Deep Learning Based Brain Tumor Detection", *International Journal of Recent Technology and Engineering (IJITEE)*, Volume 9, Issue 7, pp. 874–877, May 2020.

23. M. Patel, S. Tanwar, R. Gupta, N. Kumar. "A Deep Learning based Cryptocurrency Price Prediction Scheme for Financial Institutions", *Journal of Information Security and Applications*, Volume 55, pp. 1–13, 2020.

24. P. Bhattacharya, S. Tanwar, S. Tyagi, N. Kumar, "BINDaaS: Blockchain Integrated Deep-Learning as a Service in Healthcare 4.0 Applications", *IEEE Transactions on Network Science and Engineering*, pp. 1–14, 2019.

25. A. Bondalapati, S. N. Bhavanam, E. S. Reddy. "Moving Object Detection Based on Unified Model", *Journal of Ambient Intelligence and Humanized Computing*, Volume 12, pp. 6057–6072, June 2020.

26. B. Anjanadevi, S. Naga Kishore Bhavanam, E. Srinivasa Reddy. "An Efficient Methodology for Object Classification Using Light Weight Deep Convolutional Neural Networks", *International Journal of Recent Technology and Engineering (IJRTE)*, Volume 8, Issue 2, pp. 5965–5968, July 2019.
27. Q. He, D.-Y. Lin. "A Variable Selection Method for Genome-Wide Association Studies", *Bioinformatics*, Volume 27, No. 1, pp. 1–8, 2011.
28. D. S. Huang, C. H. Zheng. "Independent Component Analysis-Based Penalized Discriminant Method for Tumor Classification Using Gene Expression Data", *Bioinformatics*, Volume 22, No. 15, pp. 1855–1862, 2006. doi: 10.1093/bioinformatics/btl190. Epub 2006 May 18. PMID: 16709589.
29. Y. Liu. "Wavelet Feature Extraction for High-Dimensional Microarray Data", *Neurocomputing*, Volume 72, Nos. 4–6, pp. 985–990, 2009.
30. S. Li, C. Liao, J. T. Kwok. "Wavelet-Based Feature Extraction for Microarray Data Classification", *The 2006 IEEE International Joint Conference on Neural Network Proceedings*, Vancouver, BC, Canada, 2006, pp. 5028–5033.
31. L. Nanni, A. Lumini. "Wavelet Selection for Disease Classification by DNA Microarray Data", *Expert Systems with Applications*, Volume 38, No. 1, pp. 990–995, 2011.

10

Stationary Signal, Autocorrelation, and Linear and Discriminant Analysis

Bandana Mahapatra and Kumar Sanjay Bhorekar

Symbiosis Skills and Professional University

CONTENTS

10.1 Introduction

The branch of machine learning (ML) has been quite popular in recent years, which is capable of making use of successive layers for processing divergent signal types and extracting different patterns communicated. It typically uses layers of nonlinear processing units in order to build a model for high levels of abstractions within a data. The technique has gained quite a popularity because of its capability for analyzing a huge number of signals conveying a certain information pattern [1]. As one of the most powerful identification/classification tools, it has been applied in various areas. Various specialized application areas in industry, such as computer vision [2], natural language processing [3], economics [4], and bioinformatics [5], have been immensely benefited from advanced research in machine learning. In order to appreciate the contribution of ML in signal recognition and processing, we need to understand the concept of signal processing and its underlying computation.

DOI: 10.1201/9781003107026-10

FIGURE 10.1
Components of signal processing.

As per the IEEE standards, signal processing is all about electronic gadgets and machineries that work by enabling various signals, e.g., computers, radios, videos, and mobile phones. Signal processing may be considered as the branch of electrical engineering which can model and analyze data representations of physical events. Currently it is the heart of the digital world, such as speech and audio, autonomous driving, image processing, wearable technology, and communication systems [6].

A signal may be defined as the physical backbone of information communicated. As represented in Figure 10.1, signal processing can be defined as the intersection of mathematics, informatics, and physical stimuli. The physical signals here include all forms of data which can be represented in digitized forms, e.g., images, videos, audio, and sensor data. Mathematics is significant for evaluating, informatics supports the implementation, and the physical world generates the signals [7].

Machine learning for signal data needs extra steps for data processing and interpretation. Good quality signal data are quite challenging to obtain since the real data are always accompanied with much of noise factor and variability. Wideband noise, jitters, and distortions are few unavoidable characteristics that are often found in most signal data [8,9].

Currently signal processing is catching a lot of lime-light among the data analysis professionals. The physical world is a beacon of signals. The human body, the earth's environment, outer space, and even animals all emit signals that can be analyzed and understood using mathematical and statistical models. Signal processing has been used to understand the human brain, diseases, audio processing, image processing, financial signals, and more. Signal processing is slowly coming into the mainstream of data analysis with new deep learning models being developed to analyze signal data [10].

This chapter discusses the base computation over which machine learning models are built upon in Section 10.2, whereas Sections 10.3 and 10.4 are all about various machine learning approaches for various signal processing and identifications, Section 10.5 is application areas of ML in signal-based data classification of various audio- and image-based data and its contribution in various industry, and finally the chapter concludes in section 10.6.

10.2 Fundamentals of Linear Algebra and Probability Theory

Linear algebra and probability theory may be considered as a pillar or building block of the machine learning concept. The concept of ML and its application cannot be justified without a pre-required knowledge and understanding of these mathematical foundations. This section of this chapter will cover the concept and role of linear algebra and probability theory in ML with much required details [10].

10.2.1 What is Linear Algebra?

Linear algebra can be described as a niche field of mathematics which majorly focusses on vectors, matrices, and various related operations that can possibly be performed over these data structures. The concept of linear algebra can be considered as the basic building blocks for the machine learning techniques [10,11].

10.2.1.1 Important Concepts in Linear Algebra for Machine Learning

Though it is very important to have adept knowledge of major linear algebra concepts for understanding the underlying concepts behind machine learning, there are a few concepts of linear algebra that are required in order to know how machine learning works. Few of these concepts are discussed as follows:

1. **Vectors and Matrix**: The two fundamental concepts of math's that have a significant role in area of ML are the **vector** and the **matrix**. They can be considered as examples of a more complex entity known as **tensors**.

   - Tensors may be described as an *order* (or *rank*) that defines the total dimension in an array needed to represent it.
   - Vectors in math's consist of a collection of numbers, whereas a matrix comprises 2-D vectors.

   The concept of vectors plays a vital role in supervised machine learning algorithms as the target variables, whereas the features extracted from the data form the matrix. A number of operations can be performed using the matrix such as conjugate, multiplication, rank, and transformation. Two vectors with the same number of elements and dimension may be used in order to perform both subtraction and addition [11].

2. **Symmetric Matrix**: Symmetric matrix plays a vital role in both linear algebra as well as machine learning. Linear algebra matrices are majorly used in order to carry out functions. In majority of the cases, such functions are symmetrical in nature, along with their corresponding matrices. These defined functions as well as their values may be used for measuring the feature distance as well as feature covariance.

   Some of the identified features of symmetric matrices are as follows [12]:
   - The matrix and its inverse are both symmetrical in nature.
   - Eigenvalues consist of only real numbers.
   - A matrix multiplied with its transpose gives a symmetric matrix.
   - The symmetric matrices consist of the factorization property.
   - For matrices having linear independent columns, the matrix multiplied with its transpose results in a matrix which is invertible in nature.

3. **Eigenvalues and Eigenvector**: The concept of Eigenvectors can be explained as the vector showing scalar variations indicating negligible changes in the direction. The eigenvalue congruent with eigenvectors actually correlates with the

magnitude which is utilized as their scaling factor. Both the concept of Eigenvalues and eigenvectors are fundamental concepts in mathematics and computing.

While plotting a vector on an XY graph, it follows a specific direction. If linear transformation is applied over the vectors, no change in their direction can be seen. These vectors play a significant role in areas pertaining to machine learning.

Eigenvalues and eigenvectors are typically employed to reduce the noise factor in the data. These concepts can also be used to enhance the tasks that are proved to be computationally intensive. They can be further employed for measuring overfitting tendencies of bias variance trade-offs. There are multiple occurrences of scenarios where eigenvalues and eigenvectors have been proved as useful [13].

It is extremely tough to foresee the character variants of sound, textual, or image data typically stored in the 3-D format. Eigenvalues and eigenvectors are quite helpful in capturing the huge quantity of data typically stored in the form of a matrix, e.g., facial recognition [11,13].

4. **Principal Component Analysis (PCA):** In multiple cases, while dealing the machine learning-based problems, researchers generally find dimensionality as a challenge to solve. Principal component analysis (PCA) is a popular technique which is commonly used while solving problems related to feature extraction from highly correlated and relatively large-sized data sets [14].

   Typically, in a high dimensional data set, it is a challenge to uniquely identify the impact of an individual feature over the target variable. This may be justified by the fact that each individual feature consists of a high correlation factor in comparison to what is needed, which dominates the target variable in an analogous manner [13,15]. Moreover, the process of data visualization becomes challenging with high-dimensional data sets. Such issues can be easily sorted by using the PCA method which has the capability to reduce the dimension from multidimensional to 3D or 2D. The dimensionality reduction is done making sure that there should be no loss of information due to the change in the maximum variance factor. The concept of PCA is built over the orthogonal factor of mathematics which makes the computational model less complex via reducing the number of features present in the data set [14].

10.2.1.2 Role of Linear Algebra in Machine Learning

The concept of linear algebra plays a varied role in various machine learning algorithms which are discussed as follows:

1. **Importance of Linear Algebra to Excel in Machine Learning:** The concepts in linear algebra is quite important for fundamental understanding of machine learning algorithms. Concepts like integral and differential calculus assist in acquiring fundamental knowledge that is necessary for applications, such as tensors and vectors.

   Learning these techniques will help in better understanding as well as applying concepts such as the simplex method and spatial vectors [13].

2. **Prediction/Analysis in Machine learning:** The improved concepts of linear algebra not only supports in keen and clear understanding of machine learning concepts and algorithms but also adds more dimensions to it. The matrices and

vectors are helpful in increasing our vision and perspective over a specific topic. The number of dimensions that can be added is limitless. It helps us in improving our visualizing capacity as well as setting up various graphs for better analysis and understanding.

3. **Linear Algebra Helps for Creating Machine Learning Algorithms**: Linear algebra can be used to build comparatively effective supervised as well as unsupervised machine learning algorithms. Logistic regression, linear regression, decision trees, and support vector machines (SVM) are a few supervised learning algorithms that can be created from almost nothing by the support of linear algebra. Apart from that, linear algebra also plays a role for unsupervised algorithms, which includes single value decomposition (SVD), clustering, and components analysis. Linear algebra helps in developing in-depth understanding of the machine learning project as well as provides the flexibility for customizing various parameters [15,16].

4. **Linear Algebra for Better Graphic Processing in Machine Learning**: Projects based on machine learning are always constituted with various kinds of images, audio, video, or edge detection and various graphical interpretations to work on.

   Machine learning algorithms are also equipped with classifiers which can train a section of the given data set specified according to categories. Another job of classifiers is to do away with errors from the data that has already been trained.

   In this scenario, the complex computations with respect to large data sets can be performed using the concept of linear algebra, which uses techniques like matrix decomposition in order to process and handle huge data for different projects. Q-R and L-U decomposition are few popular techniques that can be used for matrix decomposition [17].

5. **Linear Algebra to Improve Your Take on Statistics**: The fundamental understanding of Linear Algebra is quite important in order to better understand the concepts of statistics needed to organize as well as integrate data in machine learning. Linear algebra consists of various methods, operations, and notations which supports the integration of advanced statistic concepts such as multivariate analysis into any given project which helps into better understanding of how increase in one variable affects another [15,16].

10.2.2 Probability Theory

The probability theory can be explained as the mathematical framework that is primarily used to quantify the data and facilitate during scenarios where being it is impossible to be certain. Probability theory can be considered as the foundation of multiple machine learning algorithms [16]. Figure 10.2 shows the mathematical representation of the probability concept.

10.2.2.1 What Is Probability?

Probability can be explained as an event that ranges anywhere between 0 and 1 value corresponding to an assumption regarding how likely is the event to happen. Considering the nature of randomness certain basic principles and methods for estimating probabilities, nearest to reality.

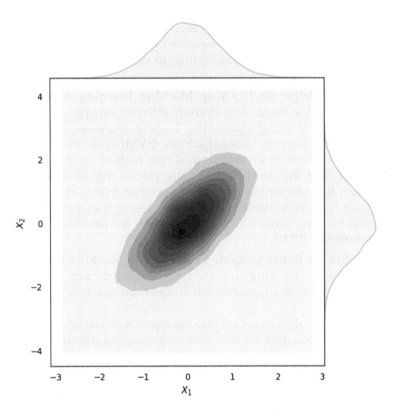

FIGURE 10.2
Mathematical representation of probability concept.

10.2.2.2 The Mathematics of Probability

Considering the mathematical framework for probability, there are important theories and axioms that are required to take full advantage of the theory as a tool for machine learning. The concept of probability is majorly about possibility of various outcomes. Here, the set of every feasible outcome is called the **sample space**. For example, the sample space for a coin flip is {heads, tails} or temperature of water is every value possible between the freezing and boiling point. At any given time only, a single outcome is possible out of the considered sample space [17].

Here, the probability of an event ω is $P(\omega)$.
Ω (capital omega) is the sample space
ω (lowercase omega) is the specific outcome.
The two basic axioms of probability can be defined as follows:

- $0 \leq P(\omega) \leq 1$
- $\sum_{\omega} P(\omega) = 1$

According to the given rule, the probability of an occurrence of any given event has to fall between 0, i.e., impossible, and 1 corresponding to certain, and the sum of the probabilities of all events should be 1. This given axiom can be further extended to the fact that the sample space must contain all possible outcomes. Hence, it is quite certain (probability 1) for one of the possible outcomes to occur.

Any **random variable** (*x*) can be defined as a variable that randomly picks on any values from a considered sample space. For example, let us say *x* represents the outcome of flipping a coin, it may be defined as holding a specific outcome as *x* = heads/tail.

Random variables can hold discrete values like the coin outcome or continuous, i.e., infinite number of possible outcomes within a range.

To define the chance of every individual possible value of any given random variable *x*, a **probability distribution can be specified**. Random variable (*x*) here can be defined as *x* ~ *P*(*x*) to indicate that it is a random number that is extracted out of the probability distribution *P*(*x*). The probability distributions factor here is described different basing upon weather the random variable is discrete or continuous [18,19].

- **Discrete Distributions**: A discrete random variable may be defined with a **probability mass function** (PMF) which maps every value given within the considered variable's sample space to the probability. For example, uniform distribution over *n* number of possible outcomes: $P(x = x) = 1/n$.

  This can be calculated as "The probability of *x* taking on the value *x* is 1 divided by the number of possible values." It's named as uniform distribution since every outcome has equal likelihood (the possibility of the outcome is uniformly extended over all possible values). Here, fair dice rolls are modeled by a uniform distribution as every face of the die has equal opportunity to occur. A loaded die is modeled with a categorical distribution, as shown in Figure 10.3, where every outcome has been attached with a different probability.

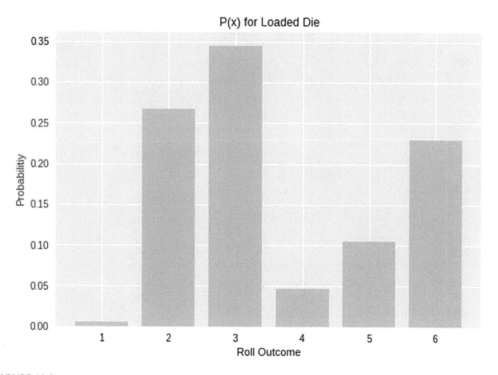

FIGURE 10.3
Probability mass function for rolling dice game.

- **Continuous Distributions**: Continuous random variables are defined by **probability density functions** (PDFs), as shown graphically in Figure 10.4, which is indicated as $f(x)$ for a random variable x. PDFs can map down any given infinite sample space to relative possible output values. For example, Gaussian (Normal) distribution commonly termed as the bell curve is majorly used in order to model various natural events like heights of every gender that are approximately Gaussian distributed. Two major parameters used here are the *mean* μ (mu) and *variance* σ^2 (sigma squared). The mean may be defined as the center of the distribution, whereas the variance specifies the width of the distribution [20].

Other factors like standard deviation σ may be defined as the square root of the variance. To indicate that x is a random variable that is drawn from a Gaussian with mean μ and variance σ^2, we can write:

$$X \, N\left(\mu, \; \sigma^2\right)$$

Where,

X is drawn from a Normal distribution with mean μ and variance σ^2.

The functional form of the PDF is defined as

$$f\left(x \,|\, \mu, \; \sigma^2\right) = \frac{1}{\sqrt{2\pi\alpha^2}} e^{-\frac{(x-\mu)^2}{2\sigma^2}} \qquad (10.1)$$

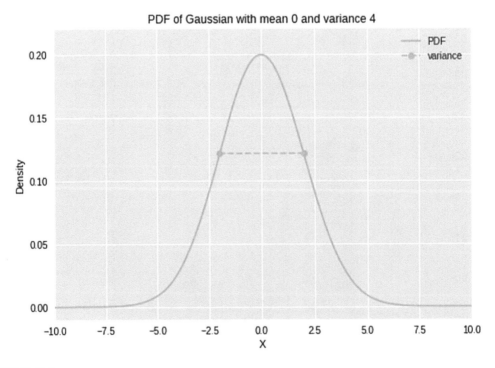

FIGURE 10.4
Probability density function for infinity sample space.

where
the PDF of x is given as μ and σ^2.

Plotting this Equation (10.1) with given $\mu = 0$ and $\sigma^2 = 4$:
Under any circumstances, the sum of all the calculated probability of every possible occurrence needs to be 1. The major challenge of how to calculate the sum over an infinity number of values within a range can be solved by adopting methods and concepts from calculus in the form of integral which can be rewritten as:

$$\int_{\Omega} f(x)dx = 1$$

(10.2)

Here, the integral of the PDF, i.e., the area under curve calculated over the sample space is 1, which can be further described as a generalized summation calculated over an infinite range of values. Hence, the area considered under the PDF corresponds to the total probability of the Gaussian [21].

- **Joint Probability Distributions**: The concept of joint probability distribution can be explained as a distribution covering a wide range of multiple random variables which can be defined as the vector **x**. The joint distribution defined over **x** specifies the probability for a particular value setting considering all random variables present in **x**, e.g., for two given random variables x and y, the joint probability factor may be defined as (Figure 10.5):

$$P(x = x, \, y = y) \text{ or just } P(x, \, y).$$

For any given random variables $X, Y, \ldots$, defined over a probability space, the joint probability distribution measured is the probability distribution which provides the probability where every value may be categorized under a particular range or the discrete set of values classified for that variable. For two random variables, it is a bivariate distribution, and when generalized to any number of random variables, it gives a multivariate distribution [17].

- **Marginal Probability Distributions**: The sum rule in case of marginal probability distribution may be defined as:

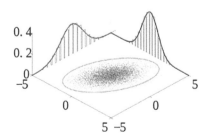

FIGURE 10.5
Graphical representation of joint probability distribution.

$$P(x) = \Sigma_y P(x, y)$$

Here, the term $P(x)$ may be defined as the **marginal probability distribution**. For example, the calculation to determine the probability of wearing a Hoodie over various ranges of seasonal options is:

I'll wear a hoodie, P(Hoodie) = P(Hoodie, Sunny) + P(Hoodie, Cloudy) + P(Hoodie, Rainy) = 3/9. The same calculation concept can be used in order to find the marginal probability for all varieties of cloths across all weather conditions.

- **Conditional Probability Distributions**: The **conditional probability distributions** of x for a given y may be defined as

$$P(x|y) = P(x, y)/P(y)$$

Here, the probability of x conditioned post observing y, i.e., in case observation is $y = y$, the probability that will be calculated as $x = x$ is $P(x, y)/P(Y)$ [18].

The conditional probability only and only exists for cases having $P(y) > 0$. In scenarios where it's impossible for y to occur, there is no observation of y to begin with.

Calculating the product of both sides of the last equation by $P(y)$, the **chain rule** of probability can be obtained as $P(x|y) = P(x, y) \cdot P(y)$.

The chain rule may be established toward hypothesizing to joint distributions with any number of random variables: $P(x, y, z) = P(x|y, z) \cdot P(y, z) = P(x|y, z) \cdot P(y|z) \cdot P(z)$.

- **Bayes' Rule**: The chain rule for two variables can be written in two equivalent ways:

  - $P(x, y) = P(x|y) \cdot P(y)$

  - $P(x, y) = P(y|x) \cdot P(x)$

If we set both right sides equal to each other and divide by $P(y)$, we get Bayes' rule:

$$P(x|y) = \frac{P(y|x) \cdot P(x)}{p(y)} \tag{10.3}$$

- **Bayes Rule**: Bayes' rule is crucially important to much of statistics and machine learning. As alluded to earlier, it's the driving force behind Bayesian statistics. This simple rule allows us to update our beliefs about quantities as we gather more observations from data. I'll definitely discuss Bayes' rule (and Bayesian statistics) some more in a later post [19].

10.2.2.3 Independence and Conditional Independence

In the previous example, we saw that $P(x|y) \neq P(x)$ because observing y gave us information about x. Is this always the case? Let's imagine that $P(x, y)$ is a joint distribution with x representing the amount of ice cream in a store and y representing the number of times per day that the moon is struck by an object. Does knowing either value give us any information about the other? Of course not! So, in this case, $P(x|y) = P(x)$! By plugging this into the chain rule, we find that in this scenario we get $P(x, y) = P(x|y) \cdot P(y) = P(x) \cdot P(y)$. This leads us directly to our definition of **independence**. Two variables x and y are said to be independent if $P(x, y) = P(x) \cdot P(y)$.

A similar concept is that of **conditional independence**. Two variables x and y are called conditionally independent given another variable z if $P(x, y|z) = P(x|z) \cdot P(y|z)$. For example, x is a random variable that indicates if it's raining and y is a random variable indicates if the outside roads are wet. It can surely signify that these events are dependent on each other. If the ground outside is wet means definitely it's been raining, and if it is raining, the ground will become wet. Now variable z can indicate if it is actually raining outside and definitely signify that my grasses are wet. So, the condition of rain has made my time of raining independent of the grass being wet!

The concept of independence and conditional independence is quite significant while representing huge joint distributions. The term independence here allows us to factorize our distribution into comparatively straight forward and noncomplex terms, facilitating efficient memory utilization as well as rapid calculations.

These mathematical concepts play the role of building up the language of probability in order to support the frame of machine learning techniques in a probabilistic light [22].

10.3 Basic Concepts of Machine Learning

Machine learning is basically a collection of algorithms which can enable a system to learn on its own with experience. Machine learning can be defined as a subset of artificial intelligence (AI), which mainly focuses over model building basing upon the sample data which is termed as "training data," that can support in making predictions or model building even in the absence of any program designed for the task. The application areas of the machine learning concept can range from email filtering to computer vision, where it is substantially tough or technically unfeasible for developing the conventional programs designed to perform the same task. The broad area of machine learning consists of a subset called computational statistics which is mainly concerned with the process of decision-making using algorithms based on statistics. However, this under no condition reflects that all machine learning can be categorized as machine learning [22].

The area of mathematical optimization mainly deals with methods and theory along with its application domains related to the field of machine learning. Data mining may be defined as the field that is related and focused more over areas like exploratory data analysis through unsupervised learning. Because of its application across business problems, machine learning can also be described as predictive analytics

The various machine learning approaches are:

- **Supervised Learning**: The concept of supervised learning mainly focuses over learning from the labeled data, i.e., for a given input X, the desired output Y can possibly be predicted.

  Some practical examples of supervised learning include the following:
  - Identifying the various components in the image.
  - Price prediction of a stock or the related features of the company.
  - Presence of malicious behavior in a file.
  - Diagnosis or identification of a disease in a patient.

- **Role of Probability in the Given Scenarios**: The mapping of X to Y can be performed in various ways. By probability distribution over possible values of Y, i.e., $P(Y \mid X)$, we obtain post observation a new sample X. Machine learning algorithm which is employed to identify this distribution is termed as **discriminative algorithms** [23,24], e.g., someone claiming he saw an animal which has fur and a long tail which is two inches tall. However, we cannot specifically identify among the possible animals and guess what it is.

  $P(Y \mid X)$ can be tried as an alternative technique, where the probability distribution is conducted over inputs carrying labels. The specific algorithms for conducting it are termed as **generative algorithms.** Considering the requirement of mice, their various features, and the possible range of values, e.g., description of the possible heights, furriness, and length of tails that mice have, is a kind of generating all possible mice.

  The concept of generative model can assist in the exercise performing of animal's classification with the help of Bias Rules. The Bias Rules states, the details of $P(Y)$, i.e., the probability of any given specific animal, can be extracted from the given training data set, where $P(X)$ can be defined as the probability of any specific feature configuration. These given terms can be explained in the form of $P(Y \mid X)$ through Bayes' rule [25].

  It's possible to learn a mapping from X to Y which is currently not in form of a probability distribution. A deterministic function f *can be attached with the* training data in order to give $f(X) \approx Y$ as the output. The criteria that can improve the distribution are certainly adopting the probabilistic model that may quantify the uncertain measures which any given regular may fail. For example, algorithms designed for illness diagnosis may pass a judgement that there is only a single month of life span needed. In such cases, function f may not be able to express the measure of confidence in the assessment. There might be few features which an algorithm never saw in the training data which clearly indicates the need of less guesswork to predict an outcome. Here, the probabilistic model **quantifies uncertainty**, where the regular function fails to do so [26].

- **Unsupervised Learning**: The concept of unsupervised learning can be explained as a broader set of techniques that supports users to understand, learn, and extract important information and patterns from an unlabeled data, representing scenarios where we have sample data series X without an output Y. Here, the common unsupervised area describes cases like the following [27,28]:

  i. **Clustering**: The concept of clustering refers to the grouping of data points having certain common functionality and features together. Clustering may be considered as a classical problem of unsupervised learning. Considering few data points that belong to various anonymous groups, it is challenging to determine the possible group it may belong to. One of the methods to solve such problems is to assume that every group is created out of varying probability distribution. Identifying the solution to this problem is more like finding the most likely configuration for these distributions.

  ii. **Dimensionality Reduction, Factor Analysis, and Embedding technique**: The concept of dimensionality reduction focuses over projecting a high dimensional data into a lower dimensional space. Dimension reduction can be explained as one of the major thrust areas of unsupervised learning.

The issues with high dimensional data are that it consumes more memory space, involves high computation, and makes it hard to interpret as well as visualize it. Moreover, there are many algorithms that may not be able to process data with high dimension. Hence, it is recommended to possibly reduce the data dimension mapping it to a lower one without compromising over the information carried by the data. One relates the problem with that of finding a distribution over a lower dimensional space which supports similar characteristics as that of distribution of original data [29].

iii. Distributed Data representation also termed as density estimation characterizes the construction of the estimate made after observing the data for an unobserved underlying probability density function. The anomaly detection can be treated as one of the major examples for density estimation.

- **Reinforcement Learning**: The area of reinforcement learning mainly deals with training artificial agents to succeed easily at a specific task. The process of learning in case of artificial agents is commenced by helping them into taking actions within the given environment as well as receiving rewards on the basis of their behavior. The agents mainly aim at maximizing the amount of expected long-term rewards or gains. The concept of probability is typically used in case of reinforcement learning in several scenarios pertaining to reinforcement learning. The process of making agents learn often focusses over the agents learning process with respect to quantifying the unpredictability regarding the utility of incorporating one specific action over the other.

10.4 Supervised and Unsupervised ML Techniques for Digital Signal Processing

10.4.1 What Is Signal Processing?

A signal may be defined as a function or a mechanism designed to convey certain information. Audio, image, electrocardiograph (ECG) signals, radar signals, stock price movement, and electricity voltage are few examples.

Signal processing as shown in Figure 10.6 may be defined as a branch of engineering which primarily focuses over synthesizing, analyzing, and modifying various signal types. Few application areas of signal processing are [30]:

- Conversion of one signal kind to another through the process of filtering, decomposition, and de-noising.
- Extracting various information and patterns from the communicated signal through computer vision, speech recognition, iris recognition, finger print recognition, etc.
- Error control and source coding via low-density parity codes (LDPC), turbo coding, linear prediction coding, JPG, and PNG.
- Detection of signals through devices like SONAR and RADAR.

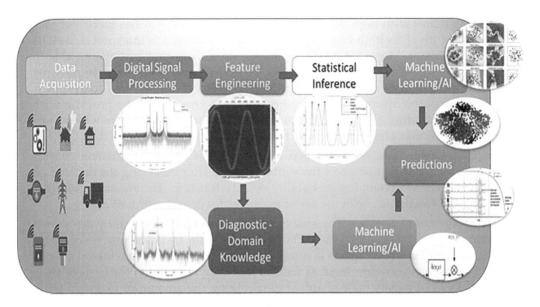

FIGURE 10.6
Signal processing using machine learning approach.

10.4.2 Machine Learning (ML) Concepts

Machine learning can be defined as an area of computer science which deals with creating algorithm or model from input data. Arthur Samuel (1959) [1] (Arthur Lee Samuel was an American pioneer in the field of computer gaming and artificial intelligence who popularized the term "machine learning" in 1959) defined the field of machine learning as "Field of study that gives computers the ability to learn without being explicitly programmed." Kevin Murphy has further stated in his Seminal Book that machine learning is merely a collection of algorithms which is capable of auto detecting or extracting various uncovered and hidden patterns in data and use them to predict future data or other important information [31].

The extraction of knowledge from data via using learning algorithms can be explained as follows:

- **Extracting Various Hidden Patterns from the Data–Example**: text patterns recognition within a set of spam emails.
- **Data Classification and Grouping into Different Categories–Example**: classification of all incoming emails into spam or nonspam.
- **Prediction of Futuristic Result Based on Current Data–Example**: prediction about the occurrence of incoming spam email.

As we know, machine learning algorithms have been segregated into four categories:

- **Supervised learning**: this is explained is a *predictive learning* approach, which mainly aims toward learning from a labeled set of input-output pairs. These sets provide examples for further processing into either classifying the data into groups or predicting the data where the inputs are named *"features"* and outputs are termed as *"response variables."*

- **Unsupervised Learning**: the category of unsupervised learning deals with averagely categorized knowledge *discovery process,* where the aim is to learn structured patterns within the data by the processing of filtering and separating them from the unstructured noisy data.
- **Reinforced Learning**: the process of reinforced learning is the process of interaction with the connected environment in order to undertake various decision-making tasks.

    Considering the above factors, the next section discusses how the synergy existing between the fields of signal processing and machine learning can add new perspective of problem-solving pertaining to various application areas.

- **Speaker Identification**: an application of ML algorithms in signal processing. Speaker identification as shown in Figure 10.7 is the process of identifying a person based on its voice characteristics. In this *supervised* **classification** application, a labeled training set of voice samples (from a set of speakers) is used in the learning process.

Steps undertaken while processing data are:

i. **Data Preprocessing**: This style of learning model cannot be used directly for either voice sample or the recording as data for processing. The considered raw data have to undergo either sampling or cleaning in order to remove the unwanted noise factor or the invalid samples that are mixed with the wanted data. These sample

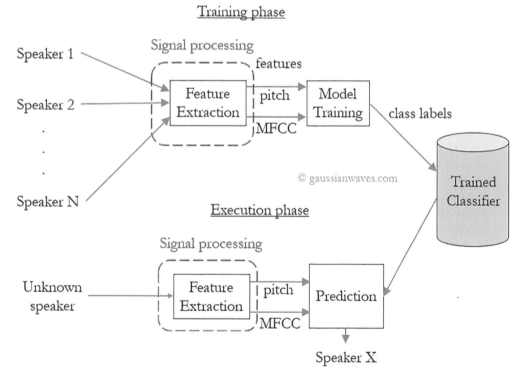

FIGURE 10.7
Speaker recognition using machine learning and signal processing.

data also have to be reformatted into suitable format appropriate to undergo further processing. The step of preparing the data in order to undergo processing is termed as *"data preprocessing."*

Apart from data preprocessing, *transformation of data* as well as *knowledge* regarding the problem collected may also be needed for certain specific ML algorithm. In order to train the machine learning model for extracting various patterns from the given voice sample data, typically signal processing is employed. Here, the features from the voice sample employed for training an ML model are pitch, Mel-Frequency Cepstrum Coefficients (MFCC) [32].

Here, the available data set can be divided into two categories: one set for the purpose of training the model, whereas the other would suffice the need of testing. The split is done at a ratio of 75%–25%. The *training set* is used in order to train the ML model, whereas the test set is used to access both the effectiveness and performance of the ML algorithm.

The training process aims at generalizing the underneath relation shared between feature vectors and class labels, where the feature vectors consist of the input provided to the supervised learning algorithm and the class labels deal with the supervised learners output. The efficiency of the ML model developed can be accessed using the verification technique called **Cross-validation**. It is equally vital for the training process to avoid **overfitting** which may lead to poor generalization as well as erroneous classification during the execution phase.

Various metrics like *accuracy, recall, and confusion* matrix are typically utilized in order to evaluate both the effectiveness as well as performance of an ML algorithm. In case of any improvement needed to be incorporated into the algorithm, the previous steps can be reiterated and changes can be applied at the previous steps.

Once the ML model is trained adequately in order to provide a satisfying outcome, the execution phase can be undertaken where an unlabeled instance of a voice sample is provided as input to the trained classifier in order to identify the person it belongs to.

ii. **Machine Learning with Digital Signal Processing of the Input DNA Sequences**: Out of the 8.7 million kind of species residing on earth, about 1.5 million distinct species have been identified, categorized as well as classified [33]. From the unidentified 86% of the species categories, it has been estimated that about 91% of them existing are marine creatures still waiting to be classified. In order to perform the challenging task of identification and classification of all the species, a considered number of varying techniques have been put forth to perform the genomic sequence as well as analysis and comparison. These proposed methods have been broadly classified into two groups:

- Alignment-based
- Alignment-free

There are multiple methods as well as software tools designed, built upon alignment-based technique, e.g., MEGA7 [3] which is built on sequence alignment using MUSCLE [4] or CLUSTALW [5,34].

Although the alignment-based methods have been proved as successful in areas like genome classification, they failed when implemented in cases that involved heavy time or memory computational cost for solving problems pertaining to multiple alignment in multigenome scale sequence data. Such methods and kinds of data typically require dependence on a prior assumption's basis. A candid, e.g., for the same is the gap penalty and threshold values as statistical parameters [7]. The next-generation sequencing (NGS) is playing a major role; it may be rather challenging to align various short reads that come from various parts of genome [8]. In order to deal with scenarios where typically an alignment-based method fails or proves to be insufficient, an alignment-free method have been put forth [9] which includes including approaches based on Chaos Game Representation of DNA sequences [10–12], random walk [13], graph theory [14], iterated maps [15], information theory [16], and category-position-frequency [17].

Though the concept adopted by alignment-free method is capable of dealing with few issues that is difficult to manage by an alignment-based method, still the method has certain challenges to cope up with which are discussed as follows:

i. No proper software implementation of the concept: Majority of the identified alignment-free algorithms are still under exploration regarding the technical foundations. They mainly lack the software implementation which are vital in order to compare various methods over a common collection of datasets.

ii. Use of simulated sequences or very small real world datasets: The majority of the existing alignment-free methods are tested using simulated sequences or very small real-world datasets. This factor makes it rather challenging to pick one tool over the other. It is hard for experts to pick one tool over the others.

iii. Memory overhead: the possible scaling done over a given multigenome data can possibly result into memory overheads with respect to word-based methods, typically in cases where long k-mers are used. Such challenges can be solved by using the concept of ML-DSP, which has a novel combination of both the supervised **M**achine **L**earning incorporated with **D**igital **S**ignal **P**rocessing performed over the input DNA sequences, as a general-purpose alignment-free method along with the software tool for genomic DNA sequence classification carried over all taxonomic levels [35].

The main contribution of ML-DSP is the *feature vector* that we propose to be used by the supervised learning algorithms. Given a genomic DNA sequence, its feature vector consists of the pairwise Pearson Correlation Coefficient (PCC) between (i) the magnitude spectrum of the Discrete Fourier Transform (DFT) of the digital signal obtained from the given sequence by some suitable numerical encoding of the letters A, C, G, T into numbers and (ii) the magnitude spectra of the DFT of all the other genomic sequences in the training set.

iii. **Machine Learning for Numerical representations of DNA Sequences**

The concept of Digital Signal Processing can be technically implemented for performing a comparative analysis over the genome sequence with context to comparative genomics since the genomic sequences can be numerically communicated as discrete numeric sequences in terms of digital signals. Numerous mathematical representations of DNA sequences have been put forth in various proposed literatures which use numbers attached to individual nucleotides, e.g., Digital Signal Processing (DSP) can be employed in the context of comparative genomics because genomic sequences can be numerically represented as discrete numerical sequences, as shown in Table 10.1 and hence treated as digital signals. Many numerical representations of DNA sequences, which employ numbers attached to individual nucleotides, have been proposed by many researchers [28], e.g., DNA sequencing numbers that are created from fixed mapping of each

TABLE 10.1

Numerical Mapping of DNA Sequence Found in Various Animal Species

Species	Human	Gorilla	Chimp	Rat	Mouse	Lemur	Rabbit	Goat	Bovine	Opossum	Gallus
Human	0	0.0038	0.0309	0.1198	0.1470	0.1604	0.1670	0.2114	0.2616	0.2696	0.2983
Gorilla	0.0038	0	0.0292	0.1206	0.1465	0.1596	0.1668	0.2100	0.2604	0.2701	0.2991
Chimp	0.0309	0.0292	0	0.1365	0.1620	0.1707	0.1782	0.2281	0.2804	0.2870	0.2988
Rat	0.1198	0.1206	0.1365	0	0.0631	0.1513	0.0987	0.1602	0.2282	0.1684	0.2583
Mouse	0.1470	0.1465	0.1620	0.0631	0	0.1208	0.0683	0.1031	0.1763	0.1393	0.2582
Lemur	0.1604	0.1596	0.1707	0.1513	0.1208	0	0.0832	0.1443	0.1608	0.1792	0.2131
Rabbit	0.1670	0.1668	0.1782	0.0987	0.0683	0.0832	0	0.1355	0.1844	0.1209	0.1940
Goat	0.2114	0.2100	0.2281	0.1602	0.1031	0.1443	0.1355	0	0.0900	0.1618	0.3215
Bovine	0.2616	0.2604	0.2804	0.2282	0.1763	0.1608	0.1844	0.0900	0	0.1921	0.3433
Opossum	0.2696	0.2701	0.2870	0.1684	0.1393	0.1792	0.1209	0.1618	0.1921	0	0.2324
Gallus	0.2983	0.2991	0.2988	0.2583	0.2582	0.2131	0.1940	0.3215	0.3433	0.2324	0

nucleotide to a random number, that carries no biological importance, i.e., using mappings of nucleotide to numerical values that has been deduced from their physio-chemical properties or extracted from the doublets or codons from which they have originated [28,29]. Various researchers claim that the choice of numerical for representation had practically no significant effect over the results obtained. The researchers have thereafter conducted a study over comparing various numerical representation techniques over small datasets [32]. Moreover, they have concluded that multidimensional representations (such as Chaos Game Representation) produced better genomic comparison outcome than any single dimensional data representations [36].

Digital signal processing typically follows choosing a suitable numeric form of representing DNA sequences, which can be applied to the output discrete numeric sequences, via process called as Genomic Signal Processing (GSP) [29]. The application areas of DSP are DNA sequence comparison, i.e., to differentiate coding regions from noncoding regions [33,35,36], to map genomic signals for classification to biological sequences [37], for whole genome phylogenetic analysis and to analyze other properties of genomic sequences [37].

10.5 Applications of Signal Based Identification Using Machine Learning Approach

Machine learning techniques have been used in various industries for signal classification based on its various features and traits which is discussed as follows.

10.5.1 ML for Audio Classification

The recent advanced trends in multimedia technologies have triggered the need for classification in audio signals in order to provide the content-based retrieval process which is more effective as well as accurate and easy to handle huge databases. The audio information plays a crucial role in grasping the overall conceptual content of the multimedia.

With the rapid growth in quantity of data, there is a demand of having automation in process of filtering the required data out as well as store more quantity of relevant data. This collected audio data can be quite resourceful in yielding important information as well as process requested results for processes like video indexing and content analysis. A human ear can perceive as well as differentiate various audio signal types by simply listening to a short segment of audio signal but faces challenge in doing so when the considered sound is weak in nature or is accompanied with noise factor [31]. Formulating a solution model for such challenges for a machine has been proved as extremely challenging, where the most difficult problem is posed in performing automated classification. Solving this problem using computers has proven to be very difficult. A major challenge in this field is the automatic classification of audio signals. Currently the audio signal classification is one of the popular technologies that has attracted the interest of many ardent researchers making it quite popular which has found its applicable areas in media services, search engines, and intelligent human-computer systems [33].

The Audio classification can be considered as important due to the following:

a. need of different processing requirement for audios of different quality and types.

b. Due to the distribution of audio into various subclasses based on its quality, the search space for retrieval of any specific audio data has been reduced significantly.

Every classified audio piece can be uniquely processed as well as indexed in order to be effective for further comparison and retrieval.

The various features extracted from the given audio signals considered for process of classification using Machine Learning approach are [29] the following:

1. **Sampling Frequency or the Rate**: rate of number of samples considered over fixed time span.

2. **Amplitude**: measure of change of sound waves over the considered period of time.

3. **Fourier Transform**: Decomposing the function of time/signal into its constituting frequencies, i.e., amplitude of each frequency present in the underlying function.

4. **Power Spectrum**: it describes the power distribution into its discrete frequency components.

5. **Cepstrum**: it is calculated by considering the Fourier transform of the logarithm of estimated power spectrum of a signal.

6. **Spectrogram**: it is the visual representation of a spectrum of frequencies over a signal considering its variations with time.

7. **Cochlea**: this is the spiral cavity located at the inner portion of human ear that contains organ of corti. It produces nerve impulse as a response to the sound vibration.

10.5.2 Audio Signals Classification

The audio signal classification as shown in Figure 10.8 can be performed over a given audio data by applying the process of feature extraction sound signals thereafter using these features in order to identify the class it can be included into. The problem of audio classification can be considered as an example of pattern recognition problem which principally deals with classifying objects into various diverse categories or classes. These classifying objects typically considered are images, signal waves, or various kinds of measurements.

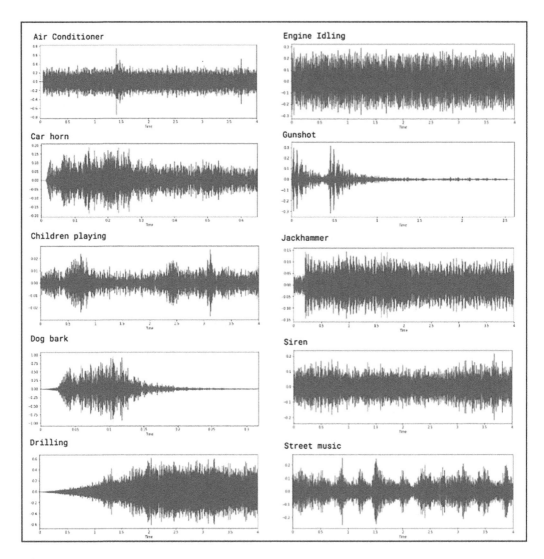

FIGURE 10.8
Audio signal classification for various sound qualities.

The problem of pattern recognition classifies these objects into various categories by developing and applying numerous algorithms that are designed to recognize various patterns in data. These algorithms have important applications in various areas like character recognition, speech analysis, image analysis, clinical diagnostics, person identification, machine diagnostics, and industrial process supervision.

The main applications of audio signal classification are discussed as following:

i. **Computing Tools**: Audio signal classification has been found to contribute into playing a major role at the front end of a system for verity of applications related to audio. Speech recognition can be considered as one of the most popular applications of ASC, where signals are categorized as phonemes and then assembled into words. ASC can be considered as a tool used to improve current speech recognition technology in multiple ways.

ii. **Automatic Bandwidth Allocation**: the audio classification has found its need in areas related to telephone network with audio classification capabilities which can dynamically allocate bandwidth to various signals that are transmitted. Extra bandwidth is allotted for music in comparison to speech transmissions, whereas no bandwidth at all in case of only background noise is detected while transmission. The concept supports the multiplexing systems into working even more efficiently. The same idea is applicable to audio streams in the data networks.

iii. **Audio Database Indexing**: the concept of audio classification is quite useful in arranging large audio files into various large audio and music database collections, e.g., the audio archives created for broadcasting facilities or sound track studios designed as an archive for the movie industry. The current technique of manual classification is quite a time- and effort-consuming job, e.g., the MP3 files stored on hard disks are often unorganized and chaotic in manner [18].

10.5.3 ML for Image Processing

Images play a crucial role in every human life as they are considered as one of the prime sense organs capable of interpreting patterns and images and perceiving them in the human brain. This fact has made the field of image processing as a one of prime areas of research in various AI and machine learning concepts. The concept of image recognition and processing has found applications in various fields including medical, military, and security. Since recent times more quantity of images have been found as a result of easily generated images and pictures via digital technology. The traditional method of processing finds it complex and challenging to adapt such huge quantity of images when compared with human vision and capability to perceive and extract patterns. As the need to increase the complexity of visionary capability of the system arises, machine learning has emerged as a promising method of handling these complex methods of processing image data with ease, making itself quite popular approach.

The increased amount of image datasets and benchmarks, approach of machine learning, and image processing have gained a lot of popularity [17,18].

Image processing can be explained as a method of performing certain operations over an image toward enhancing the image or extracting important information from it. It is basically a kind of signal processing where the input provided is an image with the output received generally being an image or characteristics/features associated with that image.

The image processing can be performed using two main approaches:

a. analogue image processing

b. digital image processing

Analogue image processing is used for the hard copies, e.g., printouts and photographs. These images can be interpreted using various fundamental interpretations for visual techniques by image analysts.

Digital image processing assists in digital image manipulation via computers.

Every data has to undergo three general phases as shown in Figure 10.9 undergoing processing using digital technique, enhancement, display, and information extraction.

The unique combination of machine learning with image processing has contributed greatly to various fields such as agriculture, healthcare, and digital information security.

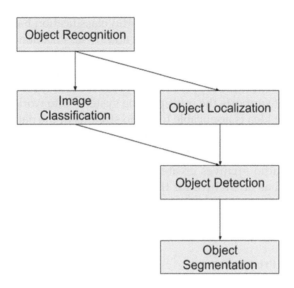

FIGURE 10.9
Phases of image processing.

10.6 Applications of ML Methods in Optical Communications

Optical communication, or **optical telecommunication**, is a communication mode conducted by lights to carry information to a specified distance. The communication can be performed both visually or through electronic devices.

An optical communication system typically makes use of a transmitter, that can encode a given message into its corresponding an optical signal, a channel, that can carry these signals to its destination, and a receiver, that can produce the message from the received optical signal. In the visual mode of communication, the person acts as the "receiver" carrying the responsibility of visually observing as well as interpreting both simple or complex signals.

Machine learning (ML) approaches have recently appeared as a new direction of research for addressing many upcoming challenges in areas pertaining to fiber-optic communications. ML-based approaches have proved to perform quite promisingly in handling scenarios where it is quite challenging to describe the underlying physics and mathematics of the problem along with its related numerical procedures, that call for significant computational resources and time [14]. In recent years, several commendable research studies have been conducted where the primary focus is ML algorithms and its applications pertaining to various aspects of optical communications, e.g., fiber nonlinearity compensation, data center optimization, intelligent testing/measurement equipment realization, network planning, and performance prediction as shown in Figure 10.10.

(i) **Optical Performance Monitoring (OPM)**: OPM can be described as a primary enabling technology in areas of emerging software-defined networks. By usage of OPMs, SDNs can possibly monitor the current network conditions as well as dynamically configure the various transceiver and network elements parameters, e.g., spectrum assignment, transmitted powers, baud rates, modulation formats,

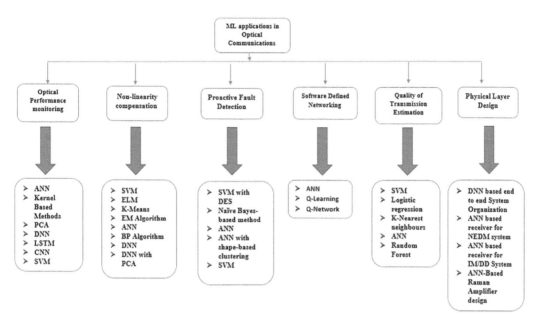

FIGURE 10.10
Some key applications of ML algorithms in optical communications.

and forward error correction (FEC) codes for achieving optimum transmission performance [2–4]. Recently ML-based OPM techniques have gained popularity for devising a cost-effective multiimpairment monitoring technique for optical networks. Few of these popular techniques include artificial neural networks (ANNs) [5,34], principal component analysis (PCA) [6,7], support vector machine (SVM) [8], deep neural networks (DNNs) [9,10], and kernel-based methods [11].

(ii) **Fiber Nonlinearity Mitigation**: ML-based algorithms are quite applicable for compensating fiber nonlinear distortions. This technique is primarily based on learning various features and properties possible over nonlinear impairments from observed data and building various probabilistic model from these impairments which may be used for either providing a compensation for these impairments or quantifying the amount of breakage introduced. Few ML-based nonlinearity compensation techniques are based on extreme learning machine (ELM) [12], stochastic back-propagation (SBP) [13], expectation maximization (EM) algorithm [14], higher-order statistical equalizer [15], and M-ary SVM [16]-based methods.

(iii) **Proactive Fault Detection/Prevention**: *Any* Reliable operation for a given optical network needs a mandate system to generate early warning along with a proactive protection working model into the network. In recent years, quite a number of ML-based techniques have been put forth by researchers for cognitive fault detection/prevention in fiber-optic networks, e.g., use of a combination of double exponential smoothing (DES) and SVM for network equipment failure prediction or proactive fiber damage detection performed by coherent receiver for identifying mechanical stress dependence.

(iv) **Software-Defined Networking**: *The* ML techniques have been able to find its application in enabling several critical functionalities in SDNs. In article [20], ANNs concepts have been used along with big data analytics for network traffic modeling. Built upon predicted traffic volume/direction, virtual network topology (VNT) has the capacity to reconfigure itself. The approach has proved beneficial in significantly reducing the needed number of transponders at the routers when compared to static VNT design approaches, resulting in reduced energy consumption and costs.

10.7 Conclusion

This chapter mainly discusses the machine learning approaches for various signal types, i.e., stationary signal, autocorrelation, and linear and discriminant Analysis. It covers the various mathematical concepts needed for identification of various signal kinds by a machine. This chapter later discusses in detail about various kinds of machine learning approaches with respect to Digital Signal Processing and its applications in classifying various data sets carrying signals representing both audio and image-based signals or other optical communications and their contributions in various industries.

References

1. Mora, C., Tittensor, D. P., Adl, S., Simpson, A. G., & Worm, B. How many species are there on earth and in the ocean? *PLoS Biol.* 2011; 9(8):e1001127.
2. May, R. M. Why worry about how many species and their loss? *PLoS Biol.* 2011; 9(8):e1001130.
3. Kumar, S., Stecher, G., & Tamura, K. MEGA7: molecular evolutionary genetics analysis version 7.0 for bigger datasets. *Mol Biol Evol.* 2016; 33(7):1870–4.
4. Edgar, R. C. MUSCLE: multiple sequence alignment with high accuracy and high throughput. *Nucleic Acids Res.* 2004; 32(5):1792–9.
5. Thompson, J. D., Higgins, D. G., & Gibson, T. J. CLUSTAL W: improving the sensitivity of progressive multiple sequence alignment through sequence weighting, position-specific gap penalties and weight matrix choice. *Nucleic Acids Res.* 1994; 22(22):4673–80.
6. Zielezinski, A., Vinga, S., Almeida, J., & Karlowski, W. M. Alignment-free sequence comparison: benefits, applications, and tools. *Genome Biol.* 2017; 18(1):1–17.
7. Vinga, S., & Almeida, J. Alignment-free sequence comparison—a review. *Bioinformatics.* 2003; 19(4):513–23.
8. Schwende, I., & Pham, T. D. Pattern recognition and probabilistic measures in alignment-free sequence analysis. *Brief Bioinform.* 2014; 15(3):354–68.
9. Song, K., Ren, J., Reinert, G., Deng, M., Waterman, M. S., Sun, F. New developments of alignment-free sequence comparison: measures, statistics and next-generation sequencing. *Brief Bioinform.* 2014; 15(3):343–53.
10. Kari, L., Hill, K. A., Sayem, A. S., Karamichalis, R., Bryans, N., Davis, K., & Dattani, N. S. Mapping the space of genomic signatures. *PLoS One.* 2015; 10(5):e0119815.
11. Hoang, T., Yin, C., & Yau, S. S. T. Numerical encoding of DNA sequences by chaos game representation with application in similarity comparison. *Genomics.* 2016; 108(3–4):134–42.
12. Almeida, J. S., Carrico, J. A., Maretzek, A., Noble, P. A., & Fletcher, M. Analysis of genomic sequences by chaos game representation. *Bioinformatics.* 2001; 17(5):429–37.
13. Yao, Y. H., Dai, Q., Nan, X. Y., He, P. A., Nie, Z. M., Zhou, S. P., & Zhang, Y. Z. Analysis of similarity/dissimilarity of DNA sequences based on a class of 2D graphical representation. *J Comput Chem.* 2008; 29(10):1632–9.

14. Qi, X., Wu, Q., Zhang, Y., Fuller, E., Zhang, C. Q. (2011). A novel model for DNA sequence similarity analysis based on graph theory. Evol Bioinform. 2011; 7:EBO-S7364.

15. Almeida, J. S. Sequence analysis by iterated maps, a review. *Brief Bioinform*. 2014; 15(3):369–75.

16. Vinga, S. Information theory applications for biological sequence analysis. *Brief Bioinform*. 2014; 15(3):376–89.

17. Bao, J., Yuan, R., & Bao, Z. An improved alignment-free model for DNA sequence similarity metric. *BMC Bioinformatics*. 2014; 15(1):321.

18. Leimeister, C. A., Boden, M., Horwege, S., Lindner, S., & Morgenstern, B. Fast alignment-free sequence comparison using spaced-word frequencies. *Bioinformatics*. 2014; 30(14):1991–9.

19. Chang, G., Wang, H., & Zhang, T. A novel alignment-free method for whole genome analysis: Application to HIV-1 subtyping and hev genotyping. *Inf Sci*. 2014; 279:776–84.

20. Reese, E., Krishnan, V. V. Classification of DNA sequences based on thermal melting profiles. *Bioinformation*. 2010; 4(10):463–7.

21. Bonham-Carter, O., Steele, J., & Bastola, D. Alignment-free genetic sequence comparisons: a review of recent approaches by word analysis. *Brief Bioinform*. 2014; 15(6):890–905.

22. Struck, D., Lawyer, G., Ternes, A. M., Schmit, J. C., & Bercoff, D. P. COMET: adaptive context-based modeling for ultrafast HIV-1 subtype identification. *Nucleic Acids Res*. 2014; 42(18):e144.

23. Remita, M. A., Halioui, A., Daigle, B., Kiani, G., & Diallo, A. B. A machine learning approach for viral genome classification. *BMC Bioinformatics*. 2017; 18(1), 1–11.

24. Kosakovsky Pond, S. L., Posada, D., Stawiski, E., Chappey, C., Poon, A. F., Hughes, G., Frost, S. D. An evolutionary model-based algorithm for accurate phylogenetic breakpoint mapping and subtype prediction in HIV-1. *PLoS Comput Biol*. 2009; 5(11):e1000581.

25. De Oliveira, T., Deforche, K., Cassol, S., Salminen, M., Paraskevis, D., Seebregts, C., Vandamme, A. M. An automated genotyping system for analysis of HIV-1 and other microbial sequences. *Bioinformatics*. 2005; 21(19):3797–800.

26. Solis-Reyes, S., Avino, M., Poon, A., & Kari, L. An open-source k-mer based machine learning tool for fast and accurate subtyping of HIV-1 genomes. *PLoS One*. 2018; 13(11):e0206409.

27. Sims, G. E., Jun, S. R., Wu, G. A., & Kim, S. H. (2009). Alignment-free genome comparison with feature frequency profiles (FFP) and optimal resolutions. In: *Proceedings of the National Academy of Sciences of the USA*. National Academy of Sciences, 2009, pp. 2677–82. doi:10.1073/pnas.0813249106.

28. Kwan, H. K., Arniker, S. B. Numerical representation of DNA sequences. In: *2009 IEEE International Conference on Electro/Information Technology*. New Jersey: IEEE Publishing, 2009, pp. 307–310. doi:10.1109/EIT.2009.5189632.

29. Borrayo, E., Mendizabal-Ruiz, E. G., Vélez-Pérez, H., Romo-Vázquez, R., Mendizabal, A. P., & Morales, J. A. Genomic signal processing methods for computation of alignment-free distances from DNA sequences. *PLoS One*. 2014; 9(11):e110954.

30. Adetiba, E., Olugbara, O. O., & Taiwo, T. B. Identification of pathogenic viruses using genomic cepstral coefficients with radial basis function neural network. In: *Advances in Nature and Biologically Inspired Computing*. Springer, Cham,2016. pp. 281–91.

31. Adetiba, E., Olugbara, O. O. Classification of eukaryotic organisms through cepstral analysis of mitochondrial DNA. In: *International Conference on Image and Signal Processing*. Springer, Cham. 2016, pp. 243–252.

32. Mendizabal-Ruiz, G., Román-Godínez, I., Torres-Ramos, S., Salido-Ruiz, R. A., & Morales, J. A. On DNA numerical representations for genomic similarity computation. *PLoS One*. 2017; 12(3):e0173288.

33. Chakravarthy, N., Spanias, A., Iasemidis, L. D., Tsakalis, K. Autoregressive modeling and feature analysis of DNA sequences. *EURASIP J Appl Signal Process*. 2004; 2004 (1), 1–16.

34. Larkin, M. A., Blackshields, G., Brown, N. P., Chenna, R., McGettigan, P. A., McWilliam, H., Higgins, D. G. Clustal W and Clustal X version 2.0. *Bioinformatics*. 2007; 23(21):2947–8.

35. Yu, Z., Anh, V., Zhou, Y., & Zhou, L. Q. (2007). Numerical sequence representation of DNA sequences and methods to distinguish coding and non-coding sequences in a complete genome. In: *Proceedings 11th World Multi-Conference on Systemics, Cybernetics and Informatics*. International Institute of Informatics and Systemics, Orlando, FL, 2007. pp. 171–6.

36. Abo-Zahhad, M., Ahmed, S. M., & Abd-Elrahman, S. A. Genomic analysis and classification of exon and intron sequences using DNA numerical mapping techniques. *Int J Inform Technol Comput Sci.* 2012; 4(8):22–36.
37. Skutkova, H., Vitek, M., Sedlar, K., Provaznik, I. Progressive alignment of genomic signals by multiple dynamic time warping. *J Theor Biol.* 2015; 385:20–30.

11

Intelligent System for Fault Detection in Rotating Electromechanical Machines

Pascal Dore, Saad Chakkor, and Ahmed El Oualkadi
University of Abdelmalek Essaâdi

CONTENTS

DOI: 10.1201/9781003107026-11

11.1 Introduction

From all the rotating systems that abound in the sectors of our daily life, asynchronous machines are among the most used because of their low manufacturing and maintenance costs on the one hand and their robustness on the other hand. Made up of countless components that are the same, the other components are prey to faults that cause them to be damaged over time, thus generating consequences both on productivity and on the human and material environment. Therefore, to ensure the availability of industrial units and the safety of goods and people, the monitoring and diagnosis of faults affecting these main components should prove to be a crucial issue not to be ignored for increased productivity within any entity that incorporates them. Thus, through this project we study the development of an intelligent system able to detect these faults in a predictive way. And if the literature allows us to understand that vibration analysis has had its share of lot in these research studies which do not date from today, it is nevertheless necessary to mention that it does not prove to be completely ideal when it is a question of the secure taking of data because the probes used are directly linked to the machine, and in case of failure, it would be necessary to go to the field to change them, which cannot be appreciable in all cases. Based on this observation and recent techniques, it was wise to think of other means of measurement, among which the stator current has proven to be one, allowing recent researchers to dispense with this problem to better focus on the real problem. It is this method that we are using in this project which moreover allows us to do without the no accessibility of these installations in case of fire. It remains to be noted that the implementation of such a sensor less technique responds to major industrial challenges in terms of the implementation of more efficient processes. Thus, the objective to be reached by this work is to find the algorithm allowing to reach such a system without using sensors.

This work is also intended to show the industrial application. This cannot be achieved without the skills required. So, we used digital signal processing to which we added the MATLAB® mathematical tool for the development of computer programs.

The objective of this work was to design an intelligent system capable of early detection of electromechanical faults in rotating machines through the analysis of the stator current, the content of this article is organized as follows: we begin with the related works to speak about the previous work carried out in the same framework, secondly we expose the asynchronous machine which contains these electromechanical systems within which these faults are detected, then in the third point we quote the main faults which attack these systems, then in the fourth place we speak about the methods of detection of the anomalies, then we give the frequency signature of these faults, and then comes an explanation on how to acquire the stator current signal of the asynchronous machine at the occurrence of the MCSA, in the seventh point we expose the ESPRIT method and these variants used to talk in the eighth point about intelligent methods of fault classification before tackling the part of the simulation in the ninth place and closing the whole with the general conclusion and perspectives.

11.2 Related Works

In the diagnosis of electromechanical faults in electric induction machines, there is not only the combination of MCSA, high-resolution signal processing (HRM) method, and learning machine algorithms as it is the case in this study. Indeed, in the past, associations such as MCSA, PCA, and signal processing methods have been used to perform the same work. Although the signal processing methods used with these techniques have produced good results, but each of them had more or less a limitation that did not allow to extend it in all cases of study. This is the case, for example, of the FFT [1] (Fast Fourier Transform) which, although it is widely used in signal processing, does not give any information about when a frequency component occurs, or the DWT (Discrete Wavelet Transform) which, although it gives an interpretation of the signal in time and frequency, offers good temporal resolution and poor frequency resolution at high frequencies, and offers good frequency resolution and poor temporal resolution at low frequencies. Moreover, these methods require a very high level of knowledge in signal processing without forgetting that PCA [2] is a linear method and therefore not applicable in most cases on conventional machines which are nonlinear. With this observation in mind, researchers have gradually migrated toward more adequate solutions; hence, the choice of this association which, in addition to dispensing with the nature of the system studied, offers an intelligent and adaptable diagnosis as the machine operates (Table 11.1).

TABLE 11.1

Technical Shortcomings of Existing Methods

Methods	Technical Deficiencies
MCSA + FFT	Does not give any information about when a frequency component occurs
MCSA + PCA	PCA is a linear method, not applicable in most cases on conventional machines which are nonlinear
MCSA + DWT	Offers good temporal resolution and poor frequency resolution at high frequencies Offers good frequency resolution and poor temporal resolution at low frequencies

11.3 Asynchronous Machines

The asynchronous machine is an alternating current machine that has no connection between the stator and the rotor. The term asynchronous comes from the fact that the rotor speed is different from the pulsation of the stator currents.

The reason for our choice to focus on the asynchronous machine is that the asynchronous machine is widely used in industrial applications, because due to its design, its cost is relatively lower than that of other machines, its electromagnetic robustness is high, and there is good standardization between different manufacturers. However, the simplicity of design of this machine hides a rather important functional complexity. It should also be mentioned that the asynchronous machine was for a long time strongly competed with the synchronous machine in high power domains, until the advent of power electronics. Today it is found in many applications, particularly in transport (metro, trains, ship propulsion), industry, and household appliances.

Originally it was only used in engines, but thanks to power electronics, it is more and more often used in generators. This is for example the case of wind turbines.

These asynchronous machines are made up of a fixed part called the stator and a moving part called the rotor which, depending on the operating mode (motor or generator) of the machine, provides the source of the induction.

We present, respectively, an asynchronous machine, a rotor, and a stator in Figures 11.1 and 11.2.

FIGURE 11.1
Asynchronous machine.

FIGURE 11.2
Rotor (before) and stator (back).

11.4 Electromechanical Faults

These machines, made up of a set of mechanical systems, are most often prey to numerous faults that affect their operation, even impacting their productivity and even the health of their material and human environment as it could be the case of a nuclear power plant. They are certainly numerous, but this article focuses on only four types of faults, as follows.

11.4.1 Bearing Fault

In the literature, the major cause of rotating machine failures is due to faults caused by fatigue spalling, lubricant contamination, excessive load, or other causes or electrical causes such as the flow of leakage currents induced by inverters [3]. Faults of bearings are at the base of several effects in rotating machines, namely: an increase of the noise level and the appearance of vibrations by the rotor's movements around the longitudinal axis of the machine [3]. This type of fault also gives rise to variations (oscillations) in the torque of the machine load inducing the blocking of the rotor. It should also be mentioned that bearings with balls are composed of two rings, one internal and the other one between which are several balls or rotating rollers. When the bearing is operating in normal conditions, the fatigue fault starts with small cracks located below the surfaces of the raceway and rolling element and propagates gradually over the contact surface. In addition, bearing faults are most often related to Eccentricity faults that induce asymmetry of the rotor. On the other hand, the faults linked to the bearing at balls can be classified as follows [3]: outer ring fault, inner ring fault, ball, and cage faults. Also, since the ball bearing supports the machine's rotor, any bearing fault could cause radial displacement between the rotor and stator. These air-gap variations caused by bearing vibrations affect the variation of the internal magnetic flux by producing harmonics in the stator current [4,5]. In Figure 11.3, we show by a diagram what a bearing looks like and the faults it can suffer, namely, the inner race damage, the outer race damage, and the cage fault (Figure 11.4).

11.4.2 Broken Rotor Bar Fault

The breakage of the bars of an asynchronous machine is a fault most commonly studied in the laboratory because of its simplicity of realization. The bar breakage causes a dissymmetry of the rotor. The result of the asymmetry is the creation of a field rotating in the opposite direction to that generated by the stator and this at the slip frequency. Consequently, an additional current is created in the stator winding [6]. A rotor bar breakage fault is shown in Figure 11.5.

FIGURE 11.3
Bearing.

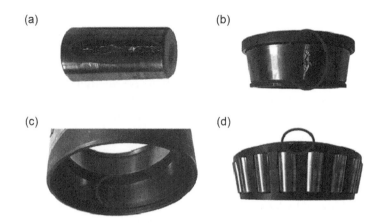

FIGURE 11.4
(a) Ball fault, (b) inner race damage, (c) outer race damage, and (d) cage fault.

FIGURE 11.5
Broken rotor bar.

11.4.3 Eccentricity Fault

These cause the variation of the air gap in the motor, the nonhomogeneous distribution of the currents in the rotor and the unbalance of the stator currents. The unbalance of the forces on the busbars generates a nonconstant overall torque. When the eccentricity becomes large, the resulting radial forces created by the stator with the rotor friction strip cause stator and rotor damage. The geometry of the rotor can present asymmetries of natural order. These fall into three categories of eccentricity of the air gap, we can see them in Figures 11.6 and 11.7:

- **Static Eccentricity**: when the stator axis coincides with the rotation axis and not with the rotor axis.

- **Dynamic Eccentricity**: when the axis of rotation of the rotor does not coincide with the axis of symmetry of the stator.

- **Mixed Eccentricity**: when the axis of rotation of the rotor does not coincide with the axes of symmetry of the rotor and stator.

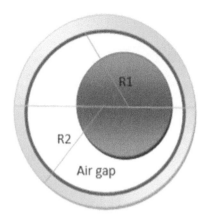

FIGURE 11.6
Eccentricity.

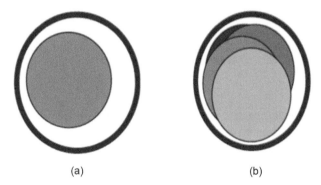

(a)   (b)

FIGURE 11.7
Static eccentricity (a) and dynamic eccentricity (b).

11.4.4 Misalignment Fault

Misalignment results from the fact that the rotation source shaft and the rotation-driven shaft do not have the same axis of rotation. Figure 11.8 shows the two most common types of misalignment.

However, if it is true that the literature and previous research focused on the diagnosis of rotating machines focus on these faults, it must nevertheless be mentioned that many analyses were needed to get to this point, among which we can talk about the methods of detection of anomalies.

11.5 Methods for Detecting Anomalies

Anomaly detection is an important part of data science (science of data processing), especially when it comes to categorizing a set of data such as in the case of a decision on the operating state of an electric induction machine as in the case of our present study. It is therefore incumbent on us to know what an anomaly is, why to detect anomalies and how to detect them.

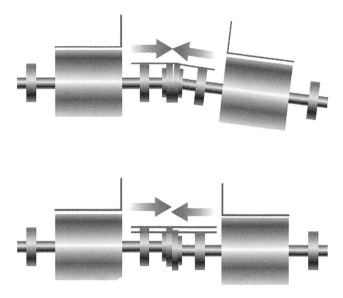

FIGURE 11.8
Misalignment (above angular misalignment, below parallel misalignment).

11.5.1 Definition

As soon as we talk about monitoring, it is like distinguishing an inappropriate operation in a batch. This is known as an anomaly. An anomaly is therefore a behavior contrary to what would seem normal. Example: a number slipped among the alphabetical letters, an order different from the normal order of a withdrawal from a bank account, an appearance of harmonics completely different from the normal harmonics of a known signal, etc.

11.5.2 Importance of Anomaly Detection

From the definition and the examples given, we immediately understand that the detection of anomalies is very important for several reasons:

- it allows you to set a limit between what would be allowed or not allowed
- it allows to monitor
- it is therefore a decision support tool (e.g., should the machine be stopped or not?)
- it thus makes it possible to avoid entering critical situations such as the explosion of an electric induction machine

In other words, to follow closely the evolution of the state of an observation to decide or wait for the right moment to act. We must also remember that without the notion of anomaly we would not be talking about the diagnosis. Otherwise, why diagnose and what to diagnose?

11.5.3 Some Techniques for Anomaly Detection

Because of its crucial stakes, as we have seen with the examples above, it is obvious that a lot of study would be accentuated by developing a set of approaches and techniques to understand the subject. The first thing to remember is to make the difference between what is normal and what is abnormal. We also talk about discretizing the data set. And then the rest of the work is just a matter of technique. Among these, we have the following: extreme value analysis, classification-based technique (RNA, decision tree, SVM), statistical techniques, proximity-based model technique (KNN, LOF, K-means), information theoretic model technique, meta-algorithm technique, and subspace-based technique (RPCA). So right away, we also understand the reason for the choice of classification algorithms for anomaly detection [7].

Thus, we can say that the diagnosis of the asynchronous machine consists of the detection of anomalies affecting them during their operating life within the entities that incorporate them. In addition, this diagnosis can be done by human intervention or in an automated way, which is, moreover, the one adopted in recent years. And earlier to use the curative way (which is very expensive), we opt for the predictive way which allows to detect the fault at its first appearance. This makes it possible to decide in time and not after the machine is damaged or caught on fire.

The only dilemma is to distinguish the characteristic frequencies of one fault from another, which has been the objective of several researchers whose results are more than convincing. We speak of a frequency signature.

11.6 Frequency Signatures

In fact, it is worth mentioning that in the annals of research on the monitoring of machines that most of the abnormal symptoms have been identified in order to develop specific models concerning each state of failure of the latter and its severity. The best way to analyze each symptom and to obtain information on its evolution is its frequency, duration of the symptom, its amplitude, its variance, and its phase. In fact, its diagnosis is based on the analysis of the harmonics contained in in the machine's supply current, flow, torque, or speed. Advanced methods have been applied in this case. They are elaborated with spectral analysis of the signals of this machine or with the comparison of the real behavior of the installation with that of the machine envisaged based on a mathematical model. Several types of research have been oriented towards the exploitation of the stator current of rotating machines and more precisely of the asynchronous machine as in the case of our present study. We analyze the spectrum of this current to extract the frequency components introduced by the fault that occurred because when a fault occurs in the asynchronous machine, it is found that this has an influence on the spectrum of the stator current. This makes it the seat of the trace of these faults. The most frequent faults in the machines and their associated frequencies are shown in Table 11.2.

In Table 11.2,

- f_0 is the power supply frequency,
- s is the slip (g) per unit,
- P is the number of poles,
- f_r is the rotor frequency,
- $f_{i,o}$ is any indoor or outdoor frequency, it depends on the dimensions and characteristics of vibration of the bearings,
- n_b is the number of balls in a bearing,
- m, k are integers [8].

TABLE 11.2

Frequency Signatures of Rotating Machine Faults

Faults	Frequency	Parameters
Broken rotor bars	$f_{brb} = \left[k\left(\dfrac{1-s}{p} \right) \pm s \right]$	$k = 1, 2, \dots$
Bearing damage	$f_{bng} = \left\| f_0 \pm k f_{i,o} \right\|$	$k = 1, 2, \dots$ $f_{i,o} = \begin{cases} 0.4 n_b f_r \\ 0.6 n_b f_r \end{cases}$
Misalignment	$f_{mis} = \left\| f_0 \pm k f_r \right\|$	$k = 1, 2, \dots$
Air gap eccentricity	$f_{ecc} = \left[1 \pm m\left(\dfrac{1-s}{p} \right) \right]$	$m = 1, 2, \dots$

Thus, we can say in one way or another that when one of these faults appears in one of the components of an electric induction machine, it affects the spectrum of the stator current, making it appear several harmonics different from each other, considered as characteristic harmonics of the faults. Therefore, in the next chapter, we will discuss the stator current to see how these harmonics are estimated from it.

11.7 The MCSA Measurement Method

Motor Current Signature Analysis (MCSA) is a condition monitoring technique for rotating machines used to diagnose problems in induction motors [9,10]. The concept originated in the early 1970s and was first proposed for use in nuclear power plants for inaccessible motors and motors located in hazardous areas [11]. But over time, it quickly gained increasing acceptance in industry. The tests are performed on-line without interrupting production with the motor running under load under normal operating conditions [11,12]. The MCSA method can be used as a predictive maintenance tool to detect common engine faults at an early stage and thus avoid costly catastrophic failures, production interruptions, and extend engine life. It can be used as a diagnostic tool and a powerful complement to vibration and heat monitoring (checking a fault with more than one technology) [13,14]. MCSA is a method in the broader field of Electrical Signature Analysis (ESA) [15], useful for analyzing not only electric induction motors, but also generators, power transformers, and other electrical equipment. The most popular of these techniques are: Current Signature Analysis (CSA), which we use and others such as VSA (Voltage Signature Analysis), EPVA (Extended Park's Vector Approach), and IPSA (Instantaneous Power Signature Analysis).

11.7.1 Modeling of the Stator Current of the Asynchronous Machine

The detection of faults in electric induction machines has been widely studied. It is based on the monitoring of their vibrations. The reliability of the results obtained is strongly dependent on the position of the accelerometers placed on these machines and elongated on their vertical, axial, and radial axes. This location is, in fact, the difficult task of this vibration modeling technique. In addition, it may also be affected by the machine's speed variation, especially when the mechanical components are deteriorated. However, these techniques are expensive, as they require additional transducers. Their use only makes sense in the case of large machines or critical applications.

The monitoring of the stator current lines is indeed the most interesting modeling basis and the most attractive for fault detection. This is so for two main reasons. Firstly, the stator current can be used to diagnose electrical and mechanical faults such as: phase imbalance, short circuit in stator windings, bearing failure, twisted shaft, broken bar, etc. Then, the stator current is very easy to access, because it is directly measurable and is used to control the machine itself. This offers an important advantage to modeling techniques indicated.

The application of the CSA stator current analysis technique for fault diagnosis in the asynchronous machine requires a precise knowledge of the various frequency and amplitude components contained in the frequency spectrum of the stator current. This current is taken from a machine in generator mode. Indeed, its analysis allows the correct discrimination of modulations and signatures faults of the asynchronous machine. For this, it is necessary to build a complex signal which models the real physical phenomenon. This analytical model of the signal must accurately describe the behavior and the evolution of the real stator current. It must contain all fault information correspondents. This current is often used for command-and-control purposes.

To study the detection of the mentioned faults, the stator current of the asynchronous machine is designated by the discrete signal $x[n]$. We obtained it by sampling direct current $x(t)$ with a step equal to $T_s = 1/F_s$. This stator current $x[n]$ of the electric induction machine in the presence of mechanical and/or electrical failures is expressed as follows [8]:

$$x[n] = \sum_{k=-L}^{L} a_k \cos\left(2\pi f_k \left(w(n)\right) \times \frac{n}{F_k} + \phi_k \right) + b[n] \qquad (11.1)$$

where

$x[n]$ corresponds to a single sample of the stator current.

$b[n]$ is a sample of Gaussian noise.

The parameter L is the number of side frequencies introduced by malfunctions. The quantities $f_k(w)$, a_k, ϕ_k correspond to frequency, amplitude, and phase, respectively. $w(n)$ is a parameter to be estimated at each instant of order n. It depends on the fault studied. It is assumed that the time and space of harmonics are not considered. The problem to be solved is treated as a statistical estimation problem. This is an estimate of the fundamental frequency, the frequencies characterizing the faults that have occurred, and the relative amplitudes. It is carried out by calculating the stator current spectrum $x[n]$.

The only problem with this signal is that it alone is not enough to properly diagnose the machine's states (for example, when you want to decide on the operating state of the machine at a given moment). It is therefore necessary to associate it with techniques capable of following the characteristic parameters of the machine's operating state. Among them are methods such as: The Fast Fourier Transform, the instantaneous power of the Fast Fourier Transform, the spectrum of the demodulated current, the wavelet analysis has proven themselves in old research. But it turns out that these techniques are very expensive in terms of time. This leads us to explore other avenues such as the technique based on variants of the ESPRIT method and intelligent faults classification algorithms.

11.8 Variants of the ESPRIT Method

ESPRIT which stands for Estimation of Signal Parameters via Rotational Invariant Techniques is a method of estimating signal parameters using the rotational invariance technique. It is an algorithm for the determination and detection of harmonics with a very high accuracy of frequency and amplitude estimation. This is independent of the window size used. It is an appropriate approach to get reliable spectral estimation results without synchronization effects [8]. It is based on shift invariance. It exists naturally between the discrete time series leading to rotational invariance and the corresponding signal subspaces. In this case, the eigenvectors U of the signal autocorrelation matrix define two subspaces (signal and noise) using two selection matrices γ_1 and γ_2.

$$S_1 = \gamma_1 U, \; S_2 = \gamma_2 U \tag{11.2}$$

The rotational invariance between the two subspaces leads to the following equation:

$$S_1 = \phi S_2 \tag{11.3}$$

where

$$\phi = \begin{bmatrix} e^{j2\pi f_1} & 0 & \cdots & 0 \\ 0 & e^{j2\pi f_2} & \cdots & 0 \\ \vdots & \vdots & \cdots & \vdots \\ 0 & 0 & \cdots & e^{j2\pi f_N} \end{bmatrix} \tag{11.4}$$

The matrix ϕ contains all the information on the N frequency components. The estimated matrices S_1 and S_2 may contain errors [8]. In addition, the TLS least-squares approach allows to find the matrix ϕ by minimizing the Frobenius standard for the error matrix. The determination of this matrix allows to obtain the estimates of the frequency defined by the following formula:

$$f_k = \frac{\mathrm{Arg}\left(\phi_{k;k}\right)}{2\pi}, \quad k = 1, 2, \ldots, N. \tag{11.5}$$

The application of all these methods makes it possible to carry out a comparison between their performances below. They are used in the detection of faults that may occur in an electric induction machine.

In this work, we use six variants which, like their roots, are used to estimate the frequencies and amplitudes contained in the stator current signal of the machine. And apart from the TLS variant which takes as an argument a third parameter which is the window length, these variants take two essential parameters, the signal vector and the number of harmonics or the mode of estimation of the number of harmonics which is based on order selection models (MOS). These variants are: ESPRIT_TLS, ESPRIT_ITCMP, ESPRIT_SVDSSA, ESPRIT_IRLBA, ESPRIT_SVD, and ESPRIT_ECON.

The procedure for estimating the frequencies and amplitudes by these variants is given in Figure 11.9.

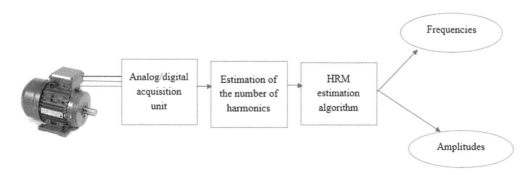

FIGURE 11.9
Fault detection procedure with an HRM.

11.9 MOS (Order Selection Model)

When recording a stator signal coming from an electric induction machine prey to a fault and operating in a more or less noisy environment, we find ourselves with a signal in the frequency domain composed of several harmonics not all of which are not explanatory of the fault or do not translate the real number of harmonics constituting the signal [16,17]. When we want to evaluate it, we use MOS.

MOS understood by model order selection is an important and fundamental problem in a variety of signal processing applications [18]. For example, the determination of the number of coefficients in a linear regression model [19], the selection of the order in the time series analysis [20], the detection of the number of clusters in the *n*-way probabilistic classification [20], the decision dimensionality for Principal Component Analysis (PCA) for the reduction of the dimension [21], and the choice of the number of sources in a linear transformation model for separating the signal and noise subspaces [22]. In general, the model order selection methods can be derived from the criteria of information theory [16], Bayesian estimation [21], and based on the deviation in an ordered sequence of parameters [22].

11.9.1 Principle

They all estimate the number of harmonics in the signal using the eigenvalues of the signal covariance matrix. If X is the recorded signal of the electric induction machine affected by the fault, then its covariance matrix is:

$$R_x = \frac{\sum_{n=1}^{M} X(n)X(n)^T}{M} \tag{11.6}$$

where
    M is the number of samples collected.

In this work, we compare five types of model order selector in order to validate the choice of the number of harmonics to be used for a rolling fault. We mention, however, that we use the formula:

$$\text{freq} = \left| f_0 \pm K \times f_{i,o} \right| \tag{11.7}$$

where

f_0 is the power supply frequency,

k is an integer and $f_{i,o}$ is any internal or external frequency; to calculate the values of the harmonics. k will take the values 1, 2, 3, and 4 and SNR will take the values between 0 and 100 dB for a number of samples equal to 26.

11.9.2 Mathematical Expressions

Before giving the results obtained with these algorithms, we present their mathematical expressions:

- **MDL**: MDL, which stands for minimum description length, was developed by Rissanen in 1978. Its mathematical expression is:

$$E_{\text{MDL}}(k) = -L\left(X/\theta_k \right) + 3G(\theta_k) \tag{11.8}$$

- **AIC**: AIC, understood by Akaike's information criteria, was developed by Akaike in 1974. Its mathematical expression is:

$$E_{\text{AIC}}(k) = -2L\left(X/\theta_k \right) + 2G(\theta_k) \tag{11.9}$$

- **KIC**: KIC, which stands for Kullback–Leibler Information Criteria, was developed by Cavanaugh in 1999. Its mathematical expression is:

$$E_{\text{KIC}}(k) = -2L\left(X/\theta_k \right) + 3G(\theta_k) \tag{11.10}$$

- **FPE**: FPE heard by final prediction error is expressed in terms of AIC. Its mathematical expression is:

$$\text{FPE}(k) = e^{\frac{\text{AIC}(k)}{T}} \tag{11.11}$$

with

$$L\left(X/\theta_k \right) = \frac{T}{2} \log \left(\frac{MG}{MA} \right)^{m-k} \tag{11.12}$$

$$G(\theta_k) = 1 + mk - \frac{1}{2}k(k-1) \tag{11.13}$$

where

$$MG = \prod_{i=k+1}^{m} \lambda_i^{\frac{1}{m-k}} \tag{11.14}$$

$$MA = \frac{1}{m-k}\sum_{i=k+1}^{m}\lambda_i \tag{11.15}$$

and where

T is the number of samples,

$L(X/\theta_k)$ is the maximum log-likelihood of the observation based on the model parameter as a function of θ_k which is the k-th order and

$G(\theta_k)$ is the penalty for model complexity given by the total number of free parameters in θ_k.

- **RAE**: The EAR heard by the adjacent eigenvalue report was presented by Liavas and Regalia (2001). It appears that the EAR has never been formally presented before. The EAR is expressed as:

$$\mathrm{RAE}\,(p) = \frac{\lambda_p}{\lambda_{p+1}}, \quad p = 1, 2, \ (m-1) \tag{11.16}$$

Thus, we get n by:

$$n = \mathrm{argmax}\left(\mathrm{RAE}(p)\right), \quad p = 1, 2, \ldots, (m-1) \tag{11.17}$$

11.9.3 Results Obtained by Each of the MOS Algorithms

The red point is the coordinate of the minimum value of the cost functions. It is this value that we then compare in order to decide which MOS algorithm to use to obtain the number of harmonics that is important for the variants of the ESPRIT method.

- **MDL-AIC**: We can see that according to Figure 11.10 the minimum value for abscissa axis is n=2 wich is the number of estimated harmonics. To know wich value of SNR and k correspond to, we plot the minimums of the values of the cost functions as shown in Figure 11.11.

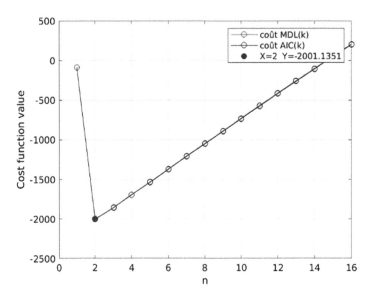

FIGURE 11.10
Value of the MDL-AIC cost function as a function of n.

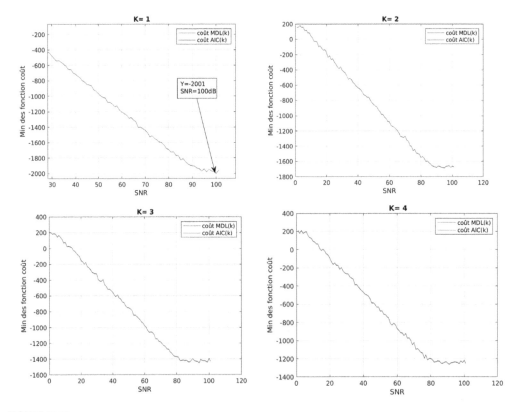

FIGURE 11.11
Minimum cost values based on SNR for each K (MDL-AIC). We realize that, this corresponds to a value of SNR equal to for a value of $k =$ and wich should estimate the n at most 2 (Figure 11.10).

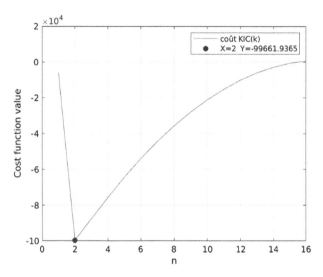

FIGURE 11.12
Value of the KIC cost function as a function of n.

- **KIC**: We can see that according to Figure 11.12 the minimum value for abscissa axis is $n = 2$ wich is the number of estimated harmonics. To know wich value of SNR and k correspond to, we plot the minimums of the values of the cost functions as shown in Figure 11.13.

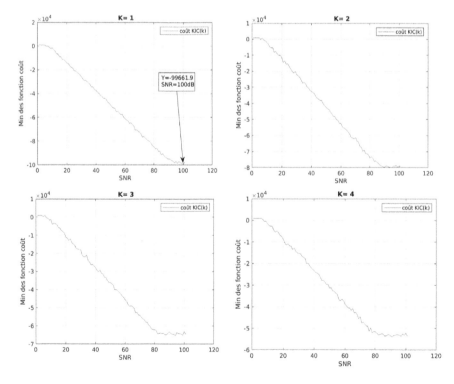

FIGURE 11.13
Minimum cost values based on SNR for each K (KIC).

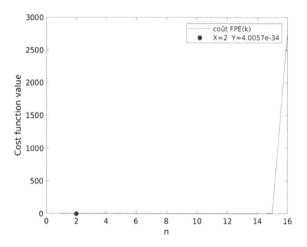

FIGURE 11.14
Value of the FPE cost function as a function of *n*.

We realize that this corresponds to a value of SNR equal to 100 dB for a value of *k* = 1 and which should estimate the *n* to at most 2 (Figure 11.12).

- **FPE:** We can see that according to Figure 11.14 the minimum value for abscissa axis is *n* = 2 wich is the number of estimated harmonics. To know wich value of SNR and *k* correspond to, we plot the minimums of the values of the cost functions as shown in Figure 11.15.

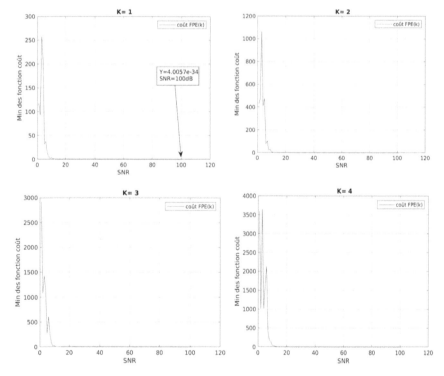

FIGURE 11.15
Minimum cost values based on SNR for each K (FPE).

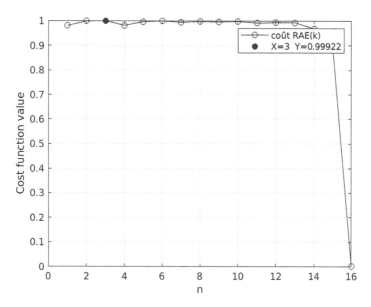

FIGURE 11.16
Value of the RAE cost function as a function of n.

We realize that this corresponds for a value of SNR equal to 100 dB for a value of $k = 1$ and which should estimate the n to at most 2 (Figure 11.14).

- **RAE**: We can see that according to Figure 11.16 the minimum value for abscissa axis is $n = 2$ wich is the number of estimated harmonics. To know wich value of SNR and k correspond to, we plot the minimums of the values of the cost functions as shown in Figure 11.17.

We realize that, this corresponds to a value of SNR equal to for a value of $k =$ and which should estimate the n at most 2 (Figure 11.16).

11.9.3.1 Conclusion

At the end of these analyses on these results, we can see that the model which gives the smallest value of the cost function is the FPE model with a value of 4×10^{-34} for a value of SNR equal to 100 dB, $k = 1$ and $n = 2$ except the frequency f_0 which would give with the two others a total of three harmonics.

11.10 Intelligent Defect Classification Algorithms

In this section, we present the algorithms that are relevant to the machine learning domain.

Their role is to detect and localize faults. They are also called artificial intelligence techniques. They are among others: ANN-AG, SVM, KNN, and ELM. We will detail in the following lines the philosophy of each of them. What is important to remember with these algorithms is that they have the possibility to pass to an autonomous functioning after learning phases. This is also appreciated for our study since the goal is to decide at any moment on the state of the machine.

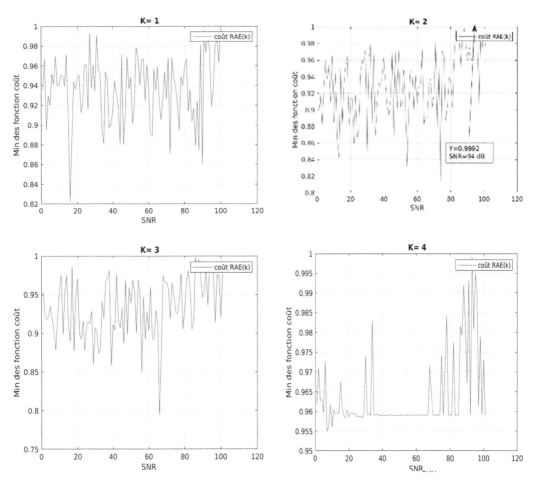

FIGURE 11.17
Minimum cost values based on SNR for each *K (RAE)*.

11.10.1 Artificial Neuronal Networks and Genetic Algorithms (ANN-AG)

Because of the difficulty to find the right architecture, by setting the parameters by hand (each time), we have chosen to associate genetic algorithms with ANNs to automate and optimize the obtaining of the architecture achieving the best classification or able to detect with the best accuracy the different states of the rotating machine. In fact, at the present time where the monitoring of rotating machines is in vogue in almost all sectors of industry, reliability is the most important criterion. This means that the systems used to monitor these machines must meet the highest standards to guarantee continuity of operation and avoid serious accidents. In the literature, it has been proven that artificial neural networks (ANNs) can be used and adapted to this type of problem [23,24]. Genetic algorithms (GA) have also been presented in several references [24,25]. In the short period of their development, the GAs has shown their superior capabilities and have been successfully applied in many areas.

11.10.1.1 Artificial Neural Networks

Artificial neural networks based on the functioning of the human brain are developed in the form of parallel distributed network models. The applications of NAS are numerous by example in data analysis, model identification and control [26,27]. And among the different types of NAS, the Multilayer Perceptron (MLP) are most popular and used in most work, as is the case in this study. In this project, the terms RNA and MLP were used for each other in the absence of other types of neural networks. Here a brief introduction to MLP is given for perfection. An MLP network consists of an input layer of source neurons, one or more hidden layers and a layer of exit. The number of neurons in the input and output layers depend on the number of input variables and number of desired classes, respectively. The number of hidden layers and the number of neurons in each hidden layer affect the generalizability of the network. For a smaller number of hidden layers and neurons, execution may not be proportionate. Consider that too much of hidden neurons may have the risk of over-adjusting the accuracy of the data. There are various heuristic and systematic methods to choose the number of hidden layers and neurons [26].

Figure 11.18 shows a typical MLP architecture consisting of three layers; M, N, and O for the input, hidden, and output layers, respectively.

The input vectors

$$X = [x_1, x_1, \ldots, x_M]^T \tag{11.18}$$

is transformed to an intermediate vector of the hidden variables U by using the activation function.

f_j: the output U_j of the hidden layer j-th neurons is obtained as follows:

$$U_j = f_j \left(\sum_{i=1}^{M} W^1_{i,j} \times x_i + b^1_j \right) \tag{11.19}$$

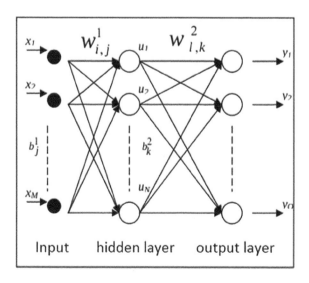

FIGURE 11.18
Example of an MLP.

where

$b^1{}_j$ and $W^1{}_{i,j}$ represent, respectively, the bias and the weight between the *j*-th neuron of the hidden layer and the *i*-th neuron of the input layer. The upper index 1 represents the (first) connection between the neurons of the input/hidden layers. The desired output vectors

$$Y = \left[y_1, y_2, \ldots, y_0 \right]^T \tag{11.20}$$

of the network is obtained from the vector of intermediate variables *U* by an activation function f_2 of the output layer. For example, the output of the neuron is expressed as follows:

$$y_k = f_2 \left(\sum_{l=1}^{N} w^2{}_{l,k} \times U_l + b^2{}_k \right) \tag{11.21}$$

where

the upper index 2 denotes the (secondary) connection between the neurons of the hidden/output layers. There are several forms of the activation functions f_1 and, f_2 such as the sigmoid function, the hyperbolic tangent, the linear function and the softmax function given by Equations (11.22)–(11.25), respectively:

$$f(v) = \frac{1}{1+e^{-v}} \tag{11.22}$$

$$f(v) = \frac{1-e^{-2v}}{1+e^{-2v}} \tag{11.23}$$

$$f(v) = v \tag{11.24}$$

$$f(v_i) = \frac{e^{v_i}}{\sum_{j=1}^{k} e^{v_j}} \tag{11.25}$$

In MATLAB, these functions are called logsig, tansig, purelin, and softmax to name a few. MLP network learning involves finding values for the connection weights, which minimize the error function between the actual results produced (calculated) and the corresponding target (desired) values in the learning set. One of the widely used error functions is the mean square error (MSE) and the most commonly used algorithms are based on the delta rule for hidden layer networks called the back-propagation rule of the error gradient. This algorithm, which has the advantage of existing, remains debatable insofar as its convergence is not proven. Its use may lead to blockages in a local minimum of the error surface. Its efficiency depends, in fact, on many parameters that must be set by the user: the gradient step, the parameters of the automaton sigmoid functions, the network architecture, the number of layers, the number of neurons per layer, the initialization of the weights. The MLP neural network, used in this work, is composed of an input layer and several hidden layers, the number of which varies between 1 and 4 whose choice is left to the genetic algorithm. The input layer had neurons representing the observations extracted from the stator current signals measured by time analysis and frequency.

These observations were used at the network entrance. The number of output O neurons has been set at 2. The values to be reached (labels) can be in binary forms which represent the different classes (normal (N) and faulty (f) states) of system operation. In MLP, the hyperbolic tangent activation functions (tansig), logsig and softmax, were used in the layers hidden and the output layer chosen by the genetic algorithm. The RNA was created, trained, and implemented in application using the MATLAB Neural Network Toolkit. The ANN was genetically formed (by the functions of the genetic algorithm) to minimize the IEM execution function between the network outputs and the corresponding target values. In addition to this, we have added to the other parameters the training and performance function.

11.10.1.2 Genetic Algorithms (GA)

The aim of using the genetic algorithm in our study is to find as quickly as possible and to lead to an optimal architecture giving a good precision in the classification of the machine condition in the context of a bearing fault. But like any genetic algorithm [28], there are steps to be respected in order to achieve its employability. In the following lines, we explain how these can cohabit without case.

11.10.1.2.1 Chromosome Coding

Chromosome coding is a crucial step in any algorithm application process genetics because it consists in defining the genes on which operations such as the mutation and crossing. Thus, by finding the nature of the genes to be used, it becomes easy to form what we want to use calls the individual or chromosome from which the candidate population for our evolutionary process will be formed during the search for elected or expected individuals. The choice, it is sometimes not easy. But it is made depending on the problem you are facing. Thus, in the framework of our study we have chosen two data types to define the types of genes used. The first which is an integer and which is the first gene and the other two genes of the string type. The chromosome was then defined as a combination of three genes:

- the number of hidden layer (integer)
- the number of neurons in each hidden layer (string)
- and transfer functions in each hidden layer (string).

Example of an individual with four hidden layers from MATLAB:
individual=$[4, [7, 6, 4, 8, 2], \text{logsig}\{4\}]$ "]]; for this individual, we read that he has four hidden layers, seven neurons in the first layer, six in the second layer, four in the third layer, and eight in the last. And the transfer functions are, respectively, each logsig. Here there is not the number of neurons in the output layer.

11.10.1.2.2 Generation of the Initial Population

The initial population consists of a set of randomly generated individuals (chromosomes). The number of individuals in a population or the size of the population is an important parameter for GA that will need to be determined. We have set it at 10 (ten). The representation of the population P is: $P = [P_1, P_2, P_3, \ldots, P_i \ldots P_{NP}]$ where P_i represents the i-th chromosome in the population and N_p represents the number of chromosomes in the population.

11.10.1.2.3 *Calculation of the Evaluation Function (Fitness)*

The evaluation function chosen is the evaluation of the architecture on the detection of the rolling fault. For this purpose, we use an algorithm to extract the five best individuals after one generation based on the max accuracy.

11.10.1.2.4 *Selection of Individuals for Reproduction*

To generate new offspring (children), in our case, parents are selected based on their accuracy in detecting the rolling fault, then crossover and mutation mechanisms are applied.

11.10.1.2.4.1 Mutation   Mutation is the process of changing the value of a gene at a given position in the chromosome. In this work, we mutated only 3 (three) out of 10 individuals from the crossing. We choose 1 individual at random for each mutation process that will serve as a donor to the individual who is to undergo the mutation also chooses randomly. Then we randomly generate the position of the gene to be modified and we proceed with the operation. The operation is repeated 3 times which corresponds to the three mutations.

11.10.1.2.4.2 Crossover   Crossing is the process by which two gene sequences from two different chromosomes are fused together. In crossbreeding, the best 5 resulting from the selection are merged into their half to give birth to 5 new individuals (children) which are added to the previous ones to give a total of 10 individuals.

11.10.2 Fusion ANN et AG

The algorithm starts with ten randomly generated individuals for a given number of hidden layers. Each individual is evaluated. For any individual in the population, if the accuracy is greater than or equal to a given max, the max is updated and saved. At the same time, each individual and its accuracy are saved. At the end of the evaluation of these ten individuals, we extract from the backup the five best ones on which we first mutate and then crossbreed by returning a candidate population to the second generation. This process is repeated until the tenth generation and the number of layers is changed hidden then we start all over again from the beginning. After evaluation on the interval of the number of layers hidden, we come out with four architectures which according to the algorithm, are the best architectures. Figure 11.19 shows the diagram of such an association

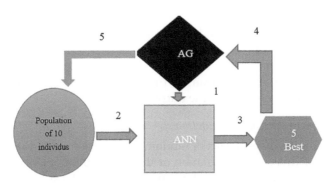

FIGURE 11.19
Association of ANN (Artificial Neural Network) and GA (Genetic Algorithm)

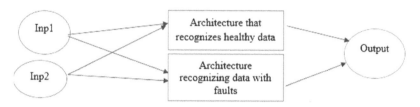

FIGURE 11.20
Association of two architectures.

11.10.3 Association of Two Architectures

The principle is to find an architecture for each state of the machine. Once they are found, network them and test them for the different SNR steps from the learning step to the 3-dB step. The result was just as good, and we present it in the part dedicated to results and analysis. Here is also a diagram that explains a little bit (Figure 11.20).

11.10.4 Support Vectors Machine (SVM)

The SVMs are classification algorithms allowing to find one or more borders between a data set [29]. They can be simple for so-called separable data, but sometimes they can be very complex for inseparable data. But what makes them powerful is that, whether it's one or the other case, they always manage to classify them. Indeed, their power is based on a powerful philosophy called kernels tricks. And yes, it must be said, that it is really a trick. They were developed by Vapnik during his work on learning theory statistics around 1998.

11.10.4.1 How It Works

The principle is to find optimal plans to separate given objects. But the first thing to remember is to do what we call learning first. The latter would allow to come up with a model capable of making decisions about new objects later on. For this, we must Label the learning data before proceeding with the learning process. Otherwise, it would be like approaching two magnets of opposite poles. And when the data are not linear, we use what is called the kernel functions. It consists in finding the solution of the dual of a problem, to find the solution of the original problem. Therefore, we use several kernels to decide which one would give the best plan to achieve the best separation. There are thus two important parameters that would help to find that optimal plan.

These are C (BoxConstraint) and gamma (KernelScale). The cores used in this work are:

- the polynomial kernel
- the Gaussian kernel
- the linear kernel.

And the resolution algorithms used are:

- the SMO algorithm
- the ISDA algorithm
- the L1QP algorithm

In Figures 11.21 and 11.22, we present the schema of an SVM and an application.

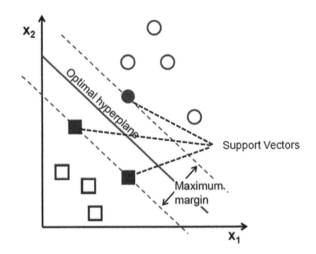

FIGURE 11.21
Example of SVM.

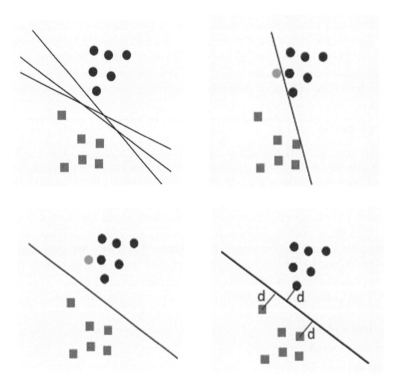

FIGURE 11.22
Search for the optimal hyperplane by SVM.

11.10.5 K-Nearest Neighbors (K-NN)

K-Nearest Neighbors from its acronym K-NN is one of the simplest classification techniques to develop a classification model. Because of its simple philosophy, it is sometimes considered as a lazy algorithm, according to which the class of an object is the class of belonging of these closest (notion of distance) neighbors. In a word, the idea is to give the class of a sample based on the class of these neighbors. This means that if you have an object in a lot and if you want to classify it, you would have to find the class of these neighbors and measure how close they are to each other with them. Example: suppose that any geometric Figure that has four sides is a quadrilateral. So, let's take another Figure would not have the same characteristic. It is then easy to say that this is not a quadrilateral. This means that samples with the same input values (or characteristic parameters) seems to belong to the same class. In other words, samples with Identical characteristics should be grouped in the same class. The expression on which become more pronounced the closer the Nearest Neighbor is. Because it's all about that. Indeed, the quantification of this expression unambiguously determines the class of a new sample. Hence, the famous K' of K-NN. If we have the right K, we will make a good classification for any classification sequence. Otherwise, if the model that is a function of K is not ideal, in the long run, it would arrive at times when the classification made does not relate to reality. We then say that we have a bad model. What we allow to announce the following: the best K-NN algorithm is the one that from a cloud of data, finds the best number of neighbors to be able to distinguish completely correctly and at all moment the belonging of each one. In the results section, you will see how this method was used to recognize the faulty or healthy condition of a bearing in a rotating machine. Figure 11.23 shows the schematic of a K-NN.

11.10.6 Extreme Learning Machines

An ELM is a new neural network-type learning algorithm with a single layer hidden unlike conventional popular learning algorithms. In addition to being of a single hidden layer, an ELM does not use the learning rules as learning machine or Machine learning that uses the concept of retro-propagation to adjust synapse weights and that are very costly in terms of computing time. This makes it 1,000 times faster in terms of time execution than its predecessors. Better than that, moreover, its application in recent research studies have proven time to give a good performance in terms of generalization on his learning. What is not the case for the neural networks known so far.

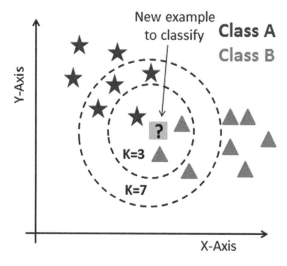

FIGURE 11.23
Principle of operation of a K-NN.

11.10.6.1 Principle or Algorithm

It works as follows [30]:

1. random assignment of the input weights (W_i) and biases of the hidden layer
2. calculation of the output matrix of the hidden layer
3. output weight calculation β

with

$$\beta = H^{\phi}T \tag{11.26}$$

where

$$H^{\phi} = \left(H^{t}H\right)^{-1} H^{t} \tag{11.27}$$

is the Moore-Penrose inverse matrix and T being the output vector.

$$T = [t_1, t_2, \ldots, t_0]^{T} \tag{11.28}$$

In Figures 11.24 and 11.25, we can see an ELM and an application.

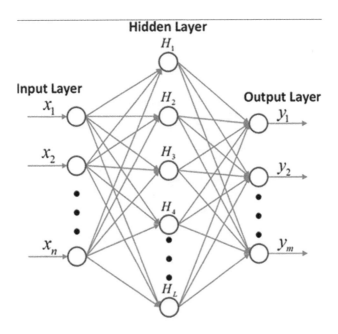

FIGURE 11.24
Diagram of an ELM.

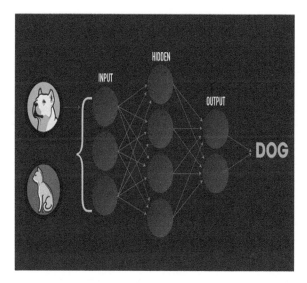

FIGURE 11.25
Example of use of an ELM.

11.11 Simulation and Analysis of Results

In this section, we present the results obtained with the different techniques above. We present first the techniques of the estimation methods, namely, the variants of the HRM ESPRIT method, and secondly the techniques from the Machine Learning. But first, we present in Table 11.3 the parameters of the simulation and at the level of each of the techniques the way in which we have prepared the simulation data (Figure 11.26).

11.11.1 High-Resolution Estimation Methods

In this technique, we will see the variants of the ESPRIT method, namely, the ESPRIT_SVD, ESPRIT_SVDSSA, ESPRIT_ITCMP, ESPRIT_IRLBA, ESPRIT_ECON, and ESPRIT_TLS algorithms. The goal is to find out which of these variants is the most suitable within the

TABLE 11.3

Parameters of the Simulation

Parameters	Value
f_r	29.01 Hz
f_0	50 Hz
n_b	12
$f_{i,o}$	139.248 Hz
F_s	1000 Hz
K	1, 2, 3, 4
SNR	[0,100] dB
Amplitude of the stator current a_0	10A
Processor	Intel Pentium (R) CPU B950 @ 2.1GHz× 2

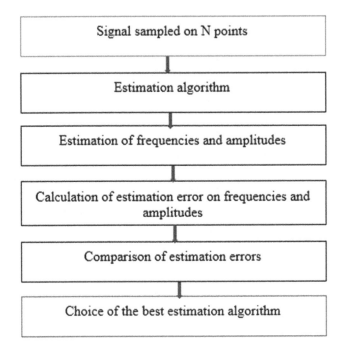

FIGURE 11.26
Execution flowchart.

framework of the objective set by this project to develop an intelligent real-time system. Otherwise, the goal is to, from the analysis of the different Figures, tell according to the SNR the most suitable algorithm in terms of execution time. This sometimes involves making compromises, as will be the case in our present work. We will go from algorithm 1 to algorithm 6 for SNR values ranging from 0 to 50 dB in 2 dB steps. Something else, these algorithms are variants of the ESPRIT algorithm which is itself a high-resolution signal processing method. We will therefore analyze together the errors on the frequencies then on the amplitudes and finally the execution times for the six (6) algorithms in order to find the best algorithm in terms of time as a function of the SNR. To do this, we will compare the error curves with the four indicators of precision, namely, in order: MSE, NMSE, the RMSE, and Normal Error.

11.11.1.1 Preparation of Simulation Data

For this part, keeping the same stator current simulation parameters, we worked with $K = 1$ to generate a sample of size $N = 1024$ with an SNR step equal to 2 dB over an interval of $[0.50]$, i.e. 26 SNR values. Moreover, using the formula that gives the frequencies as a function of K:

$$\text{freq} = \left| f_0 \pm K \times f_{i;o} \right| \tag{11.29}$$

we obtained: freq = [50, 89.248, 189.248] which represent, respectively, $f_0, f_1,$ and f_2 for values of amplitudes equal to Amp = [10, 0.2, 0.07] which represent, respectively, $a_0, a_1,$ and a_2. It should also be mentioned that the harmonic number is fixed at 2.

11.11.1.2 *Frequency Error Analysis*

- **Algorithm ESPRIT_SVD (Singular Value Decomposition):** Figure 11.27 gives the result obtained with this algorithm for the estimation of frequencies with precision indicators.

  By analyzing the estimates made with the 4 indicators, it was immediately understood that the SVD algorithm has difficulty in estimating low-frequency values for SNR values between 0 and 5 dB. This means that in a noisy environment where the SNR value would be less than 5 dB, it would be very difficult to decide on the operation of the machine. On the other hand, as soon as we go beyond that, it gives good estimates.

- **Algorithm ESPRIT_SVDSSA (SVD-Singular-Spectrum Analysis):** Figure 11.28 gives the result obtained with this algorithm for the estimation of frequencies with precision indicators.

  For this algorithm, beyond just misestimating the low-frequency values, we found more than one variation on the estimates between the values of 0 and 20 dB, which explains the instability in this SNR interval and therefore from one moment

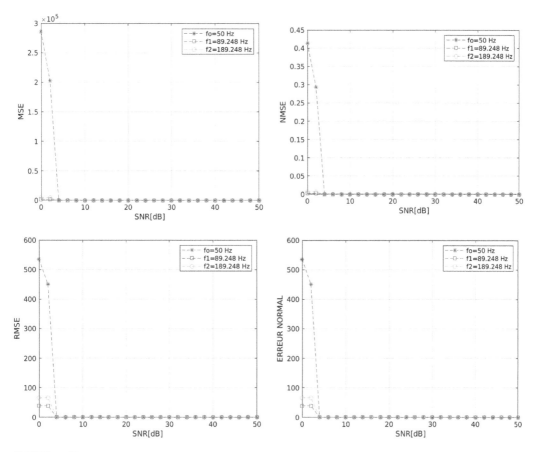

FIGURE 11.27
Variation of the frequency estimation error as a function of SNR (SVD).

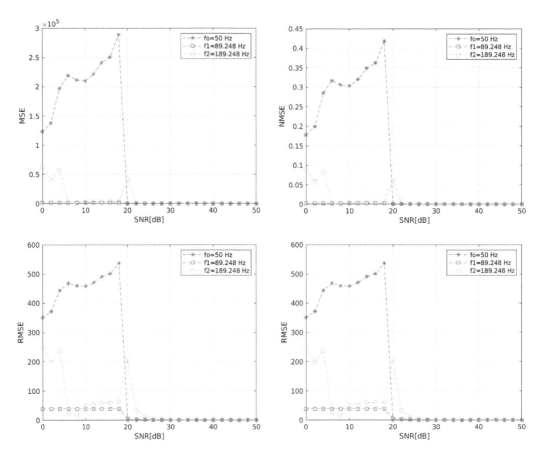

FIGURE 11.28
Variation of the frequency estimation error as a function of SNR (SVDSSA).

to another the observations can change suddenly making it difficult to monitor the machine. But beyond this SNR interval, we are gradually approaching the principle that the estimation error tends to cancel when the value of the SNR increases.

- **Algorithm ESPRIT_ITCMP (Information Theoretic Criteria and Matrix Pencil Method):** Figure 11.29 gives the result obtained with this algorithm for the estimation of frequencies with precision indicators.

  By analyzing the estimates made with the four indicators, it is easy to understand that the ITCMP algorithm has difficulty estimating low-frequency values for SNR values between 0 and 5 dB. This means that in a noisy environment where the SNR value would be lower than 5 dB, it would be very difficult to decide on the operation of the machine. On the other hand, as soon as we go beyond that, it gives good estimates.

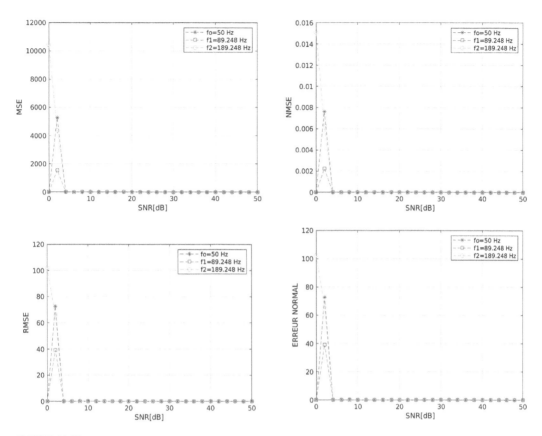

FIGURE 11.29
Variation of the frequency estimation error as a function of SNR (ITCMP).

- **Algorithm ESPRIT_IRLBA (Augmented Implicitly Restarted Lanczos Bidiagonalization Algorithm:** Figure 11.30 gives the result obtained with this algorithm for the estimation of frequencies with precision indicators.

  With this algorithm, we were able to estimate the low values of frequencies on almost all SNR values at least for the first three indicators, while the other frequencies undergo little fluctuation between the values of 6 and 16 dB, which is not normal since the value of the SNR increases.

- **Algorithm ESPRIT_ECON:** Figure 11.31 gives the result obtained with this algorithm for the estimation of frequencies with precision indicators.

  By analyzing the estimates made with the four indicators, it was immediately understood that the SVDSSA algorithm has difficulty in estimating low-frequency values for SNR values between 0 and 5 dB. This means that in a noisy environment where the SNR value would be lower than 5 dB, it would be very difficult to decide on the operation of the machine. On the other hand, as soon as we go beyond that, it gives good estimates.

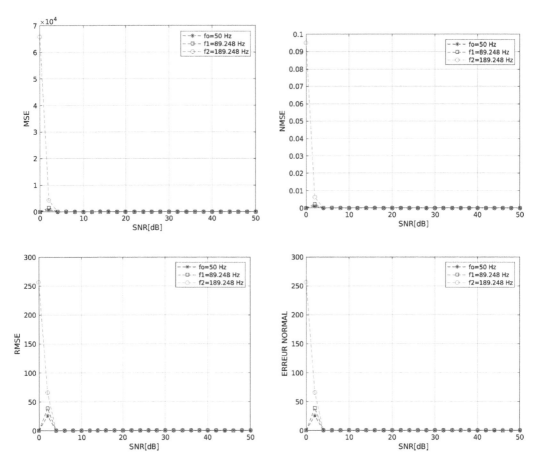

FIGURE 11.30
Variation of the frequency estimation error as a function of SNR (IRLBA).

- **Algorithm ESPRIT_TLS (Total Least Square):** Figure 11.32 gives the result obtained with this algorithm for the estimation of frequencies with precision indicators.

  This algorithm, unlike the others, estimates very well the low-frequency values over the entire SNR interval. In addition, there are almost no fluctuations in the large frequency values, but the estimation error decreases as the SNR increases. This is good for the monitoring of any electric induction machine.

- **Conclusion on frequency estimation analyses:** Beyond the analyses on the range of SNR values, it can be seen across all the curves that the NMSE indicator gives a very good estimate overall for SNR values above 30 dB. Moreover, we could notice that only the ESPRIT_TLS algorithm does not show any fluctuations or that conforms to the principle according to which the increase of the SNR reduces the value of the estimation error because the noise becomes less and the real signal much more intense.

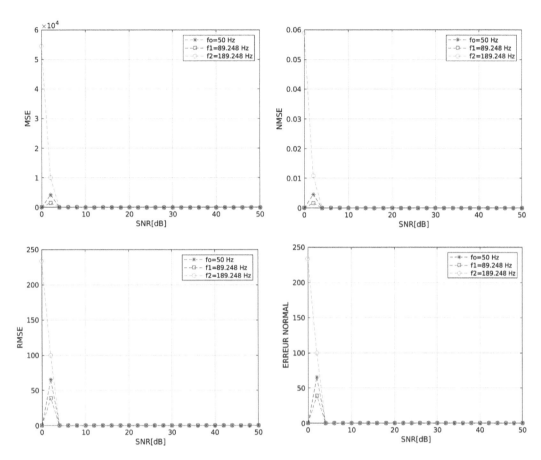

FIGURE 11.31
Variation of the frequency estimation error as a function of SNR (ECON).

11.11.1.3 Amplitude Error Analysis

- **Algorithm ESPRIT_SVD:** Figure 11.33 gives the result obtained with this algorithm for the estimation of amplitudes with precision indicators.

  This algorithm has difficulty estimating low amplitudes for an SNR value between 0 and 30 dB. But beyond this range, the estimation is good.

- **Algorithm ESPRIT_SVDSSA:** Figure 11.34 gives the result obtained with this algorithm for the estimation of amplitudes with precision indicators.

  This algorithm has difficulty estimating low amplitudes for an SNR value between 0 and 40 dB for intermediate values between 10^{-1}. But beyond this range the estimation is good.

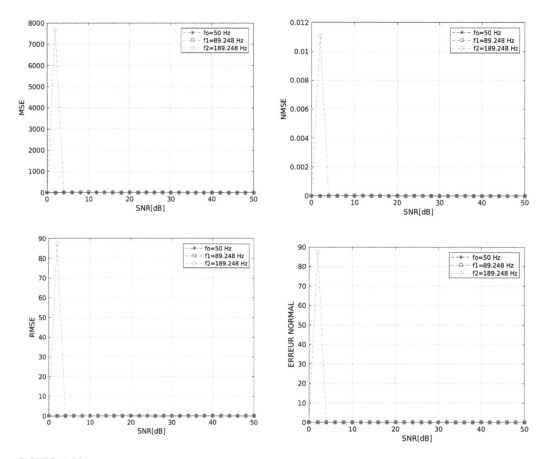

FIGURE 11.32
Variation of the frequency estimation error as a function of SNR (TLS).

- **Algorithm ESPRIT_ITCMP:** Figure 11.35 gives the result obtained with this algorithm for the estimation of amplitudes with precision indicators.

  This algorithm has difficulty estimating low amplitudes for an SNR value between 0 and 6 dB for values of intermediate amplitudes of 10^{-1} for the MSE and RMSE indicator. But beyond that the estimate is good.

- **Algorithm ESPRIT_IRLBA:** Figure 11.36 gives the result obtained with this algorithm for the estimation of amplitudes with precision indicators.

  This algorithm has difficulty estimating low amplitudes for an SNR value between 0 and 30 dB. But beyond that, the estimate is good.

- **Algorithm ESPRIT_ECON:** Figure 11.37 gives the result obtained with this algorithm for the estimation of amplitudes with precision indicators.

  This algorithm has difficulty estimating low amplitudes for an SNR value between 0 and 30 dB. But beyond that the estimate is good.

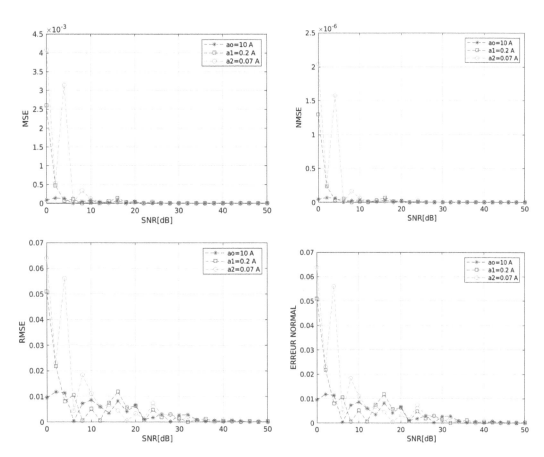

FIGURE 11.33
Variation of the amplitude estimation error as a function of SNR (SVD).

- **Algorithm ESPRIT_TLS:** Figure 11.38 gives the result obtained with this algorithm for the estimation of amplitudes with precision indicators.

  Here, although there is some variation in the estimation error over the range of 0–30 dB, it is less than that of other algorithms.

- **Conclusion on the analyses of magnitude estimates:** Beyond the analyses on the range of SNR values, we can see through all the curves that the MSE indicator gives a very good estimate on the whole for SNR values above 30 dB and more, although on the whole they have difficulty in estimating the amplitudes of low values, the ESPRIT_TLS algorithm is the one that shows this more clearly.

  In this section, we present the findings taken from the results obtained with the different techniques used for this work.

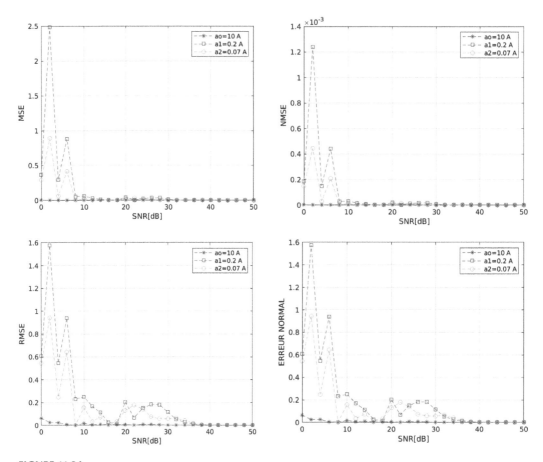

FIGURE 11.34
Variation of the amplitude estimation error as a function of SNR (SVDSSA).

11.11.1.4 Interpretations on Frequency Analysis

After frequency error analysis of the 6 algorithms for SNR ranging from 0 to 50 dB in steps of 2, it was found that the NMSE indicator is best suited for detecting the accuracy on frequency errors. To decide which algorithm to choose, we will work with Table 11.4.

We can then see from the values in the third column that the algorithm ESPRIT_TLS is the one that gives a good estimate. Therefore, it is ranked first.

11.11.1.5 Interpretations on Amplitude Analysis

If on the frequency analysis it can be noticed that the NMSE indicator was the best adapted to judge the precision of the estimation of the algorithms, however on that of the errors in the amplitudes on the six variants of the ESPRIT method, it was found too, that the NMSE indicator is the best adapted for the estimation of the errors because it is less than the three others. Table 11.5 shows the ranking of these algorithms according to this precision indicator.

We can see that the ESPRIT_TLS algorithm still occupies the first place in the ranking.

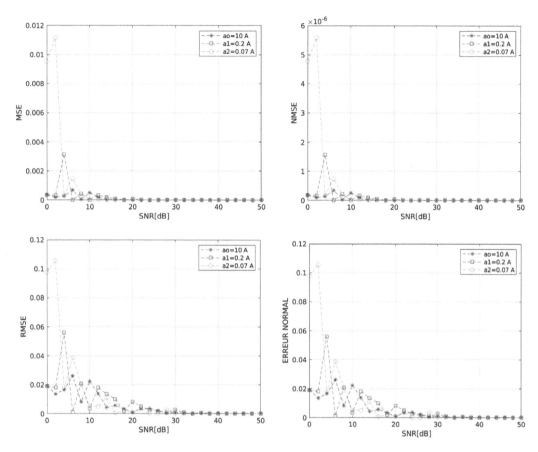

FIGURE 11.35
Variation of the amplitude estimation error as a function of SNR (ITCMP).

11.11.1.6 Interpretations on Frequency and Amplitude Analysis

Based on these two above findings on amplitudes and frequencies and by analyzing the curves corresponding to the NMSE indicator from the frequency point of view for the ESPRIT_TLS algorithm, we found that for a precision of 10^{-8} as desired precision, we can consider that all SNR values between 6 and 50 dB are suitable to minimize the error on frequencies, on the other hand for a precision of 10^{-9} as desired precision we can consider SNR values between 10 and 50 dB and for a desired precision of 10^{-11}, SNR values ranging from 18 to 50 dB are suitable. Thus, based on a precision of 10^{-8} we obtain Figure 11.39 which shows the values of the estimation error at 6 and 50 dB then by zooming on these two points we obtain Figures 11.40 and 11.41 which show, respectively, the estimation errors at 6 and 50 dB.

And proceeding for the ESPRIT_TLS algorithm on amplitudes, we found that if we wanted to consider an accuracy of 10^{-8}, that only for SNRs ranging from 10 to 50 dB were suitable; on the other hand for a precision of 10^{-9} as desired precision we can consider SNR values between 18 and 50 dB suitable. Thus, based on a precision of 10^{-8} we obtain Figure 11.42 which shows the values of the estimation error at 10 and 50 dB then by zooming on these two points we obtain Figures 11.43 and 11.44 which show, respectively, the estimation errors at 10 and 50 dB.

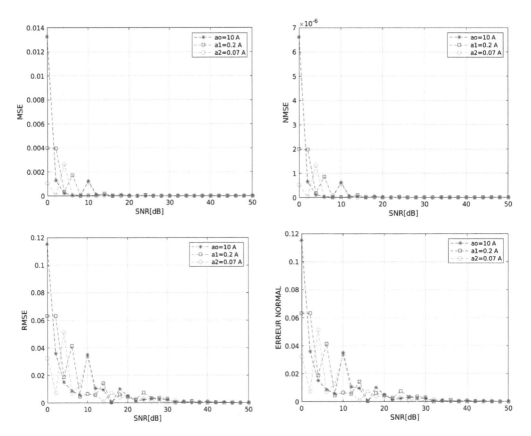

FIGURE 11.36
Variation of the amplitude estimation error as a function of SNR (IRLBA).

From these two results, we conclude that between SNR = 6 dB and 50 dB, amplitudes and frequencies have a good accuracy. So, we will can choose any SNR's value between this interval as the value that minimizes much more the errors on amplitudes and frequencies without forgetting that we retain of course as an indicator of precision, the indicator NMSE for the frequency and the amplitude.

11.11.1.7 Interpretation of Algorithm Execution Times

In this part, we will evaluate the execution times of these algorithms in order to make a ranking from the speed point of view.

After running the program for all SNRs from 0 to 50 at a rate of 20 times for each SNR, averaging for each SNR value gives Tables 11.6–11.9.

Then, by representing Tables 11.6-11.9 we have obtained Figure 11.45, what gives as graph of average execution time, Figure 11.46.

11.11.1.8 Conclusion

We conclude that, if on the frequency and amplitude estimation the best algorithm is ESPRIT_TLS, we find that the ESPRIT_IRLBA algorithm is the one that has the lowest duration on all SNRs and even at 50 dB. To conclude, we will make a comparative Table of frequency, amplitude, memory consumption, and average execution time. Table 11.11

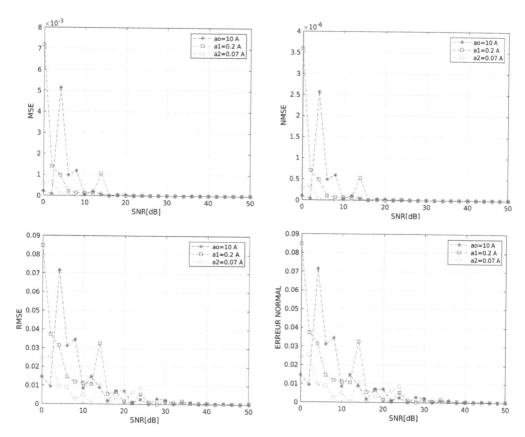

FIGURE 11.37
Variation of the amplitude estimation error as a function of SNR (ECON).

illustrates this. But well before we present the table of memory spaces occupied by these algorithms in Table 11.10.

Since frequency and amplitude cannot be dissociated but are also crucial for our study, they were therefore considered as priority 1. Then comes the time factor which is important for real-time applications as in the case of our study, so we classified it as priority 2 and finally the memory consumption because of the size of the microprogrammed circuits, so priority 3. At the end of this analysis and according to Table 11.11, we agree that the ESPRIT_TLS variant is the most suitable.

11.11.2 Fault Classification Algorithms

In this part, we are looking for, among the fault classification algorithms, the architecture capable of detecting a fault with a very good precision in order to compare it with the ESPRIT_TLS algorithm to choose the best adapted technology for the purpose of this work. The simulations here, we made them in the time and frequency domain.

11.11.2.1 Artificial Neural Networks and Genetic Algorithms

The transfer functions used in the layers are: logsig, tansig, softmax. For the drive function, we used the trainbr function which is suitable as a learning function for the transfer functions used. The performance function that is also suitable is the MSE.

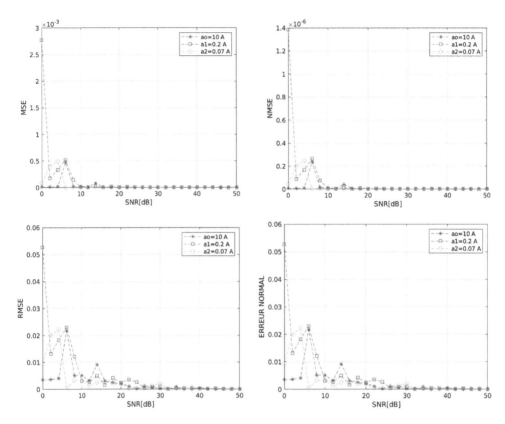

FIGURE 11.38
Variation of the amplitude estimation error as a function of SNR (TLS).

TABLE 11.4

Ranking of Algorithms on Frequency Analysis

Algorithms	Average of NMSE_{f012}	Averages of NMSE_{f_0} NMSE_{f_1} NMSE_{f_2}	Ranking
ESPRIT_SVD	$\mathrm{NMSE}_{f_0} = 0.0272$ $\mathrm{NMSE}_{f_1} = 1.71\mathrm{e}\text{-}04$ $\mathrm{NMSE}_{f_2} = 4.85\mathrm{e}\text{-}04$	0.0093	5
ESPRIT_SVDSSA	$\mathrm{NMSE}_{f_0} = 0.1167$ $\mathrm{NMSE}_{f_1} = 8.59\mathrm{e}\text{-}04$ $\mathrm{NMSE}_{f_2} = 0.0122$	0.0432	6
ESPRIT_ITCMP	$\mathrm{NMSE}_{f_0} = 2.92\mathrm{e}\text{-}04$ $\mathrm{NMSE}_{f_1} = 8.57\mathrm{e}\text{-}05$ $\mathrm{NMSE}_{f_2} = 8.22\mathrm{e}\text{-}04$	4.0033e-4	2
ESPRIT_IRLBA	$\mathrm{NMSE}_{f_0} = 3.83\mathrm{e}\text{-}05$ $\mathrm{NMSE}_{f_1} = 8.75\mathrm{e}\text{-}05$ $\mathrm{NMSE}_{f_2} = 0.0039$	0.0013	4
ESPRIT_ECON	$\mathrm{NMSE}_{f_0} = 1.76\mathrm{e}\text{-}04$ $\mathrm{NMSE}_{f_1} = 6.4\mathrm{e}\text{-}05$ $\mathrm{NMSE}_{f_2} = 0.0027$	9.728e-04	3
ESPRIT_TLS	$\mathrm{NMSE}_{f_0} = 1.95\mathrm{e}\text{-}13$ $\mathrm{NMSE}_{f_1} = 3.90\mathrm{e}\text{-}10$ $\mathrm{NMSE}_{f_2} = 4.26\mathrm{e}\text{-}04$	1.422e-04	1

TABLE 11.5

Ranking of Algorithms on Amplitude Analysis

Algorithms	Average of NMSE$_{a012}$	Averages of NMSE$_{a_0}$ NMSE$_{a_1}$ NMSE$_{a_2}$	Ranking
ESPRIT_SVD	NMSE$_{f_0}$ = 1.32e-08 NMSE$_{f_1}$ = 6.88e-08 NMSE$_{f_2}$ = 1.61e-07	8.13e-08	2
ESPRIT_SVDSSA	NMSE$_{f_0}$ = 1.14e-07 NMSE$_{f_1}$ = 8.33e-05 NMSE$_{f_2}$ = 3.41e-05	3.92e-05	6
ESPRIT_ITCMP	NMSE$_{f_0}$ = 4.53e-08 NMSE$_{f_1}$ = 9.61e-08 NMSE$_{f_2}$ = 4.4e-07	1.95e-07	4
ESPRIT_IRLBA	NMSE$_{f_0}$ = 3.16e-07 NMSE$_{f_1}$ = 2.01e-07 NMSE$_{f_2}$ = 1e-07	2.06e-07	5
ESPRIT_ECON	NMSE$_{f_0}$ = 1.55e-07 NMSE$_{f_1}$ = 2.17e-07 NMSE$_{f_2}$ = 3.26e-08	1.35e-07	3
ESPRIT_TLS	NMSE$_{f_0}$ = 1.30e-08 NMSE$_{f_1}$ = 7.77e-08 NMSE$_{f_2}$ = 1.97e-08	3.68e-08	1

11.11.2.1.1 Preparation of the Simulation Data

For the different algorithms, we used a data of size 52 composed of 26 healthy and 26 faults generated in association with the ESPRIT_TLS algorithm and the simulation parameters listed at the very beginning of this chapter. It should also be mentioned that the healthy data were obtained by noising the signal formed by the frequency f_0. While the fault data were obtained

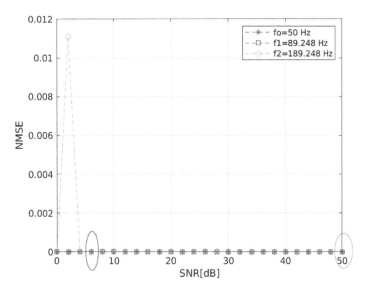

FIGURE 11.39

Precision overview for SNR = 6 dB and SNR = 50 dB.

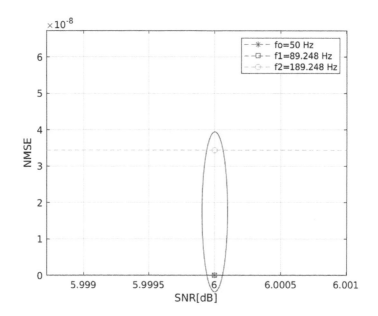

FIGURE 11.40
Precision overview for SNR = 6 dB.

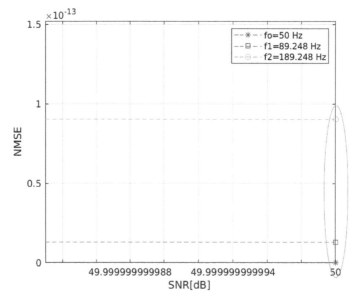

FIGURE 11.41
Precision overview for SNR = 50 dB.

by noising the signal formed by f_0 and the other harmonics. In addition, the formed data are divided into four groups. For an SNR step from 1 to 4 and for each group, the data matrix is [52 × 6], i.e., 52 rows and 6 columns. The search for the best architecture was done with 80% of all the data for learning and 20% for testing. We proceeded in two steps. A training for an

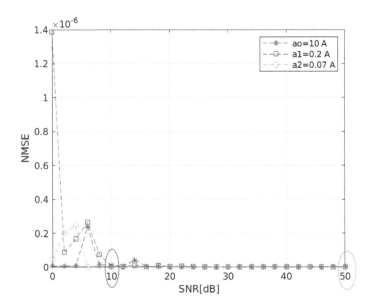

FIGURE 11.42
Precision overview for SNR = 30 dB and SNR = 50 dB.

SNR step equal to 3 and 4. After obtaining the best architecture in both cases, we test it on the data of the remaining steps to see how it generalizes its learning. The cause is that the machine operates in an environment where the noise changes at any time; thus, a variation of the SNR. The flowchart in the following Figure 11.47 explains the execution procedure.

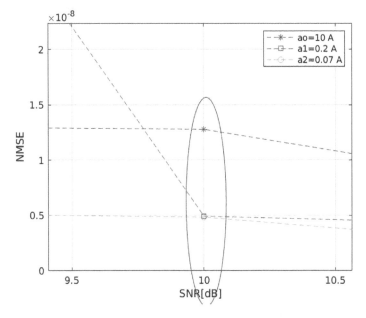

FIGURE 11.43
Precision overview for SNR = 30 dB.

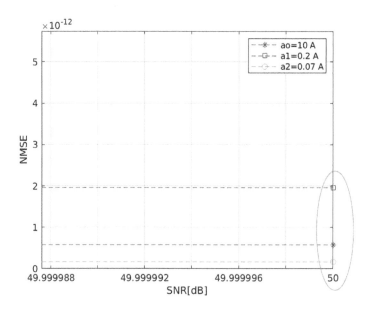

FIGURE 11.44
Precision overview for SNR = 50 dB.

TABLE 11.6

Average Running Time Values Over [0:2:14] dB

Algorithm	SNR (dB)							
	0	2	4	6	8	10	12	14
SVD	0.695	0.619	0.584	0.607	0.585	0.621	0.653	0.1615
SVDSSA	0.772	0.758	0.720	0.754	0.721	0.763	0.753	0.759
ITCMP	0.377	0.349	0.331	0.350	0.343	0.353	0.370	0.354
IRLBA	0.180	0.163	0.143	0.150	0.146	0.149	0.160	0.152
ECON	0.540	0.532	0.471	0.498	0.481	0.522	0.521	0.504
TLS	0.503	0.479	0.447	0.466	0.448	0.486	0.491	0.478

TABLE 11.7

Average Running Time Values Over [16:2:30] dB

Algorithm	SNR (dB)							
	16	18	20	22	24	26	28	30
SVD	0.608	0.623	0.629	0.610	0.671	0.677	0.631	0.629
SVDSSA	0.763	0.781	0.779	0.767	0.814	0.829	0.792	0.783
ITCMP	0.347	0.365	0.363	0.348	0.393	0.408	0.370	0.364
IRLBA	0.147	0.158	0.156	0.149	0.164	0.163	0.159	0.153
ECON	0.483	0.532	0.471	0.498	0.482	0.523	0.522	0.504
TLS	0.467	0.484	0.484	0.473	0.536	0.563	0.497	0.487

TABLE 11.8

Average Running Time Values Over [32:2:46] dB

Algorithm	SNR (dB)							
	32	34	36	38	40	42	44	46
SVD	0.634	0.643	0.647	0.646	0.641	0.664	0.645	0.659
SVDSSA	0.830	0.789	0.804	0.807	0.798	0.813	0.811	0.815
ITCMP	0.394	0.366	0.375	0.375	0.369	0.377	0.376	0.380
IRLBA	0.166	0.159	0.163	0.166	0.161	0.171	0.167	0.163
ECON	0.518	0.504	0.514	0.517	0.505	0.529	0.517	0.513
TLS	0.497	0.498	0.504	0.508	0.496	0.506	0.501	0.504

TABLE 11.9

Average Running Time Values Over [48:2:50] dB

Algorithm	SNR (dB)	
	48	50
SD	0.651	0.644
SVDSSA	0.823	0.805
ITCMP	0.377	0,376
IRLBA	0.164	0.171
ECON	0.525	0.521
TLS	0.498	0.501

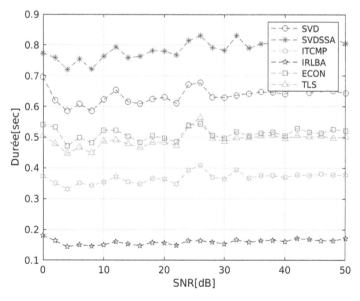

FIGURE 11.45

Execution times of the 6 algorithms.

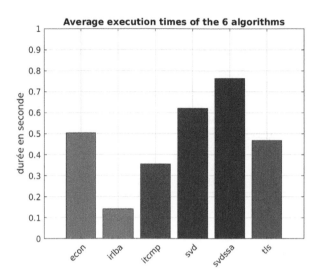

FIGURE 11.46
Average execution times of the 6 algorithms.

TABLE 11.10

Memory Size of the 6 SPIRIT Variants

Algorithm	SVD	SVDSSA	ITCMP	IRLBA	ECON	TLS
Memory (Ko)	55	55	58	55	55	55

TABLE 11.11

Ranking of Algorithms on Runtime, Memory, Frequency and Amplitude

Algorithm	Frequency (Hz)	Amplitude (A)	Memory (MB)	Average Duration (s)
SVD	3	4	5	5
SVDSSA	6	6	6	6
ITCMP	4	5	2	2
IRLBA	5	2	1	1
ECON	2	3	4	4
TLS	1	1	3	3

11.11.2.1.2 Simulation in the Time Domain

The best architectures obtained are presented in Table 11.12.

To better understand the results obtained, we have represented them in the form of a confusion matrix (The confusion matrix is a matrix that measures the quality of a classification system.) for steps 3 and 4.

For a 3 dB Step:

Figure 11.48 shows the results of learning and testing.

For this part, the best architecture was obtained with 3 dB step learning data. After obtaining it, we tested it on data where the SNR steps are 1 dB (to the right), 2 dB (bottom left) and 4 dB (bottom right). It was found that the detection accuracy for the 4 dB step is higher than the 1 and 2 dB steps due to the fact that the signal to noise ratio is higher.

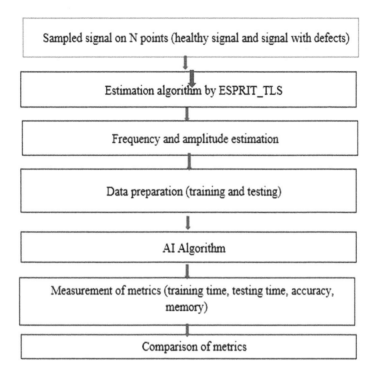

FIGURE 11.47
Flowchart of execution.

TABLE 11.12

Result for Learning in Steps of 3 and 4 in the Temporal Domain

Architecture selected	SNR Training Step (dB)	SNR Testing Step (dB)	Accuracy on Each Testing Step (%)	Duration (s)	Memory (KB)	Samples size
$[4, [7, 6, 4, 8], \text{logsig}\{4\}]$	3	3	67.3	0.2680	71	52
		1	51.9			
		2	51.9			
		4	57.7			
$[4, [9, 1, 9, 3], \text{logsig}\{4\}]$	4	4	61.5	0.2768	71	52
		1	50			
		2	53.82			
		3	51.9			

For a 4 dB Step:
Figure 11.49 shows the results of learning and testing.

For this part, the best architecture was obtained with 4 dB step learning data. After obtaining it, we tested it on data where the SNR steps were 1 dB (to the right), 2 dB (bottom left) and 3 dB (bottom right). It was found that the detection accuracy for the 2 dB step is higher than the 1 and 3 dB steps.

- **Conclusion**: Despite these results, we found that the precision in the time domain was not good in all cases.

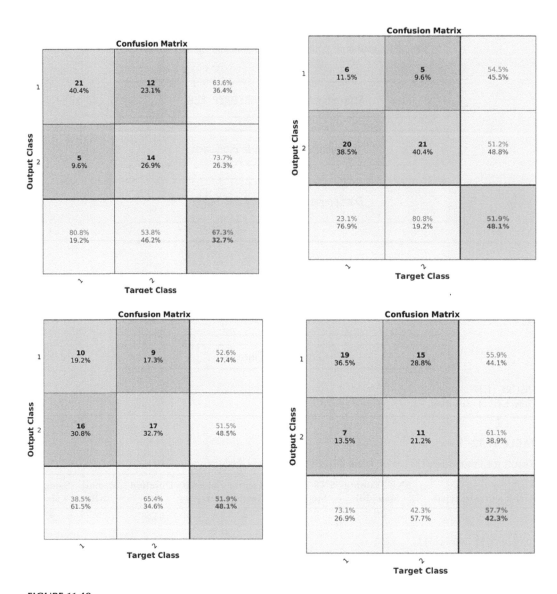

FIGURE 11.48
Time domain confusion matrices for a 3-step SNR.

11.11.2.1.3 Simulation in the Frequency Domain

The best architectures obtained are presented in Table 11.13.

To better understand the results obtained, we have represented them in the form of a confusion matrix for steps 3 and 4.

For a 3 dB Step:

Figure 11.50 shows the results of learning and testing.

For the 3 dB step, although the results are good for learning, we found that this architecture remained blind to variations in upper and lower step, and worse, the accuracy does not exceed 90% compared to the 92% on learning.

For a 4 dB Step:

Figure 11.51 shows the results of learning and testing.

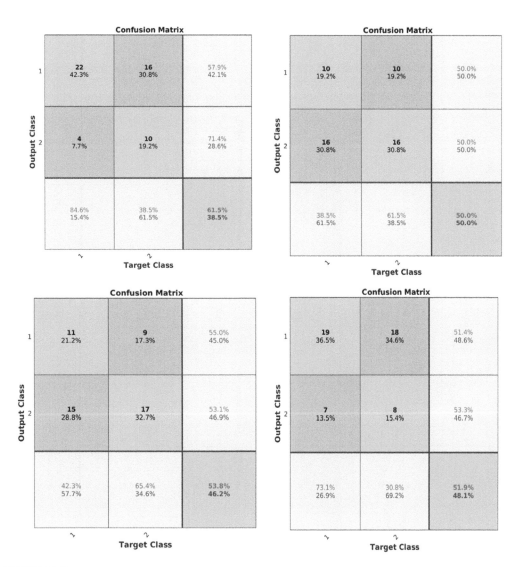

FIGURE 11.49

Time domain confusion matrices for a 4-step SNR.

TABLE 11.13

Result for Learning in Steps of 3 and 4 in the Frequency Domain

Architecture selected	SNR Training Step (dB)	SNR Testing Step (dB)	Accuracy on Each Testing step (%)	Duration (s)	Memory (KB)	Samples size
$[3, [5, 1, 10], \text{logsig}\{3\}]$	3	3	96.2	0.2702	70	52
		1	63.4			
		2	53.8			
		4	51.9			
$[3, [9, 7, 7], \text{logsig}\{3\}]$	4	4	82.7	0.2196	73	52
		1	94.2			
		2	96.2			
		3	88.4			

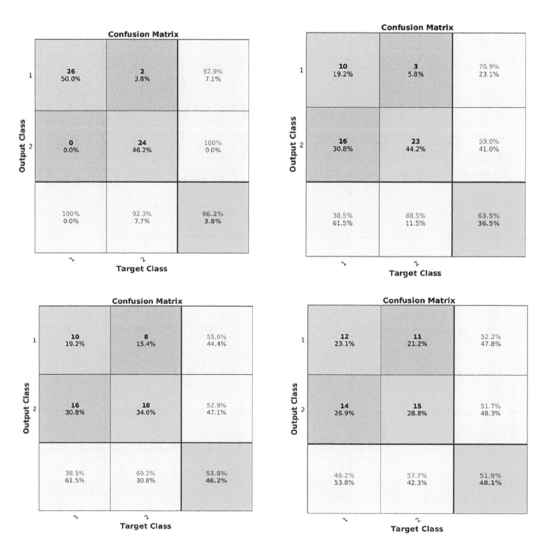

FIGURE 11.50
Frequency domain confusion matrices for a 3-step SNR.

On the other hand, for the 4 dB step, the learning accuracy exceeded 80% and for the other lower and upper steps, it exceeded 83% until reaching 96%. This shows that the architecture could be a bit generalist on the behavior of the machine state for other SNR steps, which is good.

2-Association of Two Architectures
As introduced a little previously here we will present the two networked architectures for the classification of the rolling default in our present study according to the time and frequency domains.

- **Simulation in the Time Domain**: The best architectures obtained are presented in Table 11.14.

We present this result in the form of a confusion matrix in Figure 11.52.

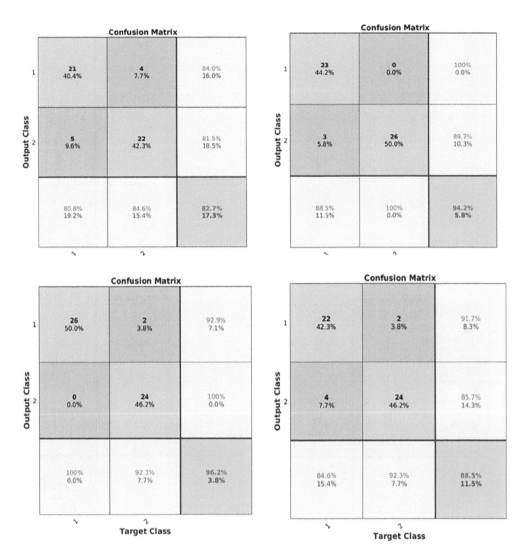

FIGURE 11.51
Frequency domain confusion matrices for a 4-step SNR.

TABLE 11.14

Result for 3 dB Step Learning in the Time Domain

Architecture Selected	SNR Training Step (dB)	SNR Testing Step (dB)	Accuracy on Each Testing Step (%)	Duration (s)	Memory (KB)	Samples Size
		3	100			
	3	1	100			
		2	100			
$[1,[6], \text{logsig}]$		4	100			
+		4	100	0.25	76	52
$[1,[8], \text{logsig}]$		1	100			
	3	2	100			
		3	100			

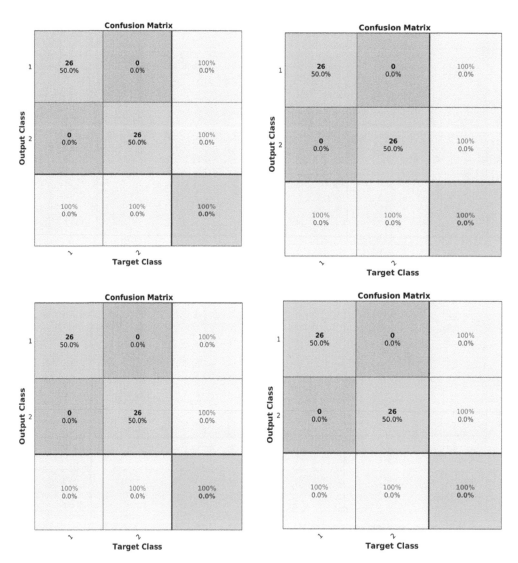

FIGURE 11.52
Time domain confusion matrices for a 3-step SNR.

The results showed that by combining two architectures, each generalist on one of the operating states of the induction machine, we obtained a network capable of detecting with a very good accuracy each state of the induction machine and this regardless of the variation of the SNR.

11.11.2.1.4 *Simulation in the Frequency Domain*

The best architectures obtained are presented in Table 11.15.

We have presented this result in the form of a confusion matrix in Figure 11.53.

The results showed that by combining two architectures, each generalist on one of the operating states of the induction machine, we obtained a network capable of detecting with a very good accuracy each operating state of the induction machine and this regardless of the variation of the SNR.

TABLE 11.15

Result for 3 dB Step Learning in the Frequency Domain

Architecture Selected	SNR Training Step (dB)	SNR Testing Step (dB)	Accuracy on Each Testing Step (%)	Duration (s)	Memory (KB)	Samples Size
$[1, [\,10\,], logsig\,]$	3	3	100	0.25	143	52
+		1	100			
$[1, [5], logsig\,]$		2	100			
		4	100			
	3	4	100			
		1	100			
		2	100			
		3	100			

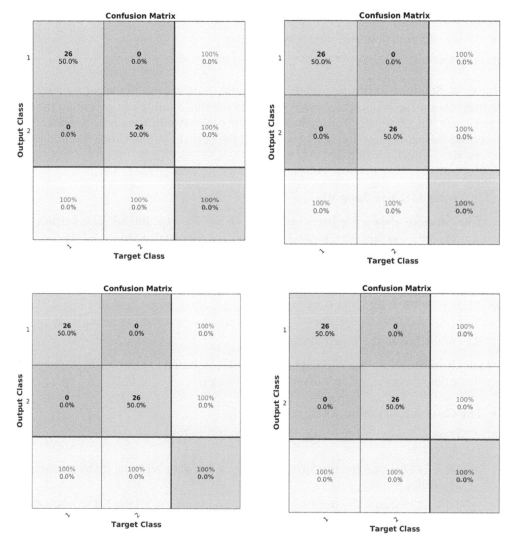

FIGURE 11.53
Frequency domain confusion matrices for a 3-step SNR.

11.11.2.2 Conclusion

The findings in the frequency and time domain have shown that the results remain the same as long as two generalist architectures are associated, respectively, on each of the states of the machine.

From the confusion matrices in the time and frequency domain, we found that unlike the frequency domain in the time domain, there is less precision on the classification of the turnover failure at any of the SNR learning steps and the other SNR steps. This was not the case for the frequency domain where the precision was good for the 4dB step on learning and testing on the other steps.

Based on these findings, we concluded that the second frequency domain architecture was the best. This architecture is characterized by:

- six neurons in the input layer.
- three hidden layers each having 9, 7, and 7 neurons, respectively.
- the transfer function in all layers being logsig.
- two neurons in the output layer.

But only for simple architectures. On the other hand, comparing it to the network architecture from the precision point of view, it would be rejected although in execution time and memory size it is preferable. In conclusion, as the difference in time is only a few tenths of a second, based on precision, we have chosen the network architecture even though its memory size is much greater.

11.11.3 Vector Machine Supports

The same previous data were used in the search for the best model. The kernels used are the polynomial kernel, the linear kernel and the Gaussian kernel and the back-end processing algorithms are the SMO (Sequential Minimal Optimization), ISDA (Iterative Single Data Algorithm) and L1QP (L1 quadratic programming) algorithms. The characteristic parameters of the model are the KernelScale γ and the BoxConstraint (C). The results obtained are presented below:

11.11.3.1 Simulation in the Time Domain

For each given kernel, we have applied the possible resolution algorithms to it. The results in the time domain are given in Tables 11.16-11.21 below:

- **The Gaussian Kernel or RBF**
  - Table 11.16 shows the results of learning and testing with the SMO resolution algorithm.
  - Table 11.17 shows the results of learning and testing with the ISDA resolution algorithm.
  - Table 11.18 shows the results of learning and testing with the L1QP resolution algorithm.

- **The Linear Kernel**
  - Table 11.19 shows the results of learning and testing with the SMO resolution algorithm.

TABLE 11.16

Result for 1 dB Step Learning in the Time Domain (RBF)

Architecture Selected	SNR Training Step (dB)	SNR Testing Step (dB)	Accuracy on Each Testing Step (%)	Duration (s)	Memory (KB)	Samples Size
Kernel = RBF	1	1	100	0.045	59	52
C = 444.747	1	2	100	0.045	59	52
Gama = 0.2413	1	3	100	0.045	59	52
Solver = SMO	1	4	100	0.045	59	52

Learning time: 49.19 s.

TABLE 11.17

Result for 1 dB Step Learning in the Time Domain (RBF-ISDA)

Architecture Selected	SNR Training Step (dB)	SNR Testing Step (dB)	Accuracy on Each Testing Step (%)	Duration (s)	Memory (KB)	Samples Size
Kernel = RBF	1	1	100	0.03	59	52
C = 0.0057	1	2	100	0.03	59	52
Gama = 0.0981	1	3	100	0.03	59	52
Solver = ISDA	1	4	100	0.03	59	52

Learning time: 51.36 s.

TABLE 11.18

Result for 1dB Step Learning in the Time Domain (RBF- L1QP)

Architecture Selected	SNR Training Step (dB)	SNR Testing Step (dB)	Accuracy on Each Testing Step (%)	Duration (s)	Memory (KB)	Samples Size
Kernel = RBF	1	1	96.5	0.03	59	52
C = 352.24	1	2	96.5	0.03	59	52
Gama = 0.755	1	3	96.5	0.03	59	52
Solver = L1QP	1	4	96.5	0.03	59	52

Learning time: 61.16 s.

TABLE 11.19

Result for 1 dB Step Learning in the Time Domain (Linear-SMO)

Architecture Selected	SNR Training Step (dB)	SNR Testing Step (dB)	Accuracy on Each Testing Step (%)	Duration (s)	Memory (KB)	Samples Size
Kernel = Linear	1	1	63.46	0.03	59	52
C = 997.56	1	2	63.46	0.03	59	52
Gama = 0.3881	1	3	63.46	0.03	59	52
Solver = SMO	1	4	63.46	0.03	59	52

Learning time: 182.14 s.

TABLE 11.20

Result for 1 dB Step Learning in the Time Domain (Linear-ISDA)

Architecture Selected	SNR Training Step (dB)	SNR Testing Step (dB)	Accuracy on Each Testing Step (%)	Duration (s)	Memory (KB)	Samples Size
Kernel = Linear C = 1.1356 Gama = 0.0011 Solver = ISDA	1	1	67.3	0.022	58	52

Learning time: 67.61 s.

TABLE 11.21

Result for 1 dB Step Learning in the Time Domain (Linear-L1QP)

Architecture Selected	SNR Training Step (dB)	SNR Testing Step (dB)	Accuracy on Each Testing Step (%)	Duration (s)	Memory (KB)	Samples Size
Kernel = Linear C = 992.99 Gama = 0.1348 Solver = L1QP	1	1 2 3 4	75	0.03	58	52

Learning time: 40.72 s.

- Table 11.20 shows the results of learning and testing with the ISDA resolution algorithm.
- Table 11.21 shows the results of learning and testing with the L1QP resolution algorithm.
- **The Polynomial Kernel**
  - Table 11.22 shows the results of learning and testing with the SMO resolution algorithm.
  - Table 11.23 shows the results of learning and testing with the ISDA resolution algorithm.

- **Conclusion:** Indeed, we could see from the results that the classification with the RBF kernel gave good details on learning and testing, but we point out that this is only a function of Γ and C. This means that the same result could be obtained with the other kernels and resolution algorithms, even if we only have the right values of the C and Γ parameters. And another important point is the learning time.

11.11.3.2 Simulation in the Frequency Domain

- **The Gaussian Kernel or RBF**
  - Table 11.24 shows the results of learning and testing with the SMO resolution algorithm.
  - Table 11.25 shows the results of learning and testing with the ISDA resolution algorithm.
  - Table 11.26 shows the results of learning and testing with the L1QP resolution algorithm.

TABLE 11.22

Result for 1 dB Step Learning in the Time Domain (Polynomial-SMO)

Architecture Selected	SNR Training Step (dB)	SNR Testing Step (dB)	Accuracy on Each Testing Step (%)	Duration (s)	Memory (KB)	Samples Size
Kernel = Polynomial	1	1	71.15	0.03	59	52
C = 97.51		2	71.15			
Gama = 40.67		3	71.15			
Solver = SMO		4	71.15			
Order = 3						

Learning time: 116.43 s.

TABLE 11.23

Result for 1 dB Step Learning in the Time Domain (Polynomial-ISDA)

Architecture Selected	SNR Training Step (dB)	SNR Testing Step (dB)	Accuracy on Each Testing Step (%)	Duration (s)	Memory (KB)	Samples Size
Kernel = Polynomial	1	1	86.53	0.03	59	52
C = 1.1532		2	86.53			
Gama = 0.9590		3	86.53			
Solver = ISDA		4	86.53			
Order = 3						

Learning time: 59.96 s.

TABLE 11.24

Result for 1 dB Step Learning in the Frequency Domain (RBF-SMO)

Architecture Selected	SNR Training Step (dB)	SNR Testing step (dB)	Accuracy on Each Testing Step (%)	Duration (s)	Memory (KB)	Samples Size
Kernel = RBF	1	1	100	0.02	37	52
C = 830.85		2				
Gama = 0.136		3				
Solver = SMO		4				

Learning time: 46.79 s.

TABLE 11.25

Result for 1 dB Step Learning in the Frequency Domain (RBF-ISDA)

Architecture Selected	SNR Training Step (dB)	SNR Testing Step (dB)	Accuracy on Each Testing Step (%)	Duration (s)	Memory (KB)	Samples Size
Kernel = RBF	1	1	100	0.03	63	52
C = 0.00102		2	100			
Gama = 0.00464		3	100			
Solver = ISDA		4	100			

Learning time: 50.69 s.

- **The Linear Kernel**
  - Table 11.27 shows the results of learning and testing with the SMO resolution algorithm.
  - Table 11.28 shows the results of learning and testing with the ISDA resolution algorithm.
  - Table 11.29 shows the results of learning and testing with the ISDA resolution algorithm.

- **The Polynomial Kernel**
  - Table 11.30 shows the results of learning and testing with the SMO resolution algorithm.
  - Table 11.31 shows the results of learning and testing with the ISDA resolution algorithm.

TABLE 11.26

Result for 1 dB Step Learning in the Frequency Domain (RBF-L1QP)

Architecture Selected	SNR Training Step (dB)	SNR Testing Step (dB)	Accuracy on Each Testing Step (%)	Duration (s)	Memory (KB)	Samples Size
Kernel = RBF	1	1	88.46	0.03	63	52
C = 0.0013		2	88.46			
Gama = 0.0648		3	88.46			
Solver = L1QP		4	88.46			

Learning time: 46.79 s.

TABLE 11.27

Result for 1 dB Step Learning in the Frequency Domain (Linear-SMO)

Architecture Selected	SNR Training Step (dB)	SNR Testing Step (dB)	Accuracy on Each Testing Step (%)	Duration (s)	Memory (KB)	Samples Size
Kernel = Linear	1	1	67.3	0.022	63	52
C = 132.408		2	67.3			
Gama = 14.546		3	67.3			
Solver = SMO		4	67.3			

Learning time: 58.31 s.

TABLE 11.28

Result for 1 dB Step Learning in the Frequency Domain (Linear-ISDA)

Architecture Selected	SNR Training Step (dB)	SNR Testing Step (dB)	Accuracy on Each Testing Step (%)	Duration (s)	Memory (KB)	Samples Size
Kernel = Linear	1	1	63.46	0.03	63	52
C = 0.0065						
Gama = 7.6596						
Solver = ISDA						

Learning time: 53.47 s.

TABLE 11.29

Result for 1 dB Step Learning in the Frequency Domain (Linear-L1QP)

Architecture Selected	SNR Training Step (dB)	SNR Testing Step (dB)	Accuracy on Each Testing Step (%)	Duration (s)	Memory (KB)	Samples Size
Kernel = Linear	1	1	61.53	0.03	63	52
C = 0.1987		2	61.53			
Gama = 3.3190		3	61.53			
Solver = L1QP		4	61.53			

Learning time: 40.72 s.

TABLE 11.30

Result for 1 dB Step Learning in the Frequency Domain (Polynomial-SMO)

Architecture Selected	SNR Training Step (dB)	SNR Testing Step (dB)	Accuracy on Each Testing Step (%)	Duration (s)	Memory (KB)	Samples Size
Kernel = Polynomial	1	1	69.23	0.03	63	52
C = 0.4923		2	71.53			
Gama = 0.2542		3	67.30			
Solver = SMO		4	69.23			
Order = 3						

Learning time: 121.10 s

TABLE 11.31

Result for 1 dB Step Learning in the Frequency Domain (Polynomial-ISDA)

Architecture Selected	SNR Training Step (dB)	SNR Testing Step (dB)	Accuracy on Each Testing Step (%)	Duration (s)	Memory (KB)	Samples Size
Kernel = Polynomial	1	1	69.23	0.03	63	52
C = 2.6343		2	71.53			
Gama = 1.353		3	67.30			
Solver = ISDA		4	69.23			
Order = 3						

Learning time: 122.05 s.

- **Conclusion**: Indeed, we could see from the results that the classification with the RBF kernel gave good details on learning and testing, but we point out that this is only a function of Γ and C. This means that the same result could be obtained with the other kernels and resolution algorithms, even if we only have the right values of the C and Γ parameters. And another important point is the learning time.

  As a result of the results obtained in both domains, we realized that all we needed was to have the right parameters, in this case KernelScale and BoxConstraint, regardless of the kernel and the resolution algorithm. The only difference found was that the training time proved to be too long in the time domain.

11.11.4 K-Nearest Neighbors

Indeed, for the K-NNs, the architecture parameters have been accentuated on the distance calculation used and the K value allowing to obtain a very good detection accuracy. The architectures obtained are presented below for both domains.

11.11.4.1 Simulation in the Time Domain

Table 11.32 shows the results of learning and testing.

- **Conclusion**: The observation is the same as the previous one. All that is needed is to find the right K value, the right distance assessor, and it doesn't matter how the SNR pitch varies.

11.11.4.2 Simulation in the Frequency Domain

Table 11.33 shows the results of learning and testing.

- **Conclusion**: The observation is the same as the previous one. All that is needed is to find the right K value, the right distance assessor, and it doesn't matter how the SNR pitch varies.

    Based on these two results, we realized that, whether in the frequency or time domain, if we have the right parameters, we can have very good detection accuracies.

11.11.5 Extreme Learning Machine

As already mentioned, ELMs have only one hidden layer. The objective is therefore to search for the right number of neurons for an acceptable rolling default detection. To do this we have varied the number of neurons in an interval from 1 to 100. Here are the results in the different domains:

11.11.5.1 Simulation in the Time Domain

Table 11.34 shows the results of learning and testing.

TABLE 11.32

Result for 1 dB Step Learning in the Time Domain (K-NN)

Architecture Selected	SNR Training Step (dB)	SNR Testing Step (dB)	Accuracy on Each Testing Step (%)	Duration (s)	Memory (KB)	Samples Size
Distance = "cityblock"	1	1	100	0.03	55	52
NumNeighbors = 1		2	100			
		3	100			
		4	100			

Learning time: 63.82 s.

TABLE 11.33

Result for 1 dB Step Learning in the Frequency Domain (K-NN)

Architecture Selected	SNR Training Step (dB)	SNR Testing Step (dB)	Accuracy on Each Testing Step (%)	Duration (s)	Memory (KB)	Samples Size
Distance = "mahalanobis"	1	1	100	0.03	58	52
NumNeighbors = 1		2	100			
		3	100			
		4	100			

Learning time: 55.51 s.

TABLE 11.34

Result for 1 dB Step Learning in the Time Domain (ELM)

Architecture Selected	Training Data (%)	Accuracy (%)	Testing Data (%)	Accuracy (%)	Time Execution (s)	Memory (KB)
Inputs weights = $[3 \times 6]$	80	57.4	20	80	0.02	12
Biases = $[3 \times 1]$						
Hidden nodes = 3						
Activation function = "logsig"						
Outputs weights = $[3 \times 1]$						

TABLE 11.35

Result for 1 dB Step Learning in the Frequency Domain (ELM)

Architecture Selected	Training Data (%)	Accuracy (%)	Testing Data (%)	Accuracy (%)	Time Execution (sec)	Memory (KB)
Inputs weights = $[72 \times 6]$	80	100	20	100	0.02	139
Biases = $[72 \times 1]$						
Hidden nodes = 72						
Activation function = "logsig"						
Outputs weights = $[72 \times 1]$						

Training data (80%) = 42 samples, Testing data (20%) = 10 samples, Final test accuracy = 61.53%

11.11.5.2 Simulation in the Frequency Domain

Table 11.35 shows the results of learning and testing.

Training data (80%) = 42 samples, Testing data (20%) = 10 samples, Final test accuracy = 100%

- **Conclusion**: By analyzing the two results, we realized that in the frequency domain the detection accuracy was clearly better than in the time domain. This led us to choose the frequency-domain architecture. It should be mentioned, however, that the architecture based on one learning SNR step will remain blind to the data of the other steps. But what makes it powerful is that it gives a very good accuracy on the test data of its learning step.

  At the end of all the results, in this section we will make a comparison of the best results obtained in the two domains in order to decide which one is best placed within the framework of the objective of our present study.

11.11.6 Comparative Table of the Different Algorithms Developed in Time and Frequency

The data below are taken from previous calculations and have been reported here in order to choose the algorithm that until then would be best suited to achieve the goal: that of having a real-time system with a very good accuracy in terms of detection of electromechanical defaults.

The precision of the ESPRIT_TLS algorithm is calculated by the following formula:

$$accuray = \left(1 - \left(n - n_{es}\right)/n\right) \times 100\% \tag{30}$$

where

$n_s - n_{es}$ is the normal error. Since the normal error has already been calculated, apply-ing this to f_0, f_1, f_2, a_0, a_1, and a_2 we obtain an accuracy equal to 99.99% for an SNR equal to 50 dB.

11.11.6.1 Comparison of Intelligent Fault Classification Algorithms in the Time and Frequency Domain

Table 11.36 shows the Time Domain Comparison of Classification Algorithms.

Algorithm	Training Time (s)	Execute Time (s)	Accuracy (%)	Memory (KB)
ANN	14	0.27	61.5	192
ANNX2	0.5	0.25	100	143
KNN	63.82	0.03	100	55
SVM	49.19	0.045	100	59
ELM	5.1×10^{-4}	0.2	61.5	12

Table 11.37 shows the frequency Domain Comparison of Classification Algorithms.

We found that the experiments carried out in the frequency domain gave very good results in terms of accuracy. This could be explained by the presence of more character-istics composing the data taken from the stator current. We speak of more informative characteristic of the data. Contrary to the time domain where these additional character-istics are missing. So, no more information to discriminate the stator current samples. So, the frequency domain is the one that is suitable for the purpose of this work.

Below we give some histograms to better understand these results.

TABLE 11.36

Time-Domain Comparison of Classification Algorithms

Algorithm	Training Time (s)	Execute Time (s)	Accuracy (%)	Memory (KB)
ANN	14	0.21	96.4	192
ANNX2	0.5	0.25	100	132
KNN	53.51	0.03	100	58
SVM	46.79	0.022	100	37
ELM	0.005	0.02	100	139

TABLE 11.37

Comparison in the Frequency Domain of Classification Algorithms

Algorithm	Training Time (s)	Execute Time(sec)	Accuracy (%)	Memory (KB)
ANN	14	0.21	96.4	192
ANNX2	0.5	0.25	100	132
KNN	53.51	0.03	100	58
SVM	46.79	0.022	100	37
ELM	0.005	0.02	100	139

11.11.6.1.1 In the Time Domain

Figure 11.54 shows Training duration of the 5 algorithms in the time domain.
Figure 11.55 shows Runtime of the 5 algorithms in the time domain.
Figure 11.56 shows Memory size of the 5 algorithms in the time domain.

11.11.6.1.2 In the Frequency Domain

Figure 11.57 shows Training duration of the 5 algorithms in the frequency domain.
Figure 11.58 shows Runtime of the 5 algorithms in the frequency domain.

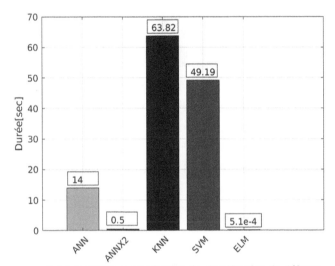

FIGURE 11.54
Training duration of the 5 algorithms in the time domain.

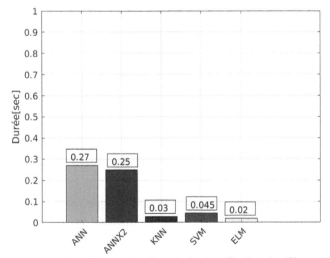

FIGURE 11.55
Runtime of the 5 algorithms in the time domain.

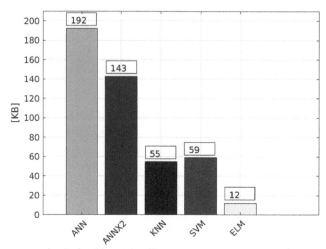

FIGURE 11.56
Memory size of the 5 algorithms in the time domain.

Figure 11.59 shows Memory size of the 5 algorithms in the frequency domain.

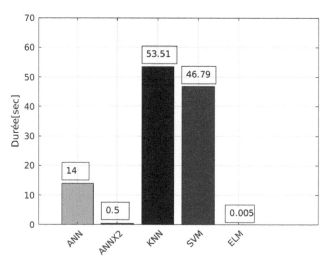

FIGURE 11.57
Training duration of the 5 algorithms in the frequency domain.

Thus, remaining in the frequency domain, we were able to observe by comparison of the differentiation indicators that the ELM (Extreme Machine Learning) algorithm is the one with the shortest training and execution time, both in terms of intelligent default classification algorithms and in comparison with the ESPRIT_TLS method, which met the desired real-time criterion and from the point of view of precision; because of its simplicity and precision, it remains the best placed. The following Table 11.38 shows these characteristics in time term, memory size, and accuracy on a rolling default analysis.

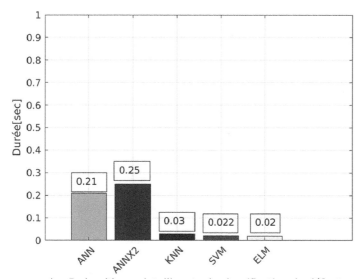

FIGURE 11.58
Runtime of the 5 algorithms in the frequency domain.

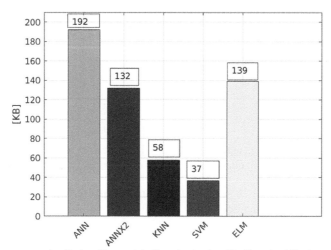

FIGURE 11.59
Memory size of the 5 algorithms in the frequency domain.

TABLE 11.38

Characteristics of the Selected ELM Algorithm

Algorithm	Training Time (s)	Execute Time (s)	Accuracy (%)	Memory (KB)
ELM	0.005	0.2	100	139

11.12 Conclusion

The aim of this work was to carry out a design study allowing the development of an intelligent system capable of detecting in real time and with a very good accuracy the electromechanical defaults of an electric induction machine. In this work, we did not present all these defaults but only that of the bearing because the principle remains the same for the others. Thus, after a rather global view of the electric induction machine and the defaults it is prey to, we lingered on the possible techniques allowing to design such a system by showing some high-resolution signal processing techniques (the variants of the ESPRIT method) and some artificial intelligence techniques (ANN-GA, KNN, SVM, ELM) in the frequency and time domain to finally decide which one would suit our purpose. And it was clear that analysis in the frequency domain allowed to have very good results in terms of not only of speed, memory size but also precision for reasons we have not forgotten to mention. After a detailed study, we have come to the conclusion that the machine learning technique ELM was best placed to meet our expectations.

It should be mentioned, however, that the study was conducted with only one SNR step for learning and testing. And this did not allow for a generalist ELM on the other steps that were not used for learning. Therefore, the ideal would be to continue the work to develop a generalist ELM. It should also be added that, according to certain theories that we did not consider in this work, one of the advantages of MLEs was their ability to detect several defects at the same time; this could be verified for a continuation of this work.

Finally, for health reasons, due to the current pandemic, we have not been able to access the university laboratory to verify the results obtained in a concrete way, which we were planning to do soon.

References

1. Chakkor, S., Baghouri, M., & Hajraoui, A. (2015). High accuracy ESPRIT-TLS technique for wind turbine fault discrimination. *International Journal of Electrical, Computer, Energetic, Electronic and Communication*, 9(1), 122–131.
2. De Ketelaere, B., Hubert, M., & Schmitt, E. (2015). Overview of PCA-based statistical process-monitoring methods for time-dependent, high-dimensional data. *Journal of Quality Technology*, 47(4), 318–335.
3. Aubert, B. (2014). Detection des courts-circuits inter-spires dans les Generateurs Synchrones a Aimants Permanents: Methodes basees modeles et filtre de Kalman etendu (Doctoral dissertation, Toulouse).
4. Chatelain, J. (1989). Machines electriques (Vol. 10). PPUR Presses Polytechniques, Lausanne.
5. Singh, G. K. (2003). Experimental investigations on induction machine condition monitoring and fault diagnosis using digital signal processing techniques. *Electric Power Systems Research*, 65(3), 197–221.
6. Bossio, G. R., De Angelo, C. H., Bossio, J. M., Pezzani, C. M., & Garcia, G. O. (2009). Separating broken rotor bars and load oscillations on IM fault diagnosis through the instantaneous active and reactive currents. *IEEE Transactions on Industrial Electronics*, 56(11), 4571–4580.
7. Krishnamurthy, S. (2019). Anamoly detection techniques and practices. Available Online at: https://fr.slideshare.net/QuantUniversity/anomaly-detection-workshop-slides.

8. Chakkor, S. (2015). E-diagnostic de processus physiques a base des methodes de haute resolution application: Machines eoliennes (Doctoral dissertation, Faculte des Sciences de Tetouan, Maroc).

9. Thomson, W. T., & Gilmore, R. J. (2003). Motor current signature analysis to detect faults in induction motor drives-fundamentals, data interpretation, and industrial case histories. In *Proceedings of the 32nd Turbomachinery Symposium*. Texas A&M University, Turbomachinery Laboratories, College Station, TX.

10. Gheitasi, A. (2012). Motors fault recognition using distributed current signature analysis (Doctoral dissertation, Auckland University of Technology, Auckland).

11. Thomson, W. T. (2009). On-line motor current signature analysis prevents premature failure of large induction motor drives. *Maintenance & Asset Management*, 24(3), 30–35.

12. Korde, A. (2002, May). On-line condition monitoring of motors using electrical signature analysis. In *Recent Advances in Condition-Based Plant Maintenance. Seminar Organized by Indian Institute of Plant Engineers* (Vol. 1718), Mumbai, India.

13. Penrose, H. W., & Old Saybrook, C. T. (2005). A multi-technology approach to motor diagnostics. *Maintenance Technology*, 18(11), 43.

14. Miljkovic, D. (2008). Review of machine condition monitoring based on vibration data. In *Proceedings MIPRO 2008* (Vol. III), CTS and CIS, Opatija, Croatia.

15. Burstein, N. M., & Ferree, D. V. (1996, November). Monitoring electric motor condition using current signature analysis: Case histories and success stories. In *International Maintenance Technology and Information Symposium*, Monterey, CA.

16. Quinquis, A., Radoi, E., Ioana, C., & Mansour, A. (2008). Digital signal processing using MATLAB (p. 424). John Wiley & Sons. https://www.amazon.com/Digital-Signal-Processing-Using-MATLAB/dp/1848210116.

17. Cong, F., Nandi, A. K., He, Z., Cichocki, A., & Ristaniemi, T. (2012, August). Fast and effective model order selection method to determine the number of sources in a linear transformation model. In *2012 Proceedings of the 20th European Signal Processing Conference (EUSIPCO)* (pp. 1870–1874). IEEE, Bucharest, Romania.

18. Stoica, P., & Selen, Y. (2004). Model-order selection: a review of information criterion rules. *IEEE Signal Processing Magazine*, 21(4), 36–47.

19. Hansen, M. H., & Yu, B. (2001). Model selection and the principle of minimum description length. *Journal of the American Statistical Association*, 96(454), 746–774.

20. Broersen, P. M., & Wensink, H. E. (1998). Autoregressive model order selection by a finite sample estimator for the Kullback-Leibler discrepancy. *IEEE Transactions on Signal Processing*, 46(7), 2058–2061.

21. Minka, T. (2000). Automatic choice of dimensionality for PCA. *Advances in Neural Information Processing Systems*, 13, 598–604.

22. Abou-Elseoud, A., Starck, T., Remes, J., Nikkinen, J., Tervonen, O., & Kiviniemi, V. (2010). The effect of model order selection in group PICA. *Human Brain Mapping*, 31(8), 1207–1216.

23. Jack, L. B., & Nandi, A. K. (2000). Comparison of neural networks and support vector machines in condition monitoring applications. In *COMADEM 2000: 13th International Congress on Condition Monitoring and Diagnostic Engineering Management* (pp. 721–730), Houston, TX.

24. Jack, L. B., & Nandi, A. K. (2000). Genetic algorithms for feature selection in machine condition monitoring with vibration signals. *IEE Proceedings-Vision, Image and Signal Processing*, 147(3), 205–212.

25. Samanta, B., Al-Balushi, K. R., & Al-Araimi, S. A. (2001, September). Use of genetic algorithm and artificial neural network for gear condition diagnostics. In *Proceedings of COMADEM* (pp. 449–456). Elsevier Science Ltd, University of Manchester, UK.

26. Jack, L. B., & Nandi, A. K. (2002). Fault detection using support vector machines and artificial neural networks, augmented by genetic algorithms. *Mechanical Systems and Signal Processing*, 16(2–3), 373–390.

27. Benahmed, N. (2002). Optimisation de reseaux de neurones pour la reconnaissance de chiffres manuscrits isoles: Selection et ponderation des primitives par algorithmes genetiques (Ecole de technologie superieure, Quebec).
28. https://towardsdatascience.com/introduction-to-genetic-algorithms-including-examplecode-e396e98d8bf3.
29. https://zestedesavoir.com/tutoriels/1760/un-peu-de-machine-learning-avec-les-svm/.
30. https://towardsdatascience.com/introduction-to-extreme-learning-machines-c020020ff82b.

12

Wavelet Transformation and Machine Learning Techniques for Digital Signal Analysis in IoT Systems

Rajalakshmi Krishnamurthi and Dhanalekshmi Gopinathan
Jaypee Institute of Information Technology

CONTENTS

12.1 Introduction

The global market trend of IoT analytics envisages the growth of a 26% compound annual growth rate (CAGR) by 2022 [1]. In today's scenario, the Internet of Things (IoT) has made extraordinary growth in academic and commercial sectors because of the various advantages and capabilities of IoT. It has improved the quality of life to a great extent by creating various applications and useful services. It has connected every object of the real world that can communicate and coordinate with each other with the help of the Internet. All the items connected to the Internet can communicate with each other with the least human efforts using the IoT. IoT is present in the environment universally, having multiple connected objects (wired or wireless) that produce the latest application and services like smart homes, smart transportation, smart energy, smart cities, and many more.

IoT is both dynamic and global networked infrastructure. It handles the self-configuring of things efficiently. Due to the vast development in the fields of technology, IoT has been involved in various other technologies like wireless sensor networks (WSN), cloud computing, etc. IoT has connected humans to objects that can be accessed anywhere and

DOI: 10.1201/9781003107026-12

anytime. IoT has its applications in every sector. It has enhanced the healthcare services as health monitoring can be done in real time. IoT has also optimized the operational cost in the transportation sector. Various house activities can be automated with the help of IoT. However, IoT also faces various challenges in successful deployments such as a huge amount of data generated by IoT sensor devices.

IoT devices produce a huge amount of data that the maintenance of such data is a complex task while maintaining data integrity. There exists a high heterogeneity in IoT devices, platforms, and operating systems. Thus, to handle the coordination among them is a difficult task. As the demand for IoT devices and services is rapidly increasing, the system should be highly scalable to maintain efficiency and effectiveness. Nowadays, as the advancement in IoT technologies is increasing, various IoT devices are surrounding people everywhere at home, work, vehicles, etc. The IoT devices can quickly determine various information related to the environment of the particular user like the habits, some patterns, etc. However, the user IoT devices cannot easily determine the other IoT devices that are present close to them physically. So, in [4], a methodology is proposed using sound chirps in which the IoT devices can discover different IoT devices near them. An audio signal and a data packet are emitted from the second device after the proximity detection system. The signal is detected through a microphone, and the packet is received. After that, to approximate the distance between both the devices, the first device uses a correlation between audio and the data packet. However, the significant challenge is to perform maintenance of IoT systems, to obtain knowledge insight from raw data generated.

In [2], a new methodology is proposed to handle the maintenance of IoT systems. The proposed method can easily find the faulty IoT nodes that are not working correctly and generating false information. Also, the continuous-time Markov chain is used to make the process of monitoring of the IoT network more efficient. Using this method, the IoT node, which is going to be faulty after the expiration of the time control period, is detected by the controller by forecasting the upcoming values of the node. After that, the controller sends a signal to replace that particular node. To collect the data in continuous time, the methodology makes a virtual sensor at the place of the faulty node so that the reliability of data is maintained even during the malfunctioning of the IoT devices. In [3], a remote facial expression monitoring system is proposed, which uses electromyography (EMG) signals at a high data rate. Wi-Fi communication is used to transfer data, and cloud computing is used for fast and efficient signal processing. This proposed mechanism can also be used in various other applications that need high data rate EMG signals.

IoT is a system of various things that together cooperate with the environment and transfer data with the help of the Internet. Millions of devices that are enabled by IoT like sensors, smartphones, etc. connect to do various tasks. IoT systems face various issues that need an effective solution like efficient energy, proper scheduling of events, data security, fault detection, node localization, etc. The solution to these kinds of problems exists in machine learning [4]. With the use of machine learning with IoT, IoT's performance has been raised significantly by exploring the already collected information and optimizing the performance without extra efforts.

IoT systems monitor dynamic environments that change rapidly. So, machine learning can make the system more adaptable so that it can handle the scenarios autonomously and efficiently. IoT systems need machine learning techniques to self-calibrate the new information to perform efficiently in unreachable settings like volcano eruption monitoring. Machine learning also plays a very important role in boosting the decision-making ability of an IoT system. The use of machine learning with IoT also has some challenges, like the IoT devices have limited resources, and the machine learning methodologies drain the energy faster.

Deep learning also plays a vital role in achieving the real-time requirements of an IoT system [5]. For example, object recognition tasks must have a significantly less latency in capturing and responding to the target tasks, etc. Various smart IoT devices that do real-time processing require a consistent network of better quality only available at limited locations. With the integration of deep learning with IoT, network connection quality will not be an issue. The IoT devices have low computing power and limited memory, due to which deep learning cannot be enabled on the IoT devices. Deep learning methods have high power consumption and need high-performance computations. Most of the deep learning libraries used third-party libraries that are not easy to move to IoT devices.

The rest of this chapter is organized as follows: Section 12.2 elaborates the role of digital signal processing techniques for IoT devices. Section 12.3 addresses the machine learning and deep learning techniques for time series analysis in IoT. Section 12.4 discusses the case study on comparison for Morlet, Mexican Hat, and Frequency B-spline wavelet toward the classification of ECG signal. Finally, the chapter closes with the Conclusion.

12.2 Digital Signal Processing Techniques for IoT Devices

Signals can be in different forms such as audio signals, video signals, seismic data, radar signals, medical signals such as ECG, electroencephalograph (EEG), etc. The signal carries information within itself. For example, the picture contains information about the brightness of RGB across the two spatial domains, and radar signals carry information about the electromagnetic waves.

The signals are broadly classified into two categories, such as continuous time-domain and discrete time-domain signals. The continuous time-domain signals, also known as analog signals, are continuous as they are present in each time step within their domain. In contrast, the discrete time-domain signals are discrete and defined in discrete time-steps. In general, most of the signals in nature are continuous signals such as human speech, electrical signals, etc. To analyze these signals in the computer, it needs to be digitized, i.e., it needs to convert into discrete signals.

Recently, IoT devices are widely used in different applications ranging from predictive maintenance to user behavior monitoring. Signals from different devices can be sounds, vibrations, images or accelerometers, vibrators, or other kinds of sensor data needing richer analytics methods. Machine learning for sensors has become widely used to train machines to detect and classify events in real-time, even with noisy, high variation data.

12.2.1 Fourier Transform

Digital signal data are generally periodic signals representing some pattern and are captured at an equally spaced interval of time. The time it takes to repeat itself is called a period, and the distance it travels during this period is called the wavelength. Fourier analysis is widely used to analyze periodic signals. It can be used to decompose the signals into various periodic components. The complex signals can be decomposed into the sum of simpler signals, which are represented as trigonometric functions such as sine and cosine waves. Similarly, different signals can be combined to form a new signal that consists of all of its components. The signals in the time-domain can be transformed into frequency-domain using the mathematical function known as Fourier transform. The function that performs the opposite function is called the inverse Fourier transform.

The fast Fourier transform (FFT) translates a digital signal of periodic signals (x) from the discrete-time domain to the frequency domain. For most of the signals, the frequency domain analysis is more useful than the time domain, and the Fourier transform is used to decompose a signal in the time domain into frequencies. The analysis of signals is then performed using the calculated amplitude and phase values which are used to classify the signals. Complex waveforms can be replicated with a sum of varying amplitude sine waves. Any waveform can be transformed into a sum of varying amplitude sine waves. The noise in the signal shows itself with the higher frequencies in the frequency domain.

Fourier transform takes the signal and decomposes the signal into its components.

Fourier transform is best suited if signals are assumed as the sum of sin waves with different frequencies. The discrete Fourier transform $X(k)$ for the time signal $x(n)$ can be expressed as follows:

$$X(k) = \sum_{n=0}^{N-1} x(n) e^{-i2\pi kn/N} \tag{12.1}$$

where

N is the number of samples,

n is the current sample,

$x(n)$ is the value of the signal at time n,

k is the frequency, and

$X(k)$ is the DFT which includes amplitude and phase of the signal.

The amplitude denotes the frequency (or energy) of the sine wave, and phase denotes the offset of a certain frequency of the sine wave (Figure 12.1).

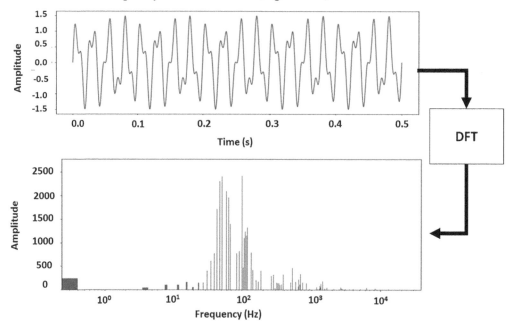

FIGURE 12.1
Converting a time signal into a frequency signal using DFT.

12.2.2 Wavelet Transform

Fourier transformation transforms a time signal into a frequency spectrum.

Fourier transform is well suited for the stationary signals where the frequencies present in the signal are not time-dependent. However, most of the signals in the real life are time-dependent like stock data, sensor data, etc. In general, the Fourier transform mainly concentrates on how the signals are localized in space. It detects the peak frequencies, and it is not able to tell when that frequency happens. It is unable to detect the time resolution of the real signal. In contrast to the Fourier transform, the wavelet transform (WT) can provide the frequency of the signals along with the time associated with those frequencies.

Compared to the Fourier transform, the wavelet transform has a high resolution in frequency and time domain. It analyzes the signal and outputs the frequency type and time at which the frequency has occurred. By analyzing the signal in large-scale and small-scale windows, the large-scale and small-scale features can be extracted. It comes in different sizes are shapes.

The wavelets are chosen depending on the type of application. The two important wavelet transform concepts are (i) scaling and (ii) shifting.

i. **Scaling**: Scaling is a process of stretching and shrinking a signal in time. Scaling is used to either reduce the frequency band of interest or determine the frequency content in a narrower time interval. The more compressed wavelets are the result of the smaller scale factor. It is used to rapidly change details from signals, like high frequency, whereas the high scaling represents a stretched wavelet, and it slowly changes. It is usually used to extract coarse features or low-frequency components.

ii. **Shifting**: Shifting a wavelet means delaying (or hurrying) its onset. In mathematical terms, the delaying function $f(t)$ by k is denoted as $f(t - k)$.

Two main transforms in wavelet are continuous wavelet transform (CWT) and discrete wavelet transform (DWT). These transforms are differed by how the wavelets are scaled and shifted. Key applications of CWT are time-frequency analysis and time localized frequency components. The key applications of DWT are denoising and compression of signals and images.

A wavelet transform is applied to a continuous signal, which breaks the signal into constituent wavelets of different scales and positions. The CWT produces wavelet coefficients as the result and multiplying scaled and shifted wavelet with these produces the constituent wavelet of the original signal

12.2.2.1 Continuous Wavelet Transform (CWT)

The output of CWT is coefficients, which are functions of scale and frequency. The given input signal is projected on a continuous family of frequency bands. The wavelet transform of a continuous signal f(t) is known as CWT and is defined in Equation (12.2) as

$$C(a, b) = \frac{1}{\sqrt{a}} \int_{-\infty}^{+\infty} s(t)\varphi\left(\frac{t - b}{a}\right) dt, \tag{12.2}$$

where

a is the scaling parameter, and b is the time-shift parameter.

$\varphi\left(\dfrac{t-b}{a}\right)$ is the mother wavelet function.

$C(a, b)$ represents the wavelet coefficients.

Wavelets are generated from the single mother wavelet $\varphi\left(\dfrac{t-b}{a}\right)$ by scaling a and shifting b; if $a > 1$ dilates, $a < 1$ contracts the signal. The coefficient $\dfrac{1}{\sqrt{a}}$ is used because the signal has to normalize for all scales. The CWT is a dot product of the original signal $s(t)$ and scaled, shifted version of the mother wavelet $\varphi(t)$.

CWT introduces a lot of duplication in the calculation of wavelet transforms, and also, it does not support multiresolution analysis (MRA) of signals. An alternative to this is using DWT, which is a sampled version of CWT. The limitations of the CWT are handled by the DWT efficiently.

12.2.2.2 Discrete Wavelet Transformation (DWT)

DWT is a powerful tool for digital signal analysis in the time domain. An original time series is broken down into various components, each of which can hold meaningful signals from the original time series. The main goal of the transition is aimed at reducing data size and/or reducing noise. Wavelets consist of mathematical functions that are used to decompose data into different components. DWT separates the input signal into different components and different scales into different frequencies. The frequency is the count of the repeated occurrences over a time unit, and the scale is the time interval of that time series. A time series with a frequency of six event occurrences per minute can be represented as a 10 s interval (scale) between events [2]. DWT transforms data into a new representation which is decomposed into multiple scales; the analysis of the transformed data is also performed at multiple resolution levels as well [3].

For different applications, wavelets display different attributes and performance. Hence, choosing a suitable wavelet filter is vital in finding the distinctive features of time series analysis. The DWT decomposes a signal into a set of mutually orthogonal wavelet basis functions in wavelet analysis. The signals are analyzed by wavelet transforms at multiple resolutions for different frequencies. In the medical domain such as EEG which is the most important for the diagnosis of epilepsy. The EEG signal is decomposed into several subbands of frequency using DWT. The intermediate results are given to the classification algorithm (e.g., artificial neural network). From the decomposed subband of EEG, ANN can classify the diagnosed patients as healthy or epileptic.

DWT plays an essential role in time series analysis, such as the reduction of dimensionality, noise reduction, and MRA. The original signal is distributed as separate signals with different frequencies with the help of the DWT function. Also, the original signal can be reconstructed from these separated signals. DWT converts the time series data into DWT coefficients. Different data analyses are then carried out on these DWT coefficients. To project a large time series into DWT coefficients, other data analyses are performed on these coefficients. Since DWT transforms the original time series data into approximation and detail coefficients, it can detect sudden changes in the signal as well. In general, the approximation features rough features, while the detailed coefficients capture the features that designate the frequent movement of the data. The detail coefficients can be analyzed to identify the sudden changes in the data by observing the peaks or spikes in the signal, which is difficult to detect from the original signal.

12.2.2.3 Computation of Discrete Wavelet Transform

Step 1: The wavelet is placed at the beginning of the signal, the inner product of the signal, and the wavelet is calculated and integrated for all times. The result is the correlation coefficient c, which provides the 'local similarity' of a part of a signal and the wavelet.

Step 2: The wavelet is then shifted to the right, and the above step is repeated until the end of the signal.

Step 3: After scaling the wavelet, the above two steps are repeated.

Step 4: Repeat steps 1 through 3 for all scales.

Calculating wavelet coefficients at every possible scale requires a lot of data. If a and b are chosen discrete, the wavelet won't generate massive amounts of data. If a and b are powers of two, then the analysis becomes much more efficient and accurate. Equation (12.3) depicts the formula to estimate the wavelet coefficients.

$$D(a,\ b) = \frac{1}{\sqrt{a}} \sum_{m=0}^{p-1} f[t_m] \varphi \frac{[t_m - b]}{a}, \tag{12.3}$$

where

a, b are scaling and shifting parameters and

$a = 2^{-j}$ and $b = k2^{-j}$,

j indicates the scale index value, and

k is the wavelet transform signal index.

$f[t_m]$ is the time-series signal, and

φ is the mother wavelet function.

Wavelet transform $D(a, b)$ can decompose a signal into different scales with different levels of resolution through the shifting of a single prototype function known as the basis wavelet φ. The DWT is widely used in the decomposition of time series signals from various domains.

For a time-series signal of length N, the DWT processes the signal in different stages. In the first stage, the signal is simultaneously convoluting the signal with a low-pass and high-pass filter. The outcome of this approach provides a set of low pass and high pass filter approximation coefficients (A1) and detail coefficients (D1), respectively. The approximation coefficients represent the low-frequency, coarse-scale signal components, while the detailed coefficients represent the high-frequency fine-scale signal components. The resultant data are down-sampled by 2. In the next step, the approximation coefficient (A1) is again decomposed into approximation coefficient (A2) and detailed coefficients (D2) using the same process. This process is repeated to produce A3, D3, and so on.

12.3 Machine Learning and Deep Learning Techniques for Time Series Analysis in IoT

Machine learning and deep learning make use of wavelet transform for feature extraction and dimensionality reduction. Features, in general, provide essential information about the data. It is the primary quantity that represents the uniqueness between different classes. Due to the time-frequency localization and adaptive multiscale properties, the wavelet transform is beneficial for feature extraction [4]. The critical aspect of using wavelet transform for feature extraction includes selecting suitable wavelet transform and the number of decomposition levels. The number of levels of decomposition is dependent on the signal's dominant frequency components. It is important to choose the decomposition levels in such a way that the signal and the frequencies preserved by the coefficients of the wavelet should be well associated. Compared to CWT, DWT is easy to implement and reduces resource and computation time. Besides, it produces sufficient information for analysis of the original signal.

The signal was broken down into different resolution levels during feature extraction. Coarse-resolution data contain information about the lower-frequency components that preserve the original signal's key characteristics, while the fine-resolution data retain information about the higher-frequency components. The detail coefficients $D1$, $D2$, etc. are the outputs of the high-frequency bands, and the approximation coefficients $A1$, $A2$, etc. are the outputs of the low-frequency bands. The extracted features known as wavelet coefficients represent the energy distribution of the signal in time and frequency.

As the IoT and pervasive computing are becoming part of our daily lives, time-series data are generated by numerous applications, including financial applications, environment monitoring, medical and healthcare, etc. Often, the high dimensionality of the time-series data is making the general-purpose machine learning algorithm underperform or fail. Hence, to extract meaningful knowledge from the time-series data, efficient algorithms are required. Time series classification (TSC) algorithms implement to classify the unknown time-series examples based on the pattern existing in the data. As the first step of classification, the dimensionality of the time series data can be reduced by using DWT to improve the classification accuracy. Also, DWT can be used to reduce the noises in time-series data for better classification performance. Implicitly, the wavelets smoothen the time-series data for more effective classification.

12.3.1 Time Series Classification Algorithms

Like general classification algorithms, the TSC algorithms also involve learning from existing labeled time series instances and utilizing the knowledge learned to classify a new unknown instance whose label is unknown. The time-series data are generated from the IoT devices and the application domain such as image and speech recognition (e.g., for recognizing spoken words), medical diagnosis (e.g., for detecting heart disease from the ECG signal), gesture detection, and so on.

The fundamental concept behind wavelet analysis is to express a signal as a linear combination of a certain set of functions (wavelet transform, WT), which is obtained by moving and dilating a single function called a mother wavelet. The signal decomposition leads to a set of coefficients called coefficients of the wavelet. Therefore, as a linear combination of wavelet functions weighted by the wavelet coefficients, the signal can be reconstructed. A sufficient number of coefficients must be calculated to achieve an exact reconstruction of the signal. Time-frequency localization is the main function of wavelets.

In general, there are two ways to integrate the DWT into a classification of time series data [11]. The first method is to apply the classification methods to the wavelet domain, and the second is to incorporate the multiresolution property into the classification process.

In the first approach, the classification is performed on the transformed data rather than the original data. Here, the main task is to identify the decomposition level, which is suitable to apply the classification. The solution to this problem mainly depends on the data and application domain. This approach can be used in many domains, such as medical, audio, and texture. Classification can be performed on the wavelet-transformed data rather than the original data. For example, in medical signal classification, the prominent features from the original signal are identified using DWT. Classification of the medical signals, for example, EEG signals were decomposed into subbands of different frequencies. After that, the wavelet coefficients are fed to a classifier like neural networks for the classification task. In [12], the authors classify the EEG signal as normal or epileptic. The DWT retains the EEG signals with significant frequencies. For this, first, the EEG signals are digitized at 200 samples. Applying DWT to each signal, the decomposed signals are generated. Each signal of level i, on decomposition, produces corresponding approximation and detail coefficients A_i and D_i of that signal. Different frequency ranges and the resultant wavelet coefficients provide meaningful information to the medical practitioners. The components that do not provide much significant information are not considered in the classification model's neural network.

The wavelet-based TSC incorporates the multiresolution property of the DWT in the classification process. The dominant features of the signals that possess the large energy values in the wavelet coefficients are chosen for classification and computed by the wavelet coefficients with large energy values that are then used for the classification.

Some of the classification algorithms used in the TSC are listed below:

i. **One Nearest Neighbor (1NN)**: 1NN classification is a specialization of a KNN where k value is set to one. In general, kNN works based on similarity measures such as Euclidean distance, Manhattan distance, etc., to compute the nearest neighbor. In time-series data, the best measure for the underlying is Dynamic Time Warping (DTW), Time Warp Edit Distance (TWED), Edit Distance on Real Sequence (EDR), Minimum Jump Cost (MJC), and kNN requiring a distance measure to find the nearest neighbors [6–8].

ii. **Shapelet Transform**: This algorithm works like a decision-tree like-classification. It tries to find the most representative subsequences from the training set as shapelet. Shapelets are representative of a class. This shapelet is then used to match unknown time-series data. By optimizing the data benefit of dividing time series data into subsequences and selecting the best candidates from the series segments, the shapelets are obtained. Besides, the Shapelet Transform (ST) is suggested to find and use top k shapelets from each class to transform datasets by measuring the distances between a sequence and each shapelet [9,10]. After transforming the time-series data into shapelets, generic classification can also be utilized for the classification of time series data.

iii. **Time Series Forest Classifier (TSF)**: works as a random forest classifier to time series data [14]. The basic steps followed by the TSF are as follows:

    a. It splits the time series signals into random intervals with random lengths and starts periods.

    b. Extracts the statistical features like mean, standard deviation, slope, etc. into a single feature vector from each random interval.

c. The extracted features are trained using a decision tree classifier.

d. The above three steps are repeated until the required number of trees have been built.

The majority vote of all trees in the forest is used to predict the class of the new series

12.3.2 Time Series Classification Using Deep Learning

The architecture for TSC using deep learning combines multiple layers to implement nonlinear functions. The multivariate time series is the input to the deep learning network [15]. The output of each layer will be input to the next layer and uses its nonlinear transformation function to produce its output.

The nonlinear transformation in each layer is controlled by a set of parameters of that layer, which links the input to the output of that layer. Three different deep learning networks used in general for TSC are (i) convolutional neural networks (CNNs), (ii) inception time, a new architecture that is based on CNN, and (iii) echo state networks, which are based on the recurrent neural networks (RNNs).

i. **Convolutional Neural Networks (CNN):** A CNN is a deep learning algorithm that takes the multivariate time-series data as input and extracts the spatial and temporal patterns. The patterns are captured by applying filters, and the extracted features are assigned a trainable weight according to the importance in general; three separate layers, such as a convolutional layer, pooling layer, and completely linked layer, are composed of CNN. A general form of applying the convolution for a centered time stamp t can be expressed as Equation (12.4) given below:

$$\text{con}_t = f\left(\omega \cdot X_{\left(\frac{t-l}{2} : \frac{t+l}{2}\right)}\right) + b, \quad \text{for all } t \in [1, T] \tag{12.4}$$

where

X denotes univariate time series data of length T with a filter ω of length l,

b denotes bias and

f denotes nonlinear function such as ReLU.

The result of the convolution is denoted by con_t.

There can be several convolutional and pooling layers that are staggered before the fully connected layer. The convolutional layer performs the convolution operation on the input series of feature maps and convolution matrix to obtain high-level features. The pooling layer extracts dominant features and is responsible for dimension reduction. The pooling layer takes a series of feature maps as input and produces a series of feature maps with lower dimensions as output. The two types of pooling used by the pooling layer are max pooling and average pooling [15]. Max pooling discards noise from the signal and is usually better than average pooling.

The fully connected layer learns the nonlinear combinations of the high-level features of the convolutional and pooling layer. In general, the fully connected layer

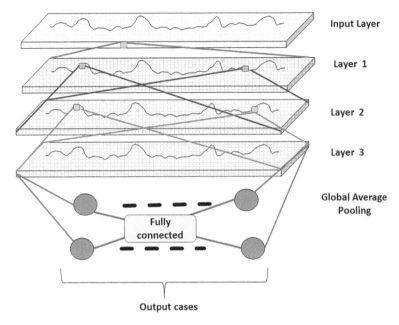

FIGURE 12.2
CNN architecture for TSC with three convolutional layers.

is implemented with a multilayer perceptron (MLP). The original time series, after several convolutional and pooling operations, are converted into a series of feature maps. The feature maps are flattened into the column vector, which is given as an input to multilayer perceptron. The output of the MLP has the number of neurons that is equal to the number of possible classes of time series. Figure 12.2 illustrates convolutional network architecture for TSC with three convolutional layers.

ii. **Inception Time**: Inception network is a deep convolutional network. In the inception network, the convolutional and pooling layers are replaced with inception modules. Inception modules in the CNN perform more computation more efficiently via dimensionality reduction with stacked 1×1 convolutions. It solves the problem of computational expense, overfitting, and other issues. The inception module learns from the same input data through multiple kernel size filters parallel rather than stacking them sequentially. For example, inception performs 1×1, 3×3 and 5×5 and more convolutional transformation and some pooling in parallel. It then stacks all the outputs of the transformation and allows the model to choose information from it.

The inception module consists of four layers. The first layer reduces the dimensionality of the input data, which reduces the computational cost and number of features. It also speeds up the training process. The second layer is the set of parallel convolutional layers of different sizes, such as 1×1, 3×3, 5×5, etc., which act on the same input feature map. The third layer is the max pooling layer. Finally, the last layer is the concatenation layer, which concatenates the parallel convolutional and Max pooling output to form the output multivariate time series of the inception module.

iii. **Echo-State Networks (ESN):** It is a type of RNN. Usually, RNN is rarely used in TSC. By removing the need to measure the gradient for the hidden layers, reducing the training time, and avoiding the vanishing gradient problem, ESN is designed to mitigate RNNs' problems [16]. The hidden layers constitute a reservoir and are initialized randomly [17]. Each neuron in the reservoir creates its nonlinear activation function for the input series. The inter-connected weights and the input weights in the reservoir are not trained. The output of the reservoir is prepared by learning algorithms such as logistic regression or ridge classifier. RNNs are based on ESNs and speed up the training process as they are very sparsely related, with most of their weights a priori set to randomly selected values [18]. After rapid preparation, they show impressive results. Besides, they are beneficial for dealing with the chaotic time series.

The basic equations of ESNs are given below in Equations (12.5) and (12.6):

$$s(n+1) = f\left(W^{\text{in}} \cdot i(n+1) + W \cdot s(n) \cdot W^{\text{back}} \cdot o(n)\right) \tag{12.5}$$

$$o(n+1) = f^{\text{out}}\left(W^{\text{out}} \cdot i(n+1), s(n), o(n)\right) \tag{12.6}$$

where

$i(n)$, $s(n)$, and $o(n)$ are input vector, state vector, and output vector of ESNs, respectively.

The terms f and f^{out} are activation functions for internal neurons of the processing unit and output unit of the reservoir, respectively.

Figure 12.3 illustrates the ESN.

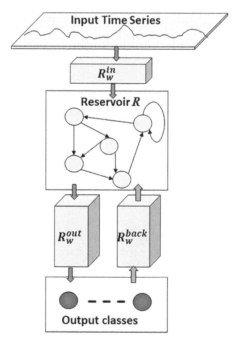

FIGURE 12.3
An echo state diagram for time-series classification.

The R_w^{in} denotes the input weight connection matrix. The connection matrix connects the input layer and the reservoir. R_w in Figure 12.3 denotes the internal weight connection matrix which connects the reservoir and internal neuron; R_w^{back} denotes the feedback weight connection matrix between the output layers. R_w^{out} denotes the output weight connection matrix that connects the reservoir and output layer which is the only key parameter that requires training.

12.4 Comparison for Morlet, Mexican Hat, Frequency B-Spline Wavelet Toward the Classification of ECG Signal

In the recent advance on IoT-based healthcare systems, the ECG exhibits a vital role in heart disease diagnosis. IoT- based biosensors are used to record these ECG signals [19–21]. The ECG signals capture the heart condition as electrical activities and convey different pathological data of heart functioning. The medical practitioners judge the heart functioning status based on the characteristics of the electrical signal of ECG. However, such a mere naked eye-based diagnosis is not possible in every patient's case. The factors such as the number of patients, limited time, and a large amount of data increase the complexity of the doctors to be efficient. Hence, the intervention of IoT sensor devices, artificial intelligence, and automated computer-aided diagnostic systems are required for ECG-based heart disease diagnosis.

In this study, the arrhythmia data from the Physionet Database of MIT- BIH Arrhythmia Laboratory are considered for experimentation purposes. The database consists of 48 records of ECG signals over 45 human subjects, where 19 females are in the age group of 23–89 years, and 26 males are in the age group of 32–89 years. In total, the MIT-BIH arrhythmia data set consists of 13,724 heartbeats. There is an annotation file that marks the complexity and heartbeat type of each signal record along with the database [22,23].

The classification of ECG signal involves differentiating between arrhythmia (ARR), congestive heart failure (CHF), and normal sinus rhythm (NSR) heart function disorders [24,25]. Arrhythmia represents the inappropriate electrical activity detected in the sinus node of the heart. Congestive heart failure occurs due to inefficient pumping of blood by the heart [13]. In these cases, the blood accumulates in the organs such as the legs, hand, liver, and lungs due to CHF. Normal Sinus Rhythm occurs due to exiting of the sinoatrial node stimulus and outspread to the left heart ventricles. Abnormal ECG signal characteristics due to NSR heart disorder are given below in Table 12.1.

TABLE 12.1

Abnormal ECG Signal Characteristics Due to NSR

Parameter	Characteristics
PR distance	≤0.20 s
QT distance	0.39 s in Female and 0.44 s in male
QRS complex	≤0.10 s
PR & ST segment	Isoelectric
P wave	0.04–0.12 s and amplitude ≤ 0.25 mv
T wave	0.10–0.25 s
Rhythm	R-R range and P-P range must be equal
Rate	60–100 per min

Generally, the raw ECG signals contain noises due to physical and technical factors. Such noises occur due to electricity line interference, baseline wander, amplifier noise, electrode contact, electromagnetic, and polarization effects [26–28]. Hence, the denoising of ECG signals is very important to carry out further analysis. ECG signal analysis involves three basic processes: signal denoising, signal wave identification, and heart disease classification, as depicted in Figure 12.4 below. Wavelet-based ECG signal decomposing, denoising, and reconstructing signals promises to be an efficient technique [29–31].

Here, this case study focuses on comparing Morlet, Mexican Hat, and Frequency Bspline Wavelet for signal denoising ECG signal. The steps involved in the wavelet transformation using the python wavelet library are as follows.

Step 1: Import the wavelet transform functions under python wavelet library
Step 2: Initialize the signal length
Step 3: Set the range of scales to accomplish the wave transformation
Step 4: Execute the continuous wavelet scaleogram with linear time.
Step 5: Compute the transform using pywt continuous wavelet function.
Step 6: Display the output of the wavelet functions

12.4.1 Mexican Wavelet Transform

Mexican wavelet is considered as the second-order derivative of the Gaussian function as given in Equation (12.7) below. This type of wavelet is popularly used for data classification problems in large-scale data analysis [32–34]. The chirp signal of the Mexican hat wavelet is given below in Figure 12.5. For this case study, the central frequency of the Mexican Hat wavelet is considered at 0.2 Hz.

$$W(t) = \left(1 - t^2\right) * e^{-\left(\frac{t^2}{2}\right)} \tag{12.7}$$

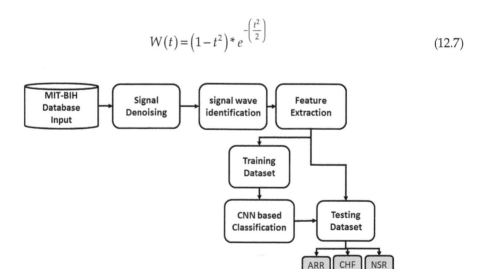

FIGURE 12.4
The basic flow of the proposed wavelet-based classification of ECG signal.

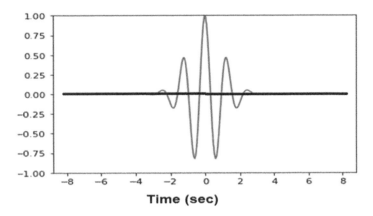

FIGURE 12.5
Chirp signal of Mexican hat wavelet.

12.4.2 Morlet Wavelet Transform

The Morlet wavelet is one of the popularly used wavelets for handling classification problem in IoT signals [35–37]. Equation (12.8) given below represents the Morlet wavelet:

$$W(t) = \frac{1}{\sqrt[4]{\pi}} * \left(e^{i\omega_0 t} - e^{-\left(\frac{\omega_0^2}{2}\right)} \right) * e^{-\left(\frac{t^2}{2}\right)} \tag{12.8}$$

Here, ω_0 represents the central frequency of the original wavelet. In this study experiment, ω_0 is considered at 0.8 Hz. Figure 12.6 below depicts the chirp signal of the Morlet wavelet.

12.4.3 Frequency B-Spline Wavelet Transform

The frequency-based B-spline wavelet is defined as the frequency domain of B-Spline performed over central frequency (w_c), integer order (ω_m), and signal bandwidth (ω_b). The chirps of frequency B-spline are depicted in Figure 12.7 below. The central frequency is considered as 1Hz. The expression for this wavelet is given in Equations (12.9) and (12.10) below.

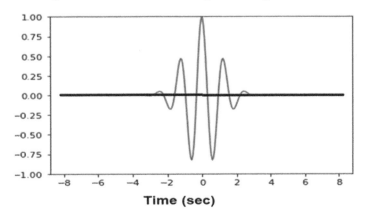

FIGURE 12.6
Chirp signal of Morlet wavelet.

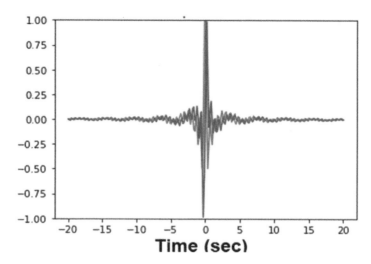

FIGURE 12.7
Chirp signal of frequency B-spline wavelet.

$$W(t) = \sqrt{\omega_b}\left[\left(\sin(w_c)\right)*\left(\frac{\omega_b t}{\omega_m}\right)\right]^{\omega_m}*e^{2i\pi\omega_c t} \tag{12.9}$$

where

$$\sin\left(w_c\right)^* = \begin{cases} 1 & *=0 \\ \dfrac{\sin^*}{*} & \text{otherwise} \end{cases} \tag{12.10}$$

First, the ECG signals are converted into scaleogram frames. These scaleogram images represent wavelet transformation based on the amplitude and frequency range of the signal [38–40]. Figure 12.8 illustrates the scaleogram of three different wavelet transform functions: Morlet, Mexican hat, and Frequency B-spline wavelet.

Here, in this study, a convolution neural network is used to perform the classification of ECG signals into three hear disorders, namely ARR, CHF, and NSR. The basic definition of Keras-based CNN is as follows:

Step 1: Initialize the model as Keras.models.Sequential

Step 2: Execute Flatten Layer (input_shape)

Step 3: Execute Dense Layer (300 with relu activation)

Step 4: Execute Dense Layer (100 with relu activation)

Step 5: Execute Dense Layer (100 with softwmax activation)

Step 6: Compile model (sparse_categorical_crossentropy loss, SGD optimizer, and Performance_Metrics for accuracy)

The classification of the ECG signal is confirmed through the confusion matrix for the prediction of heart disorder based on accuracy as performance metrics. The accuracy is estimated as the ratio between the total number of correct predictions upon the total sum of

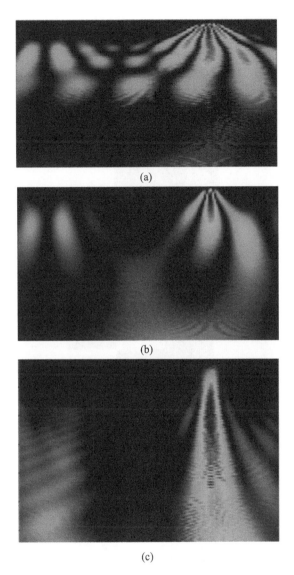

FIGURE 12.8
Scaleogram of Morlet, Mexican, and frequency B-spline wavelet transforms (a–c).

elements in the dataset. Here, the best accuracy has a value of 1, while the worst accuracy has a value of 0. Equation (12.11) given below depicts the formula for estimating accuracy:

$$\text{Accuracy} = \frac{\text{True Positive} + \text{True Negative}}{\text{True Positive} + \text{True Negative} + \text{False Positive} + \text{False Negative}} \quad (12.11)$$

Figure 12.9 depicts the confusion matrix achieved for three different wavelet transforms. At the epoch of 100 iterations, Table 12.2 depicts the accuracy achieved under different wavelet transforms. For the ARR classification, the Morlet and Mexican hat wavelet-based exhibited 98% accuracy. Frequency B-spline wavelet exhibits 99% accuracy. Next, for the

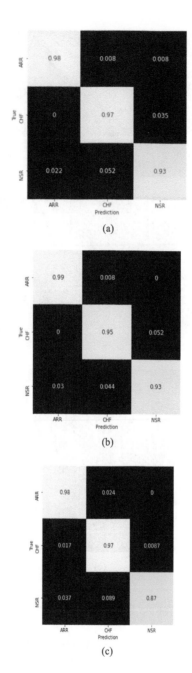

FIGURE 12.9
Confusion matrix obtained for different wavelet transforms. (a) Morlet wavelet. (b) Mexican hat wavelet.
(c) Frequency B-spline wavelet.

CHF classification, Morlet and Mexican hat wavelet-based exhibited 97% accuracy in comparison with the Frequency B-spline wavelet with 98% accuracy. Finally, for the NSR classification, Morlet wavelet-based exhibited 93% accuracy, while and Mexican hat exhibited 93% and Frequency B-spline demonstrated 87% accuracy.

TABLE 12.2

The Accuracy Achieved under Different Wavelet Transforms

Wavelet	Accuracy		
Wavelet transform	ARR	CHF	NSR
Mexican hat wavelet	0.98	0.97	0.93
Morlet wavelet	0.98	0.98	0.93
Frequency B-spline wavelet	0.99	0.98	0.87

12.5 Conclusion

This chapter focuses on various techniques of signal processing involved from the perspective of IoT. Secondly, this chapter presents different machine learning and deep learning techniques for the classification and prediction of the events in IoT sensor devices. Finally, a case study on the prediction of IoT device events using continuous wavelet transformation and machine learning models is presented. Morlet, Mexican, and Frequency B-spline wavelet transforms were considered for experimentation of ECG signal classification under three categories, namely ARR, CHF, and NSR. The performance metrics, such as accuracy was compared for three wavelets. The Morlet and Mexican hat wavelet-based ARR classification exhibited 98% accuracy in comparison with the Frequency B-spline wavelet with 99% accuracy. Next, the Morlet and Mexican hat wavelet-based CHF classification exhibited 97% accuracy in comparison with the Frequency B-spline wavelet with 98% accuracy. In conclusion, regarding NSR classification, all three classifications demonstrated 87% accuracy results.

References

1. https://www.marketsandmarkets.com/Market-Reports/iot-analytics-market-52329619.html. Accessed on 6 January 2021.
2. https://inst.eecs.berkeley.edu/~ee225b/sp18/lectures/wavelets-g&w.pdf. Accessed on 23 December 2020.
3. Chaovalit, P., Gangopadhyay, A., Karabatis, G. and Chen, Z. 2011. Discrete wavelet transform-based time series analysis and mining. *ACM Computing Surveys (CSUR)*, 43(2), 1–37.
4. Li, D. 2018. Transforming time series for efficient and accurate classification (Doctoral dissertation, University of Luxembourg).
5. Senin, P. and Malinchik, S. 2013. SAX-VSM: Interpretable time series classification using SAX and vector space model. In 2013 *IEEE 13th International Conference on Data Mining* (pp. 1175–1180). IEEE, Texas, USA.
6. Batista, G.E., Wang, X. and Keogh, E.J., 2011, April. A complexity-invariant distance measure for time series. In *Proceedings of the 2011 SIAM International Conference on Data Mining* (pp. 699–710). Society for Industrial and Applied Mathematics, Mesa, Arizona, USA.
7. Marteau, P.F. 2008. Time warp edit distance with stiffness adjustment for time series matching. *IEEE Transactions on Pattern Analysis and Machine Intelligence*, 31(2), 306–318.
8. Serra, J. and Arcos, J.L. 2012, September. A competitive measure to assess the similarity between two time series. In *International Conference on Case-Based Reasoning* (pp. 414–427). Springer, Berlin, Heidelberg.

9. Hills, J., Lines, J., Baranauskas, E., Mapp, J. and Bagnall, A. 2014. Classification of time series by shapelet transformation. *Data Mining and Knowledge Discovery*, 28(4), 851–881.

10. Lines, J., Davis, L.M., Hills, J. and Bagnall, A. 2012, August. A shapelet transform for time series classification. In *Proceedings of the 18th ACM SIGKDD International Conference on Knowledge Discovery and Data Mining*, London, United Kingdom. (pp. 289–297).

11. Subasi, A. 2005. Epileptic seizure detection using dynamic wavelet network. *Expert Systems with Applications*, 29(2), 343–355.

12. Zarei, A., & Asl, B. M. 2021. Automatic seizure detection using orthogonal matching pursuit, discrete wavelet transform, and entropy based features of EEG signals. *Computers in Biology and Medicine*, 131, 104250.

13. Siva, A., Siddharth, H., Nithin, M. and Rajesh, C. 2018. Classification of arrhythmia using wavelet transform and neural network model. *Journal of Bioengineering & Biomedical Science*, 8, 244. doi:10.4172/2155-9538.1000244.

14. Deng, H., Runger, G., Tuv, E., & Vladimir, M. 2013. A time series forest for classification and feature extraction. *Information Sciences*, 239, 142–153.

15. Fawaz, H.I., Forestier, G., Weber, J., Idoumghar, L., & Muller, P.A. 2019. Deep learning for time series classification: a review. *Data Mining and Knowledge Discovery*, 33(4), 917–963.

16. Gallicchio, C. and Micheli, A. 2017. Deep echo state network (DeepESN): a brief survey. arXiv preprint arXiv:1712.04323.

17. Chouikhi, N., Ammar, B. and Alimi, A.M. 2018. Genesis of basic and multi-layer echo state network recurrent autoencoders for efficient data representations. arXiv preprint arXiv:1804.08996.

18. Fawaz, H.I. 2020. Deep learning for time series classification. arXiv preprint arXiv:2010.00567.

19. Rai, H.M. and Chatterjee, K. 2018. A unique feature extraction using MRDWT for automatic classification of abnormal heartbeat from ECG big data with multilayered probabilistic neural network classifier. *Applied Soft Computing*, 72, 596–608.

20. Pan, G., Xin, Z., Shi, S. and Jin, D. 2018. Arrhythmia classification based on wavelet transformation and random forests. *Multimedia Tools and Applications*, 77(17), 21905–21922.

21. Kumar, S.U. and Inbarani, H.H. 2017. Neighborhood rough set based ECG signal classification for diagnosis of cardiac diseases. *Soft Computing*, 21(16), 4721–4733.

22. Jung, W.H. and Lee, S.G. 2017. An arrhythmia classification method in utilizing the weighted KNN and the fitness rule. *IRBM*, 38(3), 138–148.

23. Yildirim, Ö. 2018. A novel wavelet sequence based on deep bidirectional LSTM network model for ECG signal classification. *Computers in Biology and Medicine*, 96, 189–202.

24. Kumar, M., Pachori, R.B. and Acharya, U.R. 2018. Automated diagnosis of atrial fibrillation ECG signals using entropy features extracted from flexible analytic wavelet transform. *Biocybernetics and Biomedical Engineering*, 38(3), 564–573.

25. Kumar, M., Pachori, R. B. and Acharya, U.R. 2017. Automated diagnosis of myocardial infarction ECG signals using sample entropy in flexible analytic wavelet transform framework. *Entropy*, 19(9), 488.

26. Li, W. 2018. Wavelets for electrocardiogram: overview and taxonomy. *IEEE Access*, 7. 25627–25649.

27. Wang, H., Bai, Y., Li, C., Guo, Z. and Zhang, J. 2019. Time series prediction model of Grey Wolf optimized echo state network. *Data Science Journal*, 18(1), 16.

28. Ullah, F., Al-Turjman, F. and Nayyar, A. 2020. IoT-based green city architecture using secured and sustainable android services. *Environmental Technology &Innovation*, 20, 101091.

29. Krishnamurthi, R., Kumar, A., Gopinathan, D., Nayyar, A. and Qureshi, B. 2020. An overview of IoT sensor data processing, fusion, and analysis techniques. *Sensors*, 20(21), 6076.

30. Anavangot, V., Menon, V.G. and Nayyar, A. 2018, November. Distributed big data analytics in the Internet of signals. In *2018 International Conference on System Modeling & Advancement in Research Trends (SMART)* (pp. 73–77). IEEE, Moradabad, India.

31. Poongodi, T., Krishnamurthi, R., Indrakumari, R., Suresh, P. and Balusamy, B. 2020. Wearable devices and IoT. In *A Handbook of Internet of Things in Biomedical and Cyber Physical System* (pp. 245–273). Springer, Cham.

32. Saeed, F., Paul, A., Karthigaikumar, P. and Nayyar, A. 2020. Convolutional neural network based early fire detection. Multimedia Tools and Applications, 79, 9083–9099.

33. Vora, J., Patel, M., Tanwar, S. and Tyagi, S. Image processing based analysis of cracks on vertical walls. In *IEEE 3rd International Conference on Internet of Things: Smart Innovation and Usages (IoT-SIU 2018)* (pp. 1–5). BIAS, Bhimtal, Nainital, Uttarakhand, India, 23–24 February, 2018.

34. Mahapatra, B., Krishnamurthi, R., & Nayyar, A. 2019. Healthcare models and algorithms for privacy and security in healthcare records. *Security and Privacy of Electronic Healthcare Records: Concepts, Paradigms and Solutions*, 183–221.

35. Krishnamurthi, R. 2019. Swarm intelligence and evolutionary algorithms for heart disease diagnosis. In Sandeep Kumar, Anand Nayyar and Anand Paul (Eds.), *Swarm Intelligence and Evolutionary Algorithms in Healthcare and Drug Development* (pp. 93–116). Chapman and Hall/CRC, Boca Raton, FL.

36. Tanwar, S. (Ed.). 2020. *Fog Data Analytics for IoT Applications: Next Generation Process Model with State of the Art Technologies* (Vol. 76). Springer Nature, Singapore.

37. Tanwar, S., Tyagi, S. and Kumar, N. *Multimedia Big Data Computing for IoT Applications: Concepts, Paradigms and Solutions, Intelligent Systems Reference Library* (pp. 1–425). Springer Nature Singapore Pte Ltd., Singapore, 2019.

38. Gupta, R., Tanwar, S., Tyagi, S. and Kumar, N. 2020. Machine learning models for secure data analytics: a taxonomy and threat model. *Computer Communications*, 153, 406–440.

39. Krishnamurthi, R., Gopinathan, D. and Nayyar, A. A comprehensive overview of fog data processing and analytics for Healthcare 4.0. In Tanwar, S. (Ed.), *Fog Computing for Healthcare 4.0 Environments* (pp. 103–129). Springer, Cham.

40. Krishnamurthi, R., Aggrawal, N., Sharma, L., Srivastava, D., & Sharma, S. 2019. Importance of feature selection and data visualization towards prediction of breast cancer. *Recent Patents on Computer Science*, 12(4), 317–328.

Index

Note: **Bold** page numbers refer to tables and *italic* page numbers refer to figures.